Pluralism and the Politics of Difference

Pluralism and the Politics of Difference

State, Culture, and Ethnicity in Comparative Perspective

R. D. GRILLO

CLARENDON PRESS · OXFORD
1998

Oxford University Press, Great Clarendon Street, Oxford OX2 6DP

Oxford New York

Athens Auckland Bangkok Bogota Bombay Buenos Aires
Calcutta Cape Town Dar es Salaam Delhi Florence Hong Kong Istanbul
Karachi Kuala Lumpur Madras Madrid Melbourne Mexico City
Nairobi Paris Singapore Taipei Tokyo Toronto Warsaw

and associated companies in
Berlin Ibadan

Oxford is a registered trade mark of Oxford University Press

Published in the United States
by Oxford University Press Inc., New York

British Library Cataloguing in Publication Data
Data available

Library of Congress Cataloging in Publication Data
Grillo, R. D.
Pluralism and the politics of difference: state, culture, and
ethnicity in comparative perspective / R. D. Grillo.
Includes bibliographical references and index.
1. Pluralism (Social sciences)   2. Multiculturalism.
3. Ethnicity—Political aspects.   4. Comparative government.
I. Title.
JC330.G75   1998   305.8—dc21   98-2538
ISBN 0-19-829426-3

1 3 5 7 9 10 8 6 4 2

Typeset by Best-set Typesetter Ltd., Hong Kong
Printed in Great Britain
on acid-free paper by
Biddles Ltd, Guildford and King's Lynn

In memory of Ralph Grillo (1899–1984)
and Muriel Grillo (1902–1993)

PREFACE

As a teaching and researching anthropologist I have always worked where ethnic and racial difference has been of transparent importance. Like others who have attempted to understand it, I continually find 'ethnicity' a deeply puzzling phenomenon. This book is not, however, especially to do with ethnicity, whatever is meant by that vague but indispensable term. Instead it concentrates on another, albeit wide-ranging, issue: how do politics and political processes, working through the authoritative institutions of society (that is the state) shape and reproduce 'difference'? It is thus about pluralism, and the politicization of culture (in the anthropologists' sense) in societies where there coexist peoples who with varying degrees of consciousness, and with varying consequence, believe they are 'different' from each other in their way of life, lifestyle, language, religion, and historic identity.

This study builds on previous work on ethnic relations in France, and on linguistic pluralism in France and Britain (Grillo 1985, 1989), and I acknowledge the support of the University of Sussex, which allowed me sabbatical leave during 1993–4 to complete the first draft. I would also like to thank Oxford University Press's three anonymous readers for their detailed and constructive criticisms of the manuscript. Over many years I benefited from the encouragement, wisdom, and advice of Prof. A. L. Epstein. Frequent conversations with Dr Saul Dubow, an historian, and Dr Jeff Pratt, an anthropologist, have allowed me to try out ideas, and learn from their considerable expertise. Prof. Richard Burton's vast knowledge of France and French colonialism, and his formidable understanding of the literature on race, have influenced my thinking about the issues with which I have tried to deal. Sussex students, including those taking graduate courses in Social Anthropology and the MA in Culture, Race and Difference, have provided considerable stimulus, and supervising the research of Bruno Riccio and Ruba Salih has been a privilege and intellectual spur.

September 1997   R. G.

CONTENTS

LIST OF TABLES

1

Plural Societies

1. Crisis? What crisis?

That there is a 'crisis' of the nation-state, or at least of the concept of the nation-state (Hobsbawm 1992: 186), is, at the end of the millennium, 'a commonplace of contemporary political journalism' (Dunn 1995: 4). Arguably, it has been in perpetual 'crisis' since emerging as the predominant form of political organization in the nineteenth century: it is the chronic condition of this type of formation. European nation-states were often composed from diverse elements which had different reasons for submitting to another's hegemony, and their incorporation created new forms of differentiation and difference between and within the constituent elements. These were the fault-lines of future conflict, and nation-states thus contained their own 'mechanisms of destruction' (Grillo 1980: 25). International movement of capital and labour, and supranational forms of economic, military, and political organization, undermined the foundations of the autonomous national polity long before what we have learned to call 'globalization'.

Although for much of the last two hundred years the ramshackle apparatus appeared to hold together, there have been periods when one state alone, or several together, even the system as a whole, appeared to be in danger of collapse. Rather like the 'language question', with which of course, in Europe, it has been closely connected, the 'national question' has 'flicker[ed] in and out of the constant interplay between culture and power' (Steinberg 1987: 206), and, again like the language question, at certain moments it has assumed extreme importance. In both cases the late twentieth century appears to be one such moment: after a period of quiescence, the 'national question' is back on the agenda. Current problems appear to be multiple and reinforcing, affecting many nation-states simultaneously, and there is a questioning of the entire phenomenon. No one following events of the early 1990s in Eastern Europe and Central Asia could ignore the apparent, often bloody, persistence, or re-emergence, of ethnic, regional, national, and religious particularism: communalism seemingly replacing communism. Such things are by no means confined to the East, as regional and other movements in Western Europe confirm. And centrifugal tendencies of that kind are not the only ones. Since World War II countries such as Britain, France, Germany, Belgium, Holland, Switzerland, and in Scandinavia have through the international movement of labour (not least from former colonies and quasi-colonies) experienced new forms of internal differentiation and difference, of race, culture, and religion, again with much communal tension, as the resurgence in many European countries of extreme right-wing parties has testified. There are other pressures, too, from multinational and supranational businesses and institutions, and there now appears to be an unravelling of historic settlements: 1945, 1919, 1815, the Act of Union. As I myself wrote, prematurely perhaps, in 1980: 'The Europe of "homogeneous" nations, painfully stitched together over the last 200 years, appears to be coming apart at the seams' (1980: 25). Daniel Moynihan's word 'pandaemonium' does not seem an inappropriate title for his account of the contemporary international order (1993).

To say *the* crisis is, however, misleading. There are several crises, not all of the same kind. The contributors to John Dunn's stimulating edited collection (1995), itself entitled *Contemporary Crisis of the Nation State?* (with question mark), tend to believe that if there is a crisis it is in the realm of political economy, more to do with the *state* than the *nation-state* as such (Dunn 1995: 9, Hont 1995: 170). In much of Africa the crucial problem is the inability of the state, for economic as much as political or social reasons, to *exist*, let alone function in a manner which can satisfy the needs and aspirations of the disparate and impoverished peoples which the colonial heritage conjoined within single formations. The weakness of the state in South Asia is likewise apparent in its inability to contain periodic communalism (Kaviraj 1995). But the crisis of post-colonial nation-states should not be confounded with that faced by post-Cold War federalist states in Eastern Europe (the former Soviet Union and Yugoslavia, and their successors). Nor should *their* crises be confused with those occasioned by upsurges of regional nationalism in the apparently unified nation-states of Western Europe. What Tom Nairn called in 1977, also somewhat prematurely, *The Break-up of Britain*, is, or would be if it occurred, a different phenomenon from that of Rwanda, Sri Lanka, or Yugoslavia.

The 'national question' is thus a complex of issues, and I cannot deal with all of them, especially when it comes to the contemporary world. Instead this book concentrates on one, which, with the important exceptions of Sudipta Kaviraj and James Tully, writing on India and Canada respectively, was not generally addressed by Dunn's contributors. This is to do with the way in which nation-states conceive and handle 'difference', with what may be termed 'pluralism'. At a collective level this concerns differentiation and difference of an ethnic and cultural kind in political and economic settlements. At an individual level it pertains to person and identity, and relations with significant others, who those others are supposed to be, and what is to be done about them.

Although important in the terrain on which it operates, this is not a study of ethnicity as such, and certainly does not attempt a survey of the kind essayed by, for example, Banks (1996), Eriksen (1993), or Anthony Smith in many publications (1995). The focus is pluralism, and the comparison of different kinds of plural polities. The starting point is Gellner's observation (1983: 55) that 'culturally plural societies worked well in the past', but 'genuine cultural pluralism ceases to be viable under current conditions'. Following Gellner's example, I operate with the assumption that the interrelated working of economy, technology, and state structures provides a framework within which pluralism is enacted. This framework both shapes and is shaped by, cultural projects, through a process which may be termed an 'ethnic dialectic'.

It would be interesting to consider 'difference' in societies without the state (Chapter 2 does to a limited extent), but I concentrate on political systems in which some form of state may be readily identified. For comparative purposes three kinds of state, or rather three configurations of state and society, are of particular significance: 'patrimonial' (or 'pre-industrial' or 'early'); 'modern'; and 'post-industrial' or 'postmodern'. These, I argue, vary, *inter alia*, in their productive base, type of authority, and the space they allow difference, and I explore these links through case studies based mainly on published ethnographic and historical sources. Chapters 2 to 4 are concerned with 'patrimonial' societies, all of them non-Western, pre-industrial, and in the conventional sense pre-colonial. Chapter 2 takes three African examples (Alur, Azande, Nupe), Chapter 3 deals with Mesoamerica, concentrating on the Aztecs, and Chapter 4 with the Ottoman Empire. Although cultural and ethnic difference was not absent from such societies, it was never crucial to their operation: they were not driven by it. Their rulers were concerned less with their subjects' cultural identity and way of life than with their ability to pay taxes and tribute. They therefore offer a strong contrast with the 'modern' nation-states which developed in Europe and North America in the eighteenth and nineteenth centuries and which provided the dominant world model for the twentieth (Chapters 6–8). Chapter 5 bridges the account of patrimonialism and modern nation-states by focusing on the transformation of Africa and Mesoamerica by British, French, and Spanish colonialism. Compared with patrimonial societies, whose rulers generally engaged in what Azarya (1988) has called 'extractive' mobilization of their subjects, modern nation-states have been driven by what he calls 'normative' mobilization. They have been grounded in the fostering of a common identity and homogeneous culture. Colonial practice was in this regard ambivalent: 'patrimonial' in so far as it emphasized the extraction of resources, 'modern' in so far as the colonial powers believed they had a mission to uplift and transform their colonial subjects.

Just as colonialism was poised between two images of its project, 'modern' metropolitan nation-states were caught between two visions of the nation. In one it was an 'association', and membership of the polity was, in theory, open to anyone who accepted its principles and identified with the foundation myths. In the other, it was a 'community' related by blood and kinship, to which certain peoples by reason of race and culture were thought incapable of assimilating: Jews in France at the turn of the nineteenth and twentieth centuries, the 'new immigrants' from South and East Europe to the USA in the same period, and Commonwealth immigrants to Britain after World War II. The conflict between proponents of these two visions, in nation-states apparently committed to associational ideologies and assimilative goals, constitutes the 'crisis of assimilation', one of the (many) crises facing the nation-state as the twentieth century draws to a close. This theme is developed initially in Chapters 6 and 7 concerned with France and the USA respectively, and then in Chapter 8 focusing on contemporary Britain (with some reference to France), where it will be apparent that an understanding of ethnic and racial relations under colonialism (Chapter 5) is essential for comprehending developments in these metropolitan countries. Chapters 9 and 10 extend this discussion by examining the theory and practice of cultural pluralism in Britain, France, and the USA under conditions of postmodernity, at the end of the twentieth century.

A legitimate question is why these cases and not others? Every society is socio-historically unique, and other instances (for example, in this context, the Habsburg Empire, Tsarist Russia, the former Soviet Union, China past and present, Sri Lanka, or Malaysia) might tell us additional and possibly different things, but that is not the point. The framework of the book is the comparison of three ideotypical configurations. These do not constitute a comprehensive classification, but rather a series of models, and the case studies are intended to provide the material through which to construct a discussion of certain key themes that run through them. These models are of very wide interest, but I would not claim they are exhaustive, nor that these case studies exhaust all that might be said about them. One omission must be stated clearly. There is much to be said for distinguishing between two sources of ethnic and cultural difference in contemporary societies. Kymlicka (1995a: 10–11), for instance, contrasts 'multination states', within which several nations coexist (by 'nation' he means a 'historical community, more or less institutionally complete, occupying a given territory or homeland, sharing a distinct language and culture'), and 'polyethnic states', where diversity is the result of population movement. There is, he says, 'a profound difference between the sort of diversity created by the voluntary immigration of individuals and families, and [that] created by involuntarily incorporating entire cultures which have no desire to give up their status as separate and self-governing people' (1995b: 12). Different people are involved, and different aims: integration on the one hand, self-government on the other. Kymlicka is right to point to these two important sorts of difference though, as he himself recognizes (1995a: 17), many modern nation-states contain both, and some groups (Kymlicka says African Americans, but the situation of Jews in many parts of the world is similar) do not readily fit with either. Although the distinction is not necessarily appropriate to the pre-modern era, it would none the less have been valuable to have explored and developed it. To some extent I have done so previously in a study of language in France and Britain (Grillo 1989), but here I focus on the 'polyethnic' rather than the 'multinational' character of modern and postmodern societies. There is, after all, enough to be said about it!

Underlying this book, especially the latter part, is a question: to what extent is a plural, polyethnic, democratic society possible? 'It is hard to find a democratic or democratizing society these days that is not the site of some significant controversy over whether and how its public institutions should better recognize the identities of cultural and disadvantaged minorities', says Gutmann (1994: 3). In the late twentieth century, what were strongly homogenizing, assimilative states, have to the accompaniment of an upsurge in ethnicity become more pluralistic. This pluralism is partly a response to, partly a product of, the changing social, economic, and political conditions of post-industrial, postmodern culture which now shapes our lives in the north-western 'quadrisphere' of the global society (Chapter 10). There are, however, several kinds and degrees of pluralism ranging from an out and out separatism, through varieties of what is called 'multiculturalism', to a much looser form of generalized syncretism for which the term 'hybridity' has been proposed. Each has its advocates, though my purpose is not to proselytize on behalf of one or the other, but rather to point to the choices facing our societies as we move into the twenty-first century, and try to steer a course, as Wieviorka, puts it, between the 'Scylla of universalism and the Charybdis of differentialism' (1997: 149).

2. Varieties of pluralism

By an elastic definition, all the societies discussed in this book are 'plural'. The 'Alur', the 'Azande', the 'Nupe', the Aztec and Ottoman Empires, Britain and France, and their colonies, and the USA are (or were) polities where there coexist peoples who with varying degrees of consciousness, and with varying consequence, believe they are 'different' from each other in their way of life, their language, their religion, their historic identity. But they represent different forms of pluralism, and to call them 'plural societies', *tout court*, does little to forward the analysis. It is also unsatisfactory because the term 'plural society' has itself been pre-empted in political science to refer to a certain type of democratic society, irrespective of other considerations such as the ethnic composition of its population.

A useful starting point is Nicholls's account (1974) of what he called *Three Varieties of Pluralism*. Pluralism is both a political philosophy and an analytical category, though in each guise it has many forms. All varieties, says Nicholls, share a common concern with 'the degree of unity and the type of unity which actually exist in particular states, or which ought to exist' (1974: 1), but there are different intellectual and theoretical traditions of pluralism which address different aspects of this common concern in different ways. Some of these are relevant to the present study, some are not, at least directly. Nicholls identifies three such traditions, two of which may be conflated because they do not specifically, or consciously, deal with pluralism of a cultural or ethnic kind. Both are schools of political philosophy: one of Britain in the early years of the twentieth century, the other in and of the USA in roughly the same period. These traditions of pluralism are concerned with the distribution of power and authority in democratic systems, and crucially with the role of the state, and the balance between state and society. Plural societies are conceived as democracies in which there exist groups and institutions mediating between state and individual. In the British view, they serve to limit the autocratic tendencies of the sovereign authority by locating some power outside the central institutions. The American version, which is also concerned with 'countervailing powers', differs somewhat by emphasizing the role of groups external to the state as 'interest groups', whose task it is to promote their particularistic view. The state as 'umpire' (Nicholls 1974: 22) has the task of arbitrating and balancing. Plural societies are thus defined as non-authoritarian, non-totalitarian *democratic* societies, in which different interests are recognized as legitimate, and in which mechanisms exist for promoting those interests. That is, pluralists are concerned with the existence and strength of what others would call the institutions of 'civil society', though they would not normally use that term, just as those who speak of civil society would not normally refer to 'pluralism'. Such 'plural societies' (if the term is accepted as appropriate) are not necessarily plural in the sense that their populations differ in lifestyle, language, religion, culture, identity, and so on (Ronald Cohen 1978b: 398): for early twentieth-century British political philosophers the issue of whether they did or not was irrelevant. In the USA, however, some of those concerned with ethnicity and cultural difference did attempt to draw on a traditional philosophy of pluralism and ask how and where ethnic groups might fit into the American political configuration. That is, they were concerned with how the conventional view of pluralism might accommodate ethnic diversity (see Chapter 9).

Nicholls's third variety referred to the tradition stemming from the writings of J. S. Furnivall on colonial societies. This is definitely about pluralism of an ethnic and cultural kind, though in the course of his book Nicholls abandoned 'plural society' for the formation which Furnivall described while retaining it for the political system which he believed prevails in Britain and the USA. For societies that Furnivall called 'plural', Nicholls preferred 'segmented' (1974: 56). Furnivall's concept of the 'plural society', developed in the 1930s and 1940s, was based on his experience of colonialism in South-East Asia, though he believed it had application to a wide range of tropical colonial dependencies. Many such dependencies were, before colonial rule, heterogeneous societies, culturally and ethnically, but under the economic, political, and administrative impact of colonialism heterogeneity was transformed into cleavage. In these colonial societies there was, Furnivall argued, 'a medley of peoples'. 'It is in the strictest sense a medley, for they mix but do not combine. Each group holds by its own religion, its own culture and language, its own ideas and ways. As individuals they meet, but only in the market-place, in buying and selling. There is a plural society, with different sections of the community living side by side, but separately, within the same political unit. Even in the racial sphere there is a division of labour along racial lines' (Furnivall 1948: 304). Such societies lacked a common consensus and 'social will'. This meant that that any unity they had, was 'not voluntary but . . . imposed by the colonial power and by the force of economic circumstances; and the union cannot be dissolved without the whole society relapsing into anarchy' (p. 307). In other words there was no civil society, and Furnivall was much exercised by the process through which such configurations might make the transition from plural to democratic society (plural in another sense) when they achieved self-determination. If the plural society was, for Furnivall, typical of the tro-pical colonies, elsewhere (he mentions South Africa, Canada, and the USA, and 'lands where the Jew has not been fully assimilated into social life', p. 305) there were what he called 'mixed populations with particularistic tendencies'. In such cases, however, there are shared values and relationships other than economic, and such societies while having 'plural features', were not 'plural societies'.

Like Anderson's 'imagined communities' (1983), 'plural societies' was a brilliant, unifying concept, with the phrase itself generally better known than the writing where it emerged. It was, however, also like 'imagined communities', rather vague, and M. G. Smith, an arch-formalist, later extended Furnivall's idea that colonial societies were archetypically plural with a more specific and rigorous definition intended for understanding the Caribbean (1960*b*, 1965). For Smith, the key feature of these societies was not, as it was for Furnivall, their differentiated economies, but the coexistence within them of peoples with distinct cultural traditions: the population consisted of several sections (what Nicholls calls 'segments') distinguished from each other by their adherence to different cultural practices within the 'compulsory institutions' of kinship and marriage, property relations, religion, education, folklore, economic activity, and so on. Thus

Where cultural plurality obtains, different sections of the total population practice different forms of these common institutions; and because institutions involve patterned activities, social relations, and idea-systems, in a condition of cultural plurality, the culturally differentiated sections will differ in their internal organization, their institutional activities, and their system of belief and value. Where this condition of cultural plurality is found, the societies are plural societies (Smith 1965: 14).

The test of a pluralism was the compatibility or otherwise of the social and cultural norms which governed members of the various social sections. Where these were incompatible, there was no community of value, and the society was held together, as a society, only by force. Like Furnivall, however, Smith also recognized that many 'modern societies' were heterogeneous, but these differed from the colonial plural societies because in the latter there was found a 'formal diversity in the basic system of compulsory institutions' (Smith 1965: 82). Thus, along with Furnivall, Smith argued that the USA was a heterogeneous but not a plural society since there 'ethnicity connotes cultural differences that are quite compatible with the inclusive social order, either because they are differences within a common idiom or permitted range, or because the groups which practice these variant cultures are numerically weak' (p. 15). The ways of life of Greeks, Irish, or Italians in New York City, for example, were only 'stylistic variations' (p. 84), and no evidence for pluralism, in Smith's sense, in the USA. On the other hand, *pace* Furnivall, South Africa was very definitely a plural society. Indeed, Smith argued, 'it would be difficult to name a more extreme case' (p. 87).

The writing of Furnivall and Smith gave rise to a lively debate in the social sciences in the 1950s and 1960s, and posed a major problem: their definition of pluralism was of extremely limited application (C. Young 1976: 17). In the 1960s it was often said that South Africa was perhaps the *only* society which fully conformed to it. (Others concluded that the Ottoman Empire was a plural society in the Furnivall–Smith sense, Braude and Lewis, 1982: 1). Crawford Young, therefore, in his wide-ranging and rich study of the *Politics of Cultural Pluralism*, essayed a less stringent definition, which, *inter alia* enabled him to encompass a larger number of societies. For Young, 'cultural pluralism' existed when, within a sovereign nation-state, there was interaction between two or more 'politically significant aggregates', differentiated from each other culturally, that is by language, way of life, etc. (Young 1976: 12; Ulster might be an example). He did not, however, go as far as Cohen and Middleton, for whom plural societies are simply collectivities which are ethnically heterogeneous (1970: 8–9).

That the Furnivall–Smith model was of limited application is not necessarily a disadvantage. Their plural society represents an extreme form along a spectrum of possible social formations: at one end Furnivall and Smith's institutionally exclusive 'plural societies', a little further on Young's 'politically significant cultural aggregates', with Cohen and Middleton's ethnically heterogeneous collectivities further on still. All three point to configurations of important kinds, even if there are many more of Cohen and Middleton's (or Young's) than of Furnivall and Smith's. None, however, is adequate as the basis for a description (let alone analysis) of the forms of pluralism which characterize 'heterogeneous' societies such as Britain. These may, as is commonly done, be called 'plural' (Commission for Racial Equality 1990*a*), though in the mid-1990s the catch-all term 'multicultural' is preferred by many: Rex, for example, would retain 'plural society' for the Furnivall–Smith model (1995: 79). I am quite happy to use 'plural' to describe contemporary British society, provided that it is understood that it then refers to something much looser than Smith or Young envisaged, albeit not as vague as what Cohen and Middleton proposed, and different again from the plural society of the political philosophers.

3. Pluralism and the political order

The idea of a spectrum of pluralities is helpful so long as we are not tempted to measure (if that were possible) degrees of 'institutional exclusiveness' or 'political aggregation', with a view to saying that Britain is here, France there, the USA somewhere else along the spectrum. 'Institutional exclusiveness' and 'political aggregation' are important not because they provide ways of describing a form of society, or of comparing one society with another, but because questions about whether ethnic minorities within heterogeneous (that is plural) societies should or should not be institutionally exclusive, should or should not form political aggregates, are ones which are on the political and social agenda in such formations. There is, however, another question: is the form that pluralism takes in any way related to the political order? Can varieties of ethnic and cultural pluralism be mapped against types of polity? In developing an understanding of this question some account of the 'state' is unavoidable.

Classic definitions of the state were usually a stepping stone towards a broader theoretical perspective encompassing wide-ranging questions of power and order. For Durkheim, the state implied a 'central power' (in Giddens (ed.) 1986: 205), which was 'the sum total of social entities that alone are qualified to speak and act in the name of society' (p. 45). It was also the 'organizing centre' (p. 40) of a variety of 'secondary organs', including administrative bodies, which implemented its decisions. A primary function of the state, however, was the elaboration of 'representations' on behalf of the collectivity. It also acted as an 'organ of reflection' whose 'fundamental duty' was to call the individual 'to a moral way of life' (p. 198). The state, says Durkheim, was 'above all the organ of moral discipline' (p. 201). As always with Durkheim it is difficult to separate 'is' and 'ought'. Durkheim's definition described and prescribed, and offered a vision for the state in the society he knew best: nineteenth-century France. Durkheim like many other French scholars, not least the Marxists such as Althusser, cannot be fully understood unless it is realized that their principal example of a state, always at the back of their minds, is France itself.

Weber, who wrote more about the state than did Durkheim, offered the following: 'A state is a human community that (successfully) claims the monopoly of the legitimate use of physical force within a given territory' (in Gerth and Mills (eds.) 1961: 78). But this is no more than a starting point for what was always for Weber the crucial question: why obey? In the definition, the keyword is 'legitimate', and much of Weber's theoretical argument concerns the bases of 'legitimation' of systems of power. He was concerned with power and authority in social relations, and his key notion was authority, or legitimated power. Power may be legitimated in a limited number of ways, and depending on how that legitimation is effected, different types of organization and structure emerge. There were, he argued, four reasons for accepting the legitimacy of power: because it is traditional, for affectual, especially emotional reasons, because of a belief in its absolute value, and because it has been legally enacted. These provided the bases of legitimacy of an order, and characterized the order itself. For, he concluded, there were a limited number of types of authority which corresponded to the ways in which the order is legitimated.

These types of authority, of which Weber identified three (rational-legal-bureaucratic, charismatic, and traditional), are less relevant to defining the state than to comparing the different forms it takes. There is little to be gained by brooding over definitions, seeking to establish an apparently authoritative, seemingly universal meaning when all that is needed is to point to a certain type of political formation which, without greatly distorting the term, might be called the 'state'. The argument is not that 'this is the state', but that there is an interesting kind of political formation, with certain common characteristics, which appears, in different guises, to be widespread through time and space. In this heuristic spirit, therefore, the state may refer to a centralized *ruling* body, powerful and authoritative, within the public domain. It is an institution, or rather a complex of institutions, which *governs*. Analysis of the state as a complex of central governing institutions must place it in the widest possible context: state and society have to be seen as interrelated wholes; less states 'as such' than polities. This was the strategy followed by the classic sociologists including, most fruitfully, Weber whose analyses linked state, authority, leadership, and administrative staff, including their economic base, how they get their keep. It also informed writers such as Gellner and Elias. The latter is especially impressive for the way in which he sought to bring together a wide range of economic, technological, institutional, social, cultural factors, in his discussion of various 'figurations' ('configurations' would be better) of state and society (Elias 1978, 1982).

When, in the past, anthropologists dealt with political systems, they were concerned less with differences between types of state than between societies that have states and those that do not (see Chapter 2). Sociologists, by contrast, were exercised by what they believed to be the dissimilarity between the institutions of nineteenth-century France, Germany, or Britain, and those of early Europe and 'traditional' societies in Africa, Asia, and Australasia. This was the problem behind Durkheim's account of 'mechanical' and 'organic' solidarities in the *Division of Labour in Society*, where he argued that there were two types of society: one based on relative homogeneity, the other on relative heterogeneity. Although he had relatively little to say about institutional political organization, what he did say was very much in accord with this basic distinction which he developed in other writing. The following, for example, echoes themes from all his work from the *Division of Labour* to *Elementary Forms of the Religious Life*:

The State has ceased more and more to be what it was over a long era; that is, a kind of mysterious being to whom the ordinary man dared not lift his eyes and whom he even, more often than not, represented to himself as a religious symbol. The representatives of the State bore the stamp of a sacred character and, as such, were set apart from the commonality. But [gradually] the State has lost this kind of transcendence (in Giddens (ed.) 1986: 56).

One could imagine an *Elementary Forms of the State*. What also impressed Durkheim was the extension of state functions that had occurred in 'modern' society: 'Nowadays . . . we do not admit that there is anything in public organization lying beyond the arm of the State' (in Giddens (ed.) 1986: 59, 144), a prime example being education (p. 177). For Weber, too, the sense of change from one kind of system to another underpinned his account of the determinants of authority (that is legitimated power).

4. Three configurations of state and society

For the comparative study of pluralism, the important contrast was that which Weber drew between 'traditional' and 'rational-legal-bureaucratic' orders, and it is that contrast which informs the framework around which this book is constructed. Three types of state or rather three configurations of state and society make up that framework.

The first corresponds to societies based on traditional authority in Weber's sense, though Weber himself suggested that legitimation based on tradition was 'on the borderline' of sociologically meaningful action (1947: 116). A much more powerful term sociologically is what he called 'patrimonialism'. Patrimonial societies are those 'where authority is primarily oriented to tradition but in its exercise makes the claim of full personal powers' (1947: 347), and the patrimonial state is one in which 'the prince organises his political power over extrapatrimonial areas and political subjects—which is not discretionary and not enforced by physical coercion—just like the exercise of his patriarchal power' (Weber 1978: 1013). Patrimonialism is a mode of organization beyond 'traditional' which comes about when, with the development of a personal administrative staff, the ruler exercises power on the basis of his (or her) personal authority, and 'members are treated as subjects' (1947: 347). Crucial was the ruler–ruled relationship, at the core of which was the system of extraction. Rulers extracted products and labour (assume surpluses) from their subjects (his or her, though in the vast majority of cases the ruler was male) to support themselves, their families, their retainers, advisers, administrators, bodyguards, musicians, cooks, and hangers-on of every description, along with their courts and palaces, and the public works (temples, churches, markets, roads) which they required. Surpluses were also employed to sustain the system of control through which they were extracted: tax and tribute collectors, provincial governors, bailiffs, armies, and so forth. This was 'the patrimonial satisfaction of public wants' (Weber 1978: 1022).

In this bare account, patrimonialism must seem, and often was, thoroughly exploitative, but it was usually balanced, or said to be balanced, by reciprocity.

This emerges from Weber's discussion of the 'political subject'. Ruler and ruled in such states were joined in a 'consensual community' (Weber 1978: 1020) which did not depend on armed force. The idea of such a community was grounded in the belief in the ruler's 'traditional' legitimacy, and political subjects were those who accepted that legitimacy. The belief was sustained practically through the redistribution of extracted surpluses in the form of benefits of numerous kinds, at the very least in the form of largess. It was also sustained ideologically, and in fact for Weber the root of patrimonialism, its origins and its model, was 'patriarchy': the rule of the father in the family. Cohen, writing about the Emirate of Bornu in north-eastern Nigeria, says that the 'father–son behaviour norm is the model used by the people themselves to describe the nature of all authority relations in the society' (1967: 46). It is not that the household supplies a model for the overall form of Kanuri society, but that the relationships *within* the household provide a model for relations outside it. (Alternatively, one might say that all relations of super- and sub-ordination in such a society are shaped in the same way.) Evans-Pritchard's account of the Zande king Gbudwe (Chapter 2), or Clendinnen's description of the Aztec ruler, Moctezuma (Chapter 3), or the photograph of the Nupe ruler which forms the frontispiece of Nadel's *Black Byzantium*, each vividly illustrates the nature of patrimonial/patriarchal rule.

At the heart of the early patrimonial state, then, was patronage and clientage, a system linking ruler and ruled at all levels: king and chiefs, chiefs and village headmen, village headmen and villagers, or circumventing this hierarchy, kings and commoners. The patron–client principle (extraction balanced by reciprocity, underpinned by an appropriate and convincing ideology) was replicated at all levels. 'Citizenship', if that term can be used with reference to this configuration, meant participating in such a system as a client, a dependant, a follower, or a retainer, accepting the obligations inherent in occupying these statuses, and enjoying such benefits as were attached to them. At the top was the ruler: king, emperor, emir, paramount chief. In the early state, says Skalnik, 'the sovereign was the very pivot' (1978: 615). As Louis XIV put it (if he did, or knew what he meant when he did so), 'L'état, c'est moi.'

The mode of support of this authority meant that the patrimonial ruler met his or her needs by fees, taxes, tribute, and 'profit-making enterprise', with implications, *inter alia*, for the development of markets (Weber 1947: 351 ff.). Patrimonial rule thus encompassed what Gellner (1983) called the 'agro-literate' states of the Old Regimes in Europe (with, for comparative purposes, the emphasis on the agrarian rather than the literate), and therefore what are usually referred to as 'Absolutist States'. Szücs, who offers a good description of systems which may be termed 'patrimonial', appears to locate them outside Europe, in the Orient (1988: 298). This is mistaken: there is no fundamental distinction between a 'European' absolutism and an 'Oriental' patrimonialism. This is not to deny that there were differences (as well as similarities) between patrimonial states in Europe and elsewhere, just as there were varieties of absolutism in West, East, and 'Eastern-Central' Europe (Anderson 1974, Szücs 1988), including the way in which culture and society were interrelated, which accounts of ethnicity should address (Ingrao 1996).

The second configuration is the 'modern' state, which Weber described as 'a system of administration and law which is modifiable by statute, and which guides the collective actions of an executive staff' (Runciman (ed.) 1978: 41). This configuration had three essential characteristics. First, it claimed authority not simply over all those who were members of the state, but also over everything that occurred within its territory. Secondly, it claimed a monopoly of the use of force. Thirdly, it was a 'rational' institution: 'The bureaucratic state order . . . is precisely characteristic of the modern state'(Gerth and Mills (eds.) 1961: 82). For Weber, 'rationality', or rather the harnessing of rationality to organization, and the rationalization of state and other forms of administration in a bureaucratic mode, the development of bureaucracy to a fine art, and its extension into many spheres of civil society, were hallmarks of 'modernity'. Certainly, earlier societies had bureaucracies (the Ottoman Empire for one had a complex hierarchy of officials who produced millions of documents), but these patrimonial bureaucracies lacked the procedural predictability stemming from the systematic application of the rational rules of conduct established by modern bureaucratic procedures. They also failed to apply objective criteria of organization (for example in the selection of entrants); offices were a kind of property, and business was conducted by custom and *ad hominem*, rather than through universalistic rules. The bureaucratic turn was reflected in the rationalization of production and consumption, with the application of science and technology of an increasingly sophisticated kind to the means of production, distribution, and exchange in societies which were becoming ever more industrialized, urbanized, and large-scale: modern societies were (are) essentially 'mass' societies.

The growth of bureaucracy was also accompanied by, and reflected, the increasing willingness of the state not simply to collect taxes to provide for the rulers, or to maintain law and order, but, as Durkheim and Weber observed, to intervene directly and extensively in the economic and social affairs of the polity ('nothing beyond the arm of the State'). Keane (1988*b*: 54) has argued that Hegel provided 'a very broad licence indeed for state regulation and dominance of social life'. The modern state in this regard was very much a product of the French Revolution, with its masters frequently subscribing to what may be termed the 'Jacobin project'. This project was based on the view that through a powerful state, and acting in the name of the people, the ruling powers can and must change the world for the people's betterment (and woe betide those who stand in their way). There are many variations, stronger and weaker forms of Jacobinism. British Labourism ('the gentleman in Whitehall really does know better') falls into the latter category, whereas most communist parties espoused the former (Leninism was the apotheosis of the Jacobin project). This should not be taken to imply that Jacobinism (hard or soft) was confined to the left.

The opposite is true, and a feature of the modern state is the way it has invaded society in general, whoever is in power.

This is closely connected to the relationship between state and 'civil society'. The latter refers to 'all those social relationships which involve the voluntary association and participation of individuals acting in their private capacities . . . It involves all those relationships which go beyond the purely familial and yet are not of the state' (Tester 1992: 8, Simon 1982: 69). This concept, which in the 1980s became important in discussion of reforms in Eastern bloc countries, had an important role in Marxist thinking, especially that of Gramsci. Gramsci's general analysis of the state contained three principal terms: 'state', 'civil society', and 'political society'. Gramsci used 'state' in broader and narrower senses (Simon 1982: 71, Buci-Glucksmann 1980: 91). In the narrow sense the state was described as 'politico-juridical organisation' (Gramsci 1978: 261). This 'state-as-government', as it was sometimes called (Simon 1982: 71), was, according to Gramsci, assigned a number of functions in regard to civil society: as *veilleur de nuit* ('safeguarding public order and respect for the laws', p. 261), as 'ethical state' (the 'autonomous educative and moral activity of the secular State', p. 262, compare Durkheim), and as 'interventionist state', in economic activities.

Like other Marxists, and like Durkheim and Weber, Gramsci was primarily concerned with the nineteenth- and twentieth-century 'modern' state, and the extent to which the state did, or should, 'invade' civil society. The modern state was to a great degree the nightwatchman state *and* the ethical state *and* the interventionist state. Some polities (fascist, Nazi, communist, for example, but a similar point was made about capitalist society) were characterized by deliberate and extensive intervention in the sociocultural sphere (including cultural matters in the narrow sense). The modern state colonized civil society to an amazing degree, and very rapidly, and had no truck with pluralism. This contrasted strongly with earlier forms. 'In the most advanced states', said Gramsci, civil society had become 'a very complex structure' (1978: 235). In Tsarist Russia, on the other hand, it was 'primordial and gelatinous' (1978: 238). This variable nature of the state–civil society relationship has an obvious bearing on the comparison between patrimonial and modern societies and the way in which the two attempt, or do not attempt, to 'form' culture and society.

At the same time, and this was partly a dependent effect, and partly the outcome of the application of an autonomous ideology, political space was constructed (internally and externally) in terms of 'national' entities and boundaries: the modern, post-Revolutionary state was a 'nation-state'. Hobsbawm has summarized its characteristics as follows: 'a (preferably continuous and unbroken) territory over all of whose inhabitants it ruled, and separated by clearly distinct frontiers or borders from other such territories. Politically it ruled over and administered those inhabitants directly, and not through intermediate systems of rulers and autonomous corporations. It sought, if at all possible, to impose the same institutional and administrative arrangements and laws over all its territory' (1992: 80–1). Modern states, then, were guided by a vision of the nation-state as ideally homogeneous, and therefore sought a common, uniform, identity and a common, uniform, loyalty among its citizens. There were, however, two distinct ways in which such a polity might be constructed. From the late eighteenth century, countries such as France and the United States shared the Enlightenment assumption that nations were composed of individuals with common ideals who engaged in a mutually agreeable contract to form a mutually beneficial society. This *Gesellschaft* view of the nation as an 'association' of like-minded people, which others who accepted their political, social, and cultural principles could join without much difficulty, assumed that newcomers could be absorbed, or *assimilated*. But this view, though usually in the ascendancy, coexisted with another, that of the nation as *Gemeinschaft*, community of blood, whose proponents in the late nineteenth century tried, generally unsuccessfully, to make the basis of national adherence, *inter alia* arguing that certain peoples (Jews or Italians, for example) were 'unassimilable'. Sollors, writing about the USA, contrasts these two perspectives as ideologies of 'consent' and 'descent', and says that conflict between them is 'the central drama in American culture' (1986: 6).

Discussing contemporary Britain, Harry Goulbourne (1991: 54 ff.) alludes to these two views by drawing a distinction between a 'traditional', and a 'new' or 'ethnic' nationalism. For Goulbourne, what he calls traditional nationalism (something close to what is here termed the *Gesellschaft* view) crucially 'stopped short of trying to effectuate the congruence of "nation" and "state"' (p. 57). This 'rationalistic definition of the nation-state' was, he says, not 'dependent on an exclusive single ethnicity' in defining membership of the body politic. In consequence, 'traditional nationalism was none too clear about its project' (ibid.: 218–19). It is, perhaps, misleading to label these two basic conceptions or models of the nation and of national membership 'traditional' and 'new'. Both have been around for a long time. Moreover, they were never discrete, autonomous ideologies. Nor were they, as Chapter 6 shows, uniquely associated with different countries: *Gemeinschaft* with Germany, say, *Gesellschaft* with France. As Silverman cogently argues, the two perspectives are found 'not simply between countries . . . but within them, not simply between texts but within them' (1992: 24–5, cf. Hobsbawm 1992: 22, Räthzel 1995: 166, Silverman 1996: 154, Weil 1996). If, over a long period, one tended to prevail, as in France or the United States, or in Britain, it was always in dialogue and contestation with the other. It is with that contestation which was and is quite central to the perpetual crisis of the nation-state, that much of the second half of this book is concerned.

There were, then, radically different conceptions of how the nation might be properly constituted, but across the spectrum there was a firm belief that the body politic should be socially and culturally one. This belief was, however, constantly confronted with the reality of difference, of social and cultural heterogeneity. Goulbourne (1991) and Silverman (1992) both deal with the way in which in the late twentieth century the assimilationist model believed to underlie the British and French nation-states was severely tested not by the regional centrifugal forces which concerned Nairn, but by the presence of large numbers of people who entered those countries as immigrants in the years of economic boom after World War II. Historically, the most significant source of cultural diversity in European nation-states has been regional. Over the last century, however, large-scale population movement across national boundaries has created additional diversities. In the post-war era, tens of millions of men, women, and children left their homes, permanently or temporarily, to seek work or refuge in the core countries of Western Europe where they form some 5–10 per cent of the population. Labour migration before World War II generally involved the movement of peripheral European populations. Later came new migrants from outside Europe, often, as in the case of Britain and France, from colonial and ex-colonial territories, that is from cultural traditions perceived as very different from those of the receiving societies: the West Indies, the Asian subcontinent, North Africa, the Middle East. At first a phenomenon of men who left wives and children back home, it later involved families and independent women. In both France and Britain, as in other core countries of Western Europe, there is now a substantial immigrant family population which increased very rapidly during the 1970s, with many children born and brought up in the societies to which their parents migrated. Often these populations became heavily concentrated in the main urban and industrial conurbations: in Britain in the inner cities, in France in the peripheral suburbs.

Like their counterparts who entered the USA in the late nineteenth century, these migrants to Britain and France were perceived as challenging historic conceptions of the nation-state. This occurred at a time when both countries found themselves obliged to redefine their international roles as post-imperial, *European*, states: the very presence in the metropolitan countries of so many peoples originally from regions previously under colonial control underlined the imperial aftermath. It also happened in a context of other major changes in economic organization, national and international. Silverman, who asks whether France's 'current obsession with immigration', is not 'itself indicative of a crisis in the structure of the nation-state' (1992: 33), makes the connections explicit by drawing attention to the part played in the crisis not only by the post-colonial dilemma, but also by the development of the European Union, and the globalization of monetary and cultural relations.

The emergence of supranational economic and political entities, accompanied by the globalization of production and culture, have created multiple and reinforcing points of crisis in modern nation-states; the 'grand narrative' which held them together has now gone. This leads to the third configuration of state and society, the postmodern and post-industrial. The concepts are complex ones, and will be discussed in greater detail in Chapter 10. Briefly, however, these terms attempt to capture a range of economic, social, technological, and political changes that have, in the view of many, transformed local, national, and international relations in the last decades of the twentieth century. Dahrendorf (1959), Bell (1973), Touraine (1974), and others had suggested that by the late 1970s the economy and society of the 'West' was characterized by an ever-increasing reliance on scientific knowledge and a commensurately educated workforce. Production and consumption were organized on an ever greater scale with increasing centralization of key decisions. Bureaucratic modes of organization prevailed, but the 'managerial revolution' meant that the idea of the ownership of the means of production became problematic and increasingly irrelevant. The state continued to have a crucial role in defining and regulating the economic and social order. This type of society, the product of Keynesian interventionism in the transatlantic democracies in the boom years after World War II, is best described now as 'high' modernity (Wagener 1992: 475). From the mid-1970s to the 1990s, however, there have been profound changes stemming from the increasing globalization of economic (and cultural) relations and the apparent failure of the post-war economic social strategies. These changes have had important implications for the nation-state as the site of social, economic, and political relations: so far from being all-powerful, the state now seemed increasingly irrelevant, and there was a progressive disintegration of the classic forms of social and political organization associated with modernity.

So, then, what happens to ethnic and cultural difference within these configurations of state and society? The themes developed in the following Chapters are summarized in Table 1. Briefly, in 'patrimonial' states, patriarchal rulers were generally concerned less with their subjects' ethnic identity and cultural values than with their ability to render tribute, taxes, and labour. Ethnicity was not absent from such systems, but ethnic identity was not a key motif in the formation of state and society. The predominant plural theme, the predominant way in which difference was handled, was incorporation through accommodation. This involved a variety of devices including, for example, the co-option of regional elites, as in Britain, or the separation (separate development even) into distinct settlements as in the ghetto. Nowhere was the system more fully elaborated than in the Ottoman Empire with its so-called 'millet' system, in which the population was divided into partially self-governing religious faiths, often with a specialized economic role, occupying their own quarters within towns and villages.

TABLE 1. *States and Pluralism: Three Configurations*

Configuration of state and society	Plural themes	Identities
Patrimonial	Difference, Incorporation	Corporate
Modern	Homogeneity, Assimilation	Unitary
Postmodern, Post-industrial	Difference, Heterogeneity	Hybrid

In modern industrial societies with powerful and intrusive secular states, there was, by contrast, a keen interest in the form and content of social relations and social identities. Here, the predominant plural theme has been homogeneity, and the creation of a common culture and identity within a uniform *nation*-state. Ethnicity provides the ideological rationale for the existence of such a state, and thus for the building blocks of an inter*national* order. Homogeneity, however, could be achieved in two quite different ways. First, inclusively, through a policy of assimilation which stemmed from the view of the nation as an association of like-minded people. Within Europe, France provides a good example of this type of polity. But France is also an example of a society in which there circulated a different, exclusive, definition of the nation, one which emphasized blood and kinship. By reason of this definition, some groups, some societies and cultures (or, more specifically, races) were thought to be *unassimilable*. The two perspectives have long been at loggerheads in countries such as France, Britain, and the USA, and their conflict often underpins the crises of these 'modern', assimilative nation-states.

Later chapters will show how over the last three decades of the twentieth century there has been an upsurge in ethnicity in so-called 'advanced' industrial countries which may be linked to social, economic, and technological changes, conditions associated with the advent of the post-industrial society and postmodern forms of sociality. A great deal of literature, anthropological and other, on Britain, France, and the USA points to this. All these are countries which to greater or lesser degrees claim to espouse some as yet vague and contested form of cultural pluralism. Yet, if in patrimonial states difference was handled through incorporation, and in industrial states through homogenization (and assimilation), what will eventually happen in postmodern and post-industrial societies is unclear because it has yet to be determined. It is undetermined because it is emergent, the outcome of a multiplicity of international, national, and above all local and specific accommodations which often test pluralistic ideals to their limits. Pluralism is nowhere given, but in some societies and at certain times it may seem, and actually be, more given than in others. Ours is not such a time.

5. Addendum: a note on 'ethnicity' and 'nation' in social anthropology

This book is not about 'ethnicity', but ethnicity comes into it, and some discussion of the concept, and of approaches to it in my own discipline, is inevitable. Although long in circulation, 'ethnicity' only came into vogue in the social sciences in the 1960s, and in British anthropology at the end of that decade with the publication in 1969 of Abner Cohen's *Custom and Politics in Urban Africa* and Frederik Barth's edited collection *Ethnic Groups and Boundaries*. (Glazer and

Moynihan 1975 and Sollors 1986: 22 ff. trace the history of 'ethnicity' in American social science. Eriksen, 1993: 161, has a note on French usage.) By the 1970s, says Ronald Cohen, it was 'ubiquitous' (1978*b*: 379), and represented 'a shift to multicultural, multiethnic interactive contexts' of anthropological investigation (1978*b*: 386). Although it was, and remains, a disputed term, it seemed to offer a point of entry to a wide range of new problems, obliging anthropologists and others to make links between phenomena previously treated as unrelated, encouraging comparison across different contexts and sociological traditions (between 'tribalism' in Africa, for example, and 'race' in urban North America, Ekeh 1990: 660).

Subsequently, however, its use was so indiscriminate, incorporating so many disparate phenomena, that it seemed to lose all force as a unifying concept: it 'just grew and grew' (Fardon 1987: 171). This led to scepticism about the notion and what it implied, and sometimes a preoccupation with the word's historicity. Chapman, McDonald, and Tonkin, for example, attempted to dispense with the word, perhaps even the phenomenon, in its entirety (see also Banks 1996). Discussing the origins of *ethnos* in Greek, and what it meant in the classical and post-classical periods, they pointed out that early usage corresponded closely with what later, in English, came to be called 'tribe'; it was a generalized category of the 'Other' (Chapman, McDonald, and Tonkin 1989: 11–13). In modern Greek its meaning changed (Just 1989), referring to the Greeks themselves, perhaps translating the Ottoman word 'millet' (see Chapter 4). In similar vein, Sollors, who has also stressed 'ethnicity as otherness' (1986: 25), has noted that the related word *ethnikos* meant 'gentile', and was used to translate *goyim* in Greek versions of the Hebrew Bible. Later it came to mean 'heathen' (changing from a connotation of 'non-Israelite' to one of 'non-Christian').

Such observations are valuable, but lead to difficulties. Turning their attention from Greek to English, Chapman, McDonald, and Tonkin claim that ethnicity 'is an abstract noun, derived by non-vernacular morphological processes from a substantive that does not exist' (1989: 16). 'Non-vernacular' seems to mean 'professional social scientists'. Since *ethnos*, or rather its equivalent, does not exist in vernacular English, Chapman, McDonald, and Tonkin find *ethnicity* an embarrassment and argue for its demise. Instead, they propose to use *identity*, glossing that as 'a notion only existing in a context of oppositions and relativities', and one associated with the 'classification of peoples'. Then: 'It is best to regard those things that, for the moment, look like "ethnicities", as phenomena to be subsumed under the general study of the classification of people (by themselves and others). And then to regard the "classification of people" as subsumed by classification in general' (1989: 17). This is unhelpful. If 'people' means humankind in all its aspects (gender, class, height, sexual preference, etc.), then ethnicity is being subsumed into a very wide range of phenomena of different kind (possibly), with very different *implications*. If 'people' is taken in the narrower sense, more or less equivalent to *Volk*, then all the difficulties with 'ethnic' remain.

Ethnicity is obstinate: neither the word, nor the phenomena to which it generally, if inexactly, refers, will go away. Certainly it implies classification, an 'ordering of the human world into a comprehensive set of categories defined by reference to *an idea of common origin, ancestry and cultural heritage*' (Grillo 1974: 159, emphasis added), but there is little point in treating it primarily as such a system. Ethnicity is about difference and differentiation based on such an idea (difference is the subjective aspect of differentiation, the way in which social differentiation is perceived and conceived). Usually an ideology underpins the classification, specifying the relationship that should exist between those with the same or different identities, and how recruitment to the class is determined. In the American context, for example, Sollors (1986: 39) has identified two different, culturally constructed modes of recruitment (consent and descent), and shows that what is important is what is done with a system of classification, how difference is organized politically. The following reflects on how some of these issues have been tackled from within anthropology.

I suggested earlier that 'the "national question" is now back on the agenda'. It is not one that anthropologists themselves addressed very readily in the past. Before World War II Malinowski alone made any serious effort to engage with the subject, for example in his rambling, posthumously published *Freedom and Civilization* (1947). His view was quite simple. Human society everywhere was traditionally organized in tightly knit homogeneous units or tribes, groups of people who 'conjointly exercise a type of culture' (1941: 534). This 'tribe-nation', as he called it, was 'the prototype of what we define today as the nation, that is, a large group identified by a common language, a common tradition and a common culture. Nationhood is thus a primeval and fundamental fact in human evolution'(1947: 255). This conception, which was wrong, was common enough among those of Malinowski's background and generation, reflecting as it did the orthodox Romantic view. It is still widely held by those misguided enough to believe that society does not exist but nations are eternal. For Malinowski, though, 'tribe-nation' or nationhood was a positive force, 'the very instrument of freedom' (p. 257), he called it. This was not the case with the 'tribe-state', the framework of centralized political organization, and nationalism, the 'tendency toward the coalescence of the two' (1941: 536), he regarded as a dangerous force (1947: 274). Indeed it was in 'the relationship between nation and state' that he observed many of the problems of his contemporary world.

Malinowski's naive views on 'tribe-nation' outside Europe, and on 'nationhood' within it were further weakened by the model of isolated homogeneous communities which underpinned them. He did, however, offer an important suggestion regarding the link between politics and culture which anthropology did not take up for a long time. That it was not taken up in a European context was hardly surprising given the relatively little anthropological work under-

taken on that continent in the early period. Yet despite the considerable research effort in what was soon to be called the Third World, where the issue of
national independence was so salient, the theme was not explored much there
either. Of Malinowski's pupils only Lucy Mair was professionally concerned
with these matters. Before she became an anthropologist, Mair had written a
book entitled *The Protection of Minorities* (1928) concerned with the League of
Nations and the workings of the Minorities Treaties. Thirty-five years later she
published *New Nations*, which was not so much about nationalism as about
social and economic change in the Third World, and only a short passage (pp.
113–8) on 'New states' is germane to the former topic. There she echoed
Malinowski's earlier equation of tribal with national consciousness, but differentiated between tribe and nation in terms of scale (1963: 113), and identified a
fundamental opposition between what she termed 'national mindedness' and
'micro-national' interests of a local or regional kind (p. 114).

If the scattered early anthropological writing on nation had a theme it was
this: the persistence of, and opposition between, what were conceived of as
primordial loyalties of the ethnic kind, and modern forms of political centralization. This was illustrated in the American anthropologist Clifford Geertz's long
essay on 'The Integrative Revolution' (1963), subtitled 'Primordial Sentiments
and Civil Politics in the New States'. There Geertz observed, 'the world of
personal identity collectively ratified and publicly expressed' (p. 118) was
grounded in primordial ties of kinship, lineage, race, language, religion,
custom, and region, and he provided a detailed comparative study of the
politicization of such ties in situations where these primordial groups are joined
together in 'larger, more diffuse units whose implicit frame of reference is not
the local scene but the "nation"' (p. 153). This was also the question posed by
Worsley's account of cargo cults in Melanesia (1957), where the transcendence
of local interests was seen as essential to the struggle against colonialism.
Normally, however, anthropologists preferred to leave the running to
others: the standard books on nationalism in Nigeria, Ghana, and Uganda were
by American political scientists, and even when the ethnographic monographs written by anthropologists can now be seen in retrospect to contain
valuable insights, they made little impact on the subject at large, and on other
disciplines.

Until the mid-1970s the picture in Europe was similar. Nation-state and
nationalism were either ignored, or subsumed within other topics. John Davis's
survey of anthropological research in the Mediterranean complained that 'the
linkages between village or tribal communities and the nation-state are rarely
explored' (1977: 18). In his own account, however, the 'state' made only a brief
appearance, mainly as a bureaucratic intrusion into local societies mediated by
patrons. Nation and nationalism (along with religion) appeared not at all apart
from a brief reference (pp. 3–4) to the use of ethnology by nationalist
movements. At the same time, John Cole also criticized anthropologists for
seeing rural Europe, amoeba-like, as little more than a series of isolated,

homogeneous, 'traditional' communities. Cole, however, detected a growing attention to the way in which such communities were undergoing economic transformation and becoming progressively part of 'larger social entities' (1977: 367). He himself emphasized the political economy of this process, arguing by reference to the so-called underdevelopment thesis that integration involved the conjoining of localities in subordinate relationships with powerful centres. These surveys did not cover everything written by anthropologists working in Europe, but anyone looking for guidance would find rather less here than in the scattered work on the Third World. If a theme was emerging it was little more than that of the 'integrative revolution', to use Geertz's striking phrase, in a different context and in a slightly different form.

Why this lacuna? There was, certainly, a sense that the formation of nation-states and national identity was not the province of anthropology: the anthropological forte was the micro-focus; the macro was best left to others, and anthropologists should content themselves with 'shedding light' on their insights. Thus Loizos on Cyprus: 'an anthropological study of a small community may prove a valuable complement to the nation-centred studies of the political scientist' (1975: 2). Other disciplines certainly saw anthropology in those terms: I was once asked to talk about nationalism to a conference mainly of historians and political scientists in a session entitled 'National identity from below'. The use of the phrase presumably reflected the idea that anthropological research is generally conducted not among educated, literate elites, but at 'street', or at least village level, so to speak, where it is concerned with 'what actually happens, on the ground' among those who are generally powerless and often muted.

Although the anthropological handling of nation was until recently weak to the point where the issue was virtually ignored, work on ethnicity in both the Third World and the First, provided, indirectly, a distinctive contribution to the study of the underlying phenomena. (Eriksen has suggested that theories of nationalism and anthropological theories of ethnicity have now converged, 1993: 100.) Three approaches may be mentioned. For Abner Cohen (1969, (ed.) 1974, 1974) ethnicity was always a matter of 'interest'. Ethnic groups were interest groups, and the degree of integration of a group was a function of the articulation of its interest. For example, the organization of the collectivity of Hausa people resident in Ibadan around the Tijaniyya sect of Islam stemmed from their involvement in the cattle trade. More generally, ethnicity was about the relationship between power and symbols, the 'two dimensions' of Cohen's *Two-Dimensional Man* (1974). Barth, too, was concerned with collectivities and their organization but shifted attention from 'internal constitution and history', to 'boundaries and boundary maintenance' (Barth (ed.) 1969: 3), the way in which difference and differentiation is sustained: how the boundary is patrolled. Both 'boundary' and 'interest' have since appeared in numerous accounts of ethnicity in many parts of the world. Neither has been without critics. Epstein

(1978) was particularly severe on Cohen's materialistic conception of interest. There is often, Epstein pointed out, an 'affective dimension'. Although Epstein's stance was not fully absorbed by anthropologists, perhaps because of difficulties with the psychoanalytical framework through which he developed his 'anthropology of the emotions', none the less 'identity' came to the fore-front of anthropological discussion of ethnicity, to sit alongside 'boundary' and 'interest'.

One point on which there is widespread agreement is that ethnicity is a dynamic rather than primordial or 'natural' phenomenon (Brass 1991: 16, Eriksen 1993: 54, Glazer and Moynihan 1975: 19, Roosens 1989). When Malinowski or Geertz wrote about 'tribe-nation' or other forms of local identi-fication they did so in ways that suggested that they were given and eternal. Abner Cohen, Barth, and Epstein each stressed that ethnicity is continually constructed and reconstructed, that it is 'a process or a project, rather than a structure' (Peel 1989: 200), 'always about negotiations' (Back 1996: 158). Although Epstein has called in question some of the more extreme claims of those who see ethnicity as a totally constructed economic and political identity or group commitment which, to cite Barth from another context, could be 'assumed and shed at will' (Barth 1959: 2), it is the dynamic character of ethnicity which stands out from these and other anthropological accounts (Ronald Cohen 1978b, Fardon 1987, Jenkins 1994). One consequence of this is that anthropological work on ethnicity has been increasingly grounded as much in historical as in contemporary ethnographic evidence.

The relationship between ethnicity and history in anthropology is by no means a simple one. Consider McDonald's study of contemporary Breton identity (1986), which she approaches through a type of discursive method-ology she calls an 'Anthropology of history'. This involves 'an account of the way in which the people studied construct the past, and of the moments, situations, relations, or structural contexts in which that history is told, written or comes alive' (1986: 345). This is a powerful perspective, though in it history (and identity) are seen as heavily text-rooted, that is based on what people say about themselves, with each 'text' apparently equally weighted (Spencer 1989: 160). There are other problems, too. Chapman, McDonald, and Tonkin have sought to replace what they believe to have been the traditional question of ethnic studies: 'How far did the past create the present?' with: 'How did the present create the past?' (1989: 5). Peel has lodged a forceful objection to what he calls this 'presentism', the insistence on seeing history only in relation to contemporary constructions of the past, and thence ethnicity as only some-thing which people do with the past. He himself has stressed the desirability of a 'properly cultural and historical explanation of ethnicity', but has also emphasized that 'culture' is no 'mere precipitate or bequest of the past. Rather, it is an active reflection on the past, a cultural *work*' (1989: 198; cf. Eriksen 1993: 72, 92).

What the present does with the past is an important question, and a valuable guide to understanding historical and anthropological writing about ethnicity. The problem with the perspective proposed by McDonald *et al.* is that it eliminates the possibility of a genuinely historical anthropology, indeed of any social history, independent of what contemporary writers, thinkers, or activists make of it. But it is insufficient to describe how 'men make their own history', we must also investigate the circumstances in which they do so. Ethnicity is not simply a mental or conceptual activity, using history as a series of validating texts, carried out in an economic, or political or social void. At the very least, construction must be seen to be embedded in context. Moreover, no matter how difficult it might be to obtain an answer, that question should not preclude another: 'What was the past *like?*'

In *The Gaelic Vision in Scottish Culture*, Malcolm Chapman has discussed what he calls 'symbolic appropriation', the way in which one society, in this case English or at any rate Lowland society, constructed the identity of and for another: Highlanders. This perspective (the 'Gaelic vision' is decidedly a view 'from above') is echoed in Chapman, McDonald, and Tonkin: 'The capacity of a successful self-defining entity like a nation to define and create its relevant history, both as it happens and in retrospect, has the corollary that minority, sub-national entities within it simply cannot compete on the same scale, They are, in important senses, history-less and event-less by comparison' (1989: 7–8). They go on:

for a minority or underprivileged group in a modern nation-state, independent history is in important senses missing. This is not *only* to say that the history was unrecorded or ignored, but also that, to an important degree, it did not happen; and to note, also, that the temporal grain of action and interpretation is not one that can be readily inspected for histories other than that sanctioned by majority perception (ibid.).

There is no denying the significance of this in specific contexts: the notion of the construction of the Other through the discourse of the powerful has been a compelling one in writing on or about the Third World in recent years. Yet what is often left out is the politics, and the contestation. Jenkins, for example, who emphasizes the importance of processes of categorization, argues that they must be placed in the informal and formal contexts in which they occur, ranging from 'routine public interaction' to 'official classification' (1994: 210 ff.). Other writers, whose perspective might be termed 'postmodernist' have also called for 'strategically situated ethnography' (Marcus 1986: 172), 'meshing . . . political economy and interpretative concerns' (Marcus and Fischer 1986: 84) in the manner pioneered by the so-called Manchester School of social anthropology. An example would be ethnic and cultural pluralism in the colonial world, where it is sometimes argued that the colonial state 'created' ethnicity in top–down fashion (see Chapter 5). In reality, ethnicity, as Taylor says of identity, has a 'dialogic character' Taylor (1994: 32), and much more complex processes are at work for which I find 'ethnic dialectic' an appropriate term. The colonizers of

Africa or the Americas, or the rulers of the Ottoman Empire, did not impose or operate solely with their own preformed system of classification, nor did they adopt existing systems wholesale. In the shaping and reshaping of indigenous ethnic and cultural pluralism there was, in colonialism, a complex interplay between these forces. Similarly, in contemporary Britain or the USA, 'cultural essentialism', the idea that a population may be defined by its presumed cultural specificity, although encouraged from above does not of itself generate cultural and ethnic diversity. Ethnic policies in complex ways sometimes reflect an underlying polyethnic reality, sometimes give it a particular direction, rarely do they create it out of whole cloth.

The anthropology of ethnicity has also stressed that it is not a single, undifferentiated, phenomenon, but must be treated as a 'variable rather than a unit of analysis' (Cohen and Middleton 1970: 31, Brass 1991: 13). This implies an overarching systemic, comparative perspective which places this variation in an appropriate context. Earlier approaches coupled with more recent thinking are of value here. It will be recalled that a crucial issue for Malinowski was the relationship between the 'tribe-nation' and the 'tribe-state', and that further the dominant issue of post-war anthropological writing on nationalism was the 'integrative revolution'. If the underlying thesis now smacks of discredited ideas of 'modernization', this writing was none the less concerned with the important question of the different ways in which 'ethnicity' and 'state' were conjoined. For this reason, the construction of ethnicity must be located within analyses of the kind undertaken by Gellner; one might call it the comparative political economy approach to ethnicity and nationalism, even if at times Gellner himself undervalues the role of culture.

The 'view from below' with which anthropology is associated, and with which it associates itself, is also an important one: Edmund Leach incessantly reminded anthropologists of the need to ask 'what actually happens, on the ground?' Hobsbawm's insistence that nations are 'constructed from above, but . . . cannot be understood unless also analysed from below' (1992: 10), might, however, be turned round as a methodological injunction for anthropology. The view from below should not be the limit of anthropology's ambition when it comes to discussing national identity or ethnicity. The analysis of ethnic and national identity encompasses both broad macro-structures, and the individual, villager or townee, activist or not, for whom identification with the nation is in some way meaningful. It is important not to confuse what happens on one level with what may or may not be happening on another, or read in what may not be there. The voluble and accessible nationalist literature often beguiles into believing what activists claim, and identity has to be inferred as much from the inexplicit, the casual, and informal (and sometimes seemingly trivial) as from conscious articulation. In terms of the personal (not to be confused with the psychological) an important issue is what Althusserians call 'interpellation': how the 'I' (and hence the 'We') is constituted so that the individual becomes a subject in several senses. This again is important, though determinism and reductionism must be avoided. It should not be imagined that all that is necessary is to identify the appropriate Ideological State Apparatus which jerks the subject into life like Pinocchio. The terrain is highly contested: identity, like myth, is a 'language of argument, not a chorus of harmony' (Leach 1954: 278).

2

Pluralism and the Patrimonial State: Pre-Colonial Africa

Hundreds of thousands of people of different ethnic origins all jumbled up—the ethnologist in Africa may sometimes sigh for some neat little Polynesian or Melanesian island community!

(Evans-Pritchard 1971: 67.)

1. Patrimonial states in social anthropology

There is a story, surely apocryphal, that after the Battle of the Boyne (1689), the victor, the Protestant King William III, William of Orange, was ferried across the river. 'Who won?', asked the boatman. 'What's it to you!', replied King Billy. There are many such apocryphal tales told to point a moral about conflict in contemporary Ulster (Vincent 1993: 128). This one serves as an allegory for understanding ethnic and cultural pluralism before the modern era. The present chapter begins the comparative study of the politics of difference by examining three pre-colonial African 'early', patrimonial states, in which authority was based on what Weber called 'tradition': the Alur, the Azande, and the Nupe. Chapters 3 and 4 continue the analysis with extended accounts of a Mesoamerican society (the Aztecs or Mexica), and the Ottoman Empire.

In writing about the state, Weber, and in this he was followed by Elias, was concerned with the consequences of basing a political system on a certain type of authority and form of rule. This led him to ask about devices employed by rulers to address problems generated by the logic of the systems in which they were engaged: finance, administration, armies, and so on. Except for a short, but subsequently highly influential piece which emphasized its socially constructed nature (1978: 385–98), he had relatively little to say about ethnicity. It is largely absent from his discussion of modern states, and scarcely mentioned in his account of patrimonialism, apart from brief references to the organization of the Ottoman Janissary corps (Weber 1978: 1016 ff.). Ethnic differentiation and difference were not among the difficulties which seemed to confront the rulers of early states. None the less, many or most such states were polyethnic in character: subjectively perceived by rulers and ruled to be in varying degrees, and with varying degrees of significance, comprised of different peoples. If this did not constitute, or was not seen to constitute a 'problem', in the way that currently it is often thought to be, then that is a notable fact. In any event, what ethnic and cultural difference meant in early states, and how, if at all, it was imbricated with the political order, are, to say the least, interesting questions.

Despite reservations about 'typologizing', the different forms that social and political systems take continue to exercise social anthropologists. As I said in Chapter 1, originally, and given the history of the discipline this focus was to be expected, British anthropologists were less concerned with different types of state than the contrast between centralized and non-centralized societies. A crucial text was *African Political Systems* (1940), which divided pre-colonial African political systems into two principal types: 'Group A', represented by the Zulu, the Ngwato, the Bemba, the Ankole, and the Kede, in which there was some kind of centralized authority, and 'Group B', the Nuer, the Tallensi, and the Luhya, or Bantu Kavirondo, as they were then called, which lacked it (Fortes and Evans-Pritchard 1940: 5). There is some truth in the view that the importance of this distinction derived less from anthropology than from colonial administration. In administrative terms, the differences between centralized and non-centralized peoples were considered to have important implications for policies of indirect rule associated, in Africa, with Lord Lugard (Lugard 1922: 197, and Chapter 5 below). Lugard, writing on Nigeria, had himself distinguished three types of African society: the Muslim states of the north; the 'primitive tribes' of the south-east; and what he called the 'advanced pagan communities' in the south-west. Fortes and Evans-Pritchard's two types, Group A and Group B, certainly corresponded very closely to Lugard's first two categories, and Lugard contributed the preface to Nadel's *Black Byzantium*, an important study of a centralized society in Nigeria. That an issue was important for colonial administration, however, did not mean that it lacked theoretical interest and significance, and by and large the anthropologists of *African Political Systems* would not have concerned themselves with something which was solely of interest to administrators (Fortes 1975 describes the genesis of the book).

Without doubt, the contrast between centralized and non-centralized societies was important sociologically. For example, the fundamental unit from which the political organization was constructed was very different in the two types of society. In centralized societies these were hierarchically ordered territorial units; in non-centralized they were clans or lineages organized on a segmentary basis (though often lineages did have an important territorial affiliation): what Durkheim called 'segmental societies with a clan base' (1964: 175). The arena within which political activity occurred was on a different scale. In centralized societies many people were joined in a single polity, whereas the effective limit of political relations in non-centralized societies was generally very small. Distinctions of rank and status pervaded centralized peoples. In non-centralized societies these were non-existent or insignificant: segmentary societies were egalitarian. Conflicting or competing interests were balanced in different ways: in centralized societies by constitutional devices relating to rules of succession, the distribution of power through the administrative system, and conventions of reciprocity binding rulers and subjects; in non-centralized societies through the mutual self-interest of the segments. In non-centralized societies the right to use force was widely distributed, and there was a pervading philosophy of self-help; in centralized states it was concentrated at the centre, and help was sought from above, from patrons, or through a judicial system. Finally, in centralized societies mystical values were located in a single person (the 'king'). In non-centralized societies all segments partook of them.

African Political Systems inaugurated systematic exploration of such differences, and for the next twenty years most British political anthropology responded to its agenda. In Africa this led to two somewhat separate branches of study. One dealt with non-centralized peoples, largely those with acephalous lineage systems, and was concerned with the relationship between lineage structure and the political order, including territorial relationships, the nature of offices, and the exercise and control of violence. The second dealt with kingdoms and concentrated on rulers, their families, and non-royal administrators. It was principally concerned with mechanisms of rule, such as ritual, with modes of succession, and with stratification. While the use of ideal types or models of political systems, along the lines advocated by Weber, is indispensable for comparative analysis, the authors of *African Political Systems* and their successors unfortunately assumed that the comparative task involved the setting up of comprehensive classificatory typologies of social and cultural systems rather in the way that their linguistic colleagues were establishing typologies of African languages. The self-defeating nature of this exercise was described by Leach (1961) as 'butterfly collecting'. One problem was that having started with two types which did not cover the whole spectrum of political systems, much time was wasted deciding where other examples might fit in, for example the so-called 'segmentary states' (below). More important, however, was the absence of a sense of the theoretical or developmental relationship between the two types, stemming from a naivety about economics and an imperviousness to history. For these and other reasons, including a lack of interest in the political anthropology of large-scale institutional complexes, from the early 1960s onwards mainstream British anthropology added little to the understanding of centralized societies except in certain specific contexts (mainly South Asia). Outside that mainstream, however, and outside Britain, the study of what was called the 'early state' flourished.

This research was focused on a group of scholars, they might be called a 'school', who in the 1970s and 1980s drew on older traditions of nineteenth- and early twentieth-century anthropology and political science, especially Marxism and cultural materialism, which the British anthropologists of *African Political Systems* and after had generally ignored. (See Claessen and Skalnik, 1978a: 5–17, for an account of the intellectual heritage.) One issue with which they were concerned, almost totally ignored by British anthropology, was the 'origins' of the state in Africa, South and South-East Asia, and Mesoamerica: the emergence of the state from pre-state conditions, and its 'evolution' from one form to another. It is right to be sceptical about the possibility of saying anything in general concerning the 'origins' of the state. None the less, it is obvious that states (even if defined in the loosest possible way) did not spring fully fledged into the world, and in individual cases their origins might be identified, assuming evidence is available. One should be equally sceptical of interpretations of evolution which involve necessary 'stages' of development. On this point Claessen and Van de Velde seem to want it both ways:

In general evolutionary terms the early state can be considered as one of various stages in polity formation. Historically, or in specific evolutionary terms, however, it is impossible to relate the early state to any chronological era. Certainly, for each specific case a beginning and an end can be approximately indicated, but early states are found in widely divergent historical periods (Claessen and Van de Velde 1987: 5).

Many of whose who have contributed to the theory of early states have never quite managed to break with an evolutionary perspective embedded in historical materialism, and continue to engage with debates empty of intellectual interest (see *inter alia* Claessen and Skalnik 1978*a*: 8–9 on the 'Asiatic Mode of Production'). At the same time they have generated many important insights, and certainly rejection of an 'evolutionist' approach should not lead, as it led the authors of *African Political Systems*, into static, ahistorical, functionalist analyses of the political.

Claessen and Skalnik offer as their 'working definition' of the early state: 'the organization for the regulation of social relations in a society that is divided into two emergent social classes: the rulers and the ruled' (1978*a*: 21). Later they refine this:

The early state is a centralized socio-political organization for the regulation of social relations in a complex, stratified society divided into at least two basic strata, or emergent social classes—viz. the rulers and the ruled—whose relations are characterized by political dominance of the former and tributary relations of the latter, legitimized by a common ideology of which reciprocity is the basic principle (Claessen and Skalnik 1978*b*: 640).

They identify the following characteristics. Population size is sufficient for stratification and specialization; there is a fundamental relationship between citizenship and birth/residence within the state's territory; there is centralized government capable of maintaining law and order; the state is independent and its institutions are capable of holding potentially centrifugal forces at bay, and defending the state against external forces; the system of production enables the generation of a regular surplus; there is an emergent ruling class whose right to rule is sustained by a common ideology (Claessen and Skalnik 1978*a*: 21).

Despite difficulties posed by applying such terms as 'class' and 'citizenship' in these contexts, their sketch of the early state gives a good sense of the type of system that is involved. As their own and others' comparative analyses show (Claessen 1978b, Claessen and Skalnik 1978a, 1978b, Shifferd 1987), these configurations occur in many different eras and in many different regions (Africa, Asia, the Americas, and Europe) in a remarkably similar form.

Claessen and Skalnik do not say so explicitly, but in practice most early states were 'patrimonial' in Weber's sense (see Chapter 1). In each of the twenty-one cases discussed by the contributors to Claessen and Skalnik (eds.) 1978 there is 'a sovereign and kin and an aristocracy' (Claessen 1978b: 548), and this pattern is replicated in numerous other instances. Not every pre-modern society with some recognizable form of the state had these elements: a counter-example would be the 'republics', such as the Greek city-states of the European classical period. The great majority, however, had what convention requires be called 'kingship', and many, if not most, were also located in pre-industrial, agricultural economies, often embedded in complex, wide-ranging systems of exchange and trade (Vansina's account of the Kuba, 1978, is an excellent illustration of one such agrarian-based society). There can never be a simple correlation between economic and political order: patrimonialism, said Weber, 'is compatible with household and market economy, petty-bourgeois and manorial agriculture, absence and presence of capitalist economy' (1978: 1091). None the less, there are links between the economic and the political in this type of system (not least in their inherent fragility) which will be apparent in much of what follows.

An old theory of early states said they arose through conquest. Few now accept it, or any single cause for the emergence of the state: commerce, for example, or large-scale agricultural works such as irrigation. It is none the less striking that in many instances, conquest, invasion, at the very least people coming in and taking over, had a significant role. Indigenous history and myth certainly emphasize this, as all the cases discussed here testify (Alur, Azande, Nupe, Aztecs, Ottomans). Such examples, however, also show that it was not just in their origins (mythical or otherwise) that conquest and invasion were important. Expansion, with or without force of arms, continued to be a major factor in the history of these states, right up until their end, which in those, and many other instances, came with another form of conquest: colonialism. The Alur and the Aztecs might be at the opposite poles of the spectrum of violence employed as policy in the expansion of their respective states, but the crucial point is that both were expanding throughout the period of which we have record. The early patrimonial state was inherently predatory.

Writing about states in medieval Europe, which he compared with non-European kingdoms such as that of Ethiopia (1982: 18), Elias emphasized what might be called an imperative to expand. This stemmed internally from the demands of the ruler–ruled relationship, and externally from surrounding competitor states. Mainly interested in how and why large-scale 'absolutist' states subsequently emerged in Europe, Elias argued that in the medieval period, a variety of factors (the barter economy, demographic change, the system of rewarding retainers and clients) propelled rulers to seek beyond their immediate domain for tribute, taxes, booty, land, and labour. The system generated demands which could not be sustained internally; to survive they had to expand, and did so in competition with other states bent on the same objective. Such societies were inherently fragile (Southall 1988: 77), and other factors contributed to this fragility. Populations were vulnerable to disease, and the agricultural economy to adverse climatic and horticultural conditions. In the mid-fifteenth century, for example, Aztec rule virtually collapsed for a short time, after several seasons of crop failure: the ruler's reserves of maize were exhausted and he had nothing to give out. For a year or two it was everyone for themselves, with many families forced to sell their children into slavery in other more fortunate zones: 'It is the will now of the lord of the Heavens that each of you go his own way to seek his own salvation' (Moctezuma I, in Duran 1964: 147). Fragility is also revealed in the frequent movement within and between such states (if one patron could not fulfil his side of the bargain, then others might be found who would), and in histories which speak of internal fission especially at the time of succession, with rebellions by vassal states, provincial governors, subordinate chiefs, and princes (Gluckman 1963, 1965). All of this has implications for the meaning of citizenship (below).

2. Segmentary states

By no means universally, but certainly very generally, early states emerged in clusters. Over wide areas of East-Central and West Africa, and Mesoamerica, to cite three examples, there were congeries of states, sometimes sharing a myth of common ancestry (such as Mesoamerican states which laid claim to the Toltec heritage), or a common source (for example Hausa-Fulani emirates in West Africa). The system of interstate relations (not 'international', because 'national' begs the question) was itself usually grounded in the same principles of patronage and clientage which governed the states internally, and was generally characterized by shifting alliances, changing allegiances, conquests, rebellions, and reconquests, in a seemingly endless cycle. Consistent with this general environment, and contributing to it, was the 'segmentary' form that many of these states took.

The concept of the 'segmentary state' was devised by Aidan Southall (1956) in his account of Alur society, developed by him (1965, 1988), and taken up elsewhere, notably by writers on South Asia. Weissleder (1978: 188) relates the idea to Aristotelian thinking about the relationship between the *oikia* (household) and the *polis* (polity). Briefly, dissatisfied with the simple contrast between Fortes and Evans-Pritchard's Group A and Group B typology, Southall drew attention to differences, within Group A, between 'unitary states', where there was a strong, centralized authority, backed by a specialist administration, which exercised a monopoly of power over a defined territory; and segmentary states where 'specialised political power is exercised within a pyramidal series of segments tied together at any one level by the oppositions between them at a higher level' (1956: 260). Southall (ibid.: 248 ff.) identified the following typical features of such societies:

There are zones of increasingly restricted authority;

There is centralized government, but also 'numerous peripheral foci . . . over which the centre exercises only limited control';

There is a 'specialised administrative staff at the centre . . . repeated on a reduced scale' in the peripheral foci;

'Monopoly of the use of force is successfully claimed to a limited extent and within a limited range by the central authority, but legitimate force of a more restricted order inheres at all the peripheral foci';

There are 'several levels of subordinate foci . . . organised pyramidally in relation to the central authority';

'The central and peripheral authorities reflect the same model . . . Similar powers are repeated at each level with a decreasing range';

Peripheral authorities change from one pyramid to another. Segmentary states are 'flexible and fluctuating, even comprising peripheral units which have political standing in several adjacent power pyramids which thus become interlocked'.

Above all, in segmentary states 'spheres of ritual suzerainty and political sovereignty do not coincide. The former extends widely towards a flexible, changing periphery. The latter is confined to the central, core domain' (1988: 52).

'Segmentary state', which combined key terms from both Group A and Group B in Fortes and Evans-Pritchard's schema, was derived by Southall partly from an analogy with the way in which fission and fusion, with complementary opposition between segments, occurred in (non-centralized, acephalous) segmentary lineage systems (Stein 1980: 264). It also stemmed from his observation that in the Alur system the proliferation of chiefs and chieflets actually followed lines of lineage segmentation: in the classic metaphor, the system spread 'amoeba-like'. Southall did not, however, wish to confine application of the term to societies which had segmentary lineage systems. In his view, it was generalizable, and patrimonial states may frequently be described as 'segmentary', in a slightly broader sense. It is possible that Gramsci was groping towards a formulation of this kind when he wrote:

In the ancient and medieval state, both politico-territorial and social centralization were minimal . . . the state was a mechanical bloc of social groups, often of different races. Under the constraint and military-political pressure that bore on them, and could at certain moments assume an acute form, the subaltern groups maintained a life of their own, with specific institutions (Notebook 3, 18, quoted in Buci-Glucksmann, 1980: 274).

Burton Stein, in adapting Southall's schema for his analysis of the medieval Chola State, has argued that in South India there were 'numerous "centres" of which one had primacy as a source of ritual sovereignty' (1980: 274), and suggested that such systems were characterized by what he termed a 'dual sovereignty': political control, which may be decentralized; and a wider-ranging ritual hegemony. Whether or not this dual sovereignty occurred elsewhere, two features found in the Chola State and in other segmentary states are of particular significance. First, as Southall put it, 'central and peripheral authorities reflect the same model'. There was repetition of centre–periphery relations at each level. Beneath the kings or chiefs were 'little kings (Stein 1980: 274), what Southall called 'chieflets'. Secondly, segmentary states were 'fragile structures of great flexibility' (Southall 1956: 260). He says: 'The central authority at the top of the pyramid, while often enjoying . . . absolute power locally, is only able to enforce its will throughout the area nominally subordinate to it if it is able to call upon the self-interest of segments in one quarter of the realm to crush recalcitrance in another' (Southall 1956: 251). In consequence, the boundaries of such states, their very existence, were fundamentally impermanent. It also meant that segmentary states were all, to some extent 'empires', directly and indirectly incorporating in their patron-client systems many groups which in other ways were relatively autonomous 'vassal states', as they are usually called. Relations between the ruler and both 'internal' subordinate segments and such 'external' vassal states were thus very similar, though the contrast between 'internal' and 'external' segments is not necessarily a valid one, implying as it does a stronger sense of 'boundary' than was usually found in such systems. Both internally and externally, however, the way in which the relationship with the central ruler operated has frequently suggested an analogy with the British imperial arrangement of indirect rule, as has been noted by many writers familiar with the workings of colonial administration.

3. Patrimonial states as plural societies

In one of the most interesting and subtle overviews of the literature on the early state, Ronald Cohen (1978a), although rejecting the view proposed by Thurnwald in the 1930s that they were, by definition, stratified polyethnic societies, none the less argues that 'once the state emerges multi-ethnicity becomes possible, even inevitable' (1978a: 65), and 'multiethnicity and statehood are two sides of the same coin' (1993: 233). In a general survey, Claessen and Skalnik (1978b: 646) concluded that Cohen's contention was 'not universally valid'. Certainly there were some states (including perhaps Tahiti, discussed by Claessen himself, 1978a) where ethnic differentiation was non-existent. None the less, in the pre-modern era in Africa, the Americas, Asia, and Europe, there was a high probability that any conceivable collectivity on any significant scale would include peoples speaking different languages and dialects and following different cultural practices. The situation 'on the ground' in those regions where early states emerged, may be described simplistically as one in which there were (traditionally, pre-state) many small, face-to-face 'communities' (African acephalous lineage systems are one though by no means the only or typical example), often highly localized, with relatively self-sufficient subsistence economies, sometimes occupying a distinct ecological niche. This was a landscape in which there was, over a given region, a high degree of linguistic and cultural variation. Less simplistically, there were rarely strong boundaries between one 'people' and another, no sharp breaks, but linguistic and cultural continua (Southall 1976), and a 'penumbral or fading quality to the boundary concept' (Cohen and Middleton 1970: 15), well illustrated by Goody's difficulty in identifying, and locating, the 'Lodagaa' in northern Ghana (1962).

These localized societies, with their restricted arenas of political action, may have been relatively autonomous, but they were only relatively self-sufficient. Ecological variation meant that regionally there was generally some specialization in the gathering and processing of flora, fauna, and other natural resources, so that salt, for example, or iron or ochre had to be traded, often across vast distances, as in Aboriginal Australia. Besides trade, there was migratory movement on a considerable scale and over long periods. Thus, Cohen and Middleton (1970: 5, 15) were right to point out that in Africa, and in Mesoamerica, the interaction of peoples from different cultural traditions had always occurred. When states emerged in such landscapes, there was a likelihood that any governed collectivity would be a polyethnic collectivity, and would coexist with other states (as well as with 'stateless' peoples) in regional systems which were likewise polyethnic. Evans-Pritchard used the term 'Zande complex' to refer to one such system: not only was the Zande state a polyethnic state, but the Zande complex was a polyethnic complex, and the Alur, the Nupe, and the Aztecs discussed later were all similarly situated.

To speak of early states (or complexes of states) as being in some objective sense polyethnic (from the viewpoint of an observer versed in ethnic and cultural pluralism as it seems to be elsewhere) begs the question whether or not they were 'lived' as polyethnic in some subjective sense, and if so, how. What salience, if any, did ethnic and cultural pluralism have in such configurations? Did it ever appear in the 'construction of the political sphere' (Eisenstadt, Abitbol, and Chazan, 1988: 18), and in the construction of the political subject? On the face of it, rulers of early states looked to their subjects primarily for material resources and obedience: this is what 'citizenship' meant in this type of system. To what extent, then, did, or could, ethnic identity play any part in it? Did ethnicity determine the way in which political subjects fell into different categories or classes, with different and distinct rights and obligations? Was the obligation to be a client ever constructed through ethnicity?

The rest of this chapter explores these questions through three cases of somewhat increasing complexity. The sources employed are similar: detailed ethnographies by British anthropologists (Southall on the Alur, Evans-Pritchard on the Azande, and Nadel on the Nupe) whose fieldwork was undertaken during the penultimate phase of colonial rule, between 1926 and 1952. As well as documenting the societies as they found them, each attempted to reconstruct the pre-colonial order, using such indigenous historical evidence, mainly oral histories and accounts of informants born in the nineteenth century, as were available. They also drew on the writings of early European and Arab explorers and traders, and on the reports of colonial administrators, to locate these specific societies in the wider context of adjacent peoples and cultures with whom they interacted. It will become apparent that evidence drawn from such sources sometimes poses great difficulties of interpretation, as does the descriptive and analytical language that the anthropologists themselves employed. It will also become apparent that each of these anthropologists viewed 'their' people with considerable sympathy: they were 'pro-Alur', 'pro-Azande', and 'pro-Nupe' in ways which sometimes obscure a broader view of these societies.

4. Alurization: ethnic incorporation in a segmentary state

Aidan Southall conducted fieldwork among the Alur of north-west Uganda and the Congo (Zaire) in 1949–52. It is not possible to speak of '*the* Alur' as a single, unitary 'society'. Southall described them as a 'tribe made up of dominant groups, themselves of heterogeneous origin, which have incorporated members of many different tribes into a series of politically independent chiefdoms' (1956: 14). Indeed to speak of them as a 'tribe', which was commonly done at the time Southall was writing, is itself problematic, with connotations, most of them unfortunate, almost all misleading. Cohen and Middleton commented:

Earlier travellers, missionaries and explorers spoke of 'peoples', 'kingdoms', 'sultanates', and 'customs', but only rarely of tribes. However, by the early twentieth century, colonial administrators and those reporting on African territories were using the term to describe what they believed to be clear-cut and stable groups, each having distinct cultural traditions (1970: 2).

Early maps of the interior of Africa frequently did not mention peoples so much as places, often centres, the main villages or 'courts' of powerful persons. The usage survives in contemporary place-names: for example, Mumias in western Kenya, originally 'Mumia's', the village of Mumia, an important Luhya chief at the time of the arrival of the British. Southall himself has remarked that the way in which 'a state in Africa is always referred to as a tribe' was an African counterpart of 'orientalism' (1988: 55). It is best, therefore, to think of the Alur not as a tribe if this implies, as Cohen and Middleton suggest, a 'clear-cut and stable group', but rather as a complex of heterogeneous peoples, of different origins and speaking different languages, coexisting under the loose hegemony of a variety of chiefs and chieflets who themselves used the name 'Alur'. In this regard, Alur, Azande, and Nupe were very similar.

The Alur complex, which spread across the border between what became the British colony of Uganda and the Belgian Congo (later Zaire), encompassed about 250,000 people shortly before colonial occupation at the end of the nineteenth century (1956: 18). It covered a wide variety of ecological zones, from fertile agricultural uplands, also good cattle country, through a less densely populated and Tsetse-infested midland region, down to an unhealthy lowland area on the shores of Lake Albert producing fish and salt. It had a long and complicated history. Alur speak a Nilotic language, one of the Lwoo group found among peoples such as the Nuer and Dinka to the north in the Sudan, and the Kenyan Luo. From about 450 years before the present there was a southwards migration of Lwoo-speakers into the parts of Uganda and Zaire now occupied by the Alur. The migrants then moved east through Uganda (where they emerged as Acholi and Lango), and then south along the eastern shores of Lake Victoria, where they became the Luo, the second largest ethnic group in Kenya, of whom elements subsequently moved into Tanzania. There was also a southward movement on the western side of Uganda, into the area of the interlacustrine Bantu kingdoms of Bunyoro and Buganda. The ruling dynasty of the Nyoro state was of the Babito clan which it is generally accepted was of Nilotic origin though by the nineteenth century their descendants had become thoroughly 'Nyoro-ized', and spoke a Bantu language (Beattie 1971: 51–2, Southall 1956: 19). There may also have been at some stage a return migration of Nilotic-speakers from the Nyoro-dominated complex back to Alurland, though whether this represented a reincorporation of returned Nilotics or an incorporation of local Bantu-speaking groups into a Nilotic-dominated system is not clear.

The Alur system constituted a 'segmentary state' similar to those found throughout the region among neighbouring peoples. These included the Nyoro, whose kingdom, says Beattie was a 'loose association of semi-independent politics' among which there was 'political dependency without integration' (1971: 28–9). Not that Nyoro was exactly like Alur. Rather, across a wide area there were several states of a similar, more or less predatory character, dominated by different groups (Southall 1988: 56). In understanding the particular form that the segmentary state took in Alur it is best to begin with the 'segmentary'. Like many other peoples in this region, Nilotic and non-Nilotic, with and without chiefs, Alur had (and have) agnatic lineages, groups tracing descent in the male line from some common ancestor. Typically in such systems, descent provides the framework through which social solidarity and distance are expressed. A group calling itself the 'X', for example, would claim a common ancestor: they are the descendants of 'X' thus distinguishing themselves from the descendants of 'Y'. But 'X' and 'Y' may share a common ancestor in 'Z', and this in turn distinguishes 'X' and 'Y' together from another, more distantly related group. Common in such societies is the process of lineage 'fission', described in great detail by Middleton (1960) for the Lugbara, a Sudanic-speaking people who live in the same general area of Uganda as the Alur. When a local descent group, consisting of a number of closely related agnates, grows to a certain size, or more properly when it attains a certain sociological status, with a son or brother having his own family etc., a fraction may break off to found their own independent homestead. Alur lineages operate in much this way (Southall 1956: 38 ff.), with the effective local grouping, the descendants of a common ancestor sharing a homestead, called a *paco*. This term refers both to the social group and the terrain it occupies, and the coincidence of the two is an Alur ideal: 'lineages which matter, and which conform to the idea of what a lineage should be, are those which maintain their local corporate identity' (Southall 1956: 61). On the ground the situation is not usually so simple. Lineages are frequently dispersed, and settlements often contain families and individuals who are not of the local descent group, indeed may not be Alur.

Paco has (or had) a wider connotation than 'homestead', being applied to an area occupied by a lineage or clan, and also to the domain of a chief, though the more usual term for this was *ngom*, glossed by Southall as 'soil', 'earth', 'terri-tory', or 'world'. There was, however, no 'chief of the Alur'. Rather there were a number of major and minor chiefs (chieflets), the latter spinning off, fission-like, from a major chieftaincy. Chiefs belonged to one of a number of chiefly, as opposed to commoner, clans or lineages. Southall mentions two in particular, the Atyak and the Ucibu, both of which spawned a number of chiefs and chieflets. These were clans which had historically been dominant, and accepted as dominant, and there was some movement between chiefly and commoner status. Chiefship was closely connected with ancestor worship, and chiefs built two shrines: the 'shrine of the Lwoo', and the 'shrine of the subjects'. Over time, chiefs or a chiefly line, might decline in influence, losing followers or subjects, and the head might be reduced to building only one shrine: there is no point in building a 'shrine of the subjects' if there are none. Southall quotes the descendants of one such line who said: 'We have become distant, we have become like commoners' (1956: 110).

Chiefs, therefore, had subjects, and chiefship was the focal point of political relations in Alur. Traditionally, chiefs often had two or three homesteads, though they generally stayed in one to make themselves available to petitioners (Southall 1956: 76 ff.). Important chiefs had many retainers living around their homesteads, and substantial herds of cattle, often cared for by *andwaci*, people who attached themselves for protection and assistance. Between chiefs and subjects there was a 'reciprocity of goods and services in which the chief was only the main centre of exchange' (Southall 1956: 80). Besides controlling the ancestor shrines, two principal functions of chiefs were adjudication in matters of dispute between followers, and rainmaking. In return for the provision of these services, the chief received fines paid for infringements, and a share of the harvest and of the spoils of the hunt: he had the right to the hind leg of all principal game animals. Subjects also gave labour service, digging the chief's fields and building his huts and granaries, and the chief received tribute of products such as salt or dried fish from those of his subjects occupying specialized ecological niches.

The power of a chief was not constant over a given territory. There was, rather 'a series of zones radiating out from the main centres of chiefship . . . [with] a diminution in the inclusiveness and efficacy of chiefly power in these successive zones' (Southall 1956: 146–7). Consistent with this, 'Considerable political responsibility for their members was left to the heads of local groups, the chief stepping in to reinforce their authority only when directly called upon by them, or when violent and unresolved disorders required his intervention. Alur chiefs did not enforce any rigidly defined authority within strict territorial frontiers' (p. 237). Chiefs spawned chieflets, who moved off, fission-like, to establish their own domain (and lineage), and in this fashion the Alur polity expanded over new territory. The new chieflet was confirmed in office by his 'parent' (not necessarily his actual father) who 'gave him the rain', and to whom for a period he remained subordinate. A story recorded by Southall (p. 183) suggests that the subjects of a new chieflet paid tribute to the major originating chief until after his death: 'When I am no more you eat the tribute yourself. While I am alive bring it to me' (p. 184). In fact, practice was extremely varied. Certainly, chieflets received their own tribute, which was similar to, if on a lesser scale than, that of a major chief.

The detailed mechanics of rule are here of less interest than the way in which non-Alur were incorporated into the domains of chiefs and chieflets. The Alur, it will be recalled, are a Nilotic-speaking people of Lwoo descent who over several hundred years had migrated into and colonized their present area. That area included a number of non-Nilotic-speaking peoples such as the Lendu, Okebo, and Madi whose traditional social organization was similar to that of the acephalous Lugbara. As Alur lineages and chiefs spread across this terrain, these peoples were in varying degrees and in various ways brought within their system of rule, becoming subjects with the same obligations as, and more or less on a par with, Alur commoner lineages. A common theme in the oral histories collected by Southall is that those who put themselves under Alur domination did so voluntarily: they asked to be ruled. They 'kidnapped' the son of a chief to acquire a chieflet, or offered a home (and a domain) to the son of a chief who had quarrelled with his father. The story of Magwar, the first chief of Paidha, is typical.

Magwar, while trying to smoke out some bees to obtain their honey, accidentally set fire to grassland which his father was seeking to preserve for hunting. Running away to escape the latter's wrath, he was found by the Okebo and made their chief. Later, his father forgave him and gave him a drum, rain, and grass slasher, so that he might go among the Okebo and they would revere him (Southall 1956: 183; 1970a: 78–9).

Southall (1956: 202) cites two accounts, one Alur, the other Lendu, which put a slightly different gloss on the voluntaristic nature of the acceptance of Alur chieftaincy. The Alur said:

Songa [a chief] sent Andhiga [his son] among the Lendu. We did not fight with them; first of all we plundered them a little of small things. We struck them if they did not pay heed to what we told them. We helped them. Their elders came to us. Their elders looked after them but they did not look after them well. All really good things they got from us; we stayed with them on good terms. Lendu attached themselves to us because of our kindness to them; because we gave them nice food. We called them to eat, and then we sent them to dig our field, and if they liked they stayed. If they did not like us and went and attached themselves to another Alur master we had no redress. We could not get them back. They would never kill a man of chiefly descent; they respected him. Lendu work was taking messages; Lendu work was digging fields; Lendu work was building huts and constructing granaries.

The Lendu account, on the other hand, ran:

The Alur came slowly, slowly, like you British. They came friendly, and to friends you exchange food, and so they became chiefs . . . The Alur deceived us with things to eat. We had our food but the Alur gave us food and so the Lendu thought that these people would be able to look after these people well . . . [We tried to drive them away], but the Alur came and stayed among us slowly, slowly, and seduced us with food.

These accounts show that while there was clearly some violence ('we struck them' etc.), Alur incursion was not invasion or conquest by force. Secondly, there was the reciprocity, expressed here in the idiom of the exchange of food. The Lendu and Okebo submitted to Alur chiefship, and its tributary obligations, but, says Southall, gained from this clientage access to Alur chiefly office for the resolution of disputes, which it was believed provided a more peaceful mechanism than their traditional methods of self-help. They also acquired (crucially, it seems) access to the Alur chiefs' believed powers over the rain, and over witchcraft (Southall 1970a: 84). Thirdly, subject peoples, Alur commoners as well as non-Alur, were not tied irrevocably to any one chief. If they were dissatisfied with what one offered them they could try another. Southall recounts an instance when 'a chief who was more popular than he, is said to have sat in the path and remonstrated with the subject groups who were passing along that way to transfer their allegiance to his brother' (1956: 188 ff.).

This leads to 'Alurization'. Southall himself does not employ that term, which is found in Cohen and Middleton (1970: 22), though he does use 'Alurise' (1956: 124). In Alur society there was 'every degree of incorporation . . . from groups whose ethnic origin was no longer known even to themselves, to groups of Okebo or Lendu no longer speaking their own language but only Alur, to groups still mainly speaking their own language yet under Alur rule' (Southall 1970a: 75). There were also instances of Alur going the other way. One is the 'Nyoroization' of the Nilotic ruling clan of Bunyoro (see earlier).

Others included the Mambisa, Alur who migrated deep into Lendu country. They established a chiefship in which the ruling lineage became 'Lendu-ized', losing the Alur language albeit keeping a political culture closely resembling that of the Alur (Southall 1956: 220–7, 1970a: 84 ff.). Interestingly, in the same region was the Hema, a group probably of interlacustrine Bantu origin, whose Alur-like polity also became Lendu-ized.

Alurization was not a function of policy but the unintended consequence of long-term processes of interaction. Just as Alur commoner families attached themselves to the households of Alur chiefs, better to secure their share of such resources as were available, so too did Lendu and Okebo families. There was also intermarriage. Generally this appears to have involved Alur men (chiefs especially) marrying Lendu and Okebo women rather than the other way round, though Okebo did take Alur wives (Southall 1956: 174). There were no adverse effects on the status of non-Alur wives, and their sons could become chiefs (Southall 1956: 83). Incorporation was relatively easy to the extent that, despite linguistic differences, the underlying culture of these societies was similar: there was a shared universe of meaning about, for example, ancestors, lineages, witchcraft, and rainmaking (Southall 1956: 232, 1970a: 84).

Although Alurization occurred 'without excessive violence or injustice' (Southall 1956: 90), and without, it seems, imposing Alur-ness on any one, it is also clear that running through their thinking was a conviction of their own superiority (ibid.: 86). This is illustrated in the Alur myth about the Abira, who like the Lendu and Okebo are of non-Lwoo origin. Alur claimed that when they first arrived in the region they found the Abira living in caves and with tails, but they 'enticed them out of their caves with salt . . . [and] cut off their tails', thus enabling them to become 'normal members of human society' (1970a: 73). Alur superiority is revealed in their view of other people as 'bad-mannered and uncouth . . . who ate dirty and repulsive things like frogs' (1956: 86). Lendu were mocked for practising male circumcision: 'Your penis is on fire!' (1956: 203), and Southall records at least one Lendu group who abandoned the practice.

The predatory nature of the Alur state, the centrality of patron–client ties in establishing political relations and in shaping the form of the polity, the relative ease with which people could move from one political (and cultural) allegiance to another, above all the fluidity of the system of ethnic identification, are important themes which appear in the two other cases considered in this chapter.

5. Zande 'assimilation'

To the north and west of the Alur are the Azande, one of the best-known peoples in British anthropological literature because of Evans-Pritchard's first book *Witchcraft, Oracles and Magic among the Azande* (published in 1937, but based on fieldwork between 1926–30). Evans-Pritchard continued to write about the Azande over a period of some forty years, with his scattered papers on their political system finally appearing in collected and revised form in 1971, shortly before his death. Evans-Pritchard's account of the Zande polity, put together at different times, was not always consistent, perhaps reflecting his changing perceptions. It is unfortunate that the overview provided by this last book was not available earlier since it puts earlier published material in a somewhat different light. (Unless otherwise stated, page references are to Evans-Pritchard 1971.)

The Zande complex covered a large territory subsequently divided between three colonial powers: the Anglo-Egyptian Sudan, the Belgian Congo, and French Equatorial Africa. Evans-Pritchard tended to use the term 'Azande' unproblematically. Certainly, to judge from the copious native language quotations that he cites, Zande-speakers employed it themselves. It is notable, however, that neighbouring peoples such as the Mangbetu, who dominated a similar political complex to the south, referred to them as 'Avongara', the name of the Zande ruling aristocracy (p. 434), and the Azande referred to the Mangbetu, and another group, the Abandiya, in similar fashion. Within the 'Zande complex', as he called it (p. 27), Evans-Pritchard identified four categories of Zande clans or patrilineal descent groups: the ruling Avongara, who formed an 'aristocracy'; Ambomu clans, the original Zande clans and followers of the Avongara; clans of non-Ambomu origin ('named foreign stocks') but assimilated to them; and *auro* clans—'a heterogeneous collection of clans of unspecified foreign peoples, also . . . assimilated to the Ambomu, but regarded by them more as foreigners' (p. 20). Evans-Pritchard's pro-Azande bias is apparent in his remark that many clan names 'by their uncouth forms suggest a non-Zande origin' (ibid.) In fact, Ambomu clans themselves often consisted of non-Ambomu, attached peoples (individuals and groups) who claimed Ambomu membership, and it was difficult to distinguish 'true' Ambomu from the rest. Thus 'the Azande' are a complex admixture, more complex perhaps than the simple distinction between 'Azande ni Ambomu' and 'Azande ni Auro' (the latter glossed by Evans-Pritchard as 'assimilated stocks', p. 24, but see further below) might suggest.

In addition to these mainly Zande-speaking groups, there were many subject peoples, speaking their own languages, but in various ways under Avongara overlordship. The Zande term for 'subject' or 'follower' is *avuru*, and, says Evans-Pritchard, over a period of time, 'Azande' itself became 'synonymous with *avuru*, all alike being subjects of the Avongara' (p. 41), irrespective of the language they spoke. This 'vast ethnic amalgam' (p. 39), contained some fifty identifiable groups, and represented 'a most remarkable assimilation of different foreign peoples . . . as considerable achievement as can be claimed by, shall we say, the USA or Israel' (p. 21). Zande culture, or 'cultural complex' (p. 68), was itself an amalgam of beliefs and practices from many non-Zande sources. Chapters VII–IX of the 1971 book show in detail that much of it came from elsewhere. The knowledge and use of plants, clothing, arts and crafts, buildings (including granaries), circumcision, mortuary ceremonies as well as rites which in the anthropological literature have been most closely identified with them including the *benge* poison oracle (the institution, not just the 'medicine') were of 'foreign' origin. 'Azande' seems at times like an empty vessel, into which peoples and practices were poured.

In retrospect, the Zande polity looks like a classic segmentary state. There was no 'Zande state' as such, but a number of polities, large and small, having in common that they were ruled by members of the Avongara clan. Folk etymology derived 'Avongara' from 'Ngara', the supposed founder of the clan, whose name meant 'Strength' (p. 416). According to myth he had acquired the praise-name 'vo-Ngara', *vo* having something to do with 'binding'; hence 'Avongara'. (Evans-Pritchard specifically rejects a derivation from 'Avuru Ngara', 'follower of Ngara'.) All myths of origin agreed in depicting the Azande as living originally in a world of 'autonomous local groups' (p. 419), acephalous to the extent that there was no ruling dynasty, and no nobility (*gbia*, signifying 'Master' when used as a term of address, p. 414), with disputes settled by lineage elders. Then came the hero Ngara 'who gained precedence by his wisdom and liberality and whose descendants have established themselves as a ruling dynasty over the Ambomu and other Azande' (p. 419). Under the Avongara the Azande expanded their political hegemony by conquest and assimilation for some 150 years before they in turn were conquered by the colonial powers (p. 267).

Evans-Pritchard traced several lines of descent from Ngara, each spawning a number of kingdoms: by 1885, for example, there were five stemming from Ngara's grandson, Nunga, whose subjects were known as the 'Avuru Nunga'. Much of his data came from one of these kingdoms, that ruled from the 1860s until 1905 by King Gbudwe, a descendant of Nunga's brother. A kingdom was 'a territory whose inhabitants fought the inhabitants of a like territory in the name and at the orders of some scion of the royal clan' (p. 266). At the centre was the principal compound (court, *ngbanga*), of the king, from which he controlled directly, on his own account, what Evans-Pritchard called a 'province'. Other parts of the territory were allocated to 'governors', often, though not always, princes, that is his sons. A prince 'held a province under his father's suzerainty but in varying degrees independent of his control—eldest sons were almost completely independent' (p. 139). A network of paths connected the king's court to the rather smaller courts of princes which were in turn connected to the compounds of local notables. (See Evans-Pritchard's diagram at p. 170. Azande generally lived in dispersed homesteads, not villages.) All courts were organized in a similar fashion, indeed many elements of the system were replicated at all levels:

A court consisted of three parts, the *ngbanga* proper, a large cleared open space in a spot usually selected because some shady trees grew there and provided shelter during the heat of the day, where those who came to visit the ruler spent the day and where he sat with them to hear cases and discuss affairs. Round this court were huts for the members of the companies of young warriors, and sometimes one or two huts for married men, though they, being married and having families, did not usually sleep at court . . . Here also or near by, were the huts of those of the king's sons who had reached the age of puberty and were unable to enter the king's private quarters but, being as yet unmarried and without provinces to administer, had to live at court (p. 171).

At any one time courts housed a great many people: young warriors, visiting dignitaries, provincial governors and elders, the king's families (Gbudwe, for example, had many wives), craftsmen, petitioners, page-boys, and 'the lads who operated the oracles' (p. 191). Evans-Pritchard's account of the preparation and distribution of meals to this retinue bears a striking resemblance to the procedures at Moctezuma's court, described by Clendinnen, and cited in the next chapter.

Generosity had to be supported, and that meant tribute. Azande kings received various offerings from their subjects. These included substantial gifts of spears (p. 185), used for bridewealth payments by the king, or given by him to subjects who petitioned him for financial assistance with their marriage payments (p. 187), though the bulk was retained by the king for distribution in time of war. Tribute of food and labour was also collected from subjects in the province which the king controlled directly, as well as from those controlled by the princes (who also took their own share). 'A youth's labour belonged to his father [who] gave it to the king' (p. 198). A large part of that labour was used to cultivate the king's (and princes') land. Evans-Pritchard estimated that Gbudwe had several farms 'each at least a mile in length and several hundred yards in breadth' (p. 202). There were also gifts in kind, from the provinces and subject peoples: dried and smoked meats, oils, pots, iron goods, bark for dyeing, fruit, clothing, hats, mats, ivory, and captive slaves, principally women and young boys (pp. 218–23). This tributary system was replicated at all levels: princes and governors also had many mouths to feed. The task of organizing the collection of this tribute was delegated to an official or deputy, the *ligbu*, of whom there might be several, each responsible for a different part of the province. *Ligbu* were also in charge of organizing companies of warriors.

Evans-Pritchard's account of the organization of Gbudwe's kingdom inadvertently, but perhaps inevitably, presented a picture of a more static, settled, routinized polity than emerged from the historical evidence: it is an idealized version of how a kingdom should be. Gbudwe, for example, moved his court on a number of occasions (pp. 358–9, 405); boundaries between provinces were not unchanging, even in time of peace, and such times seem to have been rare; kingdoms were always expanding, contracting, and splitting, and prone to civil war, especially on the occasion of the succession. Gbudwe's father, Bazingbi was, for instance, 'constantly extending the boundaries of his kingdom and subjugating foreign peoples' (p. 285). During his lifetime the various parts of the kingdom had been allocated to his sons, with nothing for Gbudwe. His death was followed by a succession war from which Gbudwe emerged as the victor. This has a bearing on the predatory nature of the Zande system. If kingdoms were divided among sons, there were bound to be civil wars and wars of expansion. How would anyone get enough? Zande states (or rather their rulers) were inordinately predatory. As well as extending their hegemony over non-Zande peoples, or fighting their relatives in adjacent kingdoms, rulers were constantly poaching followers from other rulers. Princes encouraged subjects to move from one province to another (p. 236), and Evans-Pritchard recorded a speech (p. 253) in which a warrior affirmed support for Gbudwe declaring 'I will never leave you to serve Wando, to serve Malingindo, to serve the children of Ezo or the children of Nunga', all other dynasties, suggesting that movement between kingdoms was at least conceivable.

In sum, therefore, the Zande complex consisted of a series of states (kingdoms) within which were zones of greater or lesser authority. Provincial rulers were subordinate to the centre, but operated relatively independent of it. The system as a whole was able to expand and encompass surrounding acephalous peoples because, says Evans-Pritchard, of its superior organization. It continued to do so before the arrival of the Europeans unless and until it came up against states, such as those of the Mangbetu, organized in a similar way (p. 434). Expansion brought within the complex a great many non-Zande peoples. Some were so closely absorbed into Zande culture (itself an ever-changing phenomenon) that their origins could not readily be identified. Others retained their ethnically specific characteristics or indicated another origin through their pronunciation of 'l' and 'r', and in aspiration (p. 118).

Evans-Pritchard wrote ambiguously about Zande attitudes towards these foreign groups:

It was the traditional Zande policy to encourage submitted peoples to accept Avongara rule voluntarily, to stay in their homes, and to become Azande . . . Once a people submitted they were left with their own chiefs . . . All that was asked of the subject peoples was recognition of Azande suzerainty, that they should keep the peace, and a payment of tribute in labour and in kind to their rulers which was no more than Azande commoners contributed towards the upkeep of the courts (p. 33).

The ambiguity is in the phrase 'become Azande'. At one point Evans-Pritchard implied that Azande operated some form of indirect rule, and he mentions, with reference to the conquered Abandiya, that the Azande left them to their own rulers 'as was their policy in dealing with subjugated peoples' (p. 28). Later, however, writing about the administration of provinces including recently conquered non-Azande territories: 'It was the duty of the governors to complete the *assimilation* of these foreigners, spreading among them Zande institutions, language, and ways of life, as well as imposing ever more firmly Vongara rule' (p. 122, my emphasis). And in a discussion of commoner governors: 'It was the policy of kings to entrust commoners with the difficult task of administering and bringing about the assimilation (*zoga auro*) or, as they often put it, of pacifying them (*zelesi yo*)' (p. 145). The phrase *zoga auro*, which here Evans-Pritchard glossed as 'assimilate', consists of two words: *auro* or 'foreigner' (though literally it seems to have meant 'Easterners', the direction of the original Zande expansion, p. 48); and *zoga*, which in a later passage Evans-Pritchard translates simply as 'ruled': 'The prince ruled (*zoga*) him [the *ligbu*] and he was the man (*ra fu*) of the prince' (p. 209).

That someone was 'the man of' someone else of superior status and power was crucial. People were *avuru*, followers, subjects, of a prince, or governor or a king, and it is not at all clear that subjecthood (or 'citizenship') in Zande society required anything more than subservience to the principles of patronage and clienthood in which '*Ru ae*, the giving of things (to a prince) [was] balanced by *fu ae*, the giving of things (to his subjects)' (p. 215). 'Becoming Azande' seemed to mean becoming the subject of some lord and master (*gbia*). It did not necessarily mean becoming a linguistically and culturally practising Azande, an Azande person in some deeper sense. This view is consistent with what Evans-Pritchard argued elsewhere about commoner governors. Although Azande preferred to appoint Avongara (especially the king's sons) as provincial governors, non-royal Ambomu were used. It was through the employment of Zande (royal and commoner) governors that, Evans-Pritchard suggested, 'foreign peoples learnt the Zande tongue, to take part in affairs at court, and to adopt Zande ways of life' (p 161). In Gbudwe's kingdom, however, there were a number of governors from foreign clans (p. 160), and with regard to the appointment of lower ranking officials, 'it was service at court and loyalty, ability and character which counted, regardless of descent' (p. 161; compare p. 42: 'loyalty and efficiency overrode all other considerations in appointment to public office').

In general, Evans-Pritchard emphasized Zande tolerance of 'foreign' things, noting, for example that it was impolite to inquire too closely into someone's origins (p. 59). Real hostility towards foreigners seems to have been reserved for Arabs, Belgians, and British whom they called *abalomu* (a pejorative term), and 'dirty little barbarians with cropped heads' (p. 290). Undoubtedly there was 'Zandeisation', as Evans-Pritchard himself called it (p. 34), both in the sense of becoming a subject of a Zande lord, and in the sense of assimilating to Zande culture. But like 'Alurization', it was not a matter of policy, and although there was a pervading sense of Ambomu superiority, it appeared to have been vague and ill-defined, 'expressed in terms of obligation and manners' (p. 42). Evans-Pritchard certainly wrote ambiguously about it: on the one hand, there were 'clans of foreign origin, and therefore, by implication socially inferior' (p. 9), but on the other, 'Azande do not attach great importance to whether a man is Ambomu stock or not; there has been too much intermarriage for this to count much' (p. 25). Mixed marriage was clearly no bar to advancement: Gbudwe's mother was a war captive of a conquered people, the Akalinga (p. 284). Certainly Zande politics, with its emphasis on Avongara descent, was structured in such a way as to deny non-Azande direct access to the most powerful position in the kingdom, the kingship. But then Ambomu could not be kings either.

6. Ethnic and cultural pluralism in the Nupe state

Across the continent, in Nigeria, was the Nupe state, described in the title of S. F. Nadel's monograph as *A Black Byzantium*, a long, complex, and subtle book based on fieldwork in the 1930s (unless otherwise specified all page references in this section are to that book). The area occupied by the Nupe state was (and is) farming and cattle country midway between the dry savannah to the north, and the southern forest belt. Traditional history ascribed the founding of the Nupe state to a mythical-historical figure (Tsoede) in the late fifteenth century (p. 73 ff.). At that time Nupe society probably consisted of small chieftainships, some linked together in local confederacies, who were tributary peoples of the King of Ideh, along the Niger, himself a tributary of the Benin state. The collapse of the Benin tributary empire allowed the emergence of an autonomous state system in the Nupe region in the fifteenth and sixteenth centuries. This old kingdom of Nupe survived until the nineteenth century when the original dynasty was overthrown and the kingdom ruled as a Fulani (Muslim) emirate.

Fulani encroachment into Nupe occurred gradually: some had been employed as mercenaries in the Nupe army, others migrated into the area with their cattle, others came as wandering preachers, part of the general wave of Islamicization occurring throughout the region. Islam was 'firmly established' in Nupe (p. 71) by the time of the Fulani 'Jihad' (elsewhere Nadel refers to it as an 'intrusion', 1954: v). None the less, although Fulani were able to take advantage of a succession war in Nupe in the early nineteenth century, it was only after some years of prolonged struggle that the first Fulani ruler (Mallam Dendo) was able to capture the throne (he died in 1833). The Nupe kingdom then came under Fulani hegemony as a tributary of the Emir of Gwandu, one of the two focuses of Fulani power; the other was at Sokoto. Later, of course, Nupe acquired another master, as part of the British colony of Nigeria.

The Fulani advance into Nupe was part of a wider movement over a great part of Western Africa. To the north-east, for example, Zazzau (M. G. Smith 1960*a*), had until the nineteenth century been one of seven Habe (Hausa) states or tributary systems, themselves vassal states of the Songhai Empire. In *c.*1804, however, it was conquered by Fulani who subsequently adopted the Habe language and many aspects of Hausa culture, but ruled the state as an emirate and vassal of the Sultan of Sokoto. This followed the general pattern of the western Sudan, where a succession of powerful centres had established 'empires' of tributary states and then declined, each period of decline allowing smaller, relatively independent states to flourish until another major power stepped into the arena (Levtzion 1988: 102). North and east of Nupe were the

Kanuri, at one time part of the medieval Saharan state of Kanem. With the collapse of that system, the Kanuri rulers moved west to found the state of Bornu which at its height had a number of tributary states under its control. Bornu, too, was threatened by the Fulani advance which it managed to resist, though at the cost of the collapse of its ruling dynasty (Ronald Cohen 1967).

There were, then, three Nupe states described by Nadel: the old kingdom, the Nupe state under Fulani hegemony, and that state under the British system of indirect rule. Little was known about the first phase, and *A Black Byzantium* deals mainly with nineteenth-century Fulani-Nupe, after the consolidation of Fulani hegemony, when, as happened in Zazzau, the ruling dynasty gradually became assimilated linguistically and culturally to the local population: 'Nupe-ized' as Nadel says (p. 71). The process was not completed until quite late: Etsu Mohammed ('Etsu' is the title of the Nupe ruler) who died in 1915, was known as 'Etsu with two tongues', and was the last Fulani of his line to be able to speak that language (ibid.).

The patchwork quilt character of the old Nupe kingdom needs emphasizing. 'Nupe' itself referred to a language of five dialects (related distantly to Yoruba and Ibo) spoken over a wide area, though one not coterminous with the Nupe state. Conversely, that state included non-Nupe speakers, and 'Nupe' referred to those who belonged to it. Nupe also had the vaguer connotation of people who followed certain cultural practices. There was a sense that ' "the Nupe do this or that", "this and that is a Nupe custom" ' (p. 15), for example not eating eggs (p. 19), even when there is evidence to the contrary. This led Nadel to define a 'tribe' as a group 'the members of which claim to form a group' (p. 14): the empty vessel again. He seemed, in 1942, to be arguing that there was an idealized notion of Nupe-ness, 'a theory of the Nupe tribe' (p. 17), and came close to saying (perhaps anticipating the notion) that Nupe was a sort of 'imag-ined community'. He may also be capturing a later meaning of Nupe-ness: the sense of a community which emerged, and could only emerge, in the colonial context (compare Peel 1983: 146–7, on the Yoruba).

Nupe themselves had no word for 'tribe' (p. 12), though the term *kin* existed for what Nadel called 'sub-tribes', or 'lands'. It applied to people living in a locality or ecological niche: for example, the Kyedye (in settlements along the river system), or the Bataci (marshland farmers and fishermen), or the Kusopa ('Forest Tenders'). These numbered eleven or twelve if the Gwagba, a rela-tively recent formation, 'something between a sub-tribe and a political faction' were included (p. 19). Nadel's 'language map' of the region (p. 24) showed that there was originally a core area of what he called 'Nupe proper' (the source of the language of the Nupe state) which gradually expanded to incorporate speakers of other dialects and languages with some becoming bilingual. He characterized the development of the Nupe state as moving from 'expansion to military and political consolidation', a process which required the conquest (and the continual reconquest) of border areas. It thus involved 'more and more alien groups, all to be controlled and governed from a small nucleus-country, by a population less than one-fifth the size of the population that was brought under political control' (p. 84).

A description of Nupe political organization best begins with its smallest units. Nupe people traditionally lived in villages and small towns, though the capital, Bida, was by the nineteenth century a substantial urban centre. Villages or settlements had a number of *efu* ('wards') consisting of *emi* ('houses') or local descent groups (p. 27). Attached to villages were *tunga*, 'daughter settlements' or 'colonies', a term also applied to fiefs of absentee noble landlords (p. 36). Villages and towns were governed locally by *zitsu*, 'town-kings' or 'chiefs' (p. 44). The holder of such a position, to which access was generally though not always through inheritance (p. 51), would be confirmed in office by the Etsu. Village elders could appeal to the Etsu if dissatisfied with the chief's rule. The chief was assisted in office by a council of elders, heads of the *efu*, who held (ranked) titles conferred by the chief (p. 45). Chiefs received tithes from land, and from fish or game caught in the village territory, and had first claim on co-operative farm labour. Nadel calculated that the land tithe might bring in an income equivalent to about twice the average annual yield for a peasant farm (p. 59).

To understand how these local units, and other institutions, were incorporated into the Nupe polity, it is important to realize that at the core, and in this there were strong similarities with Alur and Zande practice, was the reciprocal relationship between patrons and clients. As Nadel described it, some people, *egi kata* ('sons of the house'), 'anxious to obtain political protection', formed a loose association with a master (p. 123). Others, poor peasants, mallams (religious clerics), craftsmen, become *bara*, much more closely tied, and rendering specific services:

The *bara* attaches himself to the household of his patron; he is servant, messenger, major-domo, soldier in his master's private army. He may rise to the position of a trusted friend and intermarry with his patron's family. If he has been accepted as a *bara* by an influential feudal lord, he may hope to be rewarded with the grant of land or a sub-fief (pp. 123–4).

For the patron, 'to have gathered around oneself a large number of *bara* or *egi kata* is the final, most undeniable, mark of success' (p. 124). Although the essence of the system was close to that found in Alur and Azande it was highly elaborated in Nupe. As in Bornu, it pervaded the whole of Nupe society, where Nadel observed 'a system of social gradation of remarkable thoroughness and indeed conspicuousness' (p. 127). It was fundamental to the system of rule.

Different parts of the kingdom were governed in different ways reflecting its patchwork quilt character. Nadel distinguished four (strictly five) governmental zones (p. 115). First, the countries of the *zazi kati*, 'Outside Peoples', the conquered territories, which were not governed directly, but were vassal states paying tribute of slaves to the Etsu Nupe, and recognized by the Emir of Gwandu as the Etsu's vassals. This tribute was collected annually by an official of the Etsu who received half as his share, the rest going to the ruler. Secondly, the relatively autonomous 'lands' of Beni and Kyedye. The latter was a 'riverain state' occupying a distinct ecological niche which formed a self-governing polity (Nadel 1940). Its ruler (Kuta), confirmed in office by the Etsu, paid taxes (in money), of which two-thirds went to the Etsu himself, while the rest was divided between the royal tax collector and the Kuta. The Kuta was responsible for the administration of justice in his domain, though certain cases had to be referred to the Etsu: the system bore a striking similarity to that which was subsequently adopted as the main form of colonial rule in northern Nigeria. Thirdly, in the bulk of the territory with the exceptions of Bida and the Fulani nomads, towns and villages like those described earlier, were parcelled out as 'fiefs' and administered by *egba*, nobles from either the royal house or from the 'office nobility' (below), who resided in the capital. A quarter of the taxes collected went to the Etsu, the rest to the *egba*, who also answered to the king for law and order in his fief (p. 117).

Bida had a distinctive form of administration directly under the Etsu and his immediate officials, and was divided into three sectors: an old quarter (*ba nin*, Inner City), Greater Bida, and the *lalemi* ('foreigner' quarters). Greater Bida says Nadel, 'included all the people who had come to Bida when it became the capital of the kingdom—the members of the ruling class, Fulani and Nupe nobility, with all their followers, hangers-on, with traders, Mallams, warriors, drummers' (p. 119). This group was free from taxation. The *lalemi* housed various immigrant groups, traders, and artisans, under their own headmen (such as the Sarkin Hausawa and the Sarkin Yorubawa) who paid market dues. Within the inner city resided the original (Beni) population of pre-Fulani Bida, taxpayers, who clearly resented their position: 'To the people of *ba nin* the people of Greater Bida, Fulani and Nupe alike, are "strangers", but in the kingdom they themselves, *kintsozi*, Owners of the Land, were a group deprived of all privileges . . . taxed exactly as the other peasants in the country' (p. 119). (This passage may reveal a bias in the source of Nadel's information towards the old, urban-based elite.) Finally, there were the Fulani cattle-herding nomads, administered via their own headman who collected and paid taxes to the Etsu, through a royal appointee. A similar system of 'ethnic fiefs' (*jilibe*) was used to incorporate Fulani nomads into the political system of Bornu (Ronald Cohen 1967: 27, 1970: 152).

Nupe had, therefore, a more complex, thoroughgoing, penetrative state than did the Alur or the Azande. It was a unitary rather than a segmentary system, though the ruler employed various direct and indirect methods of control and resource extraction (for example, vassalage). It was also more complexly and sharply stratified. The descendants of Mallam Dendo, the rulers and their families (there were three ruling houses each with their own palace in Bida between whom the Etsu-ship alternated) formed a royal nobility (*gitsuzi*, p. 93). There was also a nobility of officers of state, 'Titled Ones', grouped in three orders (p. 97): the *sarakizi*, who formed a council of the Etsu's advisers; the *ena manzi* of mallams; and the *ena wuzi*, Court Slaves, whom Nadel describes as a 'slave élite' (p. 97). There were also named and titled heads of the craft guilds, blacksmiths, glassmakers, weavers, barber-doctors, etc. People of varied backgrounds were eligible to become, and became, *saraki*. Of the 36 occupied posts listed by Nadel (pp. 100–1), 24 were held by Nupe, five by Fulani, six by Hausa, and one by a Yoruba. The list of *ena wuzi* titles (p. 108) also shows (less surprisingly perhaps) the varied ethnic origins of the those who held the slave titles in the 1930s. These were not, of course, by then, slaves themselves, though they were their descendants.

The old Nupe kingdom was never a culturally homogeneous and distinct society. Leaving aside the dialect and cultural differences between those who would call themselves Nupe, there were a variety of non-Nupe communities within the polity. Some of these were formerly 'Outside Peoples' who subsequently became 'lands', and were undergoing a process of 'Nupeization' (*a ze Nupe*, 'they have become Nupe'): for example, the Gbedegi 'believed to have been of Yoruba origin and Nupe-ized' (p. 19), and the Benu (of Bornu origin) who 'Nupe-ized themselves, intermarried with the Nupe, forgot their language, and abandoned most of their cultural traits' (p. 20). Other groups resident in Nupe were also becoming 'Nupe-ized': the Konu, or 'Yoruba-Nupe', and other former prisoners of war, enslaved and then freed; and Hausa specialists in making horse-trappings (p. 20). Some of those who remained 'Outside Peoples', such as the Gbari, were also becoming absorbed into Nupe culture in what Nadel calls a 'smooth and silent development' (p. 20). 'Nupeization' was also present among the Kakanda, though Nadel wrote that these people were not considered Nupe, 'or not yet', adding: 'It is impossible to define precisely the point when cultural assimilation warrants, or might warrant, inclusion in the tribe' (p. 21).

Nadel saw Nupeization as a process involving linguistic and cultural as well as political assimilation. Apart from the direct and indirect political mechanisms through which 'Outside Peoples' and non-Nupe 'lands' were incorporated as collectivities into the Nupe polity, how did individual 'strangers' routinely became part of Nupe society? Peel (1983: 28) cites an Ilesha proverb that 'Ijeshas [are] more welcoming to strangers than their own sons' as evidence in Yoruba society of an 'openness and eagerness' to absorb immigrants. Generally speaking, said Nadel, 'the Nupe like strangers—respectable strangers—to settle on their land' (p. 188). Those wanting to join a Nupe settlement attached themselves to the household of one of the heads of families, and were eventually treated as 'adopted' members of the house. Then, like any other family member, they could acquire land by asking the head of the family group; they could request it from the chief, as could any villager; or they could 'borrow' some from a landlord and work it on a share-cropping basis (pp. 181–2). A male stranger living in a village with his family could, as head of an *efu*, participate in the village council, and had the right to request, and be given, a title (p. 46). Thus many villages were ethnically mixed. Nadel, for instance, refers to one which was half-Nupe, half-Yoruba (p. 65). Nupeization under these conditions seems generally to have been neither difficult nor problematic: people moved to a village, attached themselves to a family, settled down, obtained some land, joined the parish council, became Nupe. The overall impression is of a system in which ethnic incorporation was relatively painless, though the evidence is not entirely unambiguous. Writing about Nupe religious ritual, for example, Nadel comments that 'if [strangers] are adopted into the community, they will also learn about the ritual and share its possession' (1954: 19–20). None the less, strangers, like women, were excluded from many if not most village rituals (1954: 81, 90, 111). Such exclusion would seem a diacritical feature of the outsider, and Nadel never clearly stated at what point strangers would cease to be strangers to the extent that they might share ownership of rituals, though they clearly could.

Incorporation at village level could be both individual and collective. Nadel refers to Bornu and Yoruba immigrants who 'arrived en bloc, maintained themselves as compact groups, and were thus integrated as segments, in the host communities' (1954: 223). He also refers to immigrant Yoruba communities 'wholly Nupe-ized in language and mode of life', but clinging to their own ceremonials (1954: 208). There may occasionally have been more to it. In the course of a discussion of checks on the power of the village chief, Nadel mentions that the elders of the village of Kutigi engaged in what he calls a 'strike' (it was rather a boycott) by refusing to attend a traditional ceremony at the chief's house (p. 59). Kutigi, he later noted, was a village in which the ruling family was of Bornu origin and had been confirmed in its position by the Etsu. Nadel commented: 'they were Mohammedans in a pagan and rather primitive country' (p. 63), but unfortunately provides no further information on an episode which might otherwise have shed a different light on intra-village ethnic tensions.

In towns the situation was more complex. Nadel (p. 40) portrayed Bida as a cosmopolitan, polyethnic city, though it is difficult to know whether this impression comes from Bida in the 1930s, or from evidence for an earlier period. Apart from the Fulani nobility and the 'old' Nupe population, there were many strangers, short-term immigrants and longer-term settlers, especially Hausa and Yoruba, living in their own quarters, 'in houses and huts built in their own tribal style and fashion' (p. 43). These stranger quarters are, of course, a common phenomenon throughout Nigeria and much further afield. Nadel noted that in the 1930s emigrant Nupe traders had their quarter in Ibadan, and in Lagos (1954: 228 ff.; compare A. Cohen 1969) Trade and crafts were closely associated with strangers and their quarters, though often in complex ways. Weavers, for example, were originally *konu*, freed war-slaves (p. 279). There were three groups: one of Yagba origin, one of Yoruba, one of Nupe. The head of the Yoruba *konu* weavers (Leshe) was 'regarded as the head of all *konu* weavers in Nupe, and used to receive from them small annual gifts or tribute' (p. 282). Nadel adds, 'the common allegiance and co-operation [of the *konu* weavers] reflects less the professional union than the tribal and cultural unity of these scattered Yoruba groups in Nupe country'. And again: 'With the weavers we find an additional motive for closeness of co-operation in the tribal and cultural unity of these alien, "Nupe-ized", groups' (p. 291). The situation of glassworkers who 'regard themselves almost as a distinct tribal group' (p. 274), living in a separate quarter of Bida, with a tradition that they originated in Egypt, and recruiting to the guild via slaves and apprentices, perhaps suggests something of the elusive nature of ethnic and cultural pluralism in Nupe.

Nadel sought to establish what, beyond force, held the Nupe state together, and provided 'the apparatus of control by means of which this heterogeneous society, severely divided by gulfs of culture, ethnic extraction, community, and class, maintains itself as a unit' (p. 135). He located it not in kinship, but in the economy, the legal system, a common interest in political gossip, royal ceremonial, and in religious ritual, especially the Muslim festival of Sallah, when 'for two days tens of thousands of people crowd the streets of Bida' (p. 144). Above all he found it in the 'fact of cultural assimilation' (p. 146). All these things together generated a realization of a collectivity 'over and above tribal sections, cultural and class divisions': 'They teach a new meaning of the word Nupe, which is the meaning of *nation*. Collective pride, otherwise vested in the tribe or the local community, and its counterpart, the aloof or critical attitude towards other groups and their culture, fuses with and is supplanted by the sentiments of national pride—patriotism' (p. 144). Allowing his flight of fancy to take him far beyond his evidence, he added that he saw this as a matter of design, of policy (p. 146). Certainly Nupe Etsu did things deliberately, but the examples he provided of this deliberate activity were to do either with the cult of the king, or with Islam, not the 'nation'. They were concerned with citizenship as subjecthood, which is what Nupeization meant in political terms. The Fulani nobility was also caught up in this process of Nupeization, though Nadel pointed out that the Nupe-ized Fulani elite (the *goizi*) retained a sense of their origin, and coexisted somewhat uneasily with the older, pre-Fulani, Nupe elite, the *kintsozi*, whose resentment at the state of affairs in Bida was noted earlier. He adds: 'Racial antagonism [between Nupe and Fulani] blending with the antagonism of class, remains alive, and even strengthens with its sentiments the inner tension of the society. It flares up with every open friction between rulers and ruled' (p. 71). Rather ominously, this perhaps anticipated future ethnic relations in another Nigeria.

7. Ethnic heterogeneity in patrimonial states

The fact of ethnic heterogeneity within the early state is less significant than the form that heterogeneity took. Although ethnic stratification cannot be said to be a defining characteristic of the early state, it is undoubtedly true that many were both polyethnic and stratified, with rulers and their families coming from a specific linguistic or cultural group (Shifferd 1987: 46). Thus the relationship between rulers and ruled, aristocrats, and commoners, had at least the potential to be framed in terms of ethnic differentiation and difference. To what extent, then, was there an ethnicity of the ruling class, and if there was, what were the consequences?

In each of the societies studied in this chapter a dominant group sharing a common origin and identity attained its position through conquest or successful predatory expansion. Among the Alur, certainly, and probably among the Azande and the Nupe, though the evidence is less clear-cut, the common identity was accompanied by a sense of superiority: they believed they were better people than others, of better stock, with superior habits. Such beliefs, however, did not form the bedrock of the political system, or offer a justification for it. There was no *system* of ethnic stratification, nor did ethnicity drive the polity. Within the dominant ethnic group there was an important, not to say overriding, distinction between the rulers (and their close relatives) and the rest, a distinction traditionally represented in anthropology through a discourse of royals (kings, princes, and the like), aristocrats, and commoners (see Southall 1988: 59 for the Alur). Whether or not such terms are appropriate, differences between more or less powerful individuals and families were clearly of great significance, and in general the position of the less powerful (commoner) members of the dominant group was little different, materially, from that of their counterparts in groups of other ethnic origin. Status (or class) was as significant as ethnic identity in the power politics of the kingdom.

Secondly, although there was a classification of peoples by reference to their origins, their language, and their cultural habits, there was in reality a great deal of fluidity and flexibility. There were no clear-cut boundaries (cultural or physical) between one group and another. Culturally, 'Azande' (the phenomenon is most apparent in that case) could be thought of as a loose label which might be attached to what at any time constituted 'Zande culture'. But that culture was a much more dynamic collection of ever-changing practices than some anthropological accounts of the time seemed to suggest. The fluidity of the culture, and the lack of embarrassment with which, for example, the Azande adopted new practices from wherever they might appear, suggests that these societies were not, in terms of culture or ethnic identity, in any way essentialist. People shifted readily across ethnic, cultural, and political boundaries, and incorporation was relatively easy, and occurred constantly, through population movement, intermarriage, the attachment of 'foreigners' to households, and so on.

The patron-client system, and the principle of extraction balanced by reciprocity, underpinned by ideology was fundamental. This linked superiors and inferiors, and provided the framework through which the political system operated on a day-to-day and on a longer-term basis. Political attachments (and political loyalties) were personal not corporate, and depended in large part on perceived reciprocity of goods and services between the more and less powerful. Rulers in such systems were generally not concerned with much beyond maintaining their power and that of their immediate families, and extracting sufficient resources from their followers to enable them to do so, bearing in mind the need to ensure that those supporters were not driven by their demands to take their allegiance elsewhere in search of a better deal. In this context, 'citizenship' was subjecthood, and rulers had little interest in promoting a common identity or common culture (their own). Certainly Alurization and so on occurred, mostly as the unintended consequence of pragmatic adaptation to the surrounding environment, but there was no '-ization' policy. This may be asserted despite Evans-Pritchard's and Nadel's statements to the contrary. In writing about the Azande and Nupe respectively they employed a discourse of assimilation which is inappropriate and contrary to the evidence they themselves provide. The term which the Azande apparently used, and which Evans-Pritchard glossed as 'assimilate' (*zoga auro*) appears to have meant much more simply 'ruling foreigners', and that in turn meant incorporating them into the Zande system of patron–client relations. 'Becoming Azande' signified becoming a loyal, tribute-paying, service-providing subject of a ruler or governor. Only in the case of certain Islamic polities in West Africa, and by no means all of them, as the Nupe case illustrates, were rulers engaged in 'normative mobilisation' (Azarya 1988).

A final point concerns what became of these pre-colonial states in Africa which were later subject to colonial rule. Writing on the Alur, Southall argued that the incorporative processes characteristic of their polity were 'sharply reversed and to a considerable extent unscrambled by colonial administration' (1970a: 72). A landscape of 'thousands of people of different ethnic origins all jumbled up' (Evans-Pritchard 1971: 67) was metamorphosed into one in which there were organized ethnic groups ('tribes') with relatively fixed (often fictive) boundaries, and codified 'customs'. The concept of 'Alur', 'Azande', or 'Nupe' took on a 'new meaning', to place Nadel's phrase in a more appropriate context. This 'transformation of ethnic space' in the colonial period will be explored further in Chapter 5.

3

Pragmatism against Morality: Ethnicity in the Aztec Empire

Our god will not be made to wait until new wars arrive. He will find a way, a market place where he will go to buy victims, men for him to eat. They will be in his sight like maize cakes hot from the griddle . . . Let our people, let our army go to this market place! Let us buy with our blood, our heads and hearts and with our lives, precious stones, jade and feathers for our wonderous Huitzilopochtli. This market place will be situated in Tlaxcala, Huexotzinco, Cholula, Atlixco, Tliliuquitepec and Tecoac. Because if we place it in remote lands such as Yopitzinco, Michoacan, the land of the Huaxtecs, or on either coast, it will be difficult. Our god does not like the flesh of those barbarous peoples. They are yellowish, hard, tasteless breads in his mouth. They are savages and speak strange tongues. Therefore our market place must be in these six cities. They will come like warm breads, soft, tasty, straight from the fire.

(Tlacaelel, cited in Duran 1964: 140–1.)

1. 'Normative' versus 'Extractive' mobilization

Cohen and Middleton identified 'incorporation', the absorption of individuals from one ethnic group into another, as a feature of pre-colonial African social life. In each of the three societies discussed in the previous chapter there occurred a process which the ethnographers described through the suffix '-ization': Alurization, Nupeization, Zandeization. Cohen and Middleton, however, rejected the term 'assimilation' for these processes, seeing them as very different from what occurs in modern states (1970: 7–8). Later chapters will confirm their judgement.

Cohen himself subsequently argued that the emergence of an administrative apparatus which organizes centre–periphery relations over a given territory is 'a selective pressure operating to create common ethnicity' (1978a: 66). 'No matter how disparate its segments are ethnically,' he argues, 'the polity tends to be a culture-creating social entity [eventually] creating a "polity induced" ethnicity' (1978c: 16). Thus through conquest, predatory, segmentary expansion, or through migration, states bring together heterogeneous social, cultural, and linguistic elements under a single rule, and centripetal forces (political, administrative, legal, economic) work towards the emergence of a uniform identity. This point may be linked and contrasted with Gellner's argument about the relationship between state and culture in agro-literate polities. In such societies, says Gellner, 'The whole system favours horizontal lines of cultural cleavage . . . The state is interested in extracting taxes, maintaining the peace, and not much else, and has no interest in promoting lateral communication between its subject communities' (1983: 10). 'In the agrarian order', he adds, 'to try to impose on all levels of society . . . a homogenized culture with centrally imposed norms . . . would be an idle dream. Even if such a programme is contained in some theological doctrines, it cannot be, and is not implemented. It simply cannot be done. The resources are lacking' (1983: 17). This provides a marked contrast with 'modern' states where assimilation, cultural uniformity, the homogenization of the citizenry, became a matter of ideology and policy. That is what building a *nation*-state usually meant.

Gellner may sometimes have overstated his case, but generally he was correct (see Grillo 1989, which develops this theme with respect to language in early modern France and Britain). In his comparison of pre-colonial West African states, Victor Azarya argues that in the mid-nineteenth century the Massina state, whose rulers followed the Qadiri creed of Islam, 'articulated a clear cultural and moral order' (1988: 113):

The state closely regulated the life of its inhabitants not merely to exert political or military control, but rather to impose on them a new transcendentally sanctioned and centrally determined morality . . . Those who could not be brought into the fold . . . were enclosed in 'enclaves of profanity' with minimal ties to the rest of the society. Massina was outstanding among precolonial West African societies in terms of its state-imposed standards of behaviour in matters usually left to the private discretion of individuals, families or local communities, such as patterns of consumption, entertainment and socialization (ibid.: 115).

In comparison with this 'normative mobilisation' (p. 117), other Islamic societies of the same period, such as 'Samori's State', 'aimed at the extraction of needed resources from the population (manpower, foodstuffs, information), rather than at the remolding of private life according to central values and principles' (p. 128). This contrast between normative and extractive mobilization (or more precisely between ideologies and practices of normative and extractive mobilization), is close to one made by Gellner between 'moralistic' and 'instrumental' states (1987: 116), and provides a helpful distinction with regard to the Mesoamerican data discussed in this chapter.

The 'Aztec' or 'Mexica' Empire (see *inter alia* Lockhart 1992: 1, Thomas 1993: xix, and Wolf 1962: 130 for discussion of the problem of naming) refers to what at the time of the Conquest (*c*.1520) was the most important system of tributary states in Mesoamerica. Situated on the lakes of the Valley of Mexico, in an area now occupied by Mexico City, the Empire was based on the so-called 'Triple Alliance' of the three cities of Tenochtitlan, Texcoco, and Tacuba. At its height, shortly before the arrival of the Spaniards, the Empire had conquered and brought within its tributary system a great many peoples over a large part of central Mexico, from the Gulf coast to the Pacific Ocean, and south into what is now Guatemala. From these conquered peoples there flowed into Tenochtitlan, the capital of the Aztecs, the most important and powerful members of the Triple Alliance, an immense quantity of tribute of food, raw materials, luxury goods, slaves, labour, sacrificial victims, enabling it to become an urban centre of about a quarter of a million inhabitants, perhaps the largest in the world in its day, filled with monumental public works of both a utilitarian and religious character.

What was the relationship between ethnicity, culture, and power in this empire? How did the rulers of the Aztec state conceive of ethnic difference, and to what extent did the system of Aztec rule frame ethnic difference in political terms? Donald Kurtz, adapting Claessen and Skalnik's terminology, has described the Aztec Empire as an 'early incorporative inchoate state' (1978: 170). The keyword is 'incorporative', and means a state 'still in the process of welding into a nation' the peoples who constituted it. Kurtz's description of this process focused on the mechanisms through which the Empire sought to incorporate both its own citizens in the city of Mexica-Tenochtitlan and its immediate environs (the core of the Empire), and those of its client states, within an Aztec polity. What emerges is a picture of a strong polity which controlled law, religion, trade, and agriculture, and engaged in extensive programmes of public works. It controlled education, and systems of information and communication, and had a policy of ensuring that its language, Nahuatl, was employed as a lingua franca throughout its domain. 'They may even', says Kurtz (p. 183), 'have been promoting it as a national language.' The Aztecs used harsh methods to 'control subjugated peoples and break their ties with local traditions' (p. 185): the dispersal of ethnic groups through the Empire, the extermination of resisting populations, the establishment of colonial settlements. Despite this, the system remained 'inchoate' because the Aztec polity was never able to achieve full incorporation of the many client states into the 'nation'.

Contrary to Gellner, and to Cohen, Kurtz implies that the Empire aimed to establish an Aztec *cultural* as well as political hegemony over a large part of Mesoamerica, and to achieve the full-scale incorporation of ethnic others into the Aztec mode of existence. The vocabulary he uses ('nation', 'education', and so on) gives the ethnography a 'modern' ring, and this must make one sceptical of such an interpretation. It also makes the Aztecs appear somewhat unusual in a comparative context. Skalnik, for example, pointed out that they were the only society in their sample of early states which seemed, on the basis of Kurtz's analysis, to have organized the socialization of its citizens (1978: 607). If Kurtz's view were correct, it would certainly make the Aztecs an exception to what has been proposed about ethnic and cultural difference in patrimonial states. What does the ethnography say?

2. The organization of Aztec society

The Aztec imperial system, which endured for less than 100 years, was by no means unique in Mesoamerica. Rather, it was typical of the structures of power found in the region before the Conquest. Over several centuries there had been a number of similar powerful centres, with the Aztec Empire following on from, and in many ways resembling, that of the Toltecs, at its height between AD 1000 and 1100 (Davies 1980: 227), which in turn resembled the Teotihuacan polity (AD 100–600). The tributary system into which the Aztecs drew their client states was also replicated at lower levels, with client states having their own allies and vassals. (See, for example, the tributary system of Texcoco, a subordinate ally of the Aztecs within the Triple Alliance, Offner 1984, and the arrangements prevailing in Tlaxcala, a long-standing opponent, Gibson 1967.)

Archaeological evidence from the Valley of Mexico, within which much of this activity was located, suggests that following the decline of the political, economic, and religious centre of Teotihuacan, a variety of semi-nomadic hunting peoples and sedentarized nomads known as 'Chichimecs' (the word means 'descendants of the dog', Wolf 1962: 119, Thomas 1993: 36–7) moved into this fertile area from the arid northern zones (Conrad and Demarest 1984: 15 ff.). Together with existing populations they formed the basis of a 'Toltec Empire', centred on the city of Tula/Tollan (Davies 1980, 1987a). This empire, though similar to that later established by the Aztecs, encompassed a smaller area, and trade and markets were of less importance (Davies 1980: 342). It collapsed c.1200, and was followed by a period in which the Valley of Mexico became 'balkanized' (Conrad and Demarest 1984: 20, 178, Davies 1973: 23), with numerous small, competing city-states forming shifting alliances, each 'seeking to impose tribute on its neighbours or to free itself from the obligation to pay tribute' (Davies 1987a: 11). During this period there was probably a further southwards migration of Chichimecs, and among those who entered the Valley at this time were the Aztecs, said to have originated in a distant place called 'Aztlan', hence their name. They eventually settled on an island in Lake Texcoco, founding their city of Tenochtitlan in c.1325–45 (Davies 1973: 36–7). Tenochtitlan was at the boundary between three relatively more powerful groups: the Acolhua, the Culhuacan, and the Tepanecs, based on the city-state of Azcapotzalco. The Aztecs were for a time clients of the latter, but in 1428 defeated them and constructed a tributary system of their own. Over the next 90 years they became the most powerful centre in the entire region. It is probable that they overstretched themselves, but their polity eventually collapsed with astonishing rapidity in the face of the Spanish Conquistadors in the 1520s.

Less than two hundred years separated the founding of Tenochtitlan from the Conquest during which there were many changes in the internal organization of the city and in its external relations. In the latter part of this period the Aztec polity was a bureaucratic-patrimonial state, with at its head the ruler or Tlatoani, meaning 'He who speaks'. Originally governed by a council of elders, in *c.*1372 (Davies 1973: 4) the Aztecs are said to have petitioned the nearby city of Culhuacan to supply them with a king. Specifically they asked for one Acamapichtli, a son of a daughter of the Culhuacan ruler, and allegedly the descendant of Aztecs who had gone to live in that city, intermarrying with the royal lineage. The significance of this is that the Culhuacan ruler claimed Toltec descent. Indeed, most of the city-states in the Valley of Mexico were by this time ruled by lineages which were able to demonstrate Toltec ancestry (Calnek 1982), and Acamapichtli's acquisition put the Aztecs on a par with others (Rounds 1982). History and myth are closely interwoven in accounts of the region in this period. The story of Acamapichtli is largely derived from later Aztec codices (pre-Conquest manuscripts in a pictorial language containing chronicles of the Aztecs and other peoples). It is couched in the language of Aztec claims to legitimacy, and veracity is beside the point.

The subsequent development of rulership in Tenochtitlan is much disputed, but it is clear that a dynasty was established which reigned in the city for the next 150 years, generating eight Speakers by filial or later fraternal succession through to the Conquest (Rounds 1982). The ruler was assisted by a Council of Four officers (some authorities doubt its existence), the most important of whom was probably the *cihuacoatl*, sometimes glossed as 'Prime Minister'. The best-known holder of this office was reputed to be Tlacaelel, a brother of Moctezuma I (1440–68), though his existence, too, has been doubted (Davies 1987*a*: 21). Throughout the fifteenth century the power and status of the ruler of Tenochtitlan as a political and ritual leader increased steadily, and he became closely identified with the Aztec patron-god, Huitzilopochtli. The patrimonial character of the Aztec ruler is vividly portrayed in this passage taken from Clendinnen's excellent study:

Moctezuma was the model of lordly giving, his palace kitchens preparing 'two thousand kinds of various foods' daily. When Moctezuma himself had eaten, the dishes were distributed between his ambassadors, lords, royal officials, noted warriors, and all the 'palace folk' down to his sandal makers and turquoise cutters. Gifts fountained from his hand to successful warriors and others who served his state. So lordly was his munificence that it was said he would take under his protection some poor commoner who saluted him pleasingly, or made him some humble gift—like so many anecdotes of benevolent kingship, hard to reconcile with the sternly policed distance between ruler and ruled, but speaking of the wistful popular fantasy of adoption into the protection of a munificent lord, for those gifts to inferiors marked them as recognized dependants of the royal household (Clendinnen 1991: 63–4).

The society also became more sharply stratified internally, and more closely administered: Duran, a sixteenth-century Catholic priest with wide experience of Mesoamerica, noted that there was 'a special official for every activity, small though it were. Everything was so well recorded that no detail was left out of the accounts. There were even officials in charge of sweeping' (1964: 183).

Across the region, the basic unit of political organization was the *altepetl*, as it was called in Nahuatl, which Lockhart (1992: 14) glosses as the 'ethnic state'. In fact *altepetl* links the ideas of 'water' and 'mountain', and thus, says Lockhart, 'refers in the first instance to territory, but what is meant is primarily an organization of people holding sway over a given territory' (1992: 14): the Spaniards called them *pueblos*. The value of the designation 'ethnic state' is questionable since Lockhart later adds: 'even the smallest and apparently most homogeneous altepetl was in a sense a confederation of distinct and competing ethnic groups' (1992: 27).

Within the *altepetl*, the principal unit of social organization was the *calpulli* or *calpolli* (Lockhart 1992: 16 ff.), originally perhaps a kin-based group, sometimes described as a 'clan', but probably a kindred (Offner 1984: 166, Thomas 1993: 8, Wolf 1962: 135–5). In the Aztec case, there were said to have been seven *calpulli* at the time of the migration from Aztlan, increasing to some twenty at the founding of Tenochtitlan, and later, with the growth of the city, to perhaps eighty. The city itself was divided into four 'Quarters', each with their own officials, with these Quarters in turn divided into *tlaxilacalli*, generally called 'wards' (Offner 1984: 338): Calnek (1976) calls them *barrios*, the modern Spanish equivalent, and Clendinnen likens them to parishes (1991: 22). These were named after the *calpulli* (Calnek 1976: 296), and the two units (*tlaxilacalli* and *calpulli*) tend to be closely identified in the literature, though evidence suggests that they should be distinguished.

Within the wards, people resided in compounds consisting of the household head, his spouse, and their children, including sometimes their married children, and their families (Calnek 1976: 298). In Texcoco the typical household had one, perhaps two, nuclear families, with, on average, some six residents (Offner 1984: 214). There is some evidence for ward endogamy (Offner 1984: 172), with a preference for virilocality, but both inter-*calpulli* marriage and uxorilocal residence also occurred (Calnek 1976: 296). Wards may have retained a core of members related by kinship, but though filiation was an important criterion of admission, it was not the only one (Offner 1984: 171). There was movement between wards and fluid membership rules enabled them to absorb 'new social and ethnic elements' (Conrad and Demarest 1984: 23–4). Some wards were occupationally and economically distinct: there were, for example, merchant *calpulli*, and Calnek mentions one ward in which goldsmiths were based (1976: 297). Architectural evidence indicates some social stratification within wards (Calnek 1976: 300). Authority was exercised by elders responsible to the ruler, to whom *calpulli* members paid tribute or taxes. In Texcoco each ward had a 'chief official' (*tecuhtli*) who had a number of assistants, and who reported to the palace (Offner 1984: 169). There may also have been a resident 'steward' (*calpizqui*) responsible for collecting the taxes due from the ward. Typically, there was a group of public buildings, a meeting house for the elders or officials, a temple for the patron gods of the *calpulli*, and the ward's *telpochcalli* or 'House of Youth', around a plaza, which housed a market (Calnek 1976: 297, Offner 1984: 168).

Calpulli were also land-holding units, and Duran's editors have argued that they were 'as much a division of land as the social group that exploited it'.

Each member of the *calpulli* was assigned a plot which he might cultivate for a certain period of time. If this 'owner' abandoned it for two years, the earth was then assigned to another member of the community . . . Although the plot could not be inherited by the sons of a farmer, certain rights permitted heirs to use it for their own benefit (Duran 1964: 336).

Calpulli-owned terrain, farmed by the *chinampa* system (raised beds on the lake), was not the only land which was worked. There were plots distributed by the ruler to the nobility, tilled by serf labour (*mayeque*), land given for life to warriors, and state-controlled land for the upkeep of the palaces and temples and the benefit of priests and officials (Davies 1973: 78–9). Similarly in Texcoco there were the king's plots, land set aside for the 'palace people', land attached to offices, land held by minor lords, land held corporately by the *calpulli* on which commoners (*macehuales*) enjoyed usufructory rights, and 'war land', land taken in war and distributed to warriors (Offner 1984: 124 ff.). Serfs, who were possibly immigrant labourers, did not have usufructory rights to the land of the lords which they worked, but appear to have been sharecroppers (Offner 1984: 127).

Mexica-Tenochtitlan society was highly stratified with two principal classes, the *pipiltin* (nobility, aristocracy) and the commoners, below whom came the serfs and slave-retainers (*tlacotin*). The distinction between nobles and commoners sharpened during the fifteenth century. In Texcoco, for example, they were tried in different courts, and suffered different, sometimes harsher, punishments for the same offence, as in the case of commoner adulterers or noble drunkards (Offner 1984: 261–4), and in Tenochtitlan nobles were thought to be preferable as sacrificial victims (Davies 1987*a*: 202). Hicks (1987: 93) describes the lot of commoners as that of 'tributary subjection': they were required to cultivate landholdings of kings and nobility and contribute tribute of goods. Commoners, however, were not a homogeneous class being divided into craftsmen, merchants, and warriors. (There were also priests, who seem to have been drawn from the nobility.) Craftsmen were exempt from tribute labour, contributing instead their products and services (Hicks ibid.). They also cultivated land, provided by the nobility in return for goods and services, which they worked for their own subsistence, and could hire out their skills on their own account. The warriors, drawn from both nobility and commoners, were themselves graded or ranked according to their experience and success in battle (for example as 'seasoned warriors'), and there were several orders of 'knights': Otomi, Jaguars, Eagles, etc. The ruler and his family and many other people, including the rich merchants, had retainers of all kinds.

3. The organization of empire

The development of the internal organization of Tenochtitlan, including its religion (below) has to be set alongside the external activities of the Aztec state which made it possible. In the fifteenth century the Valley of Mexico contained about fifty city-states each occupying an area of 100–150 km.^{2}, their rulers interlinked through complex ties of descent and marriage and shifting alliances (Calnek 1982: 54). The 'Triple Alliance' was the most powerful local grouping and gradually brought the rest of the valley under their control. Later more distant places came under their sway. Offner's description of the Texcocan Empire (1984: 17) indicates a relatively small core area of c.1300 km.^{2} with a population of c.250,000 in about fifteen centres, with a much larger area of tribute states encompassing a further 250,000, and this may have been the general pattern.

The Aztecs and other expanding states used similar methods in establishing hegemony over cities within their core areas and outside of them. Duran wrote:

We have mentioned many times that the Aztecs never provoked war against any nation. Conflicts sprang from disobedience or from crimes perpetrated against Aztecs who were sometimes killed along the roads. This is the excuse which the Aztecs gave, and they give it today. In the Chronicle I find this justification constantly: 'We did not seek trouble; they incited us, they provoked us' (1964: 202).

More commonly, though, the Aztecs retaliated first. Sometimes cities were attacked because Aztec merchants, for example, had been threatened or killed. More often they were requested to supply materials or labour, typically for the building of a temple. Compliance with the request was taken as a sign of acquiescence to clientship: refusal was not tolerated. The pattern recurs constantly in the chronicles: a reasonable demand, a rebuff, an attack, the defeat of the offending party who begs for mercy, promising tribute and eternal loyalty. Once established, client status was enforced only loosely and indirectly. Except for agents or stewards, usually a small number, located in each conquered or submitting city to ensure the payment of tribute (Davies 1973: 101, and Offner 1984: 95), client states were not policed or administered. Indeed, they were hardly controlled at all. Eternal loyalty did not endure, and eventually many states would rebel, or be taken over by another power-seeking bloc, and obliged to oppose the Aztecs. They would then have to be reconquered.

These shifts of allegiance and enmity are exemplified in the history of Tehuantepec (Duran 1964: 228–9). When the Aztecs called upon their supposedly subdued and thus faithful ally to assist them in an attack on another city, the Tehuantepec ruler, rather than responding promptly to their demand for assistance, waited on the outcome of the war. When it was clear that the attack had been successful, the inhabitants of Tehuantepec petitioned Moctezuma to allow their own king to marry one of his daughters. Subsequently, however, the Tehuantepec king 'stopped recognizing his father-in-law. He thought of himself as a fellow ruler and whatever tribute was to be paid he decided to keep for his son' (Duran ibid.). It was later claimed that information supplied by Moctezuma's own daughter was instrumental in enabling the Tehuantepec to defeat the Aztec army sent to bring them back into line.

Despite these constant setbacks, the Aztec Empire was extremely successful in extracting a vast amount of tribute from its clients. Duran filled several pages (1964: 128–31) listing tribute items: gold, gems, jewellery, feathers, cacao, cotton, cloth, clothing, live birds, wild animals, snakes, insects, seashells, sea snails, fish bones, colours and dyes, gourds, mats, maize, beans, chili, pumpkin seeds, firewood, bark, charcoal, lime, stone, wooden beams, fruits, flowers, and so on. Davies (1973: 112) cites calculations of 52,000 tons of food annually, 123,400 cotton garments, and 33,680 bundles of feathers. To these must be added the human tribute: labour, slaves, and captives. The Aztecs, said Duran, were 'the lords of all creation' (1964: 129). The Empire also benefited from extensive participation in the trading system which pre-dated it and which stretched across Mesoamerica and into Guatemala (Hicks 1987). Davies (1973: 137) suggests that imperial conquests in many places gave something like monopoly trading rights to Aztec merchants, who exchanged worthless Aztec products (he mentions worm cakes) for other people's valuables: special offers which trading partners could hardly refuse.

The Aztecs, then, had an extremely efficient system for the appropriation of other peoples' labour and produce which they used to maintain their ruler and his retinue and his works, including his temples; to provide a privileged existence for the nobility and clergy and upwardly mobile merchants; and to offer commoners the opportunity to become successful warriors and share in the booty. Tribute of labour and materials also enabled the Aztecs significantly to extend their *chinampa* farming system, for the benefit of the population of Tenochtitlan as a whole (Conrad and Demarest 1984: 49, Wolf 1962: 75–6). The nature of the Aztec Empire cannot, however, be appreciated without considering Aztec religion, which not only legitimated the Aztec state, but, it is argued, provided its driving mechanism (Conrad and Demarest 1984: 218).

Leon-Portilla (1963: 61) characterizes that mechanism as 'mystic imperialism'. The argument is as follows. Each city-state had its own patron god, or more precisely god-aspect, from within a Mesoamerican-wide pantheon. For the Aztecs this was Huitzilopochtli, originally a rather unimportant figure in the traditional pantheon whom the Aztecs elevated to the front rank through a judicious rewriting of myth and history: after the defeat of the Tepanecs of Azcapotzalco they simply burned the ancient codices (their own included) and constructed new chronicles emphasizing their Toltec connection and promoting Huitzilopochtli in the divine hierarchy (Leon-Portilla 1963: 158). 'Huitzilopochtli ceased to be the patron deity of a poor and intimidated tribe [and] appeared as the most powerful god' (Leon-Portilla 1963: 161). The Aztecs went further, however, maintaining that Huitzilopochtli represented the sun, and that his life, and thus that of the sun, had to be sustained through human sacrifice. In Mesoamerican theology, our present world is the age of the Fifth Sun. The four previous suns had terminated disastrously for the earth, and so eventually would this, but the end could be staved off, and the life of the sun extended by frequent feeding with the 'red and precious fluid'. Clendinnen (1991: 208) puts it slightly differently, though the underlying message is the same: 'man as warrior secures the human flesh and the blood needful to feed the earth so that the earth will yield its products'. The Aztecs argued, therefore, that their conquests through which they secured sacrificial victims were for the benefit of humankind as a whole. Thus Aztec religion, specifically its human requirements, drove the imperial vision. The city of Tenochtitlan, says Clendinnen (1991: 28), had an 'insatiable appetite for "ritual consumables"'.

Human sacrifice (accompanied by the flaying of victims and ritual cannibalism) had traditionally been practised on a limited scale throughout Mesoamerica, but in Tenochtitlan it became quantitatively and qualitatively different. Each successful military campaign produced hundreds, sometimes thousands, of captive victims who would be taken in triumph to Tenochtitlan, to be welcomed by the priests and congratulated on their fate. The sacrifices, which usually ended with the victim's heart torn out and offered to the gods, took place at the many festivals in the annual ritual cycle, and on special occasions such as the inauguration of a temple or the installation of a ruler: one of the first tasks of a new ruler was a campaign to secure victims for his installation. The scale appears to have increased significantly during the fifteenth century. It is said that for the inauguration of the Great Temple, in c.1487, over 80,000 were sacrificed. Perhaps there were only 2,000 (Davies 1973: 167, 334), but there is no doubt that sacrifice was both frequent and extensive. Intriguingly, the name 'Tenochtitlan' meant 'Place of the fruit of the cactus', a fruit which it was believed resembled the human heart (Davies 1987a: 192).

One reason why priests congratulated the victims was the belief that death by sacrifice, like death in battle, was good, honourable death: 'flowery death'. None the less, it is clear that the rituals terrified and were meant to do so. At the height of empire, rulers of tributary states, and states which were not yet clients, were invited, indeed required, to witness the major ceremonies, with predictable effect. Duran (1964: 164) records that 'The noble guests who had come to the feast and sacrifice [of the Matlatzinca] were horrified, beside themselves, on seeing the death of so many men.' That the ruler insisted on their presence is important. The fate of the unfaithful wife of Nezahualpilli, ruler of Texcoco, was instructive. He insisted that she and her lovers be publicly executed before an audience of all the rulers of his subject cities and their wives and daughters so, says Davies (1973: 178), 'that the lesson should be lost on none'.

By the time of the Conquest the Aztec Empire had overreached itself (Conrad and Demarest 1984). It had been extremely successful in extracting tribute, but the growing ritual and material needs of the parasitic city of Tenochtitlan and its grandiose rulers meant that increasingly onerous demands were imposed on increasingly rebellious clients. There were severe logistic problems, too, in sustaining campaigns across difficult and distant terrain in regions from, which it was impossible to transport booty in any quantity. There were 'diminishing economic returns' of conquest and expansion (Conrad and Demarest 1984: 183), and diminishing political returns, too, so that the Spaniards had no difficulty in recruiting local allies for their own campaign against the city of Tenochtitlan, which fell to them in 1521.

This suggests that if the Aztec Empire was an incorporative state, as Kurtz has proposed, then incorporation had not progressed very far. What was intended and what was accomplished may, of course, be quite different. But what evidence, if any, is there for the view that the Aztecs were bent on establishing Aztec cultural hegemony in Mesoamerica? More generally, what part was played by ethnic and cultural pluralism in the political order?

4. Ethnic distinctions in the Aztec Empire

Although the city-states at the core of the Aztec Empire shared the Nahuatl language, and a common identification with Toltec and Chichimec ancestry (below), the cities themselves were usually ethnically mixed (Calnek 1976: 289–90), and the Aztec vassal states included many non-Nahuatl-speaking peoples. The situation was similar in other tributary systems such as that of Tlaxcala and Texcoco, and Offner (1984: 10) argues that for the Texcocan rulers 'linguistic and ethnic diversity posed significant problems', citing as evidence the decree issued by one ruler in c.1400 that 'Nahuatl be spoken throughout his kingdom, especially by governmental office-holders' (ibid.: 37, Wolf 1962: 42).

Like Texcoco, Tenochtitlan had an ethnically heterogeneous population. Its growth during the latter part of the fifteenth century was in large part due to the influx of immigrants, such as the Chichimec serfs who worked the nobles' land (Davies 1987a: 82), to take on the many jobs which were available (Conrad and Demarest 1984: 55). Some wards may have housed workers from particular regions (Clendinnen 1991: 33). Similarly, Triple Alliance leaders attracted to the city many craft specialists from all over the Empire, particularly those skilled in the production of luxury goods (Hicks 1987: 96). These craftsmen, such as lapidaries from Xochimilco, and Mixtecan manuscript painters (Calnek 1976: 289), lived in wards together with others who followed the same trade (Hicks ibid.). When the Aztecs and their allies colonized the city of Oaxaca (below), a pattern of ethnically distinct wards emerged: 'the Aztecs formed a ward of their own, Texcocans another, and so did the Tecpanec, Xochimilca, and all the other groups' (Duran 1964: 143). On the other hand, Offner concludes that evidence from house design suggests that wards in Texcoco were probably ethnically mixed (1984: 220).

Neither the Aztecs, nor other Mesoamerican peoples, were ethnically blind. They had a keen sense of the differences not only between classes (nobles, merchants, commoners, slaves), but also between those who could claim Toltec heritage, or Chichimec background, and those who could not, and between those who could speak Nahuatl, and those who spoke other, lesser languages. Clendinnen (1991) frequently refers to 'barbarians', in quotes, and Duran's translators (1964: 349) use the word to translate the Nahuatl *popoloca*, which apparently meant 'unintelligible' (Wolf 1962: 41). They mention several terms used to designate the 'other' including *nonoalca* (glossed as 'mutes'), and *chontal* ('speaker of a strange tongue'), which like *popoloca* referred to languages and speakers whom Nahuatl speakers could not understand (Davies 1980: 109). Like *pinome*, which designated a particular non-Nahuatl language, they all carried 'barbaric' connotations (Gibson 1967: 1).

There were well-formed stereotypes of these barbarian others. The Tarascans were 'wild, nudist people' (translators' note in Duran 1964: 349). The Maya-speaking Huaxtecs, victims of the first Aztec war against non-Nahuatl-speakers (ibid.: 343), were 'drunkards and sodomites' (ibid.: 349). They lived in a very fertile coastal area which the Aztecs called 'Place of our Flesh', a sort of Garden of Eden, and the attendants who portrayed Huaxtecs in processions connected with the festival of Ochpaniztli appeared semi-naked, with erect penises: 'icons of male sexuality', Clendinnen calls them (1991: 34). Capturing 'mere Huaxtecs or other unregarded barbarians' (ibid.: 115) gave a senior warrior much less credit than if his captive came from a Nahuatl city. The Otomi, who spoke an Otomanguean language (Karttunen 1982: 409) and occupied a number of areas in central Mexico including the Toluca Valley to the west, were treated as inferiors by the people of Texcoco (Offner 1984: 220), and thought by Aztecs to be 'brutish and bestial in their sexual conduct' (translators' note in Duran 1964: 343). Among the indigenous inhabitants of the Tlaxcala region, when Nahuatl-speakers migrated into the area, the local Otomi were displaced to border zones, though some may have been assimilated into Tlaxcala society (Gibson 1967). By the end of the fifteenth century, they had become a 'semisubject race' (Gibson 1967: 6), used by the Tlaxcalans as labourers and soldiers. Like a number of African states, Tlaxcala appears to have had a system of loose ethnic stratification resulting from the incursion of a powerful invading group. None the less, there was intermarriage, and Gibson refers to 'a famous Tlaxcalan warrior' who was Otomi, adding that 'Otomi soldiers were highly regarded by the Aztecs as captives', and thus prized sacrificial victims. The name 'Otomi' was used by one of the orders of Aztec knights, and Clendinnen argues that the ethnic stereotype 'enriched the association, these élite warriors being regarded as the berserkers of the army' (1991: 35).

This view of Otomi as prized sacrificial victims, and Clendinnen's comment concerning the desirability or otherwise of Huaxtec captives, may be linked to what have been called the 'Flowery Wars'. Although the Aztec Empire had considerable success in gaining clients in both Nahuatl and non-Nahuatl-speaking areas, certain peoples (for example, the Tarascans to the north) were never conquered. Among these was a group of cities to the south-east of Tenochtitlan which formed an undefeated enclave surrounded by Aztec vassal states. The most prominent was Tlaxcala, itself a loose confederation of four towns, whose rulers were generally in alliance (Gibson 1967: 3). Despite numerous campaigns, and often under severe economic pressure from the Aztecs, the Tlaxcala never submitted, and later became prominent allies of the Spaniards. The so-called 'Flowery Wars' refer to wars fought with Tlaxcala and certain other centres. The idea behind them, as presented by the Aztecs, may be inferred from the speech by Tlacaelel (the possibly mythical 'prime minister' of Moctezuma I), cited at the beginning of this chapter, where he argued that they had no need to look far for victims for sacrifice.

These engagements, which Duran's editors (1964: 348) have called a 'remarkable form of institutionalized warfare whose . . . only object was that of the capturing of brave warriors to serve as sacrificial victims', have bewildered a number of observers. When one of the Conquistadors questioned Moctezuma about 'this puzzling war', Moctezuma replied that although he could have conquered Tlaxcala if he had wanted to, he had fought on 'for the sake of sacrificial victims and practice for his soldiers' (Gibson 1967: 57). This reply is said to have 'disturbed later writers' (ibid.). Conrad and Demarest also seem puzzled, but see the Flowery Wars as either a rationalization of the inability to defeat Tlaxcala, or a response to the shortage of sacrificial victims (1984: 59), itself a reflection of the increasing logistic difficulties involved in transporting captives from distant campaigns: on one occasion captives were actually sacrificed at the battle site. Duran was likewise perplexed:

[Moctezuma] did not take into consideration that fighting with Tlaxcalans, Cholualans, and Huexotzinca was like Spaniards warring against Spaniards. According to the natives' histories, all these people were of the same origin and the only difference was that they belonged to different parties. However, other nations such as the Mixtecs, Zapotecs, Huaxtecs and the coastal peoples were to them as the Moors, Turks, pagans or Jews are to us. The name 'Chichimec' of which the Aztec nation was so proud, is similar to our use of the word Castilian or Goth and the above-mentioned nations did not use this title. . . . The inhabitants of Tlaxcala etc. called themselves Chichimecs . . . So it was that Tlaxcal and Mexico fought in order to practice war and not because of enmity (1964: 238).

However, it has to be noted that the god's preference for 'soft and tasty' Nahuatl-speakers did not prevent his devouring Huaxtecs, Otomi, and many other barbarians, including, at the end, some Spaniards. The Aztecs did not appear to discriminate when it came to victims, sacrificing whoever came their way.

Summarizing these and other data, it would seem that ethnic identification took four main forms in Mesoamerican city-states: with the *altepetl*, with the Toltecs, with the Chichimecs, and with the Nahuatl language. First, the city. 'Primordial loyalties', says Clendinnen, 'clustered around devotion to a particular place and past, and a deity emblematic of both' (1991: 23; see Gibson 1967: 145–6 on Tlaxcalan 'patriotism', and Lockhart 1992: 14 ff., and 1982 for a post-Conquest perspective). Aztec 'campanilismo' (Pratt 1980), was closely associated with the worship of 'their' deity, Huitzilopochtli. It is no wonder, therefore, that sometimes they insisted that his importance be recognized (below). Secondly, Toltec heritage was claimed by many groups, including some of the Aztecs' most important rivals and opponents. Wolf calls it the 'sine qua non of political legitimacy' (1962: 120). The importance of the marriage alliance undertaken with the Culhuacans stemmed precisely from the latter's connection with Tula, possibly as an ally within the Toltec polity (Davies 1987a: 24–5, 154). The idealization of Toltec culture was widespread throughout Mesoamerica (Karttunen 1982: 409). Leon-Portilla points to the way in which Aztec teachers and philosophers stressed the Toltec origin of their ideas: *Toltecayotl*, 'Toltecness', was associated with 'everything superlative in their culture' (1963: 79, Davies 1980: 28–9). Although this distinguished them from the non-Nahuatl groups who did not share that heritage, or rather who had not rewritten their histories in such a way as to justify a claim to it, it could not, of course, differentiate Aztecs from other similar groups who were their rivals or clients, and it does not seem to have been employed as the basis for collective, political solidarity. Davies, who has written extensively on this 'Toltec heritage' does, however, see it as providing a justification for Empire: 'The Aztecs ascribed to the Toltecs a kind of universal "empire", such as they were well on the way to achieving. In this they were seeking a precedent, in order to legitimize their own claims to a pan-Mesoamerican heritage' (1980: 23). Thus they interwove the glory of the Toltecs with their own history in a tradition which 'passed faithfully from one *calmecac* [school] generation to another' (ibid.: 346).

Thirdly, identification with the Chichimecs. This referred to a tradition, held by various communities in Mesoamerica, that they had once been hunter-gatherers, who had later become settled farmers. Archaeological and other evidence suggests that there were several migrations of such peoples into the Valley of Mexico as the expanding arid zone to the north-west drove people south (Davies 1980: 412, 1987a: 73). 'Teochichimecs' was the term used for 'the true or extreme Chichimecs, depicted in codices as nomad hunters, dressed in skins and possessing neither agriculture nor fixed dwellings' (Davies 1980: 161). Hunting and gathering groups contemporaneous with the Aztecs were so described, and Lockhart (1982: 381) suggests that they were 'a general symbol of the non-sedentary'. The term appears in seventeenth-century Nahuatl documents relating to claims for corporate autonomy ('primordial titles', ibid.), and seems to imply a claim to lengthy residence: they came with the Chichimecs. Chichimec identity may also have appealed to the Aztecs and others because of its connotations of 'rugged manliness or hardiness' (Davies 1980: 162–3), highly suited to warriors. A Chichimec association with the Toltecs, which Davies signals through the term 'Tolteca-Chichimeca' (1980: 162), the result, possibly, of a previous migration into the region, also enabled the Toltec connection to be confirmed by another route. The fourth mode of identification, with the Nahuatl language, is discussed below.

5. Ethnicity and the political process in Mesoamerica

To what extent were such identities built into the political process in the Aztec Empire? Clendinnen (1991: 25) states firmly that 'subjugation did not mean incorporation'. Aztecs did not rule their clients so much as exact tribute from them; no government was put in place, except the tax stewards; the only formal requirement imposed on conquered peoples was compliance. In general, they did not disturb existing governments, but left ruling dynasties and lineages *in situ*, occasionally replacing individual office-holders with more likely collaborators. Colonization was rare. There appear to have been three occasions only when they put in settlers of Aztec or allied origin: at Oaxaca, and at Alahuitzlan and Oztoman, where the warfare had been such as to reduce the indigenous populations to a level below that necessary for the exploitation of resources. They were also situated on the borders with Michoacan 'their worst enemy' (Duran 1964: 200), on the northern frontier, watching the Tarascans who were never conquered.

Kurtz places considerable weight on the educational system. Certainly there were educational establishments in Tenochtitlan. Duran (1964: 132) cited an ordinance of Moctezuma I to this effect: 'All the wards will possess schools or monasteries for young men where they will learn religion and good manners. They are to do penance, lead hard lives, live with strict morality, practice for warfare, do bodily work, fast, endure disciplinary measures, draw blood from different parts of the body, and watch at night.' There were two kinds: the *telpochcalli* and the *calmecac*. The *telpochcalli* were generally attended, from puberty, by commoner boys, but to call them 'schools' may be inappropriate. From Clendinnen's description of the activities ('Their days were spent in work details for the ward, under the direction of a more senior lad, and in the further practice of a range of masculine skills', 1991: 113), they seem to have been centres of basic training for warriors, and she and others gloss *telpochcalli* as 'the "House of Youth" of the local warrior house' (ibid.). In Texcoco, youths were placed under a 'captain', and had to work on *calpulli* land, needing permission from their seniors before they could leave and marry. Entry to these schools, which were widespread throughout the Texcocan empire, was at age 12, and everyone attended (Offner 1984: 223). In Texcoco there was also the 'House of song' (*cuicacalli*) next to the temple which young men and women were compelled to attend.

The *calmecac*, which Leon-Portilla calls 'institutions of higher learning' (1963: 10), were generally for the sons of the nobility and for those destined for the priesthood. He quotes an account from Sahagun which describes a range of practical activities (sweeping, cleaning, bathing, gathering firewood, cooking), as well as intellectual ones: how to 'speak well', that is speak the 'lordly language' (*tecpillatolli*) as opposed to the 'language of the common people' (*macehuallatolli*), singing, poetry, astrology, and history (1963: 139 ff.). They were also taught 'the manner of respecting and obeying the state and its administrators' (in Leon-Portilla 1963: 145). Similarly, in Texcoco, pupils at the *calmecac* were 'taught to speak well, to govern, and to hear legal cases, and were also carefully instructed in esoteric religious knowledge, and warfare' (Offner 1984: 223). Kurtz is correct to point to the elite training provided by these establishments. Their pupils were a ruling class in formation (Thomas 1993: 10 likens them to Victorian public schools), but they served their city (Tenochtitlan or Texcoco) and its armies, rather than an Aztec Empire. If there was rule in the Empire, it was an extremely weak form of indirect rule, which did not require an imperial administrative class. Other cities may well have had similar educational institutions, but it seems highly unlikely that they were under Aztec control (practical or ideological) teaching an Aztec curriculum. Offner (1984: 81) says that the Texcocan ruler, Nezahualcoyotl, decreed 'mandatory, uniform public education', and hints at an extensive attempt to permeate the Texcocan empire with Texcocan, or at any rate Nezahualcoyotl's, values. But he offers no real evidence for this, and does not develop the point.

Likewise, there appears to be little hard evidence that the Aztecs attempted to make their language an imperial tongue: Davies (1987b) is quite firm on this. Nahuatl, within which there was and is considerable dialect variation, was probably related to the language spoken in Tula and perhaps by the Chichimecs. It was one of a number of Mesoamerican languages which included Mixtec, Zapotec, Tarascan, Popluca, Otomi, and various Mayan languages. Discussing why, after the Conquest, Nahuatl became the principal Indian language, used by the Spaniards themselves, Karttunen (1982: 409) has noted that it was already well established in pre-Conquest times as a lingua franca through the trading system. It was also seen as the prestige tongue of the region, not, she argues, because of the influence of the Aztecs, but from its association with the Toltecs, and, presumably, from the fact that many of the city-states in the central part of Mesoamerica were ruled by Nahuatl-speaking 'Toltec' lineages. It was the language of dominant groups generally throughout the region, not just of the Aztecs. This did not mean that Aztec rulers insisted on its use by subordinates: Ahuitzotl addressed the 'army of the various allied nations' brought together for the war against Chiapan 'through an interpreter' (Duran 1964: 186), and it seems only to have been an object of imperial policy in the internal affairs of Tenochtitlan where Moctezuma II insisted on the use of the 'lordly' variant at his court (Davies 1973: 215, Wolf 1962: 42).

The Aztecs had little interest in extending the sway of their religion: 'They might add, or impose, the cult of Huitzilopochtli, but this scarcely amounted to religious proselytization. Huitzilopochtli set the Aztecs apart from other peoples, but the diffusion of his cult did not motivate their conquests' (Davies 1973: 202). There were certainly occasions when the Aztecs appeared to have insisted upon worship of Huitzilopochtli. According to Duran (1964: 100), after the war against Tepeaca, various conquered peoples were ordered to Tenochtitlan 'to acknowledge and adore the god Huitzilopochtli as he was now their supreme lord'. Davies (1973: 107) says that the defeated Tepeacans agreed to 'include Huitzilopochtli in their pantheon'. 'Adore' may have been a post-Conquest Christian gloss on Duran's part. But were they asked to adore the god, or his worldly representative, if indeed they could be differentiated? On another occasion, the heads of tributary states were summoned to Tenochtitlan and asked to provide material help with the building of the temple to Huitzilopochtli: 'you know well that you are obliged to serve him' (Duran 1964: 92). They readily agreed:

We have heard your command and it will be done as well as possible, since it is our duty to obey in all things. Let this work be done for our lord in whose shade and protection we live and take refuge. Decide what is necessary and it will be brought to you (ibid.).

This smacks of imposing a language of subservience rather than a specifically Aztec cultural practice. 'Rulers of the Aztec empire', says Gibson (1967: 28), 'sought tribute and prisoners rather than the eradication of local deities. A subject Indian saw no inconsistency in paying tribute to a ruler who worshipped other gods.' On one occasion, the right to worship Huitzilopochtli seems to have been denied as a form of punishment. This was in the special context of the defeat of Tenochtitlan's 'twin city', and formerly good neighbour, Tlatelolco. The king 'ordered that the statue of Huitzilopochtli be removed and that the temple become a rubbish heap for the Aztecs' (Duran 1964: 159). The Tlatelolca were thus obliged temporarily to worship in Tenochtitlan, though their right to a temple of their own was later restored (Davies 1973: 131).

Although many ethnic distinctions were made, the Aztecs did not do much with them: 'tribal hatreds did not seem to exist within the Mexican body politic' (Thomas 1993: 20). Certainly, within the city-state, ethnic identity counted for much, and linguistic and cultural policies were evolved which gave the ruling class an ethnically specific formation, but there seems to have been little attempt to impose those values outside the city-state. Ethnicity provided the rhetoric of claim and counter-claim to legitimacy, and, with varying degrees of success, to allegiance, but was not a significant factor in the organization of inter-city Mesoamerican politics and political relations. City-states were not nations, and there is little or no evidence to suggest that, in the end, war, conquest, empire was much more (or less) than a matter of tribute. There is a passage in Tezozomoc's *Cronica Mexicana*, cited by Leon-Portilla (1963: 157), which seems to express a contrary view:

The death which our fathers, brothers and sons met was not because they owed anything; nor for stealing or lying. It was for the honor of our country and nation and for the valor of our Mexican Empire; and for the honor and glory of our god and Lord Huitzilopochtli.

Tezozomoc, a grandson of Moctezuma (Thomas 1993: 775), is cited by Davies and Thomas, but appears to be ignored by Clendinnen and many others (see Lockhart 1992: 389 ff. for a discussion of his background). Certainly the language suggests an interpolation from a later age, a rereading and rewording of Aztec politics in what were by then appropriate contemporary terms. 'In essence', says Wolf,

the Mexica remained little more than a band of pirates sallying forth from their great city to loot and plunder and submit vast areas to tribute payment, without altering the essential social constitution of their victims . . . they allowed the population to retain their traditional rulers, reminding them of their binding duties to Tenochtitlan only by inviting their underlings to witness a display of mass sacrifice in their lacustrine capital (1962: 149).

Far from being a proselytizing, normatively mobilizing, moralistic polity, the Aztecs, like other patrimonial societies in Mesoamerica and elsewhere, were principally interested in extraction.

Referring back to the work of Gellner, Kurtz, and Ronald Cohen, I once again find myself siding with Gellner. There was no policy of cultural homogenization affecting the subject population as a whole. There was no reason for one, nor could it have been easily implemented, though like Henry VIII of England, and François I of France, Moctezuma II was interested in the formation of an identifiably Mexica ruling class. To the extent that homogenization occurred, it was, as Cohen suggests, an unintended consequence of the operation of the political economy, as for example in the spread of the Nahuatl language.

It is sometimes argued that the Inca state was different in this regard, that the Inca set out to impose their values and their language, their 'Inca social reality' (Toland 1988: 118), on their subjects (see also Toland 1987, Claessen and Van de Velde 1987: 12, Patterson 1991: 78). Ronald Cohen summarizes this view as:

cultural assimilation to the great tradition of the dominant group and their capital citadel happens very slowly, although it does occur authoritatively in at least one instance (Inca) in which the conquest involves dispersing the new group in order to speed up assimilation (1993: 234).

Certainly the Inca made extensive use of colonies, and in this respect differed from the Aztecs (Davies 1973: 176). They also made extensive use of forms of indirect rule (Murra 1982: 257). Patterson adds that political systems drawn into the Inca empire

were no longer able to reproduce pre-Incaic structures of social relations. They became, instead, ethnic groups that occupied particular places in the imperial division of labour and state organization. The state crystallized ethnicity and formed new collective identities that reified and distorted old cultural patterns to provide the illusion of the continuity of old institutions and practices in new contexts (1991: 79).

Rather, it would seem, in the manner of the European colonizing powers discussed in Chapter 5. None the less, Rowe has argued that 'cultural unification was probably not a primary goal of Inca government' (1982: 94), and concurs with a seventeenth-century judgement that 'the whole foundation of their policy . . . rested on means designed to keep their people subject and deprive them of the zeal to revolt against them' (ibid.). Like the Aztecs, where ethnicity was concerned, the Inca were pragmatists rather than moralists.

4

Pluralism in a Patrimonial Bureaucracy: The Ottoman Empire

I am God's slave and sultan of this world. By the grace of God I am head of Muhammad's community. God's might and Muhammad's miracles are my companions. In Baghdad I am the shah, in Byzantine realms the Caesar, and in Egypt I am the sultan; who sends his fleets to the seas of Europe, the Maghrib and India. I am the sultan who took the crown and throne of Hungary and granted them to a humble slave. The voivoda Petru raised his head in revolt, but my horse's hoofs ground him into dust, and I conquered the land of Moldavia.

(Inscription of 1538, in Inalcik 1973: 41.)

1. Ethnic and cultural pluralism in a patrimonial bureaucracy

In a moving article on the destruction of the bridge at Mostar during the Bosnian war, the Croatian writer, Slavenka Drakulic, reflected on 'the countless numbers of people who have crossed it for 600 years . . . Turks and Serbs, Croats and Jews, Greeks and Albanians, Austrians and Hungarians, Catholics, Orthodox, Bogumils, Muslims' (*Observer*, 21 November 1993). Through most of those 600 years Mostar was part of the Ottoman Empire, and it is a sobering thought that what are now recalled as some of the most horrifying episodes of ethnic violence of the twentieth century (Armenian massacres, expulsions from Asia Minor, Cyprus, Lebanon, Palestine, and, by no means least, Bosnia) all occurred in territory which formed part of the 'Divinely protected well-flourishing absolute domain of the House of Osman' (Sugar 1977: 3). That apparent correlation is not the subject of this chapter, which examines relations in the Ottoman Empire principally during its 'golden age', the 150 years or so from the fall of Constantinople in 1453, before what is called 'the decline'. During that period the Empire incorporated ethnic and religious difference into its system of rule in ways which gave formally subordinate groups relative autonomy in their cultural, religious, economic, and political affairs, and allowed some of their members to rise to positions of great power and eminence.

For later generations the Ottoman Empire was a byword for ramshackle, corrupt organization, and by the nineteenth century this was probably correct. In its heyday, however, many regarded it, and, despite what happened in the successor states of the twentieth century, some continue to regard it, as a symbol of harmony.

The chapter therefore develops the analysis of pluralism in patrimonial states by taking a polity more complex and extensive than those considered so far: the 'multiethnic, multinational, multireligious, multilingual' Ottoman Empire, as Itzkowitz (1996: 35) calls it. Throughout the emphasis is on the position of non-Muslims and their relations with Muslim rulers and ruled. A brief account of the Empire's early history is followed by an outline of its mode of government and administration mainly during the period of its florescence, that is the fifteenth and sixteenth centuries. There is then discussion of two institutions most pertinent to this book's overall theme: *devshirme*, the taking into slavery of regular levies of non-Muslim children, and the 'millets', the organization of the population into relatively autonomous communities or 'confessions' based on religious affiliation.

There is a huge corpus of scholarly work on the Ottoman Empire, covering six hundred years, a vast region, and millions of primary documents. Despite the mountain of evidence, there are major gaps, and many apparently simple questions cannot be fully answered, if at all. None the less, a relatively coherent picture of relations within the Ottoman Empire of the fifteenth and sixteenth centuries does emerge. Later there were many changes, and a review of ethnic and inter-confessional relations in later Ottoman and post-Ottoman times would undoubtedly tell a different story. There seems little agreement among experts as to the transcription of Ottoman terminology: the poll tax paid by non-Muslims, for example, is variously written (for good reasons) as *cizye*, *cizya*, *jizyeh*, and *jizye*. I generally follow Shaw who has a good discussion of the problem (1976: vii).

2. The Ottoman mode of government

What became the Ottoman Empire emerged in Asia Minor in the fourteenth century as a so-called 'gazi' state of its founder, Osman I (1280–1324), in the borderlands between the empires of Byzantium and of the Muslim Seljuks (Wittek 1938). This was frontier territory disputed by numerous local rulers, tribal chiefs, or warlords who took the title of 'beys' and who were nominally dependent but practically independent tributaries of the Seljuk state at Konia (Inalcik 1976: 13–15). Christian *akritai* had a corresponding position in regard to the Byzantine Empire at Constantinople. 'Gazi' polities are so-called because they accepted the Islamic principle of *gaza* (*jihad*), the duty of holy war against the unbeliever. They saw themselves as the 'sword of god' (Wittek 1938: 14), though the drive for material gain seems to have been as important as religious fervour. A chief of such a polity won the loyalty of followers 'in return for the obligation to provide them with the means of livelihood, which meant the acquisition of booty' (Wittek 1938: 40). That entailed an endless drive for new conquests. Osman, whose followers were called 'Osmanli' (Inalcik 1976: 11), hence 'Ottoman' via Italian mispronunciation (Rustow 1996: 250), was the most successful of the gazi warlords, extending and consolidating his domains in north-western Asia Minor, adjacent to the richer parts of Byzantine territory (Sugar 1977: 15). His son Orhan (1324–59), based on the important trading city of Bursa, took advantage of the chaos in the Byzantine Empire, and moved on its European domains (Inalcik 1973: 121). In a period of shifting alliances and enmities, a variety of centres (Byzantine, Venetian, Serbian, and Bulgarian) competed for control of south-east Europe. By military and political means (Orhan's wives are reputed to have included a Serbian princess and the daughter of a Byzantine emperor; his successors made similar alliances), the Ottomans became the predominant force in the region.

To say that by the end of the fourteenth century 'most of the Balkans were under Ottoman rule' (Sugar 1977: 23) is an exaggeration if this implies the imposition of stable administration. At this period Ottoman hegemony was usually exercised through a system of vassalage (many of the gazi states were also their clients). By the beginning of the fifteenth century, however, it became clear that Ottomans had overextended themselves, and with the defeat of Bayezit I (1389–1402) by Tamurlaine at the Battle of Ankara in 1402 their hegemony collapsed. Their vassal states in Europe and Anatolia re-established their independence, and Bayezit's sons became clients of Tamurlaine. None the less, within fifty years the ground was regained, and there were further significant advances under Mehmet II 'The Conqueror' (1451–81), notably the final, successful siege of Constantinople in 1453. For the next 150 years Ottoman expansion continued both in Europe and Asia. The grandiose claims made in the inscription cited at the head of this chapter, attributed to Suleyman (1520–66), known to the Ottomans as the 'Lawgiver', to the West as the 'Magnificent', were not idle boasts. By the end of the sixteenth century the Ottoman Empire consisted of some thirty-five directly ruled provinces and a number of vassal states, stretching from the Western Mediterranean to the Caspian Sea, from the Danube to the Arabian Gulf.

The Empire encompassed an immense terrain with wide variations in the prevailing ecological, economic, social, and political conditions. The bulk of the population were, however, peasant farmers, and in many respects this was a typical agrarian state, or agro-literate polity, to use Gellner's term. None the less, commerce was very important, as was the extraction and transformation of primary materials, mainly through petty commodity production. Alongside the peasantry was an urban society of merchants, traders, and craftsmen, and together these formed the subjects (*reaya*) of the sultan. Between them there were marked differences of language, culture, and above all religion. The population of the cities, especially the larger urban centres, was particularly varied, but because of the way in which the Empire (and its economy) developed, the country districts, too, were rarely homogeneous. What form did government take in this 'complex, part-colored' society (Lybyer 1966 (1913): 25)?

What began as an increasingly independent fraction of the segmentary Seljuk polity, gradually bringing its neighbours under its hegemony as clients and vassals, became increasingly in the fifteenth century a 'unitary' state, with an elaborate apparatus of central and provincial government. This apparatus was not uniformly imposed throughout the area of Ottoman rule. There were several types of province; some regions and peoples were never fully incorporated in the system or were governed under special regimes; and there were numerous tributary-paying vassal states enjoying varying degrees of independence. In many respects, however, the Ottoman Empire was a typical patrimonial state. Weber chose it as one of his examples (see also Findley 1980), and Ottoman theory of government itself stressed the crucial and absolute position of the ruler and the centrality of his household as a model for social relations (Findley 1980: 30, Gibb and Bowen 1963: 71, Kunt 1983). The sultan was the 'shepherd' of his people, his subjects his 'flock': *reaya* originally meant, in Arabic, 'cattle at pasture' (Gibb and Bowen 1963: 237). They were also in the broadest sense his slaves ('the *reaya* and the land belong to the sultan' was a basic tenet of Ottoman law, in Inalcik 1973: 73), with the obligation to produce, 'create the riches', necessary to maintain the state and its ruler. This formed part of a 'circle of justice', as it was called: 'the rulers provided the justice and protection that the subjects had to have in order to flourish, while the subjects produced the resources indispensable for the continued functioning of the state' (Findley 1980: 18).

This tenet of a 'circle of justice' was shared with earlier Near Eastern Islamic states, and was one of several traditions on which Ottoman theory of government drew (Inalcik 1973: 66–7, Lybyer 1966 (1913): 20). It was summarized in an eleventh-century source:

In order to hold a land one needs troops and men; in order to keep troops one must divide out property; in order to have property one needs a rich people; only laws create the riches of a people; if one of these be lacking all four are lacking; where all four are lacking, the dominion goes to pieces (in Lybyer 1966 (1913): 20, and Inalcik 1973: 66).

Another tradition which the Ottomans themselves occasionally stressed was that of the generous ruler of their nomadic Turkomen ancestors (Wittek 1938: 6), represented in the advice: 'Open your treasury and distribute your wealth. Make your subjects rejoice. When you have many followers, make Holy War and fill your treasury [for] the concern of the common people is always with their bellies . . . Do not withhold their food and drink' (in Inalcik 1973: 67). Generally, though, 'Turk', meaning the Turkish peasantry of Anatolia, was a pejorative term: Ottomans, like the Aztecs, both took pride in and distanced themselves from their roots (Allen 1963: 49, Cook 1976: 2, Itzkowitz 1996: 31,

Sugar 1977: 109). Byzantium, too, contributed to Ottoman thinking, providing the basis of the sultan's claim to be 'Caesar', and a style of government, the 'trappings of imperial rule' (Shaw 1976: 24), which the sultanate established at Istanbul. In large part, however, Ottoman rulers derived their *raison d'être*, and to a degree their legitimacy, from their origins as a proselytizing Islamic polity, albeit one in which the extraction of booty had been at least as important as the propagation of the faith. These two, faith and booty, were a constant source of tension and conflict within Ottoman ruling institutions. For the most part booty won. None the less, if a first principle of Ottoman rule was that all subjects, whatever their origin, religion, or status, were producers, a second, stemming from the sultan's role as leader of the Islamic world, exemplified by the claim to the title of 'Caliph', was the differentiation of Muslims and non-Muslims.

The Ottoman, like other Islamic states, distinguished between the 'realm of Islam' and the 'realm of war' (Gibb and Bowen 1963: 20). Under the Sheriat (the holy law prescribed by the Quran) Muslims had the duty to treat non-Islamic societies and peoples as hostile terrain, open to plunder, and conversion. However, non-Muslims in an Islamic state, or who voluntarily submitted to rule by one, had in theory, and in the Ottoman Empire in practice, protected status as *Dimmis*. *Dimma* (Arabic) refers to the 'contract' which such people are said to make when they recognize the suzerainty of Islamic rulers in return for their protection. This contract gave the ruler the right to levy, and non-Muslims the obligation to pay, a special tax, the *cizye*, in theory a head tax on all adult males, but in Ottoman practice until the late seventeenth century a tax on households. On the other hand, under Ottoman rule, which followed Sunni Islamic doctrine, non-Muslims, or strictly speaking adherents of the monotheistic faiths which the Quran recognized as 'Religions of the Book': Judaism, Christianity, and, in some interpretations, Zoroastrianism, retained the right to practise their religion and adhere to their customs. There was, says Shaw,

no major effort to enforce mass conversion if for no other reason than the desire to retain the head tax as a major source of treasury revenue. Only where cities or towns resisted conquest or their rulers refused to accept Ottoman suzerainty did the populations suffer enslavement and loss of property and homes (1976: 19).

The courts in fact protected *Dimmis* from pressure to convert (Jennings 1978: 245).

Although the entire population was in some sense enslaved by the sultan, a sharp distinction was drawn between 'producers' and 'rulers', the members of the Ottoman ruling class. 'Ottoman' refers to that class: they were *Ottomanli*, or *askeri*, soldiers (Findley 1980: 45). The sultan was an absolute ruler (in theory), but by the sixteenth century there had emerged a powerful patrimonial bureaucracy (Findley 1980: 6 ff.). Writing in 1913, Lybyer distinguished two great power bases in this bureaucracy: the 'Ruling Institution' of the sultanate, the army, and the state functionaries, and the 'Muslim Institution' of clerics, teachers, and judges. They were distinguished in that the personnel of the former came largely if not exclusively from among converted slaves of non-Muslim origin, that of the latter from among free-born Muslims. Later evidence showed that patterns of recruitment were more complex than Lybyer thought (Findley 1980: 44, Kunt 1983: xvi–xvii), and the tendency now is to differentiate between a wider range of institutions and groups: the sultan's palace and household, the 'men of the sword', 'the men of the pen', and the 'men of knowledge' (the clerics).

Briefly, the palace consisted of a number of departments or chambers, staffed largely by slaves. Besides the Harem, there was the 'Inner' palace, concerned with the person of the sultan and his effects (treasury, larder, etc.), with at the centre the Privy Chamber of a small number of 'pages' in close attendance on the ruler (Inalcik 1973: 80 ff., Lybyer 1966 (1913): 126–8). There was a larger 'Outer' service of departments responsible for guarding the palace and its inhabitants, looking after the sultan's stables, falcons, and insignia, maintaining the buildings and the gardens, and feeding the many retainers, dignitaries, and visitors. The second set of institutions was that of the bureaucracy. Early on, sultans more or less abandoned any reliance on relatives and prominent non-royal families for administering the state. Brothers were thought to be danger-ous, and incoming sultans took the precaution of disposing of them. Instead, power was delegated to senior officials many of whom were slaves. At the head of this 'servile élite' (Findley 1980: 14) was the Grand Vizier, who owed his position to the sultan and who could be dismissed or even executed more or less at the sultan's will: 'death was always very near the highest officials' (Lybyer 1966 (1913): 88). The grand vizier and certain other top functionaries ('vizier' like 'pasha' was a title) together formed a council of state which in-cluded, in order of precedence, the chief judges and governors of Rumelia (south-east Europe) and Anatolia, the treasurers of Rumelia, Anatolia, and Africa, the commander of the Janissary army, the Admiral of the Fleet, and the head of the scribal service (Sugar 1977: 35–6). The officers of this council, which Western observers called 'the Sublime Porte', and which until 1475 was pre-sided over personally by the sultan, were responsible for many departments with their own hierarchically ordered staffs.

Provincial administration was complex and varied. Originally there were two provinces, Anatolia and Rumelia, whose governors or rather commanders (Beylerbey), retained high precedence in the council of state. By the end of the sixteenth century there were some thirty-five, each with its governor, and each divided into districts, Sancaks, ruled by a Sancak Bey. These covered several thousand square miles and had on average populations of c.100,000. There were regulations dealing with taxes for each Sancak (some specific to it), and regular cadastral and economic surveys, village by village, with persons and households liable for tax listed in a register (Kunt 1983: 14–15). Appointed ultimately by the sultan, though in practice by the grand vizier, provincial and district beys were generally of slave origin, and had worked their way up through posts in the chambers and departments of the palace, and in the provinces. Many of these officials were extremely wealthy.

To understand the nature of their wealth requires an account of the Ottoman system of landholding. Although some land was privately owned, in many but not all districts the greatest part of it (including land which came with conquest) was deemed to belong to the sultan (*miri* land). However, about half of this, together with the population residing on it, was distributed by the sultan in holdings given out as 'livings' (*dirlik*) from which deserving servants could draw an income from tithes of up to half the peasants' crops. These *timar* holdings were not unlike the fiefs of Western Europe. Traditionally, they had been given to soldiers who had performed well in battle, and holders had the obligation, as members of the Sipahi or cavalry, to respond to a call to arms in person, bringing such retainers as their holdings allowed them to support. The force so collected, grouped in units under a *subashi* who held a larger *timar* called a *ziamet*, and who came under the Sancak Bey, constituted what is sometimes called the 'feudal army' to distinguish it from the standing slave army discussed later. In south-east Europe this system replaced existing feudal institutions with the original Christian holders of feudal estates often becoming Ottoman *timar* holders (Kunt 1982: 55, 59), though the obligations on the peasantry to provide tithes and labour services were generally held to be less onerous under the Ottomans than they had been under Christian feudalism. Other land was distributed as *has*. Held like *timar*s to enable the holder to gain a living through extracting produce from the peasantry, *has* was 'set aside' (the literal meaning) in large estates for the benefit of governors, district heads, viziers, and other officials. Not only agricultural land was involved: the head of the Black Eunuchs, an important official in the Harem, was given Athens as his *has* (Sugar 1977: 213). The income of these officials was very substantial: a *subashi's ziamet* holding yielded ten times as much as that received by a typical *timar* holder; a Sancak Bey received ten times as much again, and the lowest Beylerbey had a yield about four times greater than that of the lowest Sancak (Kunt 1983: 27).

How were they recruited?

3. The *devshirme*: the slave elite

In the fifteenth and sixteenth centuries external observers of the Ottoman Empire were impressed with the system whereby large numbers of the ruling class of this Muslim state were slaves of non-Muslim origin. Lybyer (1966 (1913): 40) cites a Venetian visitor in 1573: 'It is a fact truly worthy of much consideration, that the riches, the forces, the government, and in short the whole state of the Ottoman Empire is founded upon and placed in the hands of persons all born in the faith of Christ.' Such use of slaves in key positions was common in Islamic states in the Middle East and elsewhere, for example northern Nigeria: only slaves were believed to guarantee absolute loyalty to the ruler. It has been suggested that the term 'slave' may not really be appropriate in the case of the 'slaves of the Porte' (the *kapi kulu*) in the Ottoman Empire (Gibb and Bowen 1963: 43, Kunt 1983: 41–2). Certainly they belonged to their master, but they could, in effect, own and transmit property (below), and the children of slaves suffered no disadvantage. Indeed, many sultans were the children of slave mothers (themselves very powerful), and fathered children by slave wives and concubines.

Ottoman practice often belied the rules on which the society was supposedly founded. Thus, according to the Sheriat, war between Muslim states was forbidden, but the Ottomans certainly invaded and conquered fellow Muslims, and managed to obtain special rulings (*fatwa*) giving their acts religious legitimacy (Inalcik 1973: 37). The Sheriat also forbade the enslavement of Muslims and, what is relevant here, that of non-Muslims under the protection of a Muslim ruler. Certainly the Ottomans tried (vainly) to suppress pirate slave raids on Christian islanders in the Mediterranean (Faroqhi 1984: 98), but they themselves were heavily involved in the practice of taking their Christian subjects into slavery through the *devshirme*. Traditionally, Muslim warlords were entitled to one-fifth of the booty taken from hostile territory, and captives taken in this way provided an important, and in Muslim terms legitimate, source of slaves. Such captives were systematically formed into military units from the late fourteenth century, but thenceforth, for a period of some 200 or more years, up to half of all slaves were obtained through the *devshirme*, the 'gathering' of slaves from among their Christian subjects, mainly in south-east Europe and the Caucasus. This practice was strictly speaking contrary to the Sheriat, though if the Ottomans had been challenged, they might have argued that these Christians had *originally* opposed Ottoman rule (Gibb and Bowen 1957: 223, Kunt 1983: 32). Gradually abandoned in the course of the seventeenth century (Faroqhi 1994: 570 ff.: the last *devshirme* was ordered but not carried out in 1703, Weissmann 1964: 14), in the sixteenth century the institution gathered about 1,000 slaves per annum from a Christian population of *c*.830,000 households in the Ottoman provinces of south-east Europe (Sugar 1977: 50–1).

It operated as follows. The *devshirme* was confined to the countryside and to unmarried Christian young men. Rural craftsmen were exempt as were Jews and probably Armenians (see, however, Weissmann 1964: 12), perhaps because they were usually townsmen or because their leaders had negotiated exemption (Shaw 1976: 114). Ottoman officials visited Christian villages, ascertaining from the priest what youths in the right age group (generally 14–18) had been baptized (Lybyer 1966 (1913): 52). The youths would be assembled and inspected, and a selection made, mainly on the basis of appearance. These officials worked to a quota, which they occasionally exceeded to obtain slaves for sale on their own account, an offence for which some were executed (Weissmann 1964: 13). Kunt (1982: 62) also refers to a sort of 'private devshirme' through which slaves were recruited (or perhaps volunteered) for service in private households. The slaves attached to one such household indicate how widely the net was cast: twenty-three Circassians, two Georgians, four Abkhazians, two Mingrelians, fifty-two Bosnians, twenty-two Hungarians, sixteen Albanians, seven Croats, seven Franks, three Germans, a Wallachian, and a Russian.

Youths gathered by the official *devshirme* were sent to Istanbul, where there was a further selection: about one in ten went into the palace service to be trained as pages, the rest were distributed among the households of rural Sipahi in Anatolia to work and learn the language and customs. Most of them were destined for the Janissary Corps (Inalcik 1973: 78, Lybyer 1966 (1913): 79, Shaw 1976: 113–14). How this 'gathering' was viewed by the rural population is not really known. Lybyer suggests that separation sometimes occasioned much grief, and families sought to purchase exemption, or marry their sons early. Others, however, welcomed the opportunity, and Turkish parents 'sometimes tried to evade the regulations by paying Christians to take their Moslem sons, and declare them as Christian children, so that they might be enrolled as the sultan's slaves' (Lybyer 1966 (1913): 54). Some urban Christian and Muslim fathers arranged for their children to be sent to the countryside in order that they would be recruited (Shaw 1976: 114), and in 1515 a thousand Bosnian Muslim converts were taken, allegedly at the request of their parents (Sugar 1977: 58). Existing recruits working in the palace also apparently suggested names of friends from their home villages to the authorities (Kunt 1982: 61). The benefits to be derived from a successful career as a slave were considerable. 'For the ambitious', as Gibb and Bowen put it, 'it was a positive advantage to be born an unbeliever' (1963: 44).

There was, of course, the matter of conversion. It is unclear whether this was forced on the recruits, though circumcision, 'the outward mark of acceptance of Islam' (Lybyer 1966 (1913): 66) appears to have been. An episode reported by a French observer, and cited by Weissmann (1964: 15), suggests that in the last resort it was voluntary (Kunt 1982: 60). There were a number of instances where recruits apparently confessed to outsiders that they had retained their Christian beliefs (Lybyer 1966 (1913): 68–9). In *c.*1600 the Pope, presumably bearing in mind this possibility, conceived a plan, which came to nothing, to tempt one grand vizier of Genoese origin back to Christianity (Frazee 1983: 78). When conversion occurred outside *devshirme*, as sometimes happened, it appears to have been based on pragmatic considerations. One frequently cited example is that of the so-called Bogomil populations of Bosnia who turned to Islam to escape Catholic persecution (for a more complex view see Rusinow 1996: 88 ff.). Frazee's discussion of the conversion of Orthodox villagers in Bulgaria to Catholicism, though it does not concern Islam, makes a similar point: 'Many of the converts had expected conversion to better their status either socially or politically, and when this did not happen, their interest in Catholicism waned' (Frazee 1983: 110).

The recruits taken into the palace underwent intensive training and education initially under the 'White Eunuchs' (the 'Black Eunuchs', in some ways a more important group, were in charge of the Harem). They then served in various chambers, and later underwent a further selection: some would be taken into the administration, the rest entered the cavalry divisions of the standing army. These cavalry units, called Sipahi, as were the horsemen of the 'feudal' army, were a separate body which Lybyer terms the 'Sipahi of the Porte' (1966 (1913): 49–50). An Italian captive, a former page named Giovanni Menavino who escaped and published his memoirs in 1548, described the ideal product of palace training as 'warrior statesman and loyal Muslim who at the same time should be a man of letters and polished speech, profound courtesy and honest morals' (in Inalcik 1973: 79). By polished speech he meant *Osmanlika*, the elite spoken and written dialect used in ruling circles. Certainly, descriptions of their training call to mind the education of pupils in Victorian English public schools (or in Aztec *calmecac*), being prepared for service in government and empire. Like them, the *kapi kulu* were destined for high office: district and provincial governorships, important departments in the Outer service (less frequently the scribal services), senior commands in the army (Inalcik 1973: 80). They could also become grand vizier.

In the fourteenth and early fifteenth centuries the sultans had employed members of prominent Muslim families as their grand viziers: six members of the Candarli family, a key group in a very small Muslim elite, held the post between 1359 and 1499. After the fall of Constantinople, however, it became increasingly the practice to promote *kapi kulu* to this position. Of the forty-nine viziers who served between 1453 and 1632 only five were Turkish. There were eleven Albanians, eleven Slavs, six Greeks, an Armenian, a Georgian, an Italian, and thirteen other Christians (Arnakis 1969: 78). Two examples suffice to illustrate career patterns:

Mehmet Köprülü, born in Albania of a Christian father, recruited via the *devshirme*, entered the palace to work in the imperial kitchen as a pastry cook (Sugar 1977: 197). He then went to the Treasury and the office of the Chamberlain (Husrev Pasha), whose protégé he became. Transferring to the cavalry, he was based in the village of Köprü in Anatolia, whence his name. He acquired a *timar*, and married the Sancak Bey's daughter. When Husrev Pasha became head of the Janissaries, Mehmet followed him. Later, he became head of the market police in Istanbul and, rising through a succession of important offices, grand vizier in 1656 (Shaw 1976: 207–8).

Ali Pasha, born in Dalmatia, was recruited via the *devshirme* into the palace service, later becoming gate-keeper and chief taster. Moving outside he became a cavalry commander, then head of the Janissary Corps. Thereafter he was Beylerbey of Rumelia, then Pasha of Egypt, returning to Istanbul to become third vizier and in 1561 grand vizier (Lybyer 1966 (1913): 87).

There were many others, including the Ottoman's first admiral of the fleet, known to the West as Barbarossa, who was a Greek.

The power and wealth of such *kapi kulu* again needs emphasizing. These 'grandees' (Findley 1980: 35) maintained very substantial households, modelled after the sultan's, with hundreds if not thousands of slaves and retainers. As-suming they were not purged and their assets confiscated, and Ottoman palace politics were extremely rough, they could consolidate and pass on their advan-tages to their children. Although, according to the Sheriat, slaves could not own property, the *kapi kulu* were in a strong position to buy houses and estates, and amass great wealth: 'few among them neglected to do so' (Gibb and Bowen 1957: 169). The institution of pious foundations (*vakif*) offered one way in which this wealth could be transmitted to heirs. In Ottoman society, many tasks performed by the modern state (the construction of roads, bridges, water works, lighthouses, schools, and hospitals and their maintenance) were under-taken by religious foundations, Christian as well as Muslim (Gibb and Bowen 1957: 167, Lybyer 1966 (1913): 147). The foundations which provided these services were endowed with land to give them an income, just as a *timar* or *has* provided a living. By making such endowments, a rich man could ensure that benefits passed to his family in two ways: they could enjoy the foundation's 'residual income', and/or they could become its administrators (Gibb and Bowen 1957: 168). It was also possible to establish 'family foundations' from which members could benefit directly from all the revenues (ibid.). In addition, *kapi kulu* sons (and, for example, cavalrymen of the Sipahi of the Porte) could obtain their own *timars*, and were thus 'honorably conveyed from the Ruling Institution into the Moslem population' (Lybyer 1966 (1913): 101). There was also a special unit in the standing army to which these sons might be attached, receiving a training alongside the sons of vassal rulers kept in the capital as hostage.

This process of Ottomanization and gradual absorption into Muslim, Turkish, society was replicated, albeit generally at a lower level, by the other *devshirme* recruits who did not enter the palace. After receiving their cruder basic training in Anatolia, some of these returned to Istanbul to work in the outer services of the palace, but their principal destination was the Janissary Corps. The Sipahi, the *timar*-holding cavalry, constituted an army which could be called up when required. From the late fourteenth century, however, sultans increasingly relied on a standing army of slaves which until the mid-seventeenth century was recruited via the *devshirme*. This army, consisting of a number of infantry, cavalry, and artillery units, of which the most famous was the Janissary Corps, was for a time the most formidable force in the region, and one of the reasons for the successful expansion and consolidation of the Empire. Its commanders were extremely powerful.

Entering the Corps, the 'novice' recruits, were subjected to strict military and social training in a relatively closed, self-contained institution, with its own traditional grades, jargon, rituals, and ceremonials, many of which revolved around metaphors of cuisine. A popular nickname for the Corps was 'The people of the Et-meidan Square' from their habit of taking out their cooking pots (their insignia) and assembling there when they had a grievance (Weissmann 1964: 89). Janissaries were supposed to follow a strict code, with injunctions against marriage, engaging in trade, and the consumption of alcohol. In fact, in its later years, many of these were regularly breached, and there seems to have been a long-standing association of the Corps with liquor, which perhaps derived from its close attachment to the Bektashi dervish order whose founder was the Corps's patron saint. The Bektashi order or 'path' of Islam had a syncretic creed incorporating belief in the Trinity, confession, and absolution, which may well have appealed to those with a Christian upbringing (Gibb and Bowen 1957: 191 ff.). The attrition rate in the Corps must have been considerable, given the campaigns it fought, but those who survived were able to acquire *timar*s of their own, or otherwise find a comfortable billet for their retirement (Gibb and Owen 1963: 125).

Writing of the *kapi kulu*, Inalcik (1973: 80) says 'no matter whether the boys were in origin Greek, Serbian, Bulgarian, Albanian, Hungarian, or Russian, they severed all ties with their past'. This was not always so: the grand vizier Mehmet Sokullu (1505–79), for example, a Christian from Herzegovina (Allen 1963: 46), placed his brother, a monk named Makarios, in the post of patriarch of the Slavonic rite Orthodox Church based at Ipek/Pec (Arnakis 1969: 80). Kunt (1974: 235) argues that officials revealed a continuing attachment to their place of birth by endowing foundations for its development: Sokullu funded the construction of the famous 'Bridge over the Drina' in his home region (Andric 1994). Kunt also claims that officials who shared a common origin (*cins*, meaning also 'genus' or 'sex') formed factions within the government and administration. He has identified two of these: one based on south-east Europe including Albanians and Bosnians (1974: 237), the other on the Caucasus (Abkhazians, Georgians, Circassians). Powerful individuals certainly had their own networks of 'connections' (*intisap*) and protégés (Findley 1980: 33, Shaw 1976: 166), but evidence for their regional basis is thin, and it is clear from elsewhere that regional connections were not everything. Thus among Sokullu's opponents in a serious disagreement about a proposed invasion of Cyprus were a Croat, an Albanian, and a Herzegovinian from Sokullu's own village (Allen 1963: 55).

4. The millets: the organization of religion

Lybyer wrote that Ottoman government

secured its own interests and managed to the best advantage its own affairs, which cared little for the welfare of the great majority of the people of the empire, and which had dealings with them and attended to their affairs only when obliged to do so by the pursuit of its own aims (1966 (1913): 149–50).

Much of society, much of the time, was left to its own devices, conducting its business through relatively autonomous, self-governing corporations whose leaders represented the interests of their members to the authorities. Charitable foundations were one example of this 'corporative' nature of Ottoman rule. Another was the guild system for the organization of trades and crafts, with each having its internal hierarchy of masters and apprentices, its 'agent' or headman (*kethüda*), organizing committee, patron saint(s), festivals, and often its own quarter of a town (Gibb and Owen 1963: 281 ff., Inalcik 1973: 152 ff., Sugar 1977: 82 ff.). A third was the organization of people of different faiths into 'millets', a term glossed by Findley (1980: 20) as 'autonomous confessional communities'.

The name comes from *milla*, which, says the *Encyclopaedia of Islam* (vol. vii, p. 61), is a word of non-Arabic origin, used in the Quran for 'religion': *al-milla* with the definite article, 'the religion', meant Islam. In Ottoman Turkish *milla/millet* meant 'religious community'; in modern Turkish (and Persian), 'nation'. There has been much controversy about their meaning and significance. On the one hand, there is what Findley (1980: 21) has called the 'old interpretation'. This emphasized their corporate character, with a clerical leadership, confirmed in office by the Ottoman state, and authority in religious, legal, and judicial areas 'that fell under the scope of its religious law' (Findley 1980: 21), and a lay leadership on whom was devolved the responsibility for collecting the *cizye* tax on their *Dimmis* (Jennings 1978: 237). Such systems pre-dated the Ottomans, and were found in Constantinople before the fall, and in parts of the Islamic world, such as Cairo and Baghdad (Gibb and Bowen 1957: 212–13, 217), before their absorption into the Ottoman Empire. The Ottomans simply adapted a pre-existing mode of organization, and extended its application. (The foreign trading communities accorded special privileges through treaties known as 'Capitulations' were based on the same principle, Frazee 1983: 67–8, Ursinus 1993: 62, and Inalcik, 1994: 190–1, calls them 'millets'.)

This interpretation, says Findley, 'appears to have overestimated the elaboration of communal structures, the scope of communal privilege, and the formalization of relations that existed between non-Muslim religious leaders and Ottoman officials' (1980: 21). The 'sources of the error' he goes on, are 'self-serving accounts emanating from some of the non-Muslim religious leaders, and . . . the projection into earlier periods of conditions resulting from reforms in the mid-nineteenth century', points stressed by Braude (1982: 69), Bardakjian (1982) for Armenians, and Hacker (1982) for Jews; Faroqhi (1994: 604–5) draws heavily on Braude. The controversy hinges partly on whether the term 'millet' in the sense of 'religious community' was applied to both non-Muslims and Muslims before the nineteenth century. Benjamin Braude, one of the chief exponents of a revisionist view of millets has placed a great deal of weight on this point (1982: 69–70), contending that the Ottoman Empire

had many defined and functioning institutions . . . the absence of an explicit technical term is highly significant in such a term-conscious bureaucracy [and] suggests the absence of an institutionalized policy toward non-Muslims. As for the so-called millet system, or, perhaps better, the communal system, it was not an institution or even a group of institutions, but rather it was a set of arrangements, largely social, with considerable variation over time and place (Braude 1982: 74).

'The current view of relations between the Ottoman state and its non-muslim subjects is', he concludes, 'a distortion of both fact and framework' (p. 77).

The issue of the nature of the millets, and more generally of relations between Muslims and *Dimmis* is clearly a highly contested and fraught subject which obviously *matters* to contemporary writers (for example, Bardakjian 1982, Hacker 1982). Taking issue with some of the extreme revisionists, Ursinus cites documents from 1473 onwards to show that although 'millet' did refer to Muslims, it had, well before 1800, 'become an accepted element in the administrative language of the central bureaucracy to indicate the non-Muslim religious communities of the Ottoman empire' (1993: 62). Acknowledging that 'millet' was only used regularly by the central administration, Ursinus concludes that

the individual religious communities, which, on the local level, had to live under conditions which were varying according to place and time, in the perspective of the central government were seen as parts of religious and juridical communities which, under the leadership of their (ecclesiastical) heads, ideally had an empire-wide dimension (p. 63).

From the seventeenth century, millet was 'probably current' in the offices of the central government to express this perspective. In sum, then, millets were institutions which were quite heavily organized at the top and at the centre (in Istanbul) and thus 'existed' in some sense from the point of view of the bureaucracy and their own leaders. In the towns and villages of the provinces, however, the form of the institution, and the degree of institutionalization varied greatly; in some places they must scarcely have existed at all. This leads Itzkowitz (1996: 30) refer to 'the millet mentality', rather than 'the millet system'.

Jennings's account of the Anatolian town of Kayseri in the sixteenth century (1976: 27–33) provides some evidence in support of this. In 1500, 86 per cent of Kayseri's population, as recorded in surveys undertaken to establish the basis for tax returns, was Muslim, 14 per cent *Dimmi*, the great majority 'Ermeni' (Armenians), the rest 'Rum' (Orthodox Christians). The city had two *Dimmi* quarters out of 37: one for Ermeni and one for Rum, and the whole of the Armenian population resided in their quarter. Population growth in the sixteenth century led to an increase in the number of Armenian quarters, actually termed *cemaat* ('communities') in the official documents (Braude 1982: 72), and eventually to the Ermeni being more finely distinguished according to the See to which individuals paid allegiance. In the course of the century the Armenians ceased to be concentrated in one or two quarters and gradually dispersed across the town. By 1583 there were 72 quarters in Kayseri, 13 *Dimmi*, and nine mixed, almost all the latter predominantly Muslim with small numbers of non-Muslim residents. Though in Trabazon none of the 14 *Dimmi* quarters (10 Orthodox, one Armenian, and three 'Frank', that is Latin Christians) out of a total of 23 were mixed (p. 45), in other cities there was a 'relatively substantial' integration of different communities within quarters (p. 40). Generally, mixed quarters increased through the sixteenth century as the population of the towns grew (p. 55). Clearly the differences between Ermeni, Rum, Frank, and Yahudi (Jews) were felt to be of some significance, else why did the authorities bother to distinguish them as 'communities' in the tax returns?

It is in settings of this kind that the local organization of millets must be understood. The process of extending existing ways of dealing with the ethnico-religious communities began shortly after the fall of Constantinople with the appointment in 1453 of Gennadius Scholarius as Patriarch with civil and religious authority over members of the Orthodox faith (Shaw 1976: 59). Soon after, a similar arrangement was made for members of the Armenian Church when the Bishop of Bursa was moved to Istanbul as its patriarch in 1461, and for Jews with the appointment of the Rabbi of Istanbul as 'Haham Pasha' who in Ottoman protocol had precedence over other millet heads, *millet-i bashi* (Sugar 1977: 48). All millet heads received the title of pasha, and Todorova, 1996: 49, describes the millet pasha as a 'very Ottoman figure' (Braude, 1982: 81, denies the existence of the Haham Pasha, but see Epstein 1982: 104–5). Contributing to the controversy over millets is the fact that no document authorizing the establishment of the Armenian and Jewish communities and providing the appropriate licence exists before the nineteenth century (1834 in the case of the Jews), when a number of millets were formally created for the first time (including those for Roman Catholics and Protestants). None the less, as Gibb and Bowen say, 'the Jews and certain other communities were administered as millets for centuries before being formally recognized as such' (1957: 216, Sugar 1977: 44).

The Armenian millet illustrates their form and function (*pace* Bardakjian 1982). This millet was not coterminous with, and not to be confused with, the ethnic Armenian population. Indeed at the time of its creation, the bulk of that population was outside the Ottoman Empire. It was based on the Armenian Christian Church, though not confined to it. The main theological principle differentiating Armenians from Orthodox and Latin Christians was the Armenian belief in the Unity in Christ of the divine and the human (Artinian 1988: 12). They were 'monophysites', as were other Christian communities in the Near East who were later added to the Armenian millet. This became 'the millet of the heretics' (Gibb and Bowen 1957: 232) including Syrian Jacobites, Ethiopians, Chaldeans, Georgians, Copts, and perhaps, Bogomils. Each kept their own leaders under the Armenian patriarch from whom they had to obtain permits for marriages, funerals, travel, and so on (Artinian 1988: 11, Sugar 1977: 277).

The millet head had virtually complete jurisdiction over its internal affairs: the appointment of priests, bishops, and other officials, and the running of the millet's charitable foundations. He also had his own court and prison (at

Istanbul), and was responsible for trying cases and punishing offenders except where these were charged with offences against criminal law or public security (Artinian 1988: 15): religious dignitaries had very limited powers in penal matters (Jennings 1978: 251). To understand the nature of these judicial powers requires some account of the Ottoman legal system. As an Islamic state the Ottoman Empire implemented the Sheriat, but was also governed by laws promulgated from time to time by sultans. These laws, which pertained to matters not covered by the Sheriat, but which strictly speaking had to be in accordance with it, were 'sultan's prerogative' laws (Inalcik 1973: 71, Shaw 1976: 120), that theoretically endured only for the sultan's reign. Muslim law was administered by a hierarchy of learned clerics functioning as judges (kadi). The legal hierarchy was headed by the Sheyhu'l-Islam (the Mufti of Istanbul) and the chief judges of Rumelia and Anatolia, who nominated the judges in the districts attached to the regions over which they had jurisdiction. These judges were graded according to the size and importance of the districts and cities to which they were attached (Gibb and Bowen 1957: 121–2). They traditionally levied a charge of 2.5 per cent 'on the object of litigation' (ibid.: 125), though this amount could be increased significantly at their discretion. A great many matters did not come before the kadi, being dealt with by customary methods outside the court system (ibid.: 127). The Sheriat applied only to the Muslim population, and in a wide range of matters, the members of the non-Muslim communities were governed by their own religious codes, administered by their own officials within their 'millet', though non-Muslims could appeal to the kadi if they felt aggrieved by a decision of their communal court (Jennings 1978: 282). Relations between Muslims and non-Muslims, however, and therefore cases involving persons from different millets came under the jurisdiction of the Muslim courts.

An episode in 1707 illustrates the interplay between the millet court and that of the judges. For a number of years Armenian Christians had been targeted for possible conversion to Rome by various Latin missionaries (especially Jesuits) who entered the Ottoman Empire under the protection afforded to Catholicism by the trade Capitulations. Despite opposition from the Armenian hierarchy, they met with some success. In 1707, however, eight Armenian clerics in Smyrna, suspected of being involved in the conversions, were arrested and brought before the millet court charged with 'disturbing the nation's peace and of traitorous action against the sultan' (Frazee 1983: 182). The millet court found them guilty and put the case to the kadi, who made the traditional offer of death or conversion to Islam. One declined the invitation, and was beheaded. The opposition of the Armenian hierarchy to the activities of these missions coincided with the interests of the Ottomans, who were opposed to sectarian proliferation (Artinian 1988: 33).

Locally, priests and bishops were key figures in the organization of co-religionists, though there were other local dignitaries. In towns, where each religious group tended to live in its own quarter, there was a headman who,

along with the priest or rabbi, represented the local population to the authorities. In his account of Kayseri, Jennings refers to the head (*kethüda*) of the
Dimmis of each quarter (1978: 228). In rural south-east Europe, there were local
village headman known as *knez*, in Slavic, or *demogeron*, in Greek (Arnakis 1969:
73, Faroqhi 1984: 251, Karpat 1985: 105, Weissmann 1964: 73). Additionally, in
the towns and cities where Armenians, like Jews, engaged in crafts and commerce, the organization of the guilds and of the parishes may have formed a
seamless web. Artinian (1988: 20 ff.), noting the importance of the guilds for the
internal government of the Armenian millet in a later period, also draws attention to the position of the 'magnates' as he calls them, the wealthier members
of the community such as merchants and bankers who had a significant
financial role in underwriting the system of tax-farming (below), or who
worked for the Ottoman government as doctors, furriers, architects, interpreters, and suppliers of goods and services. These magnates often mediated between the patriarch and the sultan, and gave extensive financial support to the
patriarchy for the upkeep of churches and schools.

Much of the evidence for the detailed organization of the millets comes from
later periods, and it seems almost impossible to determine the situation on the
ground in the fifteenth and sixteenth centuries. The evidence also comes, if not
from 'self-serving' memoirs, then at least from the capital, and thus focuses on
relations between the millet *prominenti*, the Ottoman establishment, and the
representatives of foreign powers. Two examples, both concerning the Orthodox millet, illustrate the interplay of forces (in Frazee 1983: 84–5, 92–3). Kyrillos
Loukaris was the Orthodox Patriarch at Istanbul several times in the early
seventeenth century. He had been born on Crete, and educated in Italy, going
on to serve in Alexandria and then the Ukraine. He was influenced by the
Reformation, and was interested in reorganizing Orthodoxy along Calvinist
lines (Gibb and Bowen 1957: 235). His opposition to reconciliation with Rome
led to a conspiracy between the French ambassador and the Jesuit mission to
replace him with another more favourable to their cause. This was achieved
with the help of a large bribe in 1623. Kyrillos, however, had the support and
financial backing of the Dutch, and within a year was back in office. Later, in
1627, a monk named Metaxas imported a Greek printing press to Istanbul, and
began issuing anti-Catholic tracts. The authorities in Rome saw this as a threat,
and the French ambassador, again with Jesuit support, persuaded the Grand
Vizier that passages in one of Metaxas's booklets were treasonable. Metaxas
was arrested and the press destroyed. The British and Dutch ambassadors,
however, convinced the Grand Vizier that he had been tricked, and thus
secured the expulsion of the Jesuits from Istanbul. Much of the material on
millets is concerned with such great games and tells us little about what was
happening in the towns and villages.

If Ottoman theory and practice constituted people in the first instance as
subjects who produced wealth, Muslim and *Dimmis* together, it also constituted
them as *religious* subjects, as devotees of the Religions of the Book, and as

practitioners of specific groups of faiths. Arnakis (1969: 81) argues that for this reason 'Vlachs, Serbs, Bulgars, Albanians, or Greeks, in whatever part of the realm they happened to be, were as likely to call themselves "Christians" as to mention their ethnic origin. For a long period the term "Christian" tended to eclipse all national identity.' He does not say how 'Armenians' fitted into this classification, and to stress a 'Christian' identification is perhaps misleading. For whatever terms of self-ascription were used, the Ottomans constituted 'Christians' as three distinct groups, Orthodox, Armenians, and Latin Catholics (Ermeni, Rum, and Frank), putting each of them in this respect on a par with Jews and Muslims. Although 'Rum' covered a wide range of peoples in different regions of Europe, Asia, and Africa, of different ethnic origins, speaking different languages, it was nevertheless accepted by educated and wealthier Orthodox Christians as a marker distinguishing them from Monophysites and Catholics (Braude and Lewis 1982: 13). The liturgical languages (and scripts which originated with them) also united peoples within a faith (ibid.: 26–7).

'Christians' in the broad sense, were not collective political actors on the scene, nor were undifferentiated *Dimmis*, though Faroqhi (1984: 186) has an intriguing reference to 'representatives of the non-Muslim mineworkers' who took their complaints to the kadi's court, and Jennings to headmen in Anatolian towns who represented all *Dimmis* before officialdom (1978: 288). But then, neither were the 'national identities' to which Arnakis refers. Gibb and Bowen make an interesting comment on this when they say that the Ottomans 'took little or no cognizance of . . . national or racial differences' (1957: 234), adding that so far as Bulgarians were concerned 'so complete was their absorption in the Greek millet that in the first place there is actually no mention of them by name in Ottoman official documents until [after about the eighteenth century], except as Voynuks'. *Voynuk* was in fact an occupational status, concerned with horse-breeding; among other things *Voynuk*s were exempt from the *cizye* tax. 'Eclipsing', 'taking no cognizance of', however, beg serious questions about the relationship in this period between the Ottoman state and the collectivities which later became the basis for national identities (Karpat 1985: 99), and about the extent to which identities such as 'Bulgarian' or 'Serbian' could be said to have 'existed' in the fifteenth or sixteenth centuries, or as some would have it, earlier. (What could a 'Serbian' or 'Bulgarian' state, as they are usually called, have meant in 1389?)

What the millet system did, or attempted to do, was create a framework for political control, and political action, by conflating a great many pre-existing ethnico-religious groups into three or four very broad categories. This conflation seems to have had little long-term effect on the internal differentiation of the confessions. Certainly the lumping together of the 'heretics' in the Armenian millet did not change what were clearly important pre-existing and active modes of identification. Similarly, the yoking of the Greek and Slavic rites of the Orthodox faith did nothing to undermine an important source of differentiation within the Orthodox population. The modern nationalisms which emerged in the eighteenth and nineteenth centuries cut the cake a different way again. As Todorova suggests: 'Balkan nationalism . . . irrevocably destroyed the imagined community of Orthodox Christianity' (1996: 68). At the same time there is evidence that something else was happening at the grass roots. Throughout Rumelia and Anatolia the similarities between the 'folk' practice of Christianity, Orthodox or other, and of Islam, which was not itself a uniform or unified religion, revealed a convergence of belief and ritual (Braude and Lewis 1982: 17, Gibb and Bowen 1957: 192, Kunt 1982: 58, Rusinow 1996: 87–8, Sugar 1977: 52 ff.). This convergence, an example of which was probably the Bektashi sect favoured by Janissaries, was hindered by 'the existence in each camp of upper classes that upheld the "exclusivist" claims of their respective faiths' (Gibb and Bowen 1957: 192, see also Lewis 1963: 153, 155), and by the millet organization which separated them.

5. Ottoman pluralism: an overview

For Braude and Lewis the Ottoman Empire was a plural society in the Furnivall–Smith sense (1982: 1). Yet the impression given by, among other things, the 'old interpretation' of the millet system, that religious and ethnic relations in the Ottoman Empire were relatively tolerant and easygoing, live and let live, is not a misleading one. In Kayseri, for example, Jennings found that in the period 1603–27 'intercommunal relations seem to have been relatively tranquil, without mutual hatred or antagonisms' (1978: 289), and 'violence and oppression towards *zimmis* seems foreign' (p. 285). Conversions were very rare, certainly in the fifteenth century (Jennings 1978: 241). There was no forced conversion of *Dimmis*, except in the context of the *devshirme*, which in any case allowed Christian converts access to the highest offices of the state. The millet system at the very least allowed religious elites their own arenas in which to exercise power, and gave the practitioners of each religion considerable autonomy (Kymlicka, 1995*a*: 157, describes it as a non-liberal instance of ethnic and religious tolerance since individual freedom of conscience was not recognized). In other ways, too, non-Muslims could generally go about their business without too much trouble, and make a considerable success of it.

The position of Jews illustrates this. In the late fifteenth century there was an influx of Sephardic and Ashkenazim Jews from Spain and Northern Europe, seeking refuge from persecution, and attracted by the Ottoman reputation for tolerance. They settled in the big cities, Istanbul, Salonika, Smyrna, living, like other confessional groups, in their own quarters with their own leaders and institutions, and a thriving intellectual life: a Jewish printing press existed in Istanbul by 1494 (Inalcik 1973: 174). Concentrated in manufacturing (clothing industry, armaments), trade, and banking, they were closely connected with Ottoman central and local elites. One prominent figure was Joseph Nasi (1515?–1579), born João Miguez in Portugal, who migrated first to Antwerp thence in

1554 to Istanbul, bringing substantial resources with him (Braude 1982: 71, Epstein 1982: 111–12, Inalcik 1994: 212, Sugar 1977: 267). He had a close relationship with Selim II, and secured the monopoly of the wine trade through Moldavia (Inalcik 1973: 132). He was appointed Duke of Naxos, with its revenues, and is said to have had ambitions of becoming King of Cyprus, and establishing a homeland for the Jews (Frazee 1983: 111). Like their Armenian counterparts, Jewish bankers were later prominent in tax-farming, either underwriting bids or contracting or subcontracting the collection (Faroqhi 1984: 253, 300–1, Inalcik 1994: 209 ff., McGowan 1981: 139–40). Like Jews and Armenians, Greeks such as the so-called Phanariote families (traditionally from the Istanbul quarter of Fener, which housed the Patriarch) could also achieve prominence in Ottoman life, without conversion to Islam. They had a monopoly of certain key positions which formed what Findley (1980: 92) calls their 'cursus honorum'. These included agencies in Moldavia and Wallachia (both vassal states of the Ottomans), various important translatorships in Istanbul, and ultimately the rulerships (as *hospodars*) of Moldavia and Wallachia. Wealthy and powerful within these domains (they sent their children to university in Italy) they were, within the Greek community, viewed as 'patrimonial dignitaries of awesome scale' (ibid.).

If Muslims and *Dimmis* were all, in the end, subjects, sharing in the inequality of that status, some were formally more unequal than others. In theory, this applied to *Dimmis* as a whole who, under the Sheriat, were subject to various restrictions and disadvantages, including legal disadvantages:

their evidence is not accepted against that of a Moslem in a Kadi's court; the Moslem murderer of a *Dimmi* does not suffer the death penalty; a *Dimmi* may not marry a Moslem woman, whereas a Moslem man may marry a *Dimmi* woman . . . *Dimmis* are obliged to wear distinctive clothes so that they may not be confused with true believers, and are forbidden to ride horses or carry arms. Finally, though their churches may be, and in practice frequently have been, converted into mosques, they are not to build new ones. The most they may do is to repair those that have fallen into decay (Gibb and Bowen 1957: 208).

It is not always clear whether Gibb and Bowen represent the 'ideal' application of the Sheriat or actual Ottoman practice. The point about the courts is repeated elsewhere, but documentary evidence for what happened is rarely cited. The author of one detailed study agrees that 'one of the most severe legal disadvantages of *Dimmis* was their inability under any circumstances to testify as witnesses against Muslims' (Jennings 1978: 257), though he later notes that the word of a *Dimmi* witness 'could not be accepted as decisive proof against a Muslim in court' (p. 287). However, they could and did go to the sharia court to testify for and against other *Dimmis*, and on behalf of Muslims, and Muslims could and did appear in court to testify for *Dimmis*. The latter also had the right (indeed obligation) to reply to charges brought against them by Muslims, and could take an oath of innocence. They could also act as witnesses to an agreement or transaction when the parties were themselves *Dimmis* and the matter was uncontested. In addition, *Dimmis* were able to seek redress through the courts against high-handed or illegal behaviour by Sipahis and Janissaries (p. 269 ff.), and in general Jennings concludes that 'the court exercised justice with patience and forbearance. The *Dimmi* may have had as much hope for justice and fairness as his Muslim counterpart' (p. 289). So far as clothing was concerned, sultans from time to time issued edicts reminding the population of their obligations, for example, requiring *Dimmi* women to wear skirts made of a certain type of cloth (Faroqhi 1984: 127). But these and other edicts (for example, those against *Dimmis* owning slaves) were *repeatedly* issued, suggesting they were by and large 'ineffective' (Inalcik 1973: 151).

The interesting case concerning the butchers of Istanbul (Faroqhi 1984: 228 ff.) reveals the complexities of the Ottoman system. In order to secure the food supply of the city, the Ottomans forcibly recruited wealthy businessmen into appointments in the butchery trade, which was apparently considered unprofitable. Sixty per cent of the candidates considered for these positions were non-Muslim. There was, however, a special loan fund on which butchers could draw, but to which other wealthy businessmen were required to contribute: it was thought of as a payment in lieu of service as a butcher. In 1580 Jewish businessmen were allowed to buy exemption from the butchery trade, because they were unable to work on the Sabbath, adding that 'their repugnance . . . towards anything to do with non-kosher meat was well known' (ibid.: 236). Instead they paid special taxes including one for 'repairs to mining installations', which in turn exempted them from contributing to the butchers' loan fund.

Many authorities agree that in the fifteenth and sixteenth centuries Ottoman rule was generally accepted by, and acceptable to, both peasants and townsmen. Inalcik (1976: 34) has argued that their land policies in the administered territories of south-east Europe abolished local feudal rights, thus improving the lot of peasants, who preferred the Ottomans to their traditional overlords: under Serbian feudal law, they had been required to work for their feudal master for two days a week, but under the Ottomans they were required to give only three days' labour a year on the Sipahi's land (Inalcik 1973: 13, see also Gibb and Bowen 1963: 157, Shaw 1976: 61, Sugar 1977: 32–3). There was, it is also suggested, a considerable degree of tolerance between Muslims and non-Muslims. 'In Constantinople', according to Mansel, 'the words pogrom, ghetto, inquisition had no meaning' (1995: 16). In the countryside, say Gibb and Bowen (1957: 256), mixed populations were 'comparatively free from sectarian prejudice, partly because they were bound by common interests and like ways of life, partly because countrymen of both faiths tended to be latitudinarian in matters of religion', adding in a footnote that 'the *Dimmis* of Bosnia, for instance, were on especially good terms with their Muslim compatriots'.

In a paper reflecting on the contemporary condition of Eastern and Central Europe, Charles Ingrao has suggested that the imperial polities that ruled the region before the modern era were never obliged to change and become nation-states in the way that occurred in Western Europe where 'agencies of statebuilding molded each of [its peoples] into a single nation' (Ingrao 1996: section 1). In line with the argument of this book, he concludes that the Ottoman sultans were: 'archetypal oriental despots: In theory they claimed to have absolute power over everyone and everything; in practice, they cared less about how their empire was run, so long as each of their dominions provided them with a steady supply of revenue and recruits for the army' (section 3). The Ottoman polity was 'extractive' rather than 'normative', and unlike the rulers of modern nation-states, or the Muslim rulers of Massina, Ottomans never 'articulated a clear cultural and moral order' (Azarya 1988: 113), nor sought to impose on their subjects a 'a new transcendentally sanctioned and centrally determined morality' (ibid.: 115), except perhaps in their most strident 'gazi' phase.

This 'diffidence', as Ingrao calls it, had two long-term consequences: the prevalence of backwardness and corruption (1996: section 3), and of linguistic and cultural particularism (section 1), into the twentieth century. On the other hand, the millet system was, he believes. an ' infinitely more humane approach to religious diversity' than that found in other parts of Europe, one which 'promoted autonomous cultural development among the Balkan peoples, as well as remarkably relaxed relationships between neighbors belonging to different millets' (section 3), as portrayed in Andric's *Bridge over the Drina*. By World War I, however, 'the nation-state had wholly replaced an Ottoman model that had been discredited not because it was based on multiethnic coexistence, but because it was associated with other, patently dysfunctional Turkish political institutions' (section 5).

By the end, of course, many things had changed. *Timars* became estates with holdings consolidated and given over to production for the market, and the conditions of the peasantry seriously deteriorated from the seventeenth century onwards. In Moldavia and Wallachia, governors and landlords had, by the end of the eighteenth century, contrived to 'bring almost the entire peasant class . . . into complete subjection, legislating progressively more oppressive corvée requirements' (McGowan 1981: 73). This was in a 'Grecized', vassal state (Gibb and Bowen 1963: 171), but throughout south-east Europe peasants and townsmen were faced with extortionate tax demands from corrupt Ottoman officials and heightened exploitation from Ottoman landlords. Although the oppression of subjects did not distinguish between Muslims and *Dimmis*, in south-east Europe the result was an increasing polarization between an Ottoman, Turkish, Muslim ruling class and their non-Muslim, nationally minded, subjects (Sugar 1977: 229, Brown 1996). This was the real decline of the Ottoman Empire.

5

Ethnic and Cultural Pluralism in the Colonial Social Order

As Roman imperialism laid the foundations of a modern civilisation, and led the wild barbarians of these islands along the path of progress, so in Africa today we are repaying the debt and bringing to the dark places of the earth, the abode of barbarism and cruelty, the torch of culture and progress, while ministering to the material needs of our own civilisation.

(Lugard 1922: 618.)

1. The 'Dual Mandate'

'Gold', said Christopher Columbus, 'is the most precious of all commodities . . . he who possesses it has all he needs in the world, as also the means of rescuing souls from purgatory, and restoring them to the enjoyment of paradise' (quoted in McAllister 1984: 80–1). The Conquistador Bernal Diaz was less portentous: 'We came here to serve God, and get rich' (Christianity combined with 'earthly motives', Thomas 1993: 60). Commenting on Diaz's sentiment, Lynch described Spanish colonialism in the Americas as a 'twofold endeavour' with a 'strange ambivalence' towards the Indians (1958: 172). Colonialism was ever thus. In Africa, says Young, the colonial state sought far more than 'a mere tributary suzerainty over distant populations. It aspired to impose upon them new social and cultural patterns, identified with "civilization"' (1985: 69). Though Young himself sees the project of bringing 'civilization' to the continent simply as a mask for domination, it must be admitted that many of those engaged in French and British colonialism firmly believed in the idea of a mission. Victor Hugo believed that France was 'composing a magnificent poem that has as its title: the colonization of Africa . . . to be occupied by France is to begin to be free, for a city of barbarians to be burned by France is to begin to be enlightened' (in W. B. Cohen 1980: 273–4). And one minister wrote in 1902 of 'Extending overseas to regions only yesterday barbarian the principles of a civilization of which one of the oldest nations in the world has the right to be proud . . . creating . . . so many new Frances . . . protecting our language, our customs, our ideals, the French and Latin glory' (in Betts 1961: 29). For Lord Lugard, the doyen of British colonial administrators, there was a 'Dual Mandate':

the civilised nations have at last recognised that while on the one hand the abounding wealth of the tropical regions of the earth must be developed and used for the benefit of mankind, on the other hand an obligation rests on the controlling Power not only to safeguard the material rights of the natives, but to promote their moral and educational progress (1922: 18).

The colonial state represented a new type of polity which emerged in Europe from the sixteenth century onwards. One of the characteristics of the 'modern' state, it is often argued, is that it increasingly assumes responsibility for its citizens, and the right to intervene widely and deeply in social and cultural affairs: 'nothing beyond the arm of the State' as Durkheim had it. In fact, as Raymond Betts, a leading authority on the colonial period, correctly points out, in general the nineteenth-century state was by instinct non-interventionist, ruling 'lightly and haphazardly', mainly concerned with order and taxes (1985: .198); intervention on the grand scale came later (1976: 188). Yet colonial states, both early states such as Spain or Portugal, and later 'mature' states such as Britain and France, differed fundamentally from the patrimonial polities discussed earlier, and from their contemporary metropolitan societies, until, for the most part, the twentieth century. Patrimonial states had little interest in 'civilizing' and transforming their subjects, even when they happened to consider them 'barbarian'. By contrast, although extraction remained a fundamental objective, colonial states sought also to transform societies and cultures. In this respect they anticipated and in certain respects epitomized, 'modernity', as did French colonial policies of assimilation, grounded as they were in the ideals of the Revolution and the Enlightenment (below). At the same time, and this reveals the complexity of the topic, opposition to the theory and practice of assimilation, led both French and British colonialism in yet another direction, towards the creation or entrenchment of 'difference', and its institutionalization in the political process, in ways which reflect debates in the contemporary, postmodern era of the late twentieth century.

2. The transformation of ethnic space

It was not only, or especially, the 'state' in the narrow sense of government and its representatives, which was engaged in the colonial enterprise. Traders, businessmen, farmers, planters, mining companies, teachers, and missionaries were among many others involved. Such groups could of course be regarded as part of the state in a wider sense. Young makes this point about missionaries, whom he regards as 'an informal extension of the state domain' (1985: 78), because they carried forward cultural policies in fields such as language and education: sword in one hand, Bible in the other. From this point of view, missions were 'Ideological State Apparatuses', as Althusserians call them (Young does not use the term, though his sentiments reflect it). This, however, makes the 'colonial state' seem a more widely ramifying, planned, coherent, totalitarian entity than it was, and disguises the extent to which government, missions, farmers, miners, and so on often worked towards conflicting ends. Not all of these cared to share the responsibility for carrying out the dual mandate, and were frequently at loggerheads with the state and with each other over precisely this.

The haphazard nature of the colonial state's interventions should be recalled. W. B. Cohen's description of the brutal, incompetent activities of French colonial administrative officers and their 'agents' in West Africa in the late nineteenth century (1971) leaves one wondering whether such an enterprise could be identified with any sort of project, still less one which claimed the high moral ground of the dual mandate. In practice, the state was weak, and there was considerable distance (geographical, but that is not the point) between its representatives on the ground, and policy-makers in London, Paris, or Madrid. This was as true in the twentieth century as in the sixteenth. Cohen, for example, reports one former French colonial governor saying, in an interview in 1965: 'In my thirty years in the colonial administration, I never received an instruction from the ministry of colonies. We were the real rulers of the empire; no one told us what to do' (1971: 61). Even when orders were received there was no guarantee they would be followed: the governors' subordinates, their district officers, frequently left theirs unread (ibid.: 64). The multifaceted nature of colonialism, in which the state often had a feeble part, must be borne in mind when assessing the role of various forces in the shaping of ethnic and cultural pluralism during the colonial period. None the less, whether through policy or not, with or without the assistance of the state, colonialism undoubtedly created a new social order in the occupied countries, and effected a major transformation in what, adapting a phrase of Crawford Young's, may be termed the 'ethnic space' of colonized peoples.

Young argues that when the colonial powers brought to Africa the prevailing European model of the state, they 'imposed a radical reorganization of political space' with important long-term consequences for 'cultural identities and patterns of communal conflict' (1985: 60). McAllister makes a similar point about the Americas. Portuguese and Spanish presence led to a new 'colonial social order' (1984: 132) of hierarchically ordered ethnic groups which was continent-wide, though not precisely the same everywhere, and of long duration. By the twentieth century there had emerged three broad social and cultural areas within 'Central' and 'Latin' America which varied according to the population mix created during the colonial period: an 'Indo-America' in highland middle America and the central Andes; a 'Mestizo-America' in northern Mexico, central Chile, and Rio de la Plata; and an 'Afro-America' in the Caribbean and Brazil (McAllister 1984: 345).

As I noted in Chapter 1, Richard Jenkins has drawn attention to the 'necessary role of categorization in the social construction of identity', and of 'the importance of power and authority relations . . . in that process' (1994: 197). The transformation of ethnic space under colonialism illustrates this. It took a number of forms including the establishment of an overarching racial order. This entailed an amalgamation of the population into a few, broad, hierarchically ordered groups, distinguished generally on the basis of presumed racial origin, in itself an innovation of the first magnitude: this of course is what Furnivall and Smith meant by a 'plural society'. Much of this is revealed in the social language of colonialism. First, the colonizers: 'Europeans', 'settlers', 'colons', 'pieds noirs', 'petits blancs'; 'criollos' or 'Indianos', as the Spanish and other settlers from Europe were called in Mexico ('gachupines' meant Spaniards from the 'mother' country). Then the indigenous population: 'subjects' or 'sujets'; 'natives', 'indigènes', 'indigenas', 'natural', 'Africans', 'Indios' or 'Inditos', 'primitives', 'backward', 'barbarians', possibly not rational human beings at all, *gente sin razon*. Thirdly, the issue from intermarriage or concubinage between the first two: 'hijos de la chingada', 'mestizos', 'mulattos', 'cholos', 'zambaigos', 'pardos', 'coyotes', 'Anglo-Indians', 'Eurasians', 'coloureds', 'métis', 'half-castes', 'half-breeds', 'chotara'. The transformation affected persons and identities, and led to the emergence of a fourth group of colonized peoples who were seen (and often saw themselves) as socially and culturally in-between: 'detribalized', 'Europeanized natives', 'educated natives', 'évolués', 'assimilados', 'déracinés', 'Bengali babus', 'Beni-oui-oui'.

Though for some purposes and in some contexts the 'native' population was treated as homogeneous, there was in colonialism, an 'ideology and practice of classification' (Young 1985: 73) which usually divided that population into further, hierarchically ordered and stereotyped, categories. Sometimes these were very broad: Spaniards in Mexico, using the Aztec term, referred to the 'wild' nomadic Indians of the north as 'Chichimecs', or more simply as 'bravos'. Sometimes they were specific and local: 'the Azande', where 'the Azande' were supposedly a bounded entity, of the kind which in Africa and elsewhere was referred to as a 'tribe'. New unities (tribes, in Africa and America, *douar*s in the Maghreb) were created to make some sense of the often extremely fluid distribution of peoples on the ground. This kind of transformation often emerged through an 'ethnic dialectic'. In the colonial classification of indigenous populations there was a dialectical relationship between existing ethnic categories, often those of the locally dominant group with which the colonizers first established contact, or with which they had their most enduring relationship, and the categories of the colonizers' own language and culture. They did not impose or operate solely with a preformed system of classification, nor did they adopt existing systems wholesale. In the shaping and reshaping of indigenous ethnic and cultural pluralism there was a complex interplay between colonizers' systems of classification and those of the colonized (which in any case were not timeless or unchanging).

The transformation of ethnic space involved various forms of social and political incorporation. The 'strange ambivalence' in Spanish policy towards the Indians in the Americas refers specifically to the way in which that policy oscillated between drawing the Indians into the new colonial order (especially its labour force), and keeping them outside of it (Lynch 1958: 172, Borah 1982: 267). They could also be eliminated: in Canada, Colbert had debated whether to exterminate or convert the Iroquois (S. H. Roberts 1963: 96). Later, the eradication of Native Americans was tantamount to policy, and in nineteenth-century Algeria the French initially operated a policy (*refoulement*) of pushing the Arab population out of the colonizers' way, removing the indigenous inhabitants from fertile agricultural areas suitable for colonization to the harsher mountainous and arid zones. Generally, however, as in the Americas the debate came down to this. Should there be a radical social and cultural transformation, through conversion (evangelization) or other kinds of 'assimilation', in order to produce a new native 'subject', a new person with a new identity, who might be allowed a limited place within the colonial system? Or should the colonial order seek to preserve the 'natives', their societies and cultures, and if so in what form and with what consequences? This chapter explores these themes by examining, first, Spanish policy and practice in the Americas, concentrating on the work of the Catholic missions, then French and British policies of 'assimilation', 'association', and 'indirect rule'.

3. The Mission: Spain in the Americas

Aztec observers thought their conquerors were insane, possessed by a 'manic preoccupation with gold' (McAllister 1984: 80). The evidence of their own eyes told them so on the 'Terrible Night' in 1520, when the Conquistadors, driven in disarray from Tenochtitlan, threw away their weapons better to carry their booty, and were slaughtered (Thomas 1993: 407 ff.). In general, the inhabitants of the 'settlement colonies' of the first empires were more concerned with lining their pockets than with the 'social adjustment' of indigenous populations (Betts 1976: 157). In the process, many Indian communities in the areas of Spanish rule simply disappeared: fifty years after the Conquest, the 'native' population of the Valley of Mexico, through disease as much as anything, had fallen by some 80 per cent. The main device for economic exploitation was, at first, the *encomienda* system of forced labour whereby communities of Indians were treated as estates and placed in the charge of individuals or corporations with the right to collect tribute (less the 'Royal Fifth'), and use their services as they saw fit (Lynch 1958: 172, Wolf 1962: 189 ff., 212 ff.). Indians outside the *encomiendas* did not escape exploitation since the Spaniards adopted the Inca *mita* system of labour service, requiring work for some four months of the year. In Peru, where this form of recruitment was mainly for the mines, about a third of conscripts died (Lynch 1958: 180). The many attempts at reform came to nothing: a system of colonial rule in which local governors were, says Lynch 'the very archetype of erring officialdom, whose repertoire included almost every device known in the history of administrative corruption' (1958: 22) did not encourage it.

Often at odds with this effectively unrestrained exploitation was the belief that Spaniards and Portuguese had the historic mission of converting the indigenous peoples and bringing them to God. This was the long-standing view of the Spanish Crown, as Queen Isabella's instructions to the first governor of the Americas in 1503 made clear:

Because we desire that the Indians be converted to our Holy Catholic Faith and their souls be saved and because this is the greatest benefit that we can desire for them, for this end it is necessary that they be instructed in the things of our faith, in order that they will come to a knowledge of it and you will take much care to see this is accomplished (cited in McAllister 1984: 108–9).

Likewise Cortes was told that 'the first aim of your expedition is to serve God and spread the Christian faith' (Ricard 1966: 16). It is not that the Crown ignored material matters: Queen Isabella's instructions of 1503 also included permission to force the Indians to mine for gold, but it took evangelization seriously.

The stance derived from the Crown's historic role as defender of the faith in the Iberian Peninsula (McAllister 1984: 12). The Spaniards, says Lafaye (1976: 35), were 'Christians par excellence . . . a new Chosen People, whose mission was to conquer the Moslems, convert the gentiles, and lead the straying Jews back into the bosom of the church'. The discovery of the Americas coincided with an upsurge of millennial Catholicism in Europe which emphasized the 'providential mission' of the Conquistadors (Lafaye 1976: 34). This mission of both Spain and Portugal was underwritten by a series of papal bulls culminating in the so-called 'Donations' of 1493 which demarcated the areas of the new world to be assigned to the two monarchies and which laid on them the responsibility for the propagation of the Catholic faith (McAllister 1984: 78). The settlers themselves usually had more limited aims: 'exploit the natives, acquire senorios, and become wealthy. They were not much concerned about the moral and juridical aspects of dominion or about the treatment of the conquered' (McAllister 1984: 81). In 1512 a Spanish jurist had drawn up a complex formulaic statement (the 'Requerimiento', Thomas 1993: 72) to be read out to the Indians, obliging them to 'acknowledge the Pope as ruler of the world' and become vassals of the king of Castile. 'The conquerors', says McAllister, 'generally employed it in a perfunctory way, and the Indians who heard it could not comprehend its doctrine or even its language since it was read in Spanish or Latin' (1984: 90). None the less, the evangelizing mission was, from the point of view of the Papacy and the Crowns of Spain and Portugal, an integral part of the exploitation of the new world.

Until the arrival of the Jesuits in 1573, the task of converting the Indians in Mexico was in the hands of three mendicant orders: the Dominicans, the Franciscans, and the Augustinians (Ricard 1966: 2–3). There had been priests with Cortes's expedition, who apparently exerted a restraining influence on both his zeal for conversion and his extraction of booty, but the real work began with the arrival of twelve Franciscans in 1524. By 1569 the three orders numbered about 800 fathers, based in some 160 centres. How did these missionaries view the Indians, how did they set about their work of evangelization, and what were their relationships with the Crown and with the settlers?

Initially, the missions were faced with the question whether or not Indians were 'sufficiently reasonable creatures to be admitted to baptism' (Ricard 1966: 90). This was swiftly and finally resolved, from the Church's point of view, by the papal bull *Sublimus Deus* of 1536 which ruled that 'the Indians are truly men and . . . capable of understanding the Catholic faith' (McAllister 1984: 154), though the bull itself was never published in the Americas (ibid.: 454). But what kind of men were they? Initially, doctrine and instinct led the fathers to treat the Indian as tabula rasa: that is, to view their beliefs and practices as idolatrous, fit only to be extirpated and replaced by Christianity which would force a clean break with what preceded (Ricard 1966: 35). This did not mean those beliefs and practices were ignored, even if they were discounted. Sixteenth-century missionaries undertook detailed studies of Indian culture and society, and very early on the first Franciscan missionaries conducted a series of theological and philosophical dialogues ('Platonicas' or 'Coloquios') with members of the elite Aztec priesthood (but see Lockhart 1992: 205–6). Father Bernardino de Sahagun, whose studies remain one of the most important sources of ethnographic information on pre-Conquest Aztec civilization, defended his work on the grounds that in order to be able to preach effectively against idolatrous practices they must first be known and understood (Ricard 1966: 49). That required knowledge of Indian languages, especially Nahuatl, in which many of the fathers became expert. Later, there were attempts to show that certain beliefs held by the Indians, as well as other 'signs', as Lafaye (1976) calls them, indicated an ancient evangelization of the continent by the Apostle Saint Thomas, identified by some with the Aztec god-hero Quetzalcóatl. The early missionaries, however, saw their task as simply that of eradicating Indian culture, and ignored possible similarities between Christianity and the indigenous religions which they might otherwise have used as possible points of entry for conversion (Ricard 1966: 33). The Catholic doctrine they promoted was the same as that which prevailed in Spain. The Jesuits, who came later, were less inclined to oppose the assimilation of Indian beliefs to Catholic doctrine (Lafaye 1976: 57), and were more open to indigenous cultures.

At the centre of missionary activity was the convent settlement, based sometimes on existing agglomerations, sometimes on newly created concentrations of scattered rural populations, bringing together people of different tribes and language groups in an 'Indian congregation': *congregación de indios*. These 'entirely artificial' communities (Ricard 1966: 140), were considered important because it was believed that in order to become good Christians Indians must learn to 'live in polity' (Borah 1982: 269). They must 'abandon savage and rustic customs and . . . reside in ordered communities like rational men—clean, barbered, eating on tables with proper utensils, sleeping on beds, and eschewing drunkenness and sodomy' (McAllister 1984: 170). Some of these communities were substantial: that at Santa Fe, modelled after More's Utopia (Gibson 1964: 99), had a population of 30,000 (Ricard 1966: 139). Their layout followed the contemporary Spanish urban tradition of a central plaza surrounded by public buildings, with residential areas divided into quarters (*barrios*): not so different, in fact, to pre-Conquest cities such as Tenochtitlan. Ricard describes religious procedure in these centres as follows:

the catechism was held on Sundays and feast days. Early in the morning the monitors (*merinos*) of each quarter of the large towns, and the *alcaldes* of the villages, summoned their people. Each quarter or each village assembled at the church, bearing crosses and reciting prayers; roll was called at the church, and the names of those whose absence could not be explained by the merinos or alcaldes were noted. This control was exceedingly severe . . . In 1539, for example, the bishops had to forbid beating the Indians with rods, imprisoning them or putting them in irons, 'to teach them the Christian doctrines' (1966: 96).

The missions also promoted new agricultural techniques and forms of economic activity such as a silk industry (Ricard 1966: 143), and undertook public works of some magnitude including irrigation schemes. The convents had hospitals (two at Santa Fe) and schools (Ricard 1966: 155), and as well as such local centres of training, the missionaries also established, in 1536, the Colegio de Santa Cruz de Tlatelolco (Lafaye 1976: 19), which introduced a small number of children of the surviving pre-Conquest nobility to a form of secondary education (Ricard 1966: 219).

Although missionaries eschewed the use of indigenous beliefs to create bridges with Catholic doctrine, they did adopt a variety of indigenous practices to aid the process of conversion. For example, pictographic representations of the kind found in Aztec codices were used in confession: priests were equipped with pictures of every possible sin, and the penitent had merely to point, with a straw, to the appropriate one to which he or she wanted to confess, indicating with pebbles the number of times it had been committed (Ricard 1966: 120). Ricard's account of what he calls the 'spiritual conquest' of Mexico contains many examples where these and similar indigenous artifices were taken over by the missionaries. Pre-Conquest tunes were set to Christian lyrics, and dances adapted to the needs of conversion. The type of traditional dance known as 'Las Morismas', for instance, re-enacted the combat between Moors and Christians in Spain ending with the victory of the latter and the conversion of the former (Ricard 1966: 185). There was also a 'missionary theatre' (Ricard 1966: 204,

Lockhart 1992: 401–10) and ritual dramas, which again echoed pre-Conquest practice. Indian actors speaking an Indian language, performed a carefully worked-out Christian script: thus the story of Isaac was retold in such a way that it was impossible to learn that Agar had been Abraham's concubine (Ricard 1966: 201). To do otherwise would have been to expose the audience to the presence in the Bible of a form of polygyny that the missionaries were anxious to suppress. These plays were immensely popular: one, put on in 1587, was said to have had an audience of 5,000 (Ricard 1966: 204). They were also very dramatic. In the *Temptation of our Lord Jesus Christ*, St Francis, preaching, is interrupted by a drunken Indian. The saint calls up the devil, who drags the drunkard off to hell, and later inflicts the same fate on a group of female witches. According to Ricard's source:

This hell had a secret door by which all those who were within could emerge, and as soon as they had come out it was set on fire, and it burned so fiercely that it seemed no one had escaped . . . and all the souls and devils groaned and screamed (Ricard 1966: 203).

Similarly, to enliven his sermons, and illustrate his argument, one Fray Luis Caldera, 'had a kind of oven brought in, had dogs, cats and other animals thrown into it, and then lit the oven' (Ricard 1966: 104).

The primary vehicle of communication and means of instruction throughout the mission centres was an Indian language, and during the sixteenth century there was a proliferation of native language texts especially in Nahuatl. Ricard calculates that of 109 books on evangelization published between 1524 and 1572 sixty-six were on or about Nahuatl (1966: 49). The adoption of that language for proselytization derived from its importance in pre-Conquest Mexico as the Aztec language. Missionaries contributed to its consolidation as the second language of many Indian groups by extending its use to the convents outside Nahuatl-speaking areas, where it was employed in sermons, and other languages relegated to the confessional (Lafaye 1976: 17, Ricard 1966: 34, 49). Spanish (Castilian) was avoided, despite desultory attempts by the Spanish Crown to promote it. Quoting a royal edict of 1550 'that the Indians be instructed in our Castilian speech and accept our social organization and good customs', Ricard says that the Crown tried to insist on this policy of Hispanicization because it felt that the native languages were inadequate to convey the gospel (Ricard 1966: 52). This was opposed by the missionaries, who believed that Hispanicization of the Indians would expose them to exploitation and a corrupting Spanish influence. On the contrary, missionary representatives advised the King that he should order the learning of Nahuatl (Ricard 1966: 50). None the less, the missionaries did have recourse to some Castilian or Latin words for key terms in Catholic discourse which they introduced into Nahuatl rather than use misleading indigenous vocabulary: *communitlactl* for 'communicant' (Ricard 1966: 124–5), *Dios* for *teotl* (ibid.: 56, but see also Lockhart 1992: 253). Gibson gives the impression that there was a substantial, thought-out, long-term policy of Hispanicization 'devoted to nothing less than the eradication of all indigenous languages' (1964: 147). If there was, it seems to have been a programme which existed only on paper: late sixteenth-century attempts to found civil schools came to nothing as there was no money (Gibson 1964: 503 n. 46). Certainly the Hispanicization policy was ineffective. Evidence from court proceedings, which Gibson cites, shows that Nahuatl continued to be used well into the late colonial period (see also Lockhart 1992 for a sustained account of long-term linguistic change).

The policy of conversion entailed abandonment by the Indians of social and cultural practices considered sinful (polygyny, witchcraft), accompanied by some economic development, and in pursuit of it the Church 'nurtured and preserved communal forms of life among Indians' (Gibson 1964: 134–5), seeking to restrict intercourse with the colonial world. Frequent royal injunctions forbidding non-Indians (Spaniards, Negroes, mestizos and mulattos) to live in Indian communities supported this policy, though with no great success (Gibson 1964: 147, Lafaye 1976: 13, McAllister 1984: 338–9). The system was thoroughly paternalistic. Ricard (1966: 180) comments that the missionaries claimed to be the 'true father and mother of the Indians' and that 'this concept of tutelage . . . kept the Indians in a perpetual status of minors', and isolated them from other Indians as much as from the rest of the population (Ricard 1966: 153). This isolation was a constant source of tension between missions, local governors, economic interests. Although the system of placing Indians in 'reserves' under the tutelage of the missions facilitated their conversion and their control (Lynch 1958: 185), it denied the colonists access to their labour. In the Jesuit 'reductions' in Paraguay, economically and politically self-sufficient communities separate from mainstream colonial society, but under the protection of the fathers, the missionaries were, for a time, powerful enough to keep the recruiters at bay (Lynch 1958: 186). Conflict between the Jesuits and the colonists led eventually, in 1768–70, to the expulsion of the Order from the Spanish Empire and the opening up of the Indian reserves to labour recruitment (Lynch 1958: 188–9, McAllister 1984: 329).

The Spanish Crown's support for Christian proselytization in the Americas was the principal means by which a weak state intervened directly in the transformation of ethnic space in its colonies in the sixteenth–eighteenth centuries. In the case of France, too, and leaving aside extermination, or the slave trade, it was the missions who during this period articulated native policy, reflecting Richelieu's view that conversion offered a way of incorporating Indians into colonial society (Betts 1976: 157). Although missionary activity continued to be important in the nineteenth century, indeed they operated on an even greater scale, and increasingly effectively, especially in Africa, both France and Britain adopted a stance towards their native populations which, as the commonly used phrase 'civilizing mission' suggests, was a kind of secular evangelization. In the case of France, this civilizing mission was signalled through the concept of 'assimilation', an idea which was 'a governing principle' of French colonial policy, says Betts (1961: 10), 'if not a practice'.

4. 'Assimilation' in the French colonial system

Discussion of assimilation in French colonialism has concentrated on what was undoubtedly its most important aspect, namely, cultural transformation. It has come to signify the idea that colonized peoples should be socially and culturally absorbed by the colonizer with the production of a new type of person, the 'assimilated' native, the 'assimilado' (in Portuguese), exemplified in the French word *évolué*. In fact, assimilation had important economic and political as well as social and cultural dimensions. It meant that French colonies were to be treated as if they and their inhabitants were part of France, not colonies at all but metropolitan *départements*, integrated into a comprehensive network of French administrative, financial, and economic institutions. For good reason, therefore, the classic early English language account of this policy (S. H. Roberts 1963, originally published in 1926) has a lengthy section on trade and tariffs. Assimilation had as much to do with commerce as with culture (see, however, M. D. Lewis 1962: 131).

Although this idea informed French policy throughout the colonial period, opposition to it, especially in the last decade of the nineteenth century, led to a different approach ('association'), which had much in common with the contemporary British policy of indirect rule. It is not easy, however, to distinguish clearly the periods characterized by assimilation from those characterized by association. Mid-nineteenth-century French colonial rule had elements later thought characteristic of the policy of association, and despite the abandonment of formal assimilation policies (except in Senegal), not least because of their practical difficulties, cultural assimilation remained the long-term objective (Crowder 1967: 1–2). Certainly, assimilation and its consequences united the opposition to French colonial rule which emerged among *évolués* in the 1930s: Césaire, Fanon, Memmi, Senghor, and others were reacting against precisely that cultural and social assimilation which had produced them.

Betts, Cohen, Crowder, and Roberts, among others, all point to continuity between the cultural dimension of assimilation and the earlier Catholic evangelizing mission, while agreeing assimilation policy had its own distinctive origin in the Enlightenment and the French Revolution (Lewis 1962: 132): it was socially, culturally, and politically a *republican* policy. The wider significance of the Revolution for the development of thinking about the state and ethnic and cultural pluralism is discussed in the next chapter. With regard to French colonial policy, it is clear that political and administrative assimilation was fully in accord with the Jacobin tendency towards centralization. What needs to be emphasized is its harmony with Revolutionary social doctrine, and the way it reflected republican discourse. Betts (1961: 15) neatly summarizes the underlying theory: 'Reason is the virtue of the world; man is universally equal; law is everywhere applicable; societies are subject to rational alteration' (Betts 1961: 30). The French Revolution had revealed the possibility for mankind to break free of the chains of superstition and unreason. Its principals were and should be available to all, and mankind had a right and duty to embrace them. Moreover, the French as the only begetters of the Revolution had the right and duty, like the Romans before them, to assist mankind in breaking the chains and achieving liberation. In 1910 one colonial authority affirmed:

We must make countries out of these empty spaces, we must make nations out of these agglomerations of half-civilized or barbarian peoples, we must organize new states, give them traditions, morals, a political and social organization (in *Notre œuvre coloniale*, cited in Cohen 1971: 77).

Writing in the 1920s and reflecting the thinking of his age, Roberts commented: 'The aim is to inculcate the civilization of France and to convert [the natives] into pinchbeck Frenchmen, revelling in the cultural and legal traditions of the metropolis . . . the whole structure of native life is to be re-moulded' (1963: 68). The peoples of the colonial world represented the opportunity for a new beginning.

Full-scale implementation of the policy of assimilation was never really attempted, nor could it be. There were neither the resources nor the political will to integrate fully and equally into France, and on equal terms with the French, the dozens of territories and the millions of inhabitants who made up the French Empire. It was only in parts of West Africa and in the Antilles that the policy was implemented to any significant degree. Crowder's account of assimilation in Senegal makes it clear how unusual was practice in that colony compared with others in West and Equatorial Africa, and even in Senegal the policy was not applied fully and equally to all the population. In the 1820s the local governor had been instructed that he should seek 'to introduce gradually among the blacks . . . a civilization based on free labour . . . education, and public peace' (in Crowder 1967: 13). Various laws, especially those concerning the status of freed slaves, had by 1848 enabled some 12,000 Africans, but only 12,000 Africans, to acquire voting rights. The Revolution of that year gave Senegal a Deputy in the French Assembly, and the local population elected a *métis* to represent them. Voting rights were annulled in Napoleon III's counter-revolution of 1852, but restored in 1871 (thus illustrating the close relationship between the application of assimilationist policies and the fluctuating fortunes of republicanism in France). Such rights, then, when they existed, applied to a small, mainly *métis* population. For the rest (*sujets*) there was summary justice at the hands of district officials (*indigénat*) and forced labour (*corvée*).

Certainly assimilation had, by its standards, its successes. A very small number of colonial subjects, products of assimilationist education policies, broke into French society. In Senegal, an African, Blaise Diagne was elected as

Deputy in 1914. In January 1918 he became Commissioner-General of the Republic for the Recruitment of Troops in Black Africa, with status equal to that of the Governor-General of French West Africa (Crowder 1967: 27–8). Later, in 1921, he acted as President of the Second Pan-African Congress (Crowder 1967: 31), represented France at an important ILO conference, and in 1931–2 was Under-Secretary of State for the Colonies (Crowder 1967: 37). Another, and in many respects archetypal *évolué* was Félix Eboué, from French Guiana, who graduated from the École Coloniale, the college which trained French colonial administrators, before World War I. After many years in the colonial service in French Equatorial Africa he was in 1940 Governor of Chad, and the only French colonial governor publicly to support de Gaulle. Promoted Governor-General of French Equatorial Africa, based at Brazzaville (Manning 1988: 138), he was highly influential in the conference which debated post-war policy for the French colonies. 'This man', says Cohen, 'ruling in the name of France over other black men, was the perfect symbol of French assimilation' (1971: 159). In a British context it was as if a Jamaican were, in 1940, governor of Nigeria. A colleague of Eboué's in the colonial administration in Equatorial Africa was the Martiniquan, René Maran, whose novel *Batouala*, based on his African experiences, won the Prix Goncourt in 1921 (Manning 1988: 109).

The importance of education needs no underlining. In the words of Governor-General Chaudié in 1897:

The school is the surest means of action by which a civilizing nation can transmit its ideas to people who are still primitive and by which it can raise them gradually to its own standards. In a word the school is the supreme element of progress. It is also the most effective tool of propaganda for the French language that the Government can use (cited in Crowder 1967: 35).

In its original incarnation as the 'Collège cambodgienne', the École Coloniale had been founded by Félix Faure in 1885 as a centre for training a 'native' cadre selected from among the sons of South-East Asian and African dignitaries (Cohen 1971: 38). From 1889 it housed a training course in colonial administration which later became the School's *raison d'être* and the earlier programme was reduced to a 'native section' (Cohen 1971: 39). Similarly, Lyautey, the Resident-General in Morocco, established an École Professionnelle de Fez, and two Collèges Musulmans at Fez and Rabat, roughly the equivalent of French lycées, intended for 'the cream of Moroccan boys, boys from cultured, educated, upper-class Moroccan families' (Scham 1970: 153). The significance of the school as an avenue of advancement and vehicle of assimilation is vividly portrayed in the novel (and film) *Rue Cases-Nègres*, by the Martiniquan Zobel.

Critics have frequently pointed out the ethnocentric bias of the curriculum. Manning (1988: 169) reminds us of the much-quoted extract from one textbook which began 'Our ancestors the Gauls are tall and fair'. Memmi, a Tunisian, writing of schoolchildren, comments:

The history they learn is not their own. They know about Colbert, Cromwell and Joan of Arc, but not Khaznadar or Kahena. Everything seems to happen elsewhere. Their country scarcely exists or exists only by reference to the Gauls, the Franks and the Marne, to what they are not, to Christianity when they are not Christians, to the West which is beyond their reach (Memmi 1973: 133–4).

Of course, as Memmi acknowledges, the vast majority of children did not attend school: 10 per cent only in Senegal in 1938, though 70 per cent of their teachers were African (Crowder 1967: 34); 1.3 per cent in neighbouring Guinée in 1947. Nevertheless, as Crowder's description of Senegal during the Vichy era indicates, the extent to which the population at large absorbed an orientation towards France and its current institutions was considerable:

so successfully did Vichy put over its image [of Pétain] that when French West Africa joined the allies, schoolchildren . . . had to be told that the 'Maréchal' had been made a prisoner, and that their soldiers were going to fight to free him. Only later was it broken to them that the 'Maréchal' had been the enemy all the time (1967: 40–1).

Opposition to assimilation came not only from mid-twentieth-century *évolués*, however. Much earlier, in the 1890s, thinking and policy began to diverge from the principles of assimilation which had informed instruction at the École Coloniale. The change accompanied the shift in mid-nineteenth-century thinking about human evolution and about social, cultural, and above all racial difference. Whereas the Enlightenment stressed the underlying universality of human thought and peoples, Romanticism wallowed in difference. There were, however, two very distinct ways of viewing difference. One stressed the idea that it was a matter for celebration, and what challenged difference was to be eschewed. People could not be divested readily of their existing beliefs and practices to which they were profoundly attached, and which had wide-ranging implications for their social and cultural ways of life. Adherents of the second perspective believed that difference was hierarchically ordered, innate, and ineradicable. Often racist in the strict sense, this perspective led the scientist Gustave Le Bon in 1889 to dismiss 'as dangerous chimeras all our ideas of assimilating or Frenchifying any inferior people. Leave to the natives their customs, their institutions, their laws' (in Betts 1961: 68, see also Lewis 1962: 138–41). Gobineau, the mid-nineteenth-century synthesist of racism, in fact opposed the colonial project because he believed that 'civilizations are incommunicable' (in Roberts 1963: 105). There were fundamental, impenetrable barriers to assimilation.

There was, however, a third perspective which stressed the practical problems and consequences of assimilation, or, in British terms, direct rule through the Crown Colony system, and the huge costs involved. Thus in both Britain and France the idea of extending ethnic space to incorporate colonial peoples as French or British citizens gave way to an emphasis on the reordering of ethnic space within the colonies themselves.

5. Association and indirect rule

The idea of 'association' which increasingly dominated French thought from the 1880s onwards, was worked out in the colonies by officials like Paul Bert in Indochina, and administrator-soldiers such as Faidherbe, Galliéni, and Lyautey in West Africa, Madagascar, and Morocco (Lewis 1962: 148 ff.). The idea was summarized by Paul Bert's son-in-law in 1909 as follows:

This policy of association rests on the idea that the natives are, at least provisionally, inferior to the Europeans, or at least different, that they have their past, their customs, their institutions and a religion to which they adhere. Even with the aid of education their minds cannot understand and accept our concepts any more rapidly. But it is the duty of the stronger people to guide the weaker people, to aid them in the evolution of their own civilization, until that day when they are close enough to ours so that they may take from it what they deem good. While awaiting this result of education and of time, we must respect their ideas, their customs, religion and civilization (cited by Betts 1961: 152).

The new system of rule was, however, by no means what it seemed:

In every country there are leaders. The big mistake that Europeans make when they go abroad conquering is to destroy that leadership. Deprived of its framework, the country falls into anarchy. One must govern with the mandarin, not against the mandarin . . . Do not undermine traditions; do not change customs. Everywhere, there is a ruling class, born to rule. Put it to work in our interests (in Maurois 1934: 44).

This passage reports advice given to Lyautey when serving in Saigon. 'Govern with the mandarin', 'co-operate with the natives' (Lyautey speech of 1918, in Scham 1970: 29), leave space for indigenous institutions.

The idea of working through existing institutions was not new. Policies adopted in West Africa a generation earlier had pointed the way. Faidherbe, governor of Senegal in the 1850s and 1860s, had an impeccable republican, not to say Jacobin, pedigree, and believed that 'he could impose more enlightened and humane institutions on the subjugated regions' (Cohen 1971: 9): Manning draws a parallel between Faidherbe's vision of a Francized Africa, and that of his African contemporary, Al-hajj Umar's concept of West Africa as a land of Islam (1988: 13, 61). Although committed to assimilation, in practice Faidherbe implemented an early form of indirect rule through the use of traditional chiefs. He divided Senegal into administrative districts under the control of a French official, but associated with a traditional ruler who 'transmitted orders' to village chiefs. Later, most of the chiefs' powers were transferred to the French *commandants de cercles*, the cornerstone of French colonialism through to the end. None the less, the system of regional or cantonal chiefs, with subordinate village chiefs, also remained an important element (Cohen 1971: 11–12).

In the Maghreb, too, there had been, and would continue to be, a mixture of direct and indirect methods of governance. From 1830 onwards the

French sought to establish and extend their control over the formerly quasi-independent Ottoman province of Algeria, the first part of the Ottoman Empire to be detached by the West (Betts 1976: 53). Initially, they assumed that the Algerian population could be treated as homogeneous: they conceived of a ' "uniform" native' (Roberts 1963: 190), modelled after the Moorish pirates with whom they had dealt previously. From 1870, however, the perception developed that there were two kinds of native: Arabs and Berbers (or Kabyles). Although Roberts remains an important anglophone authority on French colonialism, and a valuable source of information, he is even better as a source for attitudes and stereotypes. Here, for example, in his own words, and clearly in his own opinion, he represents prevailing perceptions of Arab and Berber society:

The Berbers are the mountaineers, the descendants of the pre-Mohammedan population and the real autochthones . . . Their organization is individualistic and largely democratic. The Kabyles, being agriculturalists, were keen individualists, and always had an eye on material progress . . . although their supposed primitive virtues and the extent of their democracy have probably been exaggerated, they were fighting freemen of the hills, and with no omnipotent central organizations . . . they have, in their aversion to everything foreign, reserved a special hatred and contempt for the Arabs who usurped their land in the ninth century and enforced the word of the Prophet (Roberts 1963: 190–1).

The so-called Arabs in Algeria are not really Arabs at all: their only unifying features are the Mohammedan religion and the fact they are all non-Berbers . . . Arabs and Turks and Moors and negroes have all mixed, the result being the 'Algerian Arab' of today, a nonedescript ethnic type . . . They are nomad pastoralists, with a social polity based on the family or tribe. Organization is frankly feudal, the emphasis being on the ruler, and not, as with the Berber, on the individuals . . . the group-leader is supreme in the group. The Arab thus has less independence and individuality than the Berber: Arab men are less energetic and progressive, Arab women less free (ibid.: 191).

The world of the Arab, 'idle by habit and instinct, and with a limited intelligence' (p. 194), was contrasted with what the politician Jaurès called the 'noble Kabyle democracies' (in Roberts 1963: 573, see also Renan 1873), a people whom Roberts believed to be 'in essence white' (p. 558) because of their supposed ancestry. This view was shared by Lugard (1922: 67), who placed the sub-Saharan Fulani on a higher level than others because of their alleged Berber connections.

There were indeed important social and cultural differences between Arabs and Berbers, in their indigenous political organization and their attitude towards Islam: the more distant relationship of the Berbers with that religion is something that the French, initially, failed completely to take into account (Roberts 1963: 98). Thus Scham is right, but only up to a point, to refute the criticism of Lyautey, that his policy in Morocco 'separated' Arabs and Berbers.

Indigenous Moroccan government had certainly distinguished between Arabs and Berbers, but French colonial policy built on that distinction and incorporated it into a new and thoroughgoing system of politicized difference.

The system of rule which Lyautey established in Morocco after 1912, much admired at the time, put into practice many of the principles which Bert's son-in-law had identified as underpinning the policy of association. 'At the head of the structure', says Roberts (1963: 566) 'was the Sultan, unfettered in his religious capacity . . . but supervised in his political functions.' 'Unfettered', the whole sentence, brings to mind Lugard's definition of indirect rule in British territories: 'Rule by native chiefs, unfettered in their control of their people as regards all those matters which are to them the most important . . . but . . . subordinate to the control of the protecting power in certain well-defined directions' (1922: 197). 'Subordination' meant strict limitation of the chief's powers to raise and control armed forces or taxes, and to legislate. The sovereign power also retained the right to confirm succession to office 'in the interests of good government' (Lugard 1922: 207). Certainly, Scham's account (1970: 57 ff.) of the major changes in the central government of Morocco instituted by Lyautey leave one with the impression that, not to mince words, the Sultan was a puppet ruler, more or less under the control of the Resident General. These changes included the complete restructuring of the council of viziers and of local government (Roberts 1963: 566–7, Scham 1970: 82–5). There was a new system of tribal leaders, town leaders, and judges, which built on an existing tribal order, but transformed it. A new legal system was introduced, with echoes of Ottoman practice: Muslim and Jewish courts (there was a substantial Jewish population in Morocco) dealt with civil matters concerning their confessions, while French courts dealt with relations between the French and the indigenous inhabitants (Scham 1970: 169). Berbers, on the other hand, were regulated by what in British and French territories was called 'customary law' rather than the Sheriat. Arabs, Berbers, French, and indigenous Jews therefore had their own *statut personnel*, and ethnic difference was confirmed in the political structure.

6. Tribes and tribalism

Leaving aside its sham nature, running through indirect rule (French or British style) was the conceptualization of the native population via a 'tribal' idiom. Throughout the nineteenth century, and earlier, peoples of Africa, Asia, and the Americas, even when believed inherently capable of better, were usually thought to be at a 'lower' stage of development than that achieved by European civilization (Cohen 1980: 79). Debates of the 1960s and later about the use of the term 'tribe' in African studies reflected this connotation of the term (Ekeh 1990, Mafeje 1971, Southall 1970*b*). Characteristically, Roberts castigated the French policy of assimilation for trying to convert 'Stone-Age natives to nineteenth century Frenchmen' (1963: 69). There was a profound gulf between the societies and cultures of Africa, and those to which supposedly they were to be assimilated, though of course the idea of assimilation also implied that the gulf could be bridged (Crowder 1967: 2). Such perceptions were interwined in complex ways with thinking about race and racial difference. The debate about the origins and historicity of racist thought and practice cannot be discussed here. Cohen, writing about the French, and McAllister, about the Spanish, follow those who see racism as deeply embedded in European thought, and of very great duration, antedating colonialism and the slave trade. Others derive racism from that trade. What is undeniable is that racial thinking sharpened and deepened in the second half of the nineteenth century when in addition, after Darwin, it acquired a pseudo-scientific, evolutionary basis.

Significant here is the way in which racism informed thinking about difference, not only differences between Europeans and, say, Africans, but also between indigenous colonial peoples: all were 'natives', but some more so than others. Thus Lugard thought there were two main groups in the African population: the so-called 'Hamites', descended from invaders from the Middle East, and the 'Bantu'. The former, he believed , had 'powers of social organisation and intellectual development in advance of the pure negro stock' (Lugard 1922: 68). They were associated with Islam, for which the British, like the French, had, generally speaking, a certain respect (Cohen 1980: 257). As for the Bantu: 'the typical African of this race-type is a happy, thriftless, excitable person, lacking in self-control, discipline and foresight, naturally courageous, and naturally courteous and polite, full of personal vanity, with little sense of veracity, fond of music' (Lugard 1922: 69). They were like 'attractive children' (p. 70).

These ideas, as well as the problems of practical administration, led Lugard to differentiate, in Nigeria, between the northern Hausa-Fulani states and the 'primitive tribes' of the south-east, such as the Ibo. For the former, a system of indirect rule was devised, not unlike that introduced by Lyautey in Morocco. For the latter, there was a need to 'hasten the transition from the patriarchal to the tribal stage, and induce those who acknowledge no other authority than the head of a family to recognise a common chief' (Lugard 1922: 217). In pre-colonial Africa politics, language, and culture formed relatively unbounded systems. Even within states the situation was extremely flexible and fluid. In their case indirect rule provided fixed boundaries and authorities, and created new constellations of political units. In the case of 'acephalous' societies wholly new unities were established. Assessing the system of 'warrant chiefs' set up by the British in the Ibo areas of Nigeria in the early years of the twentieth century, Afigbo concluded that they revealed a history of 'wrong assumptions leading to wrong decisions and wrong remedies and finally . . . failure' (1972: 296). In Algeria, where the local population was pushed into restricted areas to release their land for settlement, the French categorized the population by 'tribe', though not necessarily using the same groupings which indigenous people recognized, and then by *douar*: by 1870 they had enumerated and established for administrative purposes 376 of the former and 676 of the latter (Roberts 1963: 98, 198 ff.). A detailed illustration of this kind of process is found in Tosh's account of British policy in Uganda.

In what became Lango District, in the north of the country, there were a number of peoples culturally and linguistically related to the Alur, described in Chapter 2. In this traditional 'Lango' society there was 'no institutionalized grouping above the level of village or neighbourhood, and corporate or "tribal" identity, in so far as it is experienced at all, depends on ill-defined cultural factors rather than regular patterns of social co-operation' (Tosh 1973: 474). Leadership was in the hands of heads (*rwot*) of what Tosh calls clan sections (p. 476). In the 1920s, however, in the spirit of prevailing policy, the British determined to apply the 'Ganda model' of administrative organization. The Ganda kingdom, in the south of Uganda, had traditionally a hierarchically ordered system of administration divided into units translated into British official vernacular as 'Counties', 'Sub-Counties', 'Parishes', and 'Villages', each with a 'chief'. To apply this model to acephalous Lango society meant that chiefs (and villages) had to be created, and these were selected from among the heads of clan sections. Where there was a choice, as there usually was, it was made on the basis of nearness to the arbitrarily located administrative posts which had been set up as Sub-County headquarters (p. 479). The system created new and artificial entities at all levels, new focuses of political activity (pp. 483–4), and new networks of political relations. A new identity emerged, carrying a new political salience: 'Lango' became a political actor.

Crowder had considered Senegal remarkably free of 'tribal differences', and suggested that the French policy of assimilation along with other factors such as Islam assisted in the creation of an 'indigenous homogeneity' (1967: 97). This led him to the optimistic conclusion that Senegal was or could be a sort of 'ideal' state, in an Africa where, since independence, ethnically rooted politics had become the norm. In fact, in the 1960s it became commonplace to argue that colonialism itself had created 'tribes', or if not tribes then 'tribalism' in Africa (Apthorpe 1968, Mafeje 1971, Southall 1970*b*). Young, in emphasizing the tribal element in the colonial classificatory practices, uses the term 'ethonym' to refer to the labels (such as 'Lango') which colonial authorities put on groupings they believed shared a language or culture (1985: 76). He does not, however, believe that the colonial state 'engaged in a conscious process of fabrication of ethnic groups' (1985: 75). Nor, he adds 'even where the taxonomic demiurge was most prominent, did all identities find their origin in this way'. New historical evidence available in the 1980s has in fact revealed a quite complex picture of the emergence of tribal groups and ethnic identities during the early years of colonialism (Fardon 1987, Ranger 1983).

An important contribution to understanding this phenomenon has been made by Vail, who criticizes the simplistic view that ethnicity in Africa was generated by colonial 'divide-and-rule' policies. Despite an 'element of truth' in this assertion (Southall, 1970*b*: 33, used the same phrase), he finds it wanting because, if policies were uniformly applied, it fails to explain the uneven development of ethnic consciousness, and because it portrays Africans 'as little more than either collaborating dupes or naive and gullible people, beguiled by clever colonial administrators and untrustworthy anthropologists' (Vail 1989: 2–3). There was, rather, an 'ethnic dialectic', as I call it, which in Central Africa involved not only the state, but groups such as missionaries, and indigenous peoples themselves. New identities emerged partly through the role played by what Vail calls 'cultural brokers' (p. 11), intellectuals, African and other, who engaged in the construction of ethnic ideologies, and the apparatus of ethnic differentiation (see, for example, Peel, 1989, for an account of what he calls 'Yoruba ethnogenesis'). Also important was the use of African intermediaries through the system of indirect rule, and the fact that 'ordinary people had a real need for so-called "traditional values" at a time of rapid social change' (Vail 1989: 11). In other words, ethnic ideologies made sense under the circumstances.

Vail's own account (with White) of the emergence of new, regionally based identities in Malawi (Vail and White 1989), and Jewsiewicki's description (1989) of 'Luba' identity in the Belgian Congo (Zaire), provide ample evidence for this, as does Ranger's analysis of the evolution of 'Manyika' identity in Zimbabwe. While accepting that in the case of the Zulu state there may have been a pre-colonial basis to later Zulu ethnic identity, Ranger sees in his Zimbabwean material much evidence for the alternate view that ethnicity in contemporary Africa is a modern phenomenon which emerged out of events in the colonial period. In Central Africa, where pre-colonial states existed, they had 'never pulled all their subjects together into self-conscious identities, nor had they manipulated concepts of group identity in a manner which left a lasting ethnic legacy. Between the Shona culture as a whole and the local chiefly groups there existed no intermediate concept of ethnicity' (Ranger 1989: 120). In the case of the 'Manyika', however, it was not solely, or even importantly, the colonial state which worked to create the idea of a new identity. Rather it was 'unofficial' Europeans, missionaries, who played an important part in developing a written Manyika language out of the region's dialect continuum (p. 126), and mission-educated Africans who were in the forefront of promoting it. This emergent ethnicity struck a chord, especially among migrant labourers, where it became 'not just a convenient reference group, but an ideal which sustained them during their migration' (p. 141). It corresponded to a new, different, colonial reality of new systems of agricultural production, a cash economy, and the labour market. Ekeh has also suggested that under conditions where the state was minimally involved in the provision of services (except in regard to law and order), indigenous institutions had to take on increasing responsibilities for welfare and education, and through an 'upgraded kinship system' (1990: 684) offered an ethnically based system of social welfare.

7. Continuities and discontinuities

Colonialism is important historically because *inter alia* reverberations of its 'organization' of race and ethnicity continue to this day, as we shall see in later chapters. It is also important because, as is sometimes suggested, the colonial state was in certain respects a paradigmatic instance of modernity. What the evidence of the present chapter suggests is, rather, its hybrid character. Compared with patrimonial societies, modern nation-states have been grounded in the fostering of a common identity and homogeneous culture. Colonial practice was in this regard ambivalent: 'patrimonial' in so far as it emphasized the extraction of resources, 'modern', indeed modern before modernity, so to speak, in so far as the colonial powers believed they had a mission to uplift and transform their colonial subjects. Ironically, it was the non-interventionist patrimonial societies of Africa, Asia, and 'Latin' America which found themselves colonized by the European powers, and when they did adopt proselytizing policies, as some Islamic states did, for example in West Africa in the nineteenth century, it was often in response to the colonial state's own proselytizing activities.

'We should not', says Jenkins (1994: 217), 'underestimate the capacity of one group of people to define effectively or to constitute the conditions of existence experienced by another', but we should not overestimate it either—hence the need for dynamic perspectives of the kind which Jenkins himself advocates and which is signalled here by the concept of an 'ethnic dialectic'. There were ideas and policies, and there were consequences, and the three were not always in accord. Spanish, French, and British colonialism made sustained attacks on the identity of Africans and Indians. The discourse of tribe, and the 'tribalization' of the indigenous populations (in several senses), imposed a new language of ethnic difference and new forms of ethnic and cultural pluralism, sometimes in unexpected ways. All three had some intent to produce a new model 'native'. In Spanish America in the sixteenth–eighteenth centuries the lead was taken by the Catholic Church, who saw its task as that of creating the converted Indian, delivered from idolatry, but uncontaminated by Hispanicization. In practice, as Gibson points out, Hispanicization 'proceeded in ways both planned and unpremeditated' (1964: 147). Mostly, unplanned, perhaps, none the less with important consequences in the long term. In the short term, too, although Hispanicization touched only a small fraction of the population, there did emerge, surprisingly rapidly, an Hispanicized class of *cacique*, an elite intermediary group in criollo society (Gibson 1964: 156). Similarly, despite the French state's drawing back from policies of assimilation, and despite the obvious discomfort that someone like Lugard felt at the idea of the 'Europeanized' African, missionary and other forces, not least the demands of the colonial economy, ensured that the 'evolved' native would continue to be produced. Those who did emerge in this way always had an ambiguous status in the colonial social order: the French term *déraciné* is eloquent in this respect. And it was precisely such people who were in the forefront of the anti-colonial movement.

6

The Jacobin Project: The Nation-State and the Enemy Within

The age of the Messiah came with the French Revolution.

(Maurice Bloch, 1904, in Delpech 1976: 19.)

The Jew is a different being.

(Barrès 1925 (1902): 68.)

1. The Jacobin project

Among the early states of Africa and Mesoamerica, ethnic and cultural pluralism, if not absent, played little part in the organization of the body politic and relations between states. Nor were their rulers inclined to impose on their subjects their own ethnic identity. Ottomans certainly structured the body politic in terms of blocs of an ethnico-religious kind, through the organization of the confessions (Muslim, Orthodox, Jewish, and Armenian), but until the nineteenth century ethnicity did not drive the state, nor did it provide the rationale for the state's existence. From the late eighteenth century onwards, however, Europe was increasingly organized into nation-states within which the political and the ethnic became closely linked. This form of polity was not everywhere precisely the same: there were several versions of the nation-state, though all shared the view that the world could be comprehensively divided into political entities grounded in similar modes of internal ('national') and external ('international') organization, and the assumption that subjects or citizens of a nation-state belonged to a single national community.

Compared with their predecessors (including the *anciens régimes*), these 'modern' nation-states were increasingly concerned to intervene in the economies and societies they claimed as their own, assuming responsibility for directing society's affairs and moulding its subjects (as citizens), through an ever more elaborate legislative and executive apparatus of a bureaucratic kind. As we saw in the previous chapter, Raymond Betts, writing against a background of the development of colonialism, has proposed that the strongly interventionist state was a phenomenon of the twentieth century (Betts dates it to the period after World War I, 1976: 188); the nineteenth-century state was still only a 'night-watchman', responsible for law and order and not much else (Betts 1985: 198). Certainly the heyday of the interventionist state was in practice much later, probably after World War II, but the *theory* of the nation-state which arose in the late eighteenth century demanded a new, vigorously intervening type of polity. This was one of the many 'modern' concepts which emerged at that time, especially in France, and through its association with particular parties in the French Revolution it may be termed the 'Jacobin project'.

Jacobinism was an important experiment and model for the future, both for what the Jacobins did (or hoped to do), and for the way that they did it (Terror and all). Their project entailed the view that the 'nation' can and must organize itself through a powerful state which can and should engineer society for society's betterment, and woe betide those who stand in the way. (See Chapter 5 for an account of how this view informed French colonial policy.) There have been stronger and weaker versions of this Jacobin project: the social democracy espoused by the British Labour Party in the 1940s ('The gentleman in Whitehall really does know better') was Jacobinism of a middling kind. Totalitarian parties (communist and fascist) have sought something much stronger, undertaking a full-scale colonization of state and society. Leninism, indeed, might be described as the apotheosis of Jacobinism, and with good reason an important book on the Khmer Rouge was entitled *Cambodia Year Zero*. Leninism may have been an extreme example, but even those states with laissez-faire economic policies have rarely abstained from intervening widely and deeply in society and culture, even when claiming to do otherwise. This type of state ('l'Etat "fort" à la française', Birnbaum 1989: 497) was also characterized by its deep commitment to universalism and hostility towards (collective) 'difference' (see Chapter 5 for a discussion of the relevance of this to French colonialism, and Grillo 1989: 22 ff. for an account of French language policies).

This chapter explores the modern nation-state through an extended case study of the Jewish population in France: the *fons et origo* of this type of polity. It discusses the ways in which the concept of a 'nation', specifically a French nation, was constructed in the nineteenth century, and shows that there were in fact two contrasting and conflicting models prevalent in French thought. It then considers how the Jews in France (and elsewhere) were caught up in the application of these conflicting models to their great detriment. It therefore tells part of the story of the politics of Jewish identity in the modern nation-state, but relates that story to broader themes in the ideologies and practices of nation and nationalism in Europe and elsewhere which are taken up in later chapters.

Although bearing on the issue of what is called in French *nationalisation*, how populations come together within a framework of common institutions, it is not my purpose in this chapter to address the kind of questions raised by Eugen Weber's account of the transformation of *Peasants into Frenchmen*. The case of the French Jews is instructive for other reasons. One of the key questions raised by the debates in France at the time of the Revolution (and later), remains as important now as it was two centuries ago: what if anything can or should be done for collectivities rather than for individuals? Moreover, as Birnbaum argues, the emancipation which enabled Jews to enter into modernity was granted by a state interested in universalizing liberty rather than maintaining diversity (1989: 497). Thus, as he also points out, it raises questions which are reflected in late twentieth-century debates in France and elsewhere about the rights to 'difference' and the desirability or otherwise of pluralist conceptions of society (1989: 499).

2. The French nation: the two 'legends'

Lévi-Strauss once divided societies into 'cold' and 'hot' by reference to their relationship with history (Charbonnier 1969). The material on Africa and Mesoamerica suggests that this distinction is not especially useful when applied to formations such as the early states. None the less, 'modern' states certainly have an especially strong, dynamic, ongoing relationship with their past. This is obviously true of France, where in 1994 the defence minister was obliged to dismiss the head of the army's history section when 'a study to mark the centenary of the Dreyfus Affair cast doubt on the Jewish officer's innocence' (Reuter Report in the *Guardian*, 9 February 1994), and where the 1996 debate over the celebration of the 1500th anniversary of the conversion of Clovis to Catholicism caused such a furore. The extraordinary party political broadcast transmitted during François Mitterand's 1988 presidential campaign provides further illustration. Accompanied by a powerful martial beat, it presented a montage of French history (180 images in ninety seconds) culminating with the President's face filling the screen. This is not to say that such intense engagement is absent elsewhere, even if in late twentieth-century Britain that engagement increasingly takes the form of incorporating history into the leisure industry.

Relive Britain in wartime! Step back in time 50 years to the dark days of World War II for an unforgettable adventure that's fun for all ages with Winston Churchill's Britain at War Theme Museum . . . Experience the dramatic sights and sounds of the London Blitz as you pick your way through the rubble of a bombed street and dodge falling masonry and an unexploded 'bomb', and lots lots more (*Sussex Express*, 18 February 1994).

In France, by contrast, in a way which would be unthinkable in Britain, the historian Robert Faurisson, who had denied the validity of the Holocaust, was in 1981 the subject of an action brought under Article 382 of the Civil Code for falsification of history (Seidel 1986b: 99 ff.). The point is not the validity or otherwise of Faurisson's claims (though they have a bearing on what follows), but the intense dialogue with history which characterizes French culture, and the way in which political conflict is associated with competing interpretations of that history, especially where those interpretations concern the French nation.

In French discourse of the 1970s, immigrants, usually but not only those from North Africa, could be referred to as either *étrangers* or *immigrés*, terms embedded in different ideological views of the population, and reflecting two different conceptions of French society and the place of the outsider within it (Grillo 1985). These conceptions reflect two contrasting ideas of the nation, one stemming from Enlightenment thinking, the other from Romanticism. Using vocabulary devised by the German sociologist Ferdinand Tönnies, these perspectives may be termed 'nation as community (*Gemeinschaft*)' and 'nation as association (*Gesellschaft*)' (Grillo 1989: 22–3). 'Nation as community' signified a people, a *Volk*, based on likeness, on relationships of blood and kinship, or, not to mince words, racial heritage. 'Nation as association' signified one that was constituted by people who come together voluntarily, forming a pact as fellow citizens, as Rousseau and Siéyès had imagined. The nineteenth-century historian Michelet, in writing about France, drew on a contrast of this kind. Michelet despised community ('a very ancient, barbarous and unproductive state', 1973 (1846): 175), but extolled the virtues of association, whose principles he derived from the organization of the pre-modern guilds. A nation was an association which depended on its 'legend' as Michelet called it: its historical legacy, 'our' past. It is an historical tradition, and constituted by those who share or come to share that tradition. Girardet's valuable collection of readings on French nationalism cites an interesting passage from de Gaulle's memoirs in which he recalls visiting Paris as a child and observing 'the symbol of our glories: nightfall over the Notre Dame, the majesty of the evening at Versailles, the Arc de Triomphe in the sun, captured standards fluttering in the vault of Les Invalides' (in Girardet 1966: 24). Girardet points to the great similarity between that passage and one in Michelet's *Le Peuple* of 1846, where a father takes his son 'from the Notre Dame to the Louvre and the Tuileries to the Arc de Triomphe' (Michelet 1973 (1846): 204).

It is often believed that the nationalism of France and of other countries of Western Europe is of this associative kind, in contrast with the 'blood tie' conception of national identity characteristic of Germany and Eastern Europe (see, for example, Pitt-Rivers's account of the relative importance of *ius sanguinis* and *ius soli* in the two regions, 1954: 30, and Cesarani and Fulbrook 1996: 5). This supposed difference between an 'Eastern' nationalism based on consanguinity, and a 'Western' one based on contract or will (Gellner 1983) has certainly appealed to commentators in France. In 1870 Fustel de Coulanges in an open letter to the German scholar Mommsen attacked the latter's linguistic and racial arguments which supported Germany's claims to Alsace: 'You think you have proved that Alsace is German because its population is of German race and language. I am astounded that an historian such as yourself appears not to know that race and language do not constitute nationality' (in Girardet 1966: 63). For Fustel de Coulanges national solidarity derived from ideas, interests, hopes, and memories. 'It matters little that Alsace is German by reason of race and language. By reason of nationality and patriotic sentiment she is French' (ibid.: 64). Similarly, Ernest Renan in responding to an Alsatian defence of the Prussian seizure of Alsace and Lorraine on grounds similar to those put forward by Mommsen, opposed what he called a 'politique des races', and disputed the value of ethnography and philology in establishing rights to territory: 'Put not your trust in ethnography, or rather do not put such weight on it in politics. On the pretext of the Germanic derivation of its name you claim such and such a village in Lorraine for Prussia' (1871: 457). Vienna, Worms, and Mayence may have Gallic names, Renan pointed out, but 'we will never claim those towns from you'. Should others follow the German example, he warned, the Slavs might claim Prussia, Pomerania, Silesia, and Berlin on account of their names, and before long they would be on the Elbe. A nation, he concluded 'is not synonymous with race. Little Switzerland . . . has three languages, three or four races and two religions . . . a nation is a great secular association and is not eternal' (1871: 458).

Renan developed these points further in 'Qu'est-ce qu'une nation?' (1882a). To confound race and nation was a 'grave error' (p. 887). What characterized the modern nations, in contrast to the Ottoman or Habsburg Empires was the way they 'fused' their constituent populations: France included Celts, Iberians, and Germans. There were no pure races, and ethnography should have nothing to do with the constitution of modern nations. The application of racial theory would imply that 'the German family' would have the right to gather in its scattered members, even if they did not wish to be reclaimed (1882a: 895). Neither was a nation to be based on religion or language. It was, rather, a 'spiritual principle' (p. 903), constituted by a 'rich legacy of memories', and by consent: 'the wish to live together, the will to continue to value the heritage'. A nation is 'having done great things together in the past and wanting to do so again in the future' (p. 904). For Renan it was a club which one could join: in a speech welcoming M. Cherbuliez into the Académie Française, he commented: 'According to the letter of the law you have been French for only two years. But according to your talent you have always been so' (1882b: 784–5).

In this conception of nation the role of education in transmitting the heritage or legend was vital, something which Revolutionaries like Talleyrand and Grégoire fully understood (Grillo 1989). An earlier seminal contribution was that of Rousseau. In 'Considerations on the government of Poland' of 1772 (in Rousseau 1964), he advised the Poles that they must aim to 'establish the Republic so firmly in Polish hearts that it will continue to exist despite all the efforts of its enemies' (p. 959), and urged the importance of creating in the minds of its citizens a sense of the difference between Poland and other nations. Education, above all, would instil this sense of national unity:

At the age of twenty a Pole must be nothing but a Pole. In learning to read he should read nothing but material about his country. At ten, he should know everything about its products; at twelve, he should know all about its regions, its roads and its towns; at fifteen he should know all about its history; at sixteen all its laws. There should be no fine deed, no hero which he does not know about and has taken to heart (p. 966).

Rousseau, says Taylor, provided 'the formula for the most terrible forms of homogenizing tyranny, starting with the Jacobins' (1994: 51). The French Revolutionaries certainly took this advice seriously, instituting new systems of learning firmly under central control. The Regulations of 1802 declared that 'Each Lycée should have a library of 1,500 books. Each library will contain the same books. No other book may be placed in the library without the permission of the Minister of the Interior' (in Renan 1869: 533). They also ensured an appropriate curriculum in which education and nationalism were firmly linked in the French school system in the nineteenth century (see Girardet 1966: 70–84). The connection emerges strongly in Alphonse Daudet's short story 'The last lesson'. The scene is a schoolroom in Alsace shortly after the Franco-Prussian war, portrayed through the eyes of one young pupil, Franzt. M. Hamel, the French teacher, is due to give his final lesson before being replaced the next day by a German. He talks about the French language and all its glory, then the church clock strikes midday, and M. Hamel begins to say farewell to his pupils. But he is overcome by emotion, and can only turn to the blackboard on which he chalks in enormous letters: 'vive la france' (in Girardet 1966: 46).

To contrast this 'French' mode of articulating nationalism, and admitting members to the French club (which influenced colonial policies of assimilation) with a 'German' emphasis on blood, kinship, and race is to overlook important differences *within* French thought (see *inter alia* Silverman 1992, Thom 1990). An episode during the Vichy period illustrates this. In 1942 the Académie des Sciences d'Outre-mer considered a draft constitution for the post-war colonies. Discussion turned to the status of Muslims, and one of the participants enquired: 'Surely we can ask that one broaden French laws sufficiently so that one can be both Moslem and citizen at the same time.' Another, 'speaking for the rest of the committee . . . answered: "No, no, I refuse absolutely"' (in Cohen 1971: 161). This exchange, which hinged on a view of the French nation as one in which Muslims had no part, both anticipated debates of the late twentieth century, and reflected those of the Vichy period, and much earlier, on the position of the Jews. Why were Jews and Muslims, in some eyes, disqualified from membership of the French club?

In mid-nineteenth-century Europe there was an explosion of thinking about racial difference as a fundamental characteristic of the human species. In France 'race' tended to be defined less by physical than by cultural characteristics (Todorov 1993: 153). Renan, for example, used it in an 'ethnographic' sense and characterized a very large number of human groups as 'races'. Indeed, the term was applied so widely and loosely as to become virtually meaningless. None the less, in the classification of peoples there was little room for a French 'race': 'Indo-European', 'Celtic', 'Latin', yes, but not 'French'. The fact of France, in some eyes its glory, was that it brought the Celts and Latins within the same political enterprise. The nationalist Barrès was acutely aware of this: 'It is not strictly accurate to speak of a French race. We are not a race but a nation which constantly remakes itself, and we are in danger of destroying ourselves, those whom it shelters, if we do not protect it' (1925 (1902): 20). It is something he deeply regretted: 'Alas, there is no French race, but a French people, a French nation, that is a political collectivity' (p. 85). None the less, Barrès, like others, considered France much more than an 'association'. Rejecting Renan's notion of France as a 'spiritual principle', Barrès argued that 'nationalism is the acceptance of a determinism' (p. 10). The French nation was an historical tradition, but one rooted profoundly in the eternal values represented by the language and by Catholicism. Maurras, too, that 'wholly antipathetic figure' (Warner 1991: 260), asserted that 'our fatherland is not founded on a contract or voluntary pact' (1972: 160). It is a heritage to which a simple naturalization cannot permit access; not a club that can be joined at will.

3. 'A nation within a nation'

These two visions of France, which surfaced again in the 1996 debate about Clovis, and the contemporary significance of his conversion, represented 'radically different ideas of what constitutes a fatherland' (Rebérioux 1975: 22), as opposed in their way as 'German' and 'French' conceptions. They were (and are) sustained by different visions of what form the landmarks of French history and how they are to be interpreted. For Barrès and Maurras and others of like mind there was a continuity of France over a period of 2,000 years (or at least from the Capetian dynasty) which the Revolution calamitously interrupted. For Michelet, on the other hand, whom Maurras accused of writing 'plebeian' history (1954: 74), 1789 was one of two great 'Redemptions'. The other was the Maid of Orleans, 'sister of Danton' as Michelet called her (in Contamine 1992: 401), whose actions prefigured the Revolution. Joan of Arc is an apt symbol of these two visions, not for anything that she did, but for how she has been contested by them: the Joan of Arc cult which began as an enterprise in the service of the revolutionary conception of France, became by the late nineteenth century a centrepiece of the alternative perspective (Contamine 1992, Warner 1991).

At Domremy, Joan of Arc's birthplace, are two sets of statues representing these different versions (Warner 1991: 255). There is also a visitors' book which records the sentiment: 'O saint Joan, kick the Jews out of France' (in Contamine 1992: 417). In theory, Jews had been finally expelled from 'France', the kingdom as it was then constituted, by royal decree in 1394. In fact, they continued to exist within the Hexagon, though under circumstances which are obscure. Abrahams's account of medieval European Jewry cites one monarch, urged once again to expel the Jews, responding: 'We will let them remain, but we will make them pay for the privilege' (in Abrahams 1932 (1896): 429). The Jewish communities of medieval and early modern Europe existed in a state of relative isolation from the rest of society. Restricted in what they could do, and subject to numerous financial penalties, they were also relatively self-sufficient. The synagogue was the focal point of Jewish life and of the communities which sprang up in the quarters around them, even when Jews were not legally obliged to reside in designated ghettos. Confined to certain occupations (notably trade and moneylending), the communities had a substantial degree of internal self-government, dealing with civil matters which concerned Jews alone, and sometimes with criminal matters which did not involve Christians: in Spain they were even able to inflict the death penalty until 1379 (Abrahams 1932 (1896): 64). The system of internal government was superficially not unlike that found in Ottoman millets.

In the eighteenth century, on the eve of the French Revolution, the Jewish population within the borders of France was less than 50,000. It was not homogeneous. In the south-west, around Bordeaux, there were some 1,500 Jews who had entered France from Spain and Portugal whence they had been expelled in the sixteenth century. Many of them had, while still in the Iberian peninsula, converted to what is described as a superficial form of Christianity, but by the eighteenth century had returned to Judaism. These Ladino-speaking 'Spanish' and 'Portuguese' Sephardic Jews, many of whom engaged in trade and commerce, were generally better off than Jews elsewhere in France. In the south c.3,000 Jews inhabited the important commercial and industrial centres of the papal enclaves of Avignon and the Comtat de Venaisin. There they were required to inhabit ghettos, known locally as *carrières*, which they were forbidden to leave after dark, could own no property other than their dwelling, and were obliged to wear a yellow (or black) hat (Moulinas 1976: 146 ff.). Abrahams records the prevalence elsewhere of what was known as the 'French badge', a circular patch made usually of a yellow fabric which Jews had to wear on the outer garment, under penalty of a fine (1932 (1896): 321–2). They were traders, working primarily in the papal enclaves, but their activities frequently took them into France proper. By far the largest group were the Ashkenazim or 'German' Jews of Lorraine and Alsace. Distinct from the local population by reason of dress, hairstyle, diet, and language, they spoke Yiddish or 'Judaeo-Alsatian' which they wrote in the Hebrew script. Unusually for Western Europe they were a mainly rural population, living in some 183 villages, with rare exceptions forbidden to reside in the towns, at least in Alsace (Hyman 1992: 111). Not allowed to own land, they participated in the rural economy as hawkers and traders in livestock and fodder, and as pawnbrokers. Amongst the poorest Jewish communities of Western Europe, a small number had become wealthy through acting as suppliers to the French army, and some of these were permitted to live in Strasbourg.

During the eighteenth century the term *nations juives* (plural) gained currency to describe these communities. Voltaire used it to refer to 'a distinct people, living under their own laws, often in a precarious manner, within the states where they were established' (in Godechot 1976: 52). The term was certainly employed by Jews themselves: Necheles (1976: 77) cites a letter to the Abbé Grégoire of 1789 from the 'Deputies of the Jewish Portuguese nation of Bordeaux', and Girard (1976: 27) one to Voltaire, signed by several Jews from different communities, who contrasted 'Portuguese and Spanish Jews and those of other Nations'. This usage reflected an older sense of 'nation' than it came to have in the eighteenth and nineteenth centuries, and possibly represented the Hebrew *kehilah*. Under the *Ancien Régime* a Jewish *kehilah*, like those of Medieval Europe, had a distinct status as a relatively self-governing entity. There were leaders, often called 'syndics', generally from the wealthier groups, responsible for ensuring the maintenance of order and collection of dues and taxes. In Lorraine and Alsace there was an elected 'president' and a rabbi (Godechot 1976: 50), in Bordeaux a council of thirteen elders (Poussou and Malino 1992: 253), and similar systems prevailed elsewhere. Elected rabbis had considerable power, administering the Mosaic Code and judging disputes between Jews. In each community, besides the synagogue, there were many charitable organizations concerned with health, welfare, and education, each with its own administration (Girard 1976: 25–6). Jewish internal self-government was regarded as a privilege which offset subordinate, not to say pariah, status: forbidden to enter a wide range of occupations or own land, subject to restrictions on movement, obliged to declare their identity with the French badge and other devices, viewed as deicides, hated and feared by those obliged to go to them for loans, their situation was indeed precarious. The privilege of belonging to a self-governing community was also double-edged in that it obliged all Jews to be subject to the rabbinate and a particular form of orthodox, conservative Judaism (Girard 1976: 25). This laid the community open to attack by anti-religious Enlightenment intellectuals such as Voltaire.

Such intellectuals believed there was a Jewish problem which had to be addressed, and a number of Jews had come to a similar conclusion. In 1785 a prize had been offered by the Société Royale des Sciences et des Arts of Metz for the best essay on the present and future status of the Jews. It was shared by three entries, one of which was from the radical cleric, the Abbé Grégoire. Grégoire's intervention in the Jewish question was of a piece with those that he made on language, education, the emancipation of slaves, and other liberal causes (Grillo 1989: ch. 2). His biographer, Necheles, summarizes his position as follows:

Regarding the nation as an instrument for educating citizens and for introducing reforms, he thought that it must first integrate aliens into its society before expecting them to adopt the customs of the majority. The only other alternative to gradual assimilation was to expel all foreigners, and this he believed would be a mistake. He hoped that French nationality eventually would embrace all people who shared a desire for freedom, regardless of their ancestry, religion or language. Therefore he defined citizenship on a territorial and ideological basis which transcended prejudices grounded in religious, cultural, and economic differences (Necheles 1971: 28–9; cf. 1976: 79).

This is well put, and indicates the crucial problem at this period and later: to what extent was it possible for the Jews to accept this commitment to citizenship and assimilation? In other words, could one be Jewish and French?

In a debate on citizenship in the National Assembly in December 1789, the Comte de Clermont-Tonnerre argued:

Everything must be denied the Jews as a nation and everything must be granted them as individuals. We should cease to recognize their legal system; there should be none but our own. There should be no legal protection for the maintenance of the rights claimed by their Jewish corporation. They should not form a political body or order within the state. They must be citizens individually. I will be told that they do not want that. Well, then, they should say so, and they should be expelled. It is repugnant that there should be a community of non-citizens within the state, a nation within a nation (in Archives Parlementaires, vol. x, p. 756).

Clermont-Tonnerre did not believe that Jews themselves wanted this, and many had petitioned for citizenship on the terms set out by Grégoire and himself (see Feuerwerker 1976 *passim*, and Birnbaum 1989 for discussion of the differences between the demands of Jews from south-west and eastern France). Eventually, decrees in 1790 gave citizenship to 'All the Jews known in France as Portuguese, Spanish and Avignonais' (in Girard 1976: 275), and in 1791 to all Jews who took the civic oath. By taking that oath, however, Jews would be considered to have 'renounced all privileges and exceptions previously introduced in their favour' (in Girard 1976: 276). In brief, therefore, the Revolution, Bloch's Messiah, emancipated the Jews, and this fundamental change in their status was later seen as a landmark for European Jewry as a whole.

Although the decree of 1791 gave Jews French citizenship, it left many questions unresolved, including the privileges which were to be renounced, and the future status of the Mosaic Code (Godechot 1976: 50). For a brief period during the Terror, Judaism came under attack from rationalist, anticlerical forces, and synagogues were temporarily closed. This was, however, part of the onslaught on religion in general; Jews were not singled out (Delpech 1976: 11), and some participated in the anticlerical movement as they did in other Revolutionary activities (Girard 1976: 65). It was not until 1806 that Napoleon, possibly influenced by the anti-Semite de Bonald's call for the revocation of Jewish emancipation, reopened the Jewish question.

What concerned Napoleon was the abiding issue: Do the Jews really want to become French? Hoping to find ways of 'reconciling Jewish beliefs with the duties of being French and turn[ing] them into useful citizens' (in Malglaive 1942: 96), he summoned an 'Assembly of Jewish Notables'. Members of this assembly were landholders, municipal officials, merchants, manufacturers of clocks, cloth, leather, silk, and tobacco, a banker, a physician, a shipowner, a horse dealer, an army officer (in Abrahams 1932 (1896): 269), indicating the extent of stratification in the Jewish community at this time. The proceedings were brief. A series of questions was put to the notables concerning their views on French citizens and French citizenship, including: 'Do Jews born in France and regarded by the law as French citizens consider France as their fatherland?' The answer (a unanimous 'yes') was forwarded along with the rest of their responses to another body which Napoleon, drawing on ancient Jewish tradition, called a 'Grand Sanhedrin' (Girard 1976: 78–9). This opened with great ceremony, but had no real function and was dissolved after a month.

After some delay the consultation resulted in three decrees in 1808. Two, concerned with the internal organization of Judaism, established a Jewish consistory, based on synagogues in each department with 2,000 practitioners, and administered by two notables and a rabbi. (Those in departments with less than 2,000 Jews were attached to one of these.) The ultimate control over the choice of rabbis and notables rested with the Minister of the Interior and the Minister of Cults. The third established controls over Jewish financial activities, including the regulation of rates of interest. Commercial activities of Jews were to be subject to a patent from the Prefect, and there were restrictions placed on Jewish settlement in Alsace. This, later known to Jews as the 'infamous decree', occasioned much resentment, but its provisions were not renewed after 1818.

Girard suggests that the Assembly and the Grand Sanhedrin resulted in a pact which defined future relations between Jews and Christians, and the obligations of Jews as citizens (1976: 134). French law was agreed to have priority over the Mosaic Code (marriage and divorce would be contracted under civil law first, before being conducted under religious law), and rabbis would be concerned not with Jewish law, but with custom or usage. The importance of this was that under reformed Judaism, Jewish law which contradicts civil law is treated as 'custom', and not necessarily compulsory. Later legislation confirmed the overall settlement which Napoleon had negotiated, removing the obligation on Jews to swear a special religious oath in a synagogue before giving evidence in a court (the *serment more judaico*, a relic of the *Ancien Régime*, Feuerwerker 1976: 566), providing state salaries for rabbis (Maurrus 1971: 90), and other state subventions for the work of the consistories.

4. Jewish assimilation in the nineteenth century

The debate of 1806–8 may be said to have been about conceding as much as necessary to be considered French while retaining as much as necessary to be considered Jewish. But this is territory much disputed in Jewish historiography.

Mainstream twentieth-century Jewish historians have been very critical of Revolutionaries such as Clermont-Tonnerre and Grégoire, accusing them of demanding the abandonment of a Jewish heritage (Fraenkel 1992, see also Necheles, 1976). The response of Jewish notables to Napoleon's initiative in

1806 was believed to have been 'particularly humiliating' (Fraenkel 1992: 11). These criticisms emerge in studies which viewed the emancipation of Jews as a prelude to headlong assimilation. The Reformed Judaism which became current in Western Europe in the course of the nineteenth century is treated in such accounts as 'the symbol . . . of a readiness to trade in age-old beliefs in exchange for civil equality and social acceptance' (Fraenkel 1992: 13). Western European Jewish assimilation is compared unfavourably with Eastern European traditionalism and loyalty to the community. Jonathan Fraenkel, however, argues that in the 1970s and 1980s this perspective gave way to a more nuanced view of a 'sub-world subjected to a multiplicity of conflicting forces interacting in unpredictable ways. Acculturation is no longer seen as leading necessarily to assimilation . . . The Jewish masses are no longer seen as necessarily loyal to the community' (p. 30).

This debate has an obvious bearing on the way in which social change in the French Jewish population in the nineteenth century is interpreted (see Birnbaum 1989: 501). That there were major changes of a socio-economic character is, however, incontestable. These included a significant shift in the distribution of that population. Although initially Jewish exploitation of the opportunities offered by emancipation was concentrated in the traditional regions of settlement, there was overall a move to the cities. The Jews of the (former) papal enclaves, who had already conducted much of their business in France, abandoned the ghettos of Avignon and Carpentras in favour of the cities of Nîmes, Aix, and Marseille (Moulinas 1976: 172). Similarly Lyon emerged as an important Jewish centre in the Rhône. Whereas there were only 185 Jews in the city in 1808, three-quarters of whom were very poor, by 1848 there were a 1,000, half of them hawkers, the rest small shopkeepers. By 1870 there were some 1,400, 75 per cent in trade and crafts, but with a small, growing class of businessmen, manufacturers, lawyers, etc. (Delpech 1976: 37). A move to the cities also occurred in Alsace with the village-based population drifting towards Strasbourg and Mulhouse, and later, after the Franco-Prussian war, to Paris. It was Paris, however, that became the major pole of attraction. From a tiny community of some 500–700 at the time of the Revolution (Poussou and Malino 1992: 260), by the latter part of the nineteenth century some 50,000, about half the Jewish population of France, were settled in the capital (Maurrus 1971: 31). This reflected a national trend, but in an exaggerated way.

The gradualness of these demographic shifts, and of the socio-economic changes which accompanied them, needs stressing. At the time of emancipation, Jewish communities in Alsace were rural, devout, Yiddish-speaking, engaging in a limited range of occupations, and maintaining a network of cross-frontier links with similar communities across the Rhine. Hyman shows that in the first half of the nineteenth century this picture changed slowly, though more rapidly in the towns to which some of the rural population now migrated, and there was considerable continuity in occupations and 'a steadfast adherence to the traditional features of Alsatian Jewish life' (Hyman 1992: 114).

Yiddish continued to be used in record-keeping, and Hebrew rather than French characters were employed, for example, for signatures to marriage documents. The Jewish forms of personal and family names were maintained until well into the mid-nineteenth century (Hyman 1992: 114–15). Jewish villagers also kept up traditional marriage ceremonies, though in that, says Hyman, they were no different from their non-Jewish counterparts in the conservative Alsace countryside. Likewise, the reluctance to allow sons to join the army was not confined to the families of young Jews (see also Raphael 1976). Village society thus 'promoted conformity and continuity' (Hyman 1992: 117), and villagers opposed the introduction of the new, modern, Jewish elementary schools, preferring the traditional (religious) Jewish schools until the 1840s, even then maintaining them clandestinely (ibid.: 118). In towns such as Strasbourg (2,387 Jews in 1854) and Mulhouse (1,527), where there were new economic opportunities, change was much faster. There was a rapid decline of Yiddish as a public language and for record-keeping, and religious observance was in general less marked, and less conservative: the Strasbourg Consistory made a number of attempts to introduce reforms in religious practice, in the 1830s and 1840s, for example abolishing the sale of synagogue honours (ibid.: 121).

Changing patchily and sometimes slowly, by the last quarter of the nineteenth century the Jewish population in France had become more complex and heterogeneous. The communities in Bordeaux and the papal enclaves had long been internally stratified: the Assembly of Notables of 1806 provides evidence for that. By the late nineteenth century, however, there was a titled, aristocratic elite, with at its head the Rothschild family. Beneath them was an upper class of financiers and bankers, some of whom had recently emigrated to France from Germany and the Ottoman Empire: the milieu described by Proust. There was a majority of 'shopkeepers, small-scale manufacturers, civil servants, and professional men' (Maurrus 1971: 41), and a lower middle class/working class of *c*.20,000 artisans, traders, small shopkeepers. Among professionals, journalism was important as, increasingly, was a career in politics. An active Jewish press kept a record of individual successes in education and other fields (Maurrus 1971: 44).

Maurrus defines assimilation as the 'process by which individuals of Jewish background assumed an identity which is essentially French' (1971: 2). Leaving aside, for the moment, questions of identity, it is clear that in the nineteenth century French Jews became more or less fully integrated into French economic life. There was also an increasing secularization. In the provinces community life declined, not least because of the movement of population to Paris. Attendance at synagogues was low, and important ceremonies such as the bar mitzvah were maintained in a reduced form, though a new initiation ceremony for boys and girls aged 12–13, which imitated the Catholic first communion down to the form of dress, became popular (Maurrus 1971: 58). Reflecting a general movement towards the secular, modernizing values which republican

France espoused, many voices advocated reform of religious practice, with proposals for abolishing the use of Hebrew in the liturgy, abandoning circumcision, and celebrating the Sabbath on a Sunday (Maurrus 1971: 221–4). On the other hand, few converted to Christianity (the anticlericalism of the era was perhaps against it), and endogamy prevailed. There were some intermarriages, frowned on, for religious and social reasons, by both Catholics and Jews, but generally marriages took place within the confession. And especially in the capital, the communities continued to have an important role in day-to-day life. The Paris Consistory ran a hospital, several schools, a welfare committee, a Société des Études Juives, burial societies, mutual aid clubs, and the Alliance Israélite Universelle for the 'betterment of the moral and material condition of Jews outside France' (Maurrus 1971: 77–81). It was, however, heavily dependent on the generosity of the Rothschild family: Gustave Rothschild was the president from 1858 to 1910 (Maurrus 1971: 67). Thus, concludes Maurrus, 'charitable organisation . . . the governmental apparatus of the consistoire, the rabbinate, and above all the ubiquitous Zadoc Kahn [the Chief Rabbi] and Rothschild family, seem to have enabled the Jews to maintain an indefinable, though weakened Jewish community' (1971: 82–3).

What did these demographic, socio-economic, and cultural changes mean for identity? Girard, in a manner which exaggerates the import of evidence he cites, and contradicts views he expresses elsewhere, suggests that in the nineteenth century the Jews, like Basques, Bretons, and others were 'ground down in the standardizing French mill', though not unwillingly (1976: 251). Though Albert (1992) does not cite this text, her conclusion would oblige her to take him to task. Following Eugen Weber (1976), she argues that the standard view of France as a country which in the course of the nineteenth century rapidly became socially, culturally, and linguistically 'one and indivisible' is no longer tenable, and in consequence she seeks to play down the extent of Jewish assimilation. She has a point, though it is well to remember that Weber was writing about rural France, and that from mid-century onwards the bulk of the Jewish population was urban, and specifically Parisian. Albert does, however, illuminate the difficulties surrounding the interpretation of what have otherwise been taken as important signifiers of change in Jewish identification in nineteenth-century France.

Both Girard and Maurrus based their conclusions about assimilation in part on the vocabulary which Jews used to describe themselves. In 1806 Berr Isaac Berr, a wealthy Alsatian Jew, had proposed that the word *juif* be dropped in favour of *Israélite* or *Hébreu* (Girard 1976: 140). The latter was rejected, but the former found increasing favour and became widely used in titles of organizations and publications. It has been suggested (Maurrus 1971: 2) that the term was preferred by those Jews who favoured assimilation. Albert, however, believes that Berr Isaac Berr's intervention was intended to excise a word which was redolent of previous eras of persecution and prejudice, and its rejection signalled a change of status, not necessarily a change of identification (1992: 93).

The opposition of 'Jew' and 'Israelite' she sees as a late nineteenth-century or even twentieth-century phenomenon (linked with the emergence of Zionism), and warns against reading nineteenth-century texts in the light of later concerns. She does, however, acknowledge that there was a similar debate in the nineteenth century between those who supported the appellation 'Français Israélite' as opposed to 'Israélite Français' with the former, stressing French first, favoured by assimilationists. Albert also offers an alternative reading of Clermont-Tonnerre stressing that:

What Jews were required to give up was not their ethnicity, but their corporate structure, their set of privileges and obligations as an officially recognized, unified body within French society. Once the principle of individual citizenship with personal accountability to the state was established, no more was asked of the Jews. They were free to retain their social and cultural specificity (as were the many regional and linguistic groups within the country) (Albert 1992: 91).

Thus, she argues, there was little real pressure on Jews to abandon their identity, and moreover they did not do so, as the continuities in community life testify. On the other hand, and echoing Senghor on the position of Francophone Africans, though she does not refer to him, she draws a contrast between *s'assimiler* and *assimiler*, passive absorption and active adoption. Jews, she says, were not assimilated by French society, but voluntarily drew on many features of French culture which they adopted for their own ends.

A population as varied in background and social location as the Jews in France was unlikely ever to have had a single voice over such a long period as the nineteenth century. There were, rather, a set of questions which Jews (and French) felt they had to address. One question was that implied by Clermont-Tonnerre's remark about a 'nation within a nation'. The modern nation-state demanded the undivided loyalty of its subject-citizens. Notwithstanding the natural reluctance of young Alsatian Jewish villagers to accept conscription into the French Army, a trait they shared with other peasants (Raphael 1976), Jews frequently and publicly displayed a deeply felt commitment to France (the nation) and to French values. One of the most poignant moments in the Dreyfus Affair occurs in a letter in which Dreyfus expresses shock and puzzlement that one such as himself who had dedicated his career to France and to revenge against the Prussians for their seizure of Alsace should be accused of treason. The motto of the Central Consistory was 'Fatherland and Religion': France (first) and Judaism (second). There was, says Maurrus, an 'exaltation of the idea of the fatherland to an irrational almost religious level' (1971: 117). An example was the dedication of the Jews of Lorraine to the cult of Joan of Arc, identified with Deborah in the Bible, with statues donated at Nancy and Paris in the 1890s (Maurrus 1971: 119).

Jews therefore saw themselves as passionate patriots, devoted to France and its mission. Nevertheless, there was a hesitation: assimilation, but . . . Two things stand out in that regard, continuing endogamy, and the ongoing importance of the institutions maintaining Judaism and a Jewish sense of identity. The nation had ceased to exist, but not the community. At the same time, and perhaps contributing to the hesitation, it is clear that the French state and society had never fully resolved for itself the question: in what sense could one be a Jew and French?

5. Jew or French?

What were the conditions under which it was possible to be both French and a Jew? The questions return time and again in the late nineteenth and early twentieth centuries: a publication in Vichy in 1942 was entitled *Juif ou Français?* In the 1880s and 1890s it was posed in an extreme form with the rise across Europe of a virulent anti-Semitism, and symbolized by the Dreyfus Affair.

Anti-Semitism has a long and baleful history. In a sense that history may be treated as background noise—it is omnipresent even during periods of relative quiescence, providing a discourse of imagined acts and vocabulary which may be drawn upon at any time. The nineteenth century had not been especially anti-Semitic. From the mid-nineteenth century until 1880 there was only one major pogrom in Europe, in the Ukraine (Byrnes 1950: 76). None the less events from time to time brought the anti-Semitic apparatus into play. One such was the so-called Damascus affair of 1840. A young French monk disappeared in the city. His body was never found, and the Jewish community was accused of murdering him to use the blood in the manufacture of unleavened bread (Girard 1976: 141), the notorious blood libel, a constant feature of the background. All Jewish communities in Europe were affected by this episode, but they weathered it. A similar case of alleged ritual murder in Hungary in the early 1880s likewise attracted wide publicity (Byrnes 1950: 86, 111). There was also a casual, intellectual anti-Semitism, like that of Voltaire, for example, which helped perpetuate pejorative stereotypes. Thus Michelet, the republican historian, felt able to say, in an aside, that when Alsatians emigrate, and sell their property, 'the Jew is there ready to buy' (1973 (1846): 38), or again, in a much-quoted phrase: 'The Jews, whatever is said of them, have a country—the London Stock Exchange; they operate everywhere, but are rooted in the country of gold' (p. 93). Ideas of this kind were later incorporated in an anti-Semitic discourse of the left in which Jews were equated with capital (Byrnes 1950).

None the less, the background noise does not explain the recrudescence of a widespread, popular, active anti-Semitism in the 1880s. Byrnes (1950: 4–7 ff.) suggests that it resulted from a convergence of the breakdown of the 'federative' political order in Europe and its replacement from the 1850s onwards by an aggressive form of armed national-statism, the rise of racist thought, and an extended period of difficult social and economic change, with increasing industrialization and urbanization leading to a breakdown of traditional loyalties and a great insecurity. To these may be added the economic depression of the 1880s and, in the case of France, the shocks of 1870. It would not be the last time that economic and political dislocation accompanied by a profound sense of national and personal humiliation led to a search for scapegoats.

From 1880 onwards there was an increasing climate of anti-Semitism. Contributing to it were a number of journalists and politicians, first and foremost Edouard Drumont whose two-volume *La France Juive* was published in 1886, selling 100,000 copies by the end of that year. Drumont played skilfully and at great length all the familiar anti-Semitic tunes, laying at the door of the Jews every problem that France had ever encountered. The book caught the moment: anti-Semitism in France was an idea whose time had, unfortunately, come. *La France Juive* was followed by an outpouring of anti-Semitic books, pamphlets, and newspaper articles, many by Drumont himself. and a great deal of anti-Semitic organizing, which linked a variety of unlikely bedfellows, from anarchists to reactionary Catholics. By the 1890s there were 'pools of antisemitism' across the country (Byrnes 1950: 261) in Paris, Flanders, Picardy, the West, Bordeaux, Toulouse, Lyon, Grenoble, and the East. There was widespread support among the upper classes, army officers, merchants, functionaries, liberal professions, writers, journalists, publishers, artists, and the Catholic clergy (Byrnes 1950: 262–304). None the less, by 1894 this wave of anti-Semitism appeared to be on the wane, and thus the Dreyfus Affair happened at an opportune moment for the anti-Semites.

The Affair was the most important event or series of events in French political life between 1870 and 1914. It 'crystallized anti-semitism and gave it a particular ideological and political character which had been latent but never explicit' (Kedward 1965: 55). The complexity and ramifications cannot be addressed here. Briefly, Captain Alfred Dreyfus, an Alsatian Jew and staff officer in the French Army, was accused of selling military secrets to the Germans. Found guilty, he was cashiered and sent to Devil's Island. Convinced of his innocence, his family worked quietly, collecting evidence and recruiting a number of influential supporters. It gradually emerged that in all probability Dreyfus had been framed to protect another officer. In early 1898, at a time of serious anti-Semitic rioting, first in Algeria, then in cities in mainland France, matters were brought to a head by the publication of Zola's famous article 'J'Accuse!' Dreyfus was retried, and though the military court once again found him guilty, he was eventually pardoned. The following discussion deals with two issues only: what Dreyfus represented symbolically for those who believed him guilty (the Anti-Dreyfusards), and the response of the Jewish community.

For the Anti-Dreyfusards the paramount fact about Dreyfus was simply that he was a Jew. Everything followed from that. Barrès, who was present on the occasion when Dreyfus was publicly stripped of his rank, is an eloquent witness to this. He commented: 'His foreign racial features, his callous, overbearing manner, everything about him revolted the most hardened spectator' (1925 (1902): 144). 'That Dreyfus was a traitor', he added, 'I conclude from his race'

(p. 161). On the other hand, 'since Dreyfus does not belong to our nation, how could he betray it? The Jews' fatherland is wherever they find the greatest profit. On that account one might say a Jew could never be a traitor' (p. 162). Expanding on this theme, Barrès affirmed that 'the Jewish question is linked to the national question. Assimilated with French citizens by the Revolution, the Jews have retained their distinctive character, and from being previously persecuted they have become dominant.' Jews violated the principles of the Revolution by economic speculation and cosmopolitanism. The posts they occupied in the army, the law, government, and civil service, were far more than their numbers warranted. The disparity must be overturned: 'greater respect for the true nationals, the sons of Gaul, not those of Judaea' (p. 161).

France, according to Barrès, was a nation which lacked moral unity and was 'debrained' (*décérébrée*). The cause was to be found not just in the Jews, but in all elements foreign to the nation: 'the foreigner, like a parasite, poisons us' (p. 161). He meant the foreigner in France, and Barrès, like many others, linked together Jews, Freemasons, Protestants, and foreign workers as the enemy within. His programme for the election of 1898 was a full-scale attack not just on Jews but all foreigners, including immigrants. In phrases which have a familiar ring, he claimed that there were 20,000 foreigners convicted of crimes each year. In Paris, 10,000 foreigners found shelter each night by the charitable services 'while our fellow citizens sleep on the streets' (Barrès 1925 (1902): 188). The 1,300,000 foreigners then in France 'take over all our trades and professions' (p. 190). The bosses love them because they will suffer any conditions imposed on them: 'In the North, there are Belgians who have left their families at home, and live cheek-by-jowl in a barn, eating potatoes cooked by one or other of them. Our French families couldn't live like that' (ibid.). In the South, 'the walls are covered with posters in Italian' calling for workers in the defence industries (p. 198). Urging protection for national workers who 'see their own country invaded by foreigners, while they themselves have nothing, who see national wealth taken over by foreigners, protected by French law, while they themselves have difficulty in getting a job' (p. 192), Barrès called *inter alia* for a tax on employers recruiting foreign workers, the exclusion of foreigners from employment on defence projects, and the expulsion of those on public assistance (pp. 195–9).

To describe these foreigners Maurras coined the word *métèque*. For him, as for Barrès, a further problem was democracy itself, and he united anti-Semitism and hostility to all that was foreign into a theory of what he called 'integral nationalism' which was anti-democratic, authoritarian, monarchist, and corporatist. It was a particular blend of French fascism. For Barrès, Maurras, and others of their persuasion, France, the French nation, was defined, by its Catholic heritage, in such a way as to exclude the Jews. Their answer to the question 'French or Jew?' was abundantly clear. Jews could never be French. They were, as Drumont asserted, 'incapable of assimilation' (1886: 31). This was not, it must be stressed, the prevailing view of French state or society. After all, the Dreyfusards triumphed, the Republic won, even if it was a close-run thing. None the less it remained a powerful vision throughout the first half of the twentieth century, and its time came again in 1940 when it acquired real authority in the Vichy regime.

Vichy and the Occupation remain extremely painful episodes in French life. Only in 1992, for example, did the French state feel able to recognize and mark the anniversary of one of the most shameful events of the period: the round-up of 13,000 Jews in Paris in June 1942, and their imprisonment in the cycling stadium, the 'Vel d'Hiver', before transportation to the concentration camps. There was great continuity between the Affair and Vichy. Maurras himself was an ardent supporter of Marshall Pétain, and after the war, when sentenced to imprisonment for his collaboration, Maurras cried out at the conclusion of his trial: 'It's Dreyfus's revenge.' Further continuity may be observed in a book by Gabriel Malglaive, published in 1942 in Vichy, much of which regurgitates the same fantasies and obsessions to be found in Drumont concerning the world-wide Jewish conspiracy. Malglaive's conclusion is also the same as that reached by Drumont: the Jews are 'unassimilated and unassimilable' (Malglaive 1942: 31). The book's only virtue is that it contains a clear and full record of Vichy legislation aimed at Jews, which in effect removed them from public life. The preface by Xavier Vallat, then Vichy Commissioner-General for Jewish Affairs demonstrates his anxiety to show that he was not too hard on the Jews, but neither had he 'sold out to Rothschild' (Malglaive 1942: 4). Patently conscious of his masters in Paris and in Berlin, he concludes: 'In fact it will be up to the victor, if he has it in mind to organize an enduring peace, to find the means . . . to fix the wandering Jew' (p. 12). This is the same Vallat who in the late 1960s congratulated de Gaulle on a remark of his apropos the Arab–Israeli conflict which others interpreted as anti-Semitic (Birnbaum 1992: 435). A final point of continuity emerges from the so-called 'Monument Henry'. Colonel Henry was an officer who after Dreyfus's conviction, forged certain papers, to make sure the result could not be challenged. Uncovered and imprisoned he committed suicide. His supporters rallied with a fund for the benefit of his widow. A journalist, Pierre Quillard, published the names of the several thousand sub-scribers, along with extracts from their letters. Three suffice to illustrate the point: an army doctor said he would rather 'have vivisection practised on Jews than on inoffensive rabbits' (in Byrnes 1950: 265); a country priest 'prays vehe-mently for the extermination of Jews and Freemasons' (in Girardet 1966: 178); and a cook 'would love to have the yids in her oven' (ibid.).

Like their predecessors in Spain in the fifteenth century, Jewish leaders were surprised by the anti-Semitic movement of the 1880s and 1890s (Thomas 1993: 60). Regarding their response two voices stand out. The first, probably repre-senting the majority, was that of disbelief that the anti-Semitism of the Dreyfus Affair was anything more than a passing phenomenon. Thus, Emile Durkheim wrote in 1898 that anti-Semitism in France was a 'superficial symptom of a state of social malaise', compared with Germany where it was 'chronic' (in Maurrus

1971: 99). Coupled with this was a profound belief that the republican virtues of liberty, equality, and fraternity would prevail, and that the best strategy for Jews was 'the silence of disdain' (Maurrus 1971: 141–2). This policy meant that the principal Jewish institutions played very little part in the Affair, indeed the role of the Consistory throughout the episode is best described as feeble (Maurrus 1971: 234).

There were others who might well have argued, in effect, 'We have tried to become useful French citizens, as Napoleon wanted. We have assimilated, but you still hate us. What more can we do?' The second response provided an answer, though it was one which appealed at the time to a small minority only. Maurrus finds a representative of that voice in the writing and political activity of Bernard Lazare. Lazare had moved in literary circles and been influenced by Barrès's early philosophy of the self which had an appeal well beyond anti-Semites. Later, he became increasingly sceptical of the virtues of assimilation, and criticized what he called the 'atavistic pusillanimity' of the Jews in the face of anti-Semitism (Maurrus 1971: 182). Instead, he advised that Jews should *emphasize* their Jewishness, and *accept* that Jews are a nation. Thus in 1898:

Give back to the Jews who no longer have it, reinforce in those who do have it, the sense of Jewish nationality. A people knows how to defend itself when it is conscious of itself and it knows how to defend its own who need to be defended. Let the Jewish nation arise and it will find in itself the necessary force to vanquish its enemies and to win its rights (in Maurrus 1971: 190).

Lazare, therefore, sought to confront French nationalism with nationalism of another kind, a mirror image as it were of the nationalism of Barrès, and forged a link with the emergent Zionism of the 1890s.

6. The right to difference?

As Winock suggests, anti-Semitism has always been the 'ideological cement' of the extreme right in France, in whose fantasies the Jew has always been 'the Other par excellence' (1993: 13). There are, however, other issues which need to be underlined.

Chapters 6 to 8 of this book focus in various ways on nation-states of the modern era which united around a common identity and culture, and a singular loyalty. There was a drive to define the body politic as a nation, in the late eighteenth- and early nineteenth-century sense of that term. The state, the organs of government and administration, had an important role in this, but not only as the instrument through which the transformation was affected. The identification of nation with state (in the 'nation-state') meant that ethnicity and authority were not just closely interwoven but became synonymous. There were, however, two ideological versions of this transmogrification of the body politic: 'nation as association', 'nation as community', distinguished in part by their possible modes of recruitment. In an association membership could be achieved, in a community it was ascribed. In theory, the dominant French ideology asserted the 'associative' mode: membership of the French nation-state was open to all; it could be earned and learned. Assimilation was then largely about the process whereby individuals and groups were absorbed into this new entity. In practice, many in France yearned for the ascriptive mode, which prevailed elsewhere, not least in Germany, and in which membership was not always achievable; some groups would always be incapable of assimilation.

The reasons why nation-states rallied to a single identity and culture are complex. Gellner locates the source of this drive in 'the structural requirements of industrial society' (1983: 74; see also Grillo 1989: 38–42, and later chapters in this book). Whatever the reason, and whichever mode of nationalism they adopted, nation-states exhibited hostility towards difference. In the case of France, Clermont-Tonnerre's statement that there could be 'no nation within a nation' was echoed by other Revolutionaries, for example in Barère's intervention in the language debate of 1794 in which he asserted that one of the heinous faults of the *Ancien Régime* was that it allowed 'several nations in one', with the result that the body politic was divided, socially, culturally, and linguistically (in Grillo 1989: 27). The emphasis on homogeneity meant that the nation-state was incapable of tolerating difference, at least of a collective kind: the latter was tantamount to treason.

Clermont-Tonnerre had argued that the Jews should be accepted individually, but not as a collectivity. The tragedy of the Dreyfus Affair was that it revealed that in many minds that distinction could not be made: Dreyfus had to be a traitor because he was a Jew. This failure of Clermont-Tonnerre's vision may be linked with the Napoleonic intervention. In practice, as Albert rightly says, French-style policies of assimilation were never really implemented in a thorough and systematic way: as with linguistic unification the means were not available (not least in education) until well into the nineteenth century. Napoleon's attempt to resolve the Jewish question was a compromise, which reproduced some of the forms and principles associated with the *Ancien Régime*: Girard argues that the consistories of 1860 had many similarities with the *kehilah* of the *Ancien Régime* (1976: 251). The state gave Jews a firm indication of the direction in which they should move, and placed Judaism under what was in theory strong central state control: the rabbis were in effect paid state functionaries. But the consistorial system permitted, indeed encouraged, the maintenance of religious and cultural specificity, practices different from those of mainstream French society. This compromise was of a piece with other Napoleonic interventions; he was happy enough to allow the Alsatians to retain their language as 'they sabre well enough in French' (cited in Grillo 1989: 40).

If there was compromise on the part of the French, there was also compromise on the part of many Jews. In the 1840s, for example, there were voices, some not many, which, opposing comprise, called for a form of separatism, urging, as did Créhange, 'a separate Jewish society, a sort of voluntary ghetto which would engage only in commercial relationships with Christian society' (Girard 1976: 144). This, suggests Girard, was a claim to a 'right to difference', a century in advance of its time. To an extent, the Napoleonic pact conceded the right to be different though in a highly restricted and controlled form. The pact foundered eventually, however, because it failed to reconcile the real difficulties which such an arrangement posed for the principles on which the nation-state itself was founded. There are a number of continuities in the 'Jewish question' in France over a long period, from the final years of the *Ancien Régime* through to Vichy and beyond, and this is another. The extent to which a nation-state can or should permit within itself an alternative nation or national community remains an unresolved problem, as does the right of such communities to demand to be different. Later chapters return to these issues in a more recent period and in other contexts.

7

'Nation of Many Nations'? The United States and Immigration, 1880–1930

> I believe in the immigrant. He has in him the making of an American, provided a sympathetic hand guides him and smoothes the path which leads to assimilation. The hand of the native-born can best do this . . . in every community where the men of southeastern Europe have settled, the redemptive forces necessary to raise the foreigners from inefficiency and ignorance, from anti-social habits and gross superstition, are available, provided they are marshaled, supported, and set to work by patriotic men.
>
> (P. Roberts 1912: vii.)

1. The 'new immigration'

Walt Whitman described himself as 'One of the Nation of many nations' (1926: 38). Between 1880 and 1930 some 28 million immigrants entered the USA, nearly half from Central, Eastern, and Southern Europe. This 'New Immigration', as it was called, raised serious questions for the body politic: could, should, the USA 'assimilate' such peoples, and what would their assimilation mean, for the immigrants themselves and for existing members of the receiving society? A minority of Americans opposed their entry in the belief that their social, cultural, and racial background made them unassimilable; another minority, and one which probably grew smaller during the period under consideration, actively welcomed them, believing that America should open its doors to the 'wretched refuse of your teeming shore', as Emma Lazarus's famous poem put it. The prevailing view, however, was something between these two. The USA required immigrants to continue the opening up of the country, and to provide labour for its burgeoning industries, but these immigrants would need to change; they had to become 'Americanized', and would need assistance in doing so.

It is with the theory and practice of assimilating and 'Americanizing' the immigrant that this chapter is principally concerned. From the mid-nineteenth century through to the present era mass labour migration and the displacement of populations through religious, political, or ethnic persecution have moved hundreds of millions of children, women, and men across the globe in search of work and/or security away from their homeland, not forgetting, in the case of the Americas, the earlier forced migration of millions of Africans to the slave plantations of the New World. When migrants were 'birds of passage', who would return whence they came, the problems they posed were mainly to do with their efficient use and control. In so far as they were to become 'permanent' members of the receiving society their presence raised a different set of issues. For the nineteenth and much of the twentieth century, a polyethnic 'modern' society appeared to be a contradiction in terms: to echo Clermont-Tonnerre, there could not be a nation within a nation, and immigrants had to be 'absorbed'.

Why this was so is a complex matter, albeit one which goes to the heart of the nature of the modern nation-state. At the root of the drive towards making society and culture uniform within the political space of the nation-state was undoubtedly the rationalization of the production system (Gellner 1983; compare Grillo 1989: 42). According to Milton Gordon:

structural separation of ethnic groups . . . is dysfunctional . . . for the workable operation of society itself. The operation of modern urbanized industrial society is predicated upon the assurance of the easy interchangeability and mobility of individuals according to occupational specialization and needs. The fulfilment of occupational roles, the assignment of living space, the selection of political leaders, and the effective functioning of the educational process, among others, demand that universalistic criteria of competence and training, rather than considerations based on racial, religious, or nationality background, be utilized (Gordon 1964: p. 236).

In the nineteenth and early twentieth centuries, then, the prevailing view in both France and the USA emphasized cultural singularity, and under the circumstances pluralistic alternatives were difficult to envisage and implement.

In the early years of the twentieth century about a million immigrants a year entered the USA. Bearing in mind that the resident population in 1900 was some seventy-six million these are formidable figures. Not all stayed: many were seasonal and other temporary workers who returned home after a short stay (Nelli 1983: 43–4, P. Taylor 1971: 105): between 1908 and 1914 there were seven million arrivals, but two million departures. Though families did accompany some immigrants (perhaps increasingly during this period), many of those who arrived were young, single males (Kraut 1982: 17). Families followed later, once the household head was settled. Throughout the nineteenth century the USA maintained an open door for immigrants. In 1897 President Cleveland, opposing proposals to restrict the inflow, described USA policy as 'generous and free-handed' (in P. Davis (ed.) 1977 (1920): 376). It never had universal support. In the 1850s opposition to foreigners had been a central plank in the platform of the 'Know-Nothing' or American party which ran a presidential candidate in 1856. From the early 1880s onwards immigration restriction was increasingly hotly debated in American politics, and legislation, culminating in the Literacy Act of 1917 and the 'Quota' Acts of the early 1920s, gradually tightened entry requirements. Despite opposition, however, for much of the nineteenth and early twentieth centuries immigration was not merely tolerated but actively encouraged. A Report to the Senate in 1864 had expressed the view that there was a 'mutual interest of the USA and the immigrant', and commented, *inter alia*, that 'our system of free schools, melt[ed] in a common crucible all differences of religion, language, and race' (in Abbott (ed.) 1926: 348; see also Davis (ed.) 1977 (1920): 331). As Higham observes, 'immigration restriction did not square easily with the belief that this was a land of opportunity for all' (1984: 30). Support for immigration did, however, square with the need for labour, and many individual States undertook publicity campaigns in potential sending countries to attract immigrants to their farms and industries. Private recruiting agencies were also at work, and some firms themselves engaged in the direct recruitment of skilled workers from overseas, or maintained agents in ports of entry to direct immigrants to their employ (Korman, 1967: 22 ff., has an account of the Wisconsin campaign). Although sending countries did not always approve of these attempts to attract their populations, many welcomed the remittances which the migrants sent home (Kraut 1982: 10).

In the 1880s there was considerable concern about the hardship faced by immigrants through exploitation by unscrupulous transporters, or through the system of contract labour. In response, an Act of 1881 placed the regulation of the various Federal and State agencies handling immigration under the Secretary of State for the Treasury. Yet despite increasingly strident campaigns by the restrictionists after *c*.1880 (below), the control of immigration was, for much of the nineteenth century, lightly imposed, and mainly concerned with monitoring (and preventing) the entry of individuals with criminal records, the sick, and those 'likely to be a burden on the taxpayer' (in Abbott (ed.) 1924: 97). The increasing flow of immigrants also obliged the authorities to establish regular reception centres at which control might be exercised. The most important was at Ellis Island, in New York, which opened in 1891 and which could process over 5,000 entrants per day (Kraut 1982: 54). A very high proportion of immigrants passed through Ellis Island, nearly all Italians, for example (Nelli 1983: 47), and the photographs of their arrival are among the most powerful icons of American history (there are excellent examples in Adamic 1940).

Between 1880 and 1929 the volume and rate of immigration was not constant. (See Table 2.) In the 1880s, for example, the peak year of 1882 (788,000 immigrants) was followed by the low of 1886 (334,000). By 1892 immigration had risen again to *c*.580,000, but fell back to 229,000 in 1898. Thereafter it rose steadily to reach a high of nearly 1.3 million in 1907, with further fluctuations until the outbreak of World War I. In so far as it was demand led, with migrants pulled by conditions in the USA, immigration reflected the fortune of the economy during these decades. However, despite those periods in the 1880s and 1890s when the economy was in a depressed state, the era as whole was

TABLE 2. *Immigrants to the USA, 1880–1929*

Years	Total immigrants	Central, Southern and Eastern Europe	
		Nos.	%
1880–1889	5,248,568	830,652	15.8
1890–1899	3,693,934	1,722,659	46.6
1900–1909	8,202,388	5,822,869	71.0
1910–1919	6,347,380	3,656,318	57.6
1920–1929	4,295,510	1,302,627	30.3
Total	27,787,780	13,335,125	48.0

Source: Immigration and census data.

characterized by rapid industrial expansion. From 1880 to 1910 coal production, for example, grew from seventy to 500 million tons per annum (Roberts 1912: 50), and censuses report that between 1880 and 1920 the number of 'gainful workers' in key industries (mining, manufacturing, construction, and transport) increased by 13 million. In four states (New York, Illinois, Massachusetts, and Pennsylvania, and it was in these and similar north-eastern States that immigrants were concentrated) the labour force across all sectors grew from four to twelve million. As Kraut remarks, 'there was an abundance of jobs for new immigrants in the American economy' (1982: 75), and by 1900 'they were becoming the chief source of labor in every area of industrial production' (ibid.: 86). Despite the numerous recessions, it has been estimated that between 1890 and 1914 real wages rose by about a third, though immigrants were often in sectors most vulnerable to downturns, lay-offs, short-time working, and so on (Taylor 1971: 207). 'Wherever unskilled work is needed, the foreigner is the one who does it' (Roberts 1912: 52). These jobs were in the 'disagreeable occupations "white people" have forsaken' (ibid.: 53), not only in manufacturing, but in the service industries, and what a later generation would call the 'informal sector'. Often such jobs fell into the category that the inventor of Taylorism ('scientific management') deemed suitable for those who were 'stupid and phlegmatic', like the ox (cited in Roberts 1912: 73).

During this period there occurred what observers of the day deemed to be a significant shift in the source of incomers to the USA. In 1870 some 82 per cent of immigrants had arrived from North-West Europe and Germany, and formed what was later called the 'old' immigration. Between 1890 and 1900 there was a surge in immigration from Central, Eastern, and Southern Europe, and until the outbreak of World War I this was the predominant group, from 1896 to 1914 constituting two-thirds of all arrivals. Modern scholars warn against accepting without question the contemporary belief that there was something radically different about this 'new' immigration. Jones, for example, argues that neither 'old' nor 'new' immigrants were homogeneous, and both had much the same motives (1960: 192). Higham (1984: 20) conflates the two, drawing a different contrast between them, as a 'Second Immigration' in which Catholics predominated, with an even earlier 'First Immigration' which was mainly Protestant.

Certainly there were important differences between the various groups that formed the new immigration: 'what', asks Taylor, 'did a Jew from Minsk have in common with an Italian from Palermo?' (1971: 170). Yet despite such reservations, many commentators believe that a contrast may be drawn between the migrants from Central, Eastern, and Southern Europe after 1890 and those who arrived earlier: for Jones they were 'culturally very different' (1960: 205). The point, perhaps, is not 'objective' dissimilarity, but difference as it was perceived by contemporaries. Largely of peasant origin, though this was a trait shared with many earlier immigrants, not least those from Ireland, the Italians, Poles, Russians, Greeks, Jews, among many others who arrived, were thought *inter alia* to be of different racial origin, with a different cultural heritage, and crucially perhaps adhering to different religious traditions: Judaism, Orthodox Christianity, and a different Roman Catholicism to that practised in Northern Europe.

There are several genres of historical and social scientific writing about immigration into the USA. One focuses on the experience of migration, and a most influential contributor to it was Oscar Handlin whose Pulitzer Prize-winning book *The Uprooted* was first published in 1951. Handlin, it is often said (Barton, 1975: 2), conceived of immigration as a *rite de passage*, and certainly the way in which he constructed the experience of migration bore all the hallmarks of Van Gennep. To use another metaphor, however, migration was also represented as a kind of Calvary. First there was the rural origin, presented by Handlin (and he was not alone in this) in somewhat romantic terms as a timeless peasant past which in the late nineteenth century was severely disrupted by social and economic change driving the inhabitants of Central, Eastern, and Southern Europe from their villages. Thence the journey, arduous and expensive, by foot, cart, or train, to a sojourn at the ports of embarkation, often to fall into the hands of exploiting agents. After that the crossing, descriptions of which inevitably call to mind the 'middle passage' of the slave trade. Then the port of entry (typically Ellis Island) with the humiliation of the inspection, described in a report of 1917 in the following terms:

Many inattentive and stupid-looking aliens are questioned by the medical officer in the various languages as to their age, destination, and nationality. Often simple questions in addition and multiplication are propounded. Should the immigrant appear stupid and inattentive to such an extent that mental defect is suspected, an X is made with chalk on his coat at the anterior aspect of his right shoulder. Should definite signs of mental disease be observed, a circle X would be used instead of the plain X. In like manner a chalk mark is placed on the anterior aspect of the right shoulder in all cases where physical deformity or disease is suspected (in Abbott (ed.) 1924: 246).

Finally, bewildered and exploited, they disperse to their ultimate destinations. Handlin did not invent the genre, similar themes structure the work of Claghorn (1923), for example, and other earlier observers, though he did develop it to a fine art. Rolle calls *The Uprooted* a 'maudlin book' (1980: 23). This is both fair and unfair. It is certainly lyrical, and deeply moving, but despite its faults, which include a tendency to write of the undifferentiated 'immigrant', it is not misleading. Even if their plight cannot be truly compared with that of the victims of the slave trade, they experienced abundant hardship, humiliation, and exploitation.

Concerning the arrival and subsequent dispersal of immigrants into places of work and residence, three points stand out. First, whether arriving in groups, often from the same village or region, or individually, most had a specific destination in mind: an address, and a name. In his account of immigration to Cleveland, Ohio, Barton (1975: 49 ff.) stresses the importance of what has been called 'chain migration', that is migration through networks of contacts based on home ties. Though in Cleveland there were a significant number of what Barton calls 'solitary' migrants (he says 25 per cent), connections from 'the old country' were generally very important in determining the destination of immigrants. In the case of the Italians these chains were substantial and large-scale, with on average groups of 100 migrants coming from the same village and establishing themselves in the same place (Barton 1975: 54). Chain migration was in itself of considerable importance in the subsequent establishment of concentrations of individuals and families of the same (ethnic) background at work and in places of residence, though it was not the only factor. The predilection of employers for workers from particular areas, with, it was often believed, characteristics making them suitable for certain kinds of employment, also played a part. In the case of the Italians, the so-called 'padrone system' (D. S. Cohen (ed.) 1990: 63–7, Nelli 1970: 56–61, 1983: 78–82) was an important factor in establishing ethnically specific links with a factory or workshop. This was the practice whereby some individuals became intermediaries between employer and potential employees, perhaps meeting new immigrants from their home area as they arrived on the boat, and promising them a job. Kraut (1982: 91) suggests that *padroni* controlled 50 per cent of the New York City Italian labour force in 1900, though as Italians and similar immigrants became more familiar with American labour practices, and with the English language, they were increasingly able to dispense with the use of such intermediaries.

There was a parallel, and well-known, concentration of immigrants from the same village or region (or with the same 'nationality', below) in housing. Park and Miller (1921: 146 ff.) described in detail the settlement of Italians from different regions of Italy in different blocks of tenements on Manhattan before

World War I, for example in the area between Mulberry and Bowery streets, and East Houston and Canal. This was New York's 'Little Italy' which still exists albeit in an attenuated form. As Park and Miller showed, there were other New York Italian 'colonies', too, such as that between East 69th Street and Avenue A involving over 200 families of Sicilians from the village of Cinisi. 'Little Italys', 'Little Polands', 'Chinatowns', and so on were to be found in all the major, and many minor, cities of the north-eastern USA, where the great bulk of immigrants were destined to live.

Both at work and in the crowded tenements, the conditions that the immigrants faced were often appalling. There was, for example, a horrendous record of industrial accidents: 3,000 miners were killed in 1907 alone (Taylor 1971: 202). Claghorn's account of the problems faced by immigrants in the courts documents the tribulations of workers (or their widows) attempting to seek redress and compensation from neglectful employers. Violence meted out to protesters or those (immigrant and non-immigrant) who sought to combine in unions for better wages or conditions was another common experience. As a Report of the Massachusetts Commission of Immigration noted in 1914:

Because of his bitter experiences at the hands of petty exploiters, and because of the misrepresentation on the part of interpreters and 'shyster' lawyers through whom he seeks to obtain justice, the immigrant is learning some of the ugliest aspects of our life, and his Americanization along right lines is, for this reason, being prevented or at least rendered more difficult (in Abbott (ed.) 1924: 525).

Not surprisingly, therefore, most immigrants maintained considerable cohesion within the USA: they stuck together, constituting new communities. As many observers have noted, these communities were not, could not possibly be, reproductions of the societies from which migrants came. They were novel solutions to the problems encountered in the receiving society and to the conditions in which migrants found themselves. Thus each group developed a range of relatively autonomous institutions ranging from self-help societies (including the so-called 'immigrant banks'), to churches, 'parochial' schools (where the 'home' language might be taught), to festivals, clubs, and associations of all kinds (including criminal fraternities). Park and Miller, for example, listed dozens of Polish organizations in Chicago ranging from the Zuaves of St Stanislaw Kostka to the Society of Polish Women of St Wanda (1921: 213–15). There was also a thriving national language press, and a theatre and vaudeville.

Immigrant associational life did not evolve in the same way everywhere. Barton's investigations of Cleveland, for example, show that for reasons connected with different patterns of immigration and implantation, there were 'contrasting configurations of cultural loyalties' among the Italians, the Slovaks, and the Romanians (1975: 59). Italian associational activities were built on ties of locality (back home) whereas those of Slovaks and Romanians were based on

what Barton calls 'broader folk loyalties' (p. 61). These two groups also maintained important connections with their compatriots elsewhere in the USA. (It
is possible that Slovaks and Romanians living under Habsburg and Ottoman
rule had a different historical experience of how ethnic relations might be
shaped compared with Italians.) In the case of the Slovaks, the institutions
established during the early years of the century 'came to define the perimeters
of the ethnic group. Membership in a Slovak parish, elementary education in a
Slovak parochial school, and adherence to some local branch of a national
benefit union—these facts constituted the norm of Slovak ethnicity' (Barton
1975: 151). In the process of implantation new ethnic categories emerged. In
numerous cases (Italians, Poles, and Czechs, for example) the 'nation' as a point
of identificational reference either did not exist or had been in existence for only
a short period at the time many immigrants arrived in the USA. Supra-local
identities were often generated through the immigration experience. 'I had
never realised I was an Albanian until my brother came from America in 1909'
(in Park and Miller 1921: 146).

2. The new immigration and its critics

Taylor (1971: 170) has described the new immigration as a 'nightmare of
American social thought', a construction of the imagination of both
contemporary theorists, politicians, and social workers, and of the sociologists
and historians who came later. What shape did this 'nightmare' take, and with
what consequences?

Despite opposition, immigration was virtually unchecked by legislation, and
continued at a very high rate through to the outbreak of World War I. None the
less, there was a gradual tightening of controls under pressure from labour
leaders, and from what Higham has called the 'patrician thinkers' of the New
England establishment (1984: 49). The instrument around which opponents of
immigration rallied was a campaign for a Bill, brought before Congress on
several occasions between 1896 and 1917, which aimed to restrict entry to those
able to pass a literacy test. It was a deceptively simple device which in its final
form, in the Immigration Act of 1917, required the exclusion of 'All aliens over
sixteen years of age, physically capable of reading, who cannot read the English
language, or some other dialect, including Hebrew or Yiddish' (in Abbott (ed.)
1924: 217–18; the minimal requirement was the ability to read some thirty to
forty words). The 1917 Act, which also barred immigrants originating from
certain geographical zones, in effect Asia (Higham 1984: 52, Jones 1960: 270; see
Claghorn 1923: 309 on earlier legislation restricting the entry of Chinese into
California), was not the final measure. Five years later opponents of immigration succeeded in passing the so-called 'Quota Act' of 1921–2 which restricted
the annual number of immigrants from any source (national origin) to 3 per
cent of the number of foreign-born persons from that source resident in the

USA at the time of the 1910 Census (Abbott (ed.) 1924: 240). This 'makeshift' law, as Higham calls it (1984: 54), was stiffened in 1924 by reducing the annual quota for each nationality to 2 per cent of the numbers resident at the Census of 1890. These Acts cut drastically the numbers of immigrants entering from Central, Eastern, and Southern Europe.

Bills to impose literacy tests and the like had come before Congress on numerous occasions prior to the 1917 Act, and were twice subject to Presidential vetoes (by Presidents Cleveland and Wilson). Why were the new immigrants, against whom these measures were aimed, considered such a problem? There were three related reasons which proponents of restriction returned to time and again: racial, sociocultural, and what might be called industrial. The various elements in the case against the new immigrants were brought together in the speeches and writing of the 'patrician' Senator Henry Cabot Lodge. Lodge, who had been influenced by the writing of Gustave le Bon (Higham 1988: 142), took up the cause of the literacy test as early as 1891 (Higham 1988: 101). In his speech to Congress in March 1896 in support of the Bill, Lodge was quite candid about its effects:

The illiteracy test will bear most heavily upon the Italians, Russians, Poles, Hungarians, Greeks and Asiatics, and very lightly, or not at all, upon English-speaking emigrants or Germans, Scandinavians, and French. In other words, the races most affected . . . are those whose emigration to this country has begun within the last twenty years and swelled rapidly to enormous proportions, races with which the English-speaking people have never hitherto assimilated, and who are most alien to the great body of people of the United States (in Abbott (ed.) 1924: 193).

He went on to associate the 'races' most affected by the imposition of the literacy test with the 'slum population, with criminals, paupers, and juvenile delinquents', and with 'birds of passage' (p. 194). These were 'the most undesirable and harmful part of our present immigration', which had damaged the 'quality of our citizenship' (p. 196), and posed 'a great and perilous challenge in the very fabric of our race' (p. 197). This was the 'race stock . . . of the great Germanic tribes . . . [which] have been welded together by more than a thousand years of wars, conquests, migrations, and struggles . . . [and have] attained a fixity and definition of national character unknown to any other people' (pp. 197–8). Restriction was necessary also because of the harmful economic effects of immigration, which lowered wages, and forced down the living standard of the American working man. The 'desirable' races, on the other hand, would not be touched by the Bill. Lodge covered the same ground in an article in 1900 in which he argued that

The problem which confronts us is whether we are going to be able to assimilate this vast body of people, to indoctrinate them with our ideals of government, and with our political habits, and also whether we can maintain the wages and the standards of living among our working-men (in Davis (ed.) 1977 (1920): 52).

Such sentiments are familiar from other times and places: there is a great deal of shared rhetoric about immigration, in both the late nineteenth and late twentieth centuries.

The key element in Lodge's attack, the racial one, needs further explication. 'Nativism', which Higham (1988: 4) defines as 'intense opposition to an internal minority on the ground of its foreign ("Un-American") connections' took a number of forms in nineteenth-century America. Higham himself identifies three: anti-Catholicism, a 'fear of foreign radicals' (p. 7), and a 'racial nativism' which emphasized an Anglo-Saxon heritage (p. 9). Originally the Anglo-Saxon heritage appeared in a liberal discourse: 'In the Anglo-Saxons, or perhaps the Teutons, had been implanted a unique capacity for self-government and a special mission to spread its blessings' (p. 10): the French, of course, made similar claims for their own heritage. In the late nineteenth century the belief in a liberal and liberating Anglo-Saxon tradition became conflated with a belief in the racial superiority of the Anglo-Saxons or 'Teutons'. In identifying the context in which this occurred Higham rightly points to the convergence of an intellectual racism (which in the USA drew extensively on French thought) with, in the 1880s and 1890s, a period of rapid social and technological change, and of economic crisis. 'The spring of modern American nativism', he says, 'lay in the social and economic problems of an urban-industrial society' (Higham 1988: 98).

As in France, during the latter part of the nineteenth century 'race' came to refer to almost any human group. Racist thinking imposed order on the resultant multitude of labels by consolidating them into a limited set of higher level categories, for which new terms were usually invented, and by constructing theories about the hierarchical relationship between them. One such set popular in the USA was that promulgated by William Z. Ripley in his *Races of Europe* (1899) which employed three terms: 'Teutons', 'Alpines', and 'Mediterraneans'. The system was adopted by later racist writers such as Edward A. Ross and Madison Grant (Higham 1988: 154, Jones 1960: 267). An example of the application of Ripley's ideas was provided by a J. F. Carr, who was able to write in 1906: 'Northern Italians are of the Alpine race and have short, broad skulls, southern Italians are of the Mediterranean race and have long, narrow skulls' (in Davis (ed.) 1977 (1920): 141). Such sets of categories posed two problems for racist thinkers and those who sought to restrict immigration. The first was what to do about the Irish. They could scarcely be called Teutons, but were clearly different from 'Alpines' and 'Mediterraneans'—often believed to have 'a strong mixture of oriental blood in their veins' (Roberts 1912: 139), thus accounting for 'the ease and grace with which they take their pleasures' (p. 266). The Irish were Celts, and moreover had considerable political clout in the cities of America. Lodge resolved the problem by affirming that 'although of different race stock originally, [they] have been closely associated with the English-speaking people for nearly a thousand years. They speak the same language' (in Abbott (ed.) 1924: 196). Secondly, that, of course, was more than could be said for the

Germans, yet the Germans were unquestionably of Teutonic heritage. Or were they? The first edition of Madison Grant's book *The Passing of the Great Race*, published in 1916, had them firmly in the Teutonic category, but in the second edition, published in 1918, when the USA was at war with Germany, they became Alpines (Higham 1988: 218). These shifting labels and categories (for example Teutonic was sometimes replaced by 'Baltic') are of little interest in themselves. The crucial point is that Italians, Poles, Slovaks, etc. were 'races', and placed in the lowest category within the European order (beyond and outside this order were of course, others: 'Asiatics', 'Negroes').

It was not only their lowly place in the racial hierarchy which put a question mark over the new immigrants, but also their social and cultural distance, though this was often conflated with race. For example, the 1911 report of United States Commission on Immigration, which investigated immigration policy at great length and came out in favour of restriction, believed that 'certain kinds of criminality are inherent in the Italian race' (in Nelli 1970: 126). In these and other ways, for instance the manner in which they congregated in the tenements and at work, the new immigrants were deemed to pose a serious threat to American society, and it was seriously questioned whether they could ever be assimilated. Thus, one L. Marshall, writing in 1906 on the 'Racial effects of immigration' asked:

are [the] permanent racial characteristics [of the newcomers]—those they will retain after they have changed nationality, tongue, and customs—such as will be satisfactory to a democracy? Are they by racial disposition fitted or unfitted for the exercise of political rights? (in Davis (ed.) 1977 (1920): 239).

Senator Johnson of Indiana, speaking in the literacy clause debate of 1896, concluded:

There may have been a time when we could assimilate this undesirable immigration—the ignorant, the pauper, and the vicious class. That time has passed. Annually there are coming to our shores large numbers of people who are utterly unable to discharge their duties of American citizenship. They add to our burdens and responsibilities without adding anything whatever to our energies and resources. They strain our public and our private charities, fill our charitable and penal institutions, and are a constant menace to our free institutions (in Taylor 1971: 244).

Given the vehemence of these feelings, it is surprising that restrictive measures took so long to became law. Jones suggests that there were two reasons: immigrants themselves were becoming powerful voting blocks in many urban areas, and the measures were generally opposed by big business which needed labour (1960: 261). This did not mean that big business was unconcerned about the new immigration, far from it. As well as being worried by the involvement of immigrants in radical politics and trade unions (such as the IWW, the Industrial Workers of the World, the 'Wobblies'), most accepted the view expressed by the educationist E. P. Cubberley in 1909:

Everywhere these people tend to settle in groups or settlements, and to set up here their national manners, customs and observances. Our task is to break up these groups or settlements, to assimilate and amalgamate these people as part of our American race, and to implant in their children, so far as can be done, the Anglo-Saxon conception of righteousness, law and order, and popular government, and to awaken in them a reverence for our democratic institutions and for those things in our national life which we as a people hold to be of abiding worth (in Gordon 1964: 98).

3. The Americanization of the immigrants

In so far as they were not deemed 'unassimilable' there was therefore a strong interest in ensuring that immigrants 'Americanize' as rapidly as possible. But what did that mean? In both France and the USA the principal term used in addressing the issue of cultural uniformity and diversity in the context of the nation-state has been 'assimilation'. In France, that was generally glossed as the absorption of French values: 'becoming French'. What that meant, in practice, was usually taken, by the French, as more or less self-evident, though it will be apparent from the previous chapter that thinking about the nature of French society and identity was ambiguous and vague, and surrounded by a great deal of fuzziness. Such notions are in fact always extremely vague, inherently fuzzy (Robin Cohen, 1994: 7, comes to the same conclusion). Milton Gordon's influential *Assimilation in American Life* (1964) pointed to one very important ambiguity in the American discourse on assimilation, not relevant in the French context. Did assimilation refer to adopting the prevailing culture of an existing society, grounded in the values of the 'Founding Fathers' (what he calls 'Anglo-conformity'); or did it mean participating in the creation of something entirely novel, blending together those existing values with others in a new 'American' identity? Was the model citizen someone who conformed to the norms of the Anglo-Saxon heritage, or a new person, an amalgam of that and other traditions?

Here Gordon is referring to the idea expressed through the celebrated metaphor of the 'melting pot'. The image had been around a long time. In 1782 de Crèvecoeur, in *Letters from an American farmer*, had written of 'this American, this new man', in a country where 'individuals of all races are melted into a new race of men' (in Abbott (ed.) 1926: 419; see also Sollors 1986: 75). In 1845 Ralph Waldo Emerson had expressed the belief that 'the energy [of immigrants] will construct a new race, a new religion, a new state, a new literature, which will be as vigorous as the new Europe which came out of the smelting-pot of the Dark Ages' (cited in Jones 1960: 160–1, and elsewhere). The theme was taken up most famously in Israel Zangwill's play actually called *The Melting Pot* (1909) which described America as 'God's crucible . . . where all the races of Europe are melting and reforming' (in Gordon 1964: 120; see also Sollors 1986: 66 ff.). It was found, too, in the historian Turner's thesis on the frontier, where, he believed, 'the new immigrants were Americanized, liberated, and fused into a mixed race' (1920: 22–3, cited in Gordon 1964: 118).

National definitions, then, are rarely delineated precisely: they are almost always still 'under construction', and the conditions under which they fit neatly with some underlying reality are rarely met. That reality is, moreover, also constantly changing. National definitions therefore try to make sense of a reality which obstinately refuses to fit ideals often themselves extremely vague. In the American case there was not only vagueness about whether the ideal American was an 'Anglo-Saxon' or someone out of the smelting pot, but also about the very idea of America. Thus, for example, Franklin K. Lane, then Secretary of State for the Interior, writing in 1919 saw the 'essence of Americanism' in the Washington Monument, 'that clear, straight arm lifting to God in eternal pledge that our land shall always be independent and free' (in Davis (ed.) 1977 (1920): 620). In so far as the Washington Monument symbolized the 'American Idea', the quintessential American social and political ideals, it was an important point of reference in the definition of American identity. These ideals included (and include) along with liberty, democracy, justice, and brotherhood, 'the development of the individual for his own and the common good', as Brandeis put it in 1915 (in Davis (ed.) 1977 (1920): 640).

According to Theodore Roosevelt, Americanism was a 'matter of the spirit and the soul' (in Davis (ed.) 1977 (1920): 649), and it is not surprising that the Americanization campaigns discussed below should place such a strong emphasis on civics: the Massachusetts Bureau of Immigration declared in 1920, for example, that 'a comprehensive outline of the structure and aims of our government' would have to be a fundamental part of any campaign of assimilation or Americanization (in Davis (ed.) 1977 (1920): 492). To these civic ideals there was added the idea of betterment: the attainment of, or at least aspiration to, an American standard of living: a certain level of material prosperity, and a way of making the home, both physically and socially, in conformity with certain values, even vaguely defined (compare also Woods (ed.) 1902: 50). There was also the sharing of a common language: English. As the Massachusetts Bureau said: 'the basic factor in Americanization of the non-English-speaking foreign-born is the acquisition of a working knowledge of the English language' (ibid.: 49). 'America is too small for two languages', claimed Peter Roberts, an industrial expert and influential figure in the YMCA's Americanization campaign. English was nearly always thought a necessary condition for citizenship, even if it was not a sufficient one. Finally there was what Frances Kellor, another influential Americanizer, called an 'integral national life' (in Davis (ed.) 1977 (1920): 623), a common national identification. This meant 'no hyphens'. 'There is no room in this country for hyphenated Americans', said Roosevelt (in Davis (ed.) 1977 (1920): 648). In an address at Philadelphia in 1915 to a large company of newly naturalized immigrant Americans, President Wilson told them: 'You cannot become thorough Americans if you think of yourselves in groups. America does not consist of groups. A man who thinks of himself as belonging to a particular national group in America has not yet become an American' (in Davis (ed.) 1977 (1920): 612). This was in the shadow of a war which America would shortly join and which had already brought into conflict many of the nation-states from which immigrants new and old had originally come. It was therefore by political and social characteristics such as these that 'America' was defined. Despite the wishes of the ardent racists, it was not grounded in some physical heritage. Only occasionally, says Higham, did any-one attempt to define the American as a distinct phenotype (which of course was done quite readily in other places, notably Nazi Germany). The description essayed by Henry James (in 'The American', cited by Higham 1984: 188) was thus unusual. (It brings strongly to mind an image of Clint Eastwood.)

In the early years of the twentieth century the movement to ensure the proper Americanization of the new immigrants was led by East Coast business and civic leaders who promoted the inculcation of the English language and American civic ideals. This movement became a campaign which reached its height during World War I. Initially, the vehicle for the campaign was the North American Civic League for Immigrants, which brought together a number of powerful bankers, industrialists, and merchants (see list in Hartmann 1948: 38–9). In 1910 D. Chauncey Brewer, a Boston lawyer and prominent figure in this and later organizations, noting 'with uneasiness the changing character of our population', expressed the belief that 'the majority of immigrants entering the continent . . . are well meaning, and may become useful citizens if they receive the attention to which they are not only entitled as a matter of humanity, but which prudence necessitates because of their relation to our economic and political affairs' (in Hartmann 1948: 39–41). Of particular concern to the industrialists was the rise in support for militant trade union organizations like the IWW, and the growth of what Brewer later called 'that type of socialism which is synonymous with treason' (in Hartmann 1948: 93).

Hartmann's account of the history of the League and its dependent organiza-tions such as the powerful New York City Committee, shows that it was extremely successful in engaging support for its programmes among industrial-ists and civic authorities in the major cities. It also lobbied successfully for the creation of a Division of Immigrant Education within the Federal Bureau of Education. Until 1919, when such arrangements were abolished, this Division was funded and staffed privately by the New York Committee (Hartmann 1948: 98). The League, which as a result of internal struggles spawned the Committee for Immigrants in America in 1914, promoted not only training in the English language and in civics, but also naturalization. With the outbreak of World War I the latter was seen as an urgent priority, and in 1915, through the agency of yet another appendage, the National Americanization Day Commit-tee, plans were made to make 4 July of that year 'a day of significance in the relations existing between native and foreign-born Americans' (Hartmann 1948: 115). Frances Kellor, who had been secretary of the New York City

Committee of the North American Civic League, and who had a key role in the Americanization Day plan, called for a 'conscious effort to forge the people of this country into an American race . . . Every effort should be bent toward an Americanization which will mean that there will be no "German-Americans", no "Italian quarters", no "East Side Jews" . . . but that we are one people in ideals, rights and privileges' (in Hartmann 1948: 114).

The 1915 campaign, which had the backing of President Wilson (Hartmann 1948: 119), was well thought out, well organized, and well funded. It drew support from a wide range of private and civic institutions, and with their assistance circulated over 50,000 posters. The Committee also issued briefings for a large number of speakers. The day itself was celebrated in 150 cities. For example, in Pittsburgh 'more that 10,000 adults, chiefly aliens, heard about 1,000 school children sing patriotic airs as they formed a huge American flag' (Hartmann 1948: 121). After the success of this event, the organization decided to forward its work under the auspices of yet another body, the National Americanization Committee, which remained in being until 1919. According to Hartmann, the Committee defined Americanization as:

the union of the many peoples of the country into one nation and the use of the English language throughout the nation, the establishment of American standards of living in every community of the country, a common interpretation of American citizenship, and a recognition of foreign-born men and women in the human, social, and civic as well as the industrial aspects of American life (1948: 124–5).

Hartmann also points out, however, that there was, inevitably, a vagueness at the core. They aimed to

win over the immigrant from his foreign ways, speech and ideals, through education and inculcation as well as by good example, and thereby transform him into an individual holding the same ideals, speaking the same language, and living the same sort of life as that of his native American contemporary. Beyond this explanation they seldom went, taking for granted that the native American population to whom their literature and propaganda was chiefly addressed would fully understand what constituted 'good Americanism' (1948: 269).

In practical terms, as well as providing opportunities to celebrate the virtues of acquiring American citizenship, the Committee placed great stress on the proper preparation for naturalization, especially the need to learn English: 'English Language First' was a key slogan. To this end it worked through both State Education Boards and the private sector, especially industry. In Detroit, for example, much promotional activity was conducted through factory noticeboards, and leaflets inserted in workers' pay slips: 'immigrants were bombarded with the message that attendance at Americanization classes would get them better jobs and make them better citizens' (Carlson 1975: 113). Carlson, who notes that some managers refused to promote non-citizens, or made attendance at language classes compulsory, describes the work of

Americanization as 'social pressure and a curriculum geared to inculcate the prevailing ideology' (1975: 115–16). Thus, those who attended the language classes in the Ford factory schools were invited to 'walk to an American blackboard, take a piece of American chalk, and explain how the American workman walks to his American home and sits down with his American family to their good American dinner' (in Carlson 1975: 113–14). (Sollors, 1986: 89–91, has a description of the 'Ford English School Melting Pot' play or ceremony put on when students graduated.) Extracts from the content of course material used in English language classes in Milwaukee reinforce the point:

I hear the whistle. I must hurry. I work until the whistle blows to quit. I eat my lunch. It is forbidden to eat until then. I leave my place nice and tidy. I go home. No benefits will be paid if you are hurt while scuffing or fooling. No benefits will be paid if you are hurt or get sick as a result of having been drinking (cited by Korman 1967: 144–6).

Highly influential in the English language campaign was Peter Roberts of the YMCA whose organization had some 1,900 English language instructors in the field in 1915 (ibid.: 141). Roberts's methods provided a welcome model for teaching English as a second language which many organizations gladly adopted. That industrialists were strongly attracted to the campaign to promote English for other than nationalistic reasons is shown by the following comment from the manager of a Milwaukee shoe company in 1917:

There should be but one common language in this country, and the accomplishments of this purpose will lessen accidents and increase efficiency. By encouraging foreigners to become American citizens and to learn the English language you are taking them outside of the influence of irresponsible agitators (in Korman 1967: 183).

As Korman himself says:

To Americanizers, concerned with the general question of linguistic diversity or convinced that diversity complicated industrial discipline and fostered radicalism, factories appeared as logical classrooms for teaching English to migrants and for starting them on the road to citizenship (ibid.: 200).

It is difficult to gauge the effect of such campaigns. Meetings and leaflets were usually in English, and ideas presented in terms which appealed to 'the prosperous native, nurtured in American traditions' rather than to the immigrants (Claghorn 1923: 280). Americanizers themselves believed their activities were extremely successful, though as Korman shows on numerous occasions national committees may have been misled by reports emanating from the field. The campaign of 1919 in one Milwaukee factory was little short of a 'fiasco': it was so badly organized and taught (by unqualified and inexperienced teachers) that the director was suspended. None the less, 'the company gave the impression of being well pleased with the results', reporting that '600 employees had received a ten-week course on speaking, reading, writing, and calculating in English, and that they had attended four one-hour classes for five days each week' (Korman 1967: 189). Claghorn also draws a pertinent contrast between the violent and repressive response of the police and lawcourts to a major strike in the textile town of Lawrence (Mass.) in 1919, and an Americanization campaign being conducted at the same time. The latter embraced a variety of activities, including meetings and open forums concerned with 'education, housing, citizenship, industrial welfare, arbitration, employment, thrift and savings, health, recreation' etc., and Claghorn compares the 'beautiful principles' in the abundant literature with the reality of the brutal confrontations between strikers and the forces of law and order, 'the actual happenings of every day in the town' (Claghorn 1923: 279–80). She also records that one Russian speaker, sent by a Federal Bureau as part of its Americanization campaign, was arrested as a dangerous radical on the occasion of his lecture on Abraham Lincoln (p. 289).

These establishment organizations were not, of course, the only, or even perhaps the most important, means through which assimilation and Americanization occurred. Another type of intervention took place through the embryonic social work movement, especially the Settlement Houses. These were community centres established in slum areas, often where immigrants predominated. They were influenced by similar experiments conducted in Britain, especially at Toynbee Hall in the East End of London, in the latter part of the nineteenth century. Higham (1988: 251–3) describes their instigators as oriented towards a kind of 'liberal' Americanization: Carlson describes them as 'middle class idealists' (1975: 80). Typically Settlement workers were young (in their twenties), college-educated, with half having done some postgraduate work, and from relatively well-off 'old-stock' American families. Their stay in the Settlements generally lasted from two to three years (A. F. Davis 1967: 33–4).

One of their most influential leaders was the well-connected Jane Addams, who opened a community centre at Hull-House in a run-down area of Chicago in 1889 to promote the 'betterment' of immigrants who were 'densely ignorant of civic duties' (Addams 1960 (1910): 81; see Woods (ed.) 1898, 1902 for settlement houses in Boston). The idealism of Addams and her followers is apparent in everything they did: 'In the very first weeks of our residence Miss Starr [one of her stalwart supporters] started a reading party in George Eliot's Romola' (Addams 1960 (1910): 83). Carlson comments:

Settlement house lessons in the proper handling of the silver tea service gave immigrant women an excuse for time away from the tenements, but were hardly the most useful use of that time. Miss Starr achieved the absurd in her ceremony of the salad bowl and her concern that the color of the soups served at Hull-House not clash with the mauve dresses she always wore (1975: 82).

True, but unfair, if it is taken as typical of the activities of the Settlement Houses. Jane Addams herself, for example, had a well-deserved reputation for radicalism: she was active in campaigns against child labour and for the Eight-Hour Day, had significant contacts with the trade unions, as well as the civic authorities, and invited controversial figures such as the anarchist Kropotkin to speak at meetings at Hull-House (Addams 1960 (1910): 278). She also founded a 'Labor Museum'.

Addams argued that the Settlement was 'valuable as an information and interpretation bureau. It continually acts between the various institutions of the city and the people for whose benefit these institutions were erected', that is hospitals, county agencies, State asylums, and so on (1960 (1910): 126–7). In this Hull-House was similar to the Chicago League for the Protection of Immigrants, and there was a close connection between the two: a key figure in the League (Grace Abbott) was a long-term resident at Hull-House (Addams 1960 (1910): 163). Detailed reports referring to the work of the League and the closely associated Immigrants' Commission of Illinois are recorded in a book edited by Grace Abbott's sister, Edith (Abbott (ed.) 1924: 298–460, and 597–801). Typically these involved liaising with the authorities (and sometimes associations such as the Hebrew Immigrant Aid Society) on behalf of immigrants and their families who sought help in cases concerning restriction of entry or deportation. The humanity of the interventions (as well as their paternalism) is notable. One example suffices:

An illiterate Persian Jew had been admitted to the United States under a bond which required him to pass a literacy test within a defined period or face deportation. He had enrolled with an adult class, but despite considerable assistance from a dedicated teacher, he failed. An extension of his stay was secured through the intervention of a Congressman, and his teacher entered him for another test which he failed again. The Chicago Immigrants' Commission wrote on his behalf to the Commissioner of Immigration at Ellis Island, and he was allowed a further attempt. He failed once more, though the Supervisor of the Public Schools felt that the man had been doing very well at his studies, and believed the test to be harder than justified. The office wrote again, this time to the Commissioner of Immigration at Washington. He was allowed a further try, and after a valiant effort by his teacher he finally passed (in Abbott (ed.) 1924: 367–8).

Settlement workers introduced one further element into their work. Addams herself believed that immigrants might 'yield to our American life something very valuable' (Addams 1960 (1910): 177). On a par with their celebration of traditional working crafts, which found expression in the Hull-House Labor Museum, was the celebration of the 'traditional' way of life of the immigrants: the customs, music, costumes, etc. of the 'old countries'. This took the form, in the main, of an emphasis on 'folk' activities 'pageants and festivals to dramatize the heritage of each immigrant group' (Davis 1967: 49), though a play in Classical Greek was also performed at Hull-House. Summing up their activities, Higham judges that in general the Settlements 'did more to sustain the immigrant's respect for his old culture than to urge him forward into the new one' (1988: 236).

4. Into the melting pot . . .

The point is not what was achieved but what was intended. Higham thinks that in practice the Americanization campaign was a 'manifest failure' (1988: 269). Certainly there were three million naturalizations between 1908 and 1930, but whether these were stimulated by the campaign is difficult to determine. None the less, that there was an absorption of American culture and values, albeit over a very long period, was certainly the widely held view of Americans generally, and of historians and social scientists of immigration in particular, at least until the 1970s. Hartmann, for example, pointing out that the vast majority of immigrants never attended a language class, or had contact with a Settlement House, believed Americanization was not the result of any public policy or programme, but occurred through a 'gradual process of assimilating American customs, attitudes, speech, and ideals from their native American neighbors and from their American-born children' (1948: 271). The most important vehicle through which this was achieved was widely held to be the public school system. This is what Greer calls the 'great school legend', namely that the schools 'took the backward poor, the ragged, ill-prepared ethnic minorities who crowded into the cities, educated and Americanized them, and molded them into the homogeneous productive middle class that is America's strength' (1972: 3). So, the legend has it, the second generation, the children of the new immigrants, sometimes their grandchildren, learned to become Americans, and in World War II the Dino Crocettis, Malden Sekuloviches, Issur Demskys, Paolo Vaccarellis, or Mihailo Evanichs fought for the USA at Anzio, Omaha, and Guadalcanal, and over Berlin and Tokyo, though they may have done so as Dean Martin, Karl Malden, Kirk Douglas, Paul Kelly, or Mike Evans. (Kelly was a New York Mafioso who changed his name from Vaccarelli, Nelli 1976: 108; Evans was a Croat originally called Evanich, Adamic 1940: 59.)

When Americanization occurred, it was not without casualties. This is not so much a matter of the thousands who died in industrial accidents, or who perished in the violent labour disputes of the period (the fifteen Italian women and children burned to death at Ludlow in 1914, for example, Rolle 1980: 71). Nor is it a matter of those subjected to rough justice of the kind meted out to the eleven Italians lynched in New Orleans in 1891 (Nelli 1976: 50 ff.; the American dialect of Italian has the verb *linciare*, Rolle 1980: 40), or of the Sacco and Vanzettis, judicially murdered because of an association between 'immigrant' and 'anarchist'. Nor is it to do with the anti-Semitism, less virulent perhaps than that in France or Germany, but none the less real, which came in waves in the 1880s and 1890s and again in the early 1920s (see Higham 1984: 165 ff., for an account of the lynching of Leo Frank in 1913). The experience of 'white' immigrants scarcely bears comparison with that of 'Asiatics', Chinese, and Japanese, or of America's Blacks, of whom 1,678 were lynched between 1884 and 1900 (Carlson 1975: 75). On the other hand, Italians, Poles, Greeks, and others were often described as 'not white men' (see Roberts 1912, *passim*), and given the thinking of the day, the experience to which they were subjected had all the hallmarks of racism. It is, rather, the 'little murders' of a cultural kind which stand out in many accounts of the experience of the new immigrants.

'Told to speak a new language, learn a new skill, let the children be baseball players, keep house like an American, eat differently, dress differently—it seemed as though nothing short of total transformation would make the immigrant acceptable to this alien society' (Kraut 1982: 141). Nelli records one Italian immigrant child later recalling that when he attended school he felt 'different, odd, and in the eyes of other people, peculiar' (1970: 68). Leonard Covello, himself a teacher in New York, provided a moving account of the experiences of the Italian-American child in the school system in that city in a doctoral thesis completed in the 1940s, though not published until 1967. Such children were, says Covello, seen as 'problems' by the educational authorities. Covello, who concurred with that judgement, believed the cause was to be found in the cultural 'lag' between the children and the school (1967: 328), that is in the contrast between the life of these children, in their homes and on the streets, and the different styles of housekeeping, food, clothing, health and hygiene which the education system promoted.

A young informant told Covello:

Lunch at elementary school was a difficult problem for me . . . To be sure, my mother gave me each day an Italian sandwich, that is half a loaf of French bread filled with fried peppers and onions, or with one half dipped into oil and some minced garlic on it. Such a sandwich would certainly ruin my reputation; I could not take it to school . . . My God, what a problem it was to dispose of it, for I was taught never to throw away any bread (1967: 339).

The symbolic significance of food as a marker of cultural difference, and of cultural shame, appears in other accounts. Rolle quotes from a short story by the Italian-American writer John Fante, published in 1933, which made a similar point:

At the lunch hour I huddle over my lunch pail, for my mother doesn't wrap my sandwiches in wax paper, and she makes them too large, and the lettuce leaves protrude. Worse, the bread is homemade; not bakery bread, not 'American' bread. I make a great fuss because I can't have mayonnaise, and other 'American' things (Rolle 1980: 160).

Nelli cites another comment of Fante's, from an article published in the 1930s, in which he wrote about his father: 'I look up at him in amazement. Is that man my father? Why, look at him! Listen to him! He reads with an Italian inflection! He's wearing an Italian moustache . . . he looks exactly like a Wop' (in 1983: 175). The shame of it! Rolle, who like Nelli and other American authors of Italian origin sought in 1970s and 1980s to redress the record of the experience of Italian immigrants, also notes this highly pertinent comment by Mario

Cuomo, later Governor of New York, and one of the most successful Italian-American politicians, in 1975:

I can cry now when I think about the time when I was fourteen years old and embarrassed to bring my father to . . . meet the teachers and other parents because he didn't speak English well. Looking back now, and feeling the anguish of that recollection teaches me all I need to know about the ethnic self-hate and the melting pot myth and what it means to deny a heritage (in Rolle 1980: 42–3).

5. . . . And out again

Milton Gordon believes that the Americanization campaign was 'fundamentally misguided in its demand for a rapid personal transformation and a draconic and abrupt detachment from the cultural patterns and memories of the homeland' (1964: 106). Yet this is what the idea of the homogeneous nation required. Already by 1916 writers such as Horace Kallen had begun to argue against this idea, a theme taken up in the 1930s by others such as Adamic (1940) concerned to advocate a more pluralistic conception of American society (see Chapter 9). Notwithstanding arguments over principle, for many years the prevailing view of observers of the American scene was that for better or worse immigrants of both old and new immigrations gradually (over a generation or two) blended together within a new society which although it took on elements from the newcomers was fundamentally 'Anglo' in its cultural shape, not least in its language. In the 1960s and 1970s, however, social scientists and others, began to wonder whether the legend of the melting pot in fact corresponded to the reality. Milton Gordon, writing in 1964, came to the conclusion that it was 'too early to read the "nationalities" out of the picture entirely' (1964: 207). He argued instead that whereas a great deal of cultural assimilation had occurred (or rather that there was a convergence of the cultural practices of second and later generation Americans and those of their American-born contemporaries), American society was still characterized by what he called 'structural pluralism'. Later events suggested he was right.

In the second edition of *The Uprooted*, published in 1973, Oscar Handlin wrote, somewhat plaintively: 'Ethnicity was not a word of common currency in 1950' (1973: 274). When written, the book had seemed to draw a line under a period of American history. The social and cultural tension surrounding immigration into the USA appeared to have dissolved. There was a new era of a confident, increasingly affluent, assimilated America. The struggles were over, and *The Uprooted* was a poignant reminder of what they had been. Ethnicity, as Handlin called it in 1973, was a 'fading phenomenon, a quaint part of the national heritage' (p. 275), and pluralism 'a sentimental cultural monument to the past' (ibid.). In similar vein Jones summarized his history of immigration, published in 1960, by arguing that in the mid-twentieth century ethnic differences 'were fading rapidly from view' (Jones 1960: 307). Even the distinct and diverse immigrant/ethnic churches had been 'metamorphosed into characteristically American institutions' (p. 319). This was the standard opinion of the day, and one which reflected the extent to which ethnicity had, by and large, been written out of the historical and social scientific record, or at least the perception of it. My own first encounter (in 1963) with that marvellous study of young men in Boston in the 1930s, William Foote Whyte's *Street Corner Society*, missed completely the point that they were *Italians*, in a city by and large run by the *Irish*. Yet this is what Whyte said, quite unmistakably, if one knew how to read him.

A landmark in the changing perception of ethnicity in the USA was Glazer and Moynihan's *Beyond the Melting Pot* (originally published in 1963) in which they argued it did not happen. 'The American ethos', they said, 'is nowhere better perceived than in the disinclination of the third and fourth generation of newcomers to blend into a standard, uniform national type' (preface to first edition, p. xcvii). The ethnic group was, however, no relic of the era of immigration. It was not a persistence of the past into the present, but a new and integral part of the experience of living in the USA (or at any rate New York City). Thereafter a plethora of studies told a very different story from that found in the older literature, and in the second edition of his 1960 book on immigration, published in 1992, which includes a substantial chapter on the intervening years, Jones changed his conclusion about ethnic distinctions by inserting a crucial phrase: in the mid-twentieth century they now only '*seemed to be* fading rapidly from view' (Jones 1992: 263, my emphasis). So much did the intellectual mood change that in the 1970s the melting pot idea became what another of the older generation of scholars, Higham, called 'a subject of mockery' (Higham 1984: xi). Indeed, that metaphor was replaced by one, equally infelicitous, of the 'salad bowl' (for example in D'Innocenzo and Sirefman (eds.) 1992), and Sollors felt able to write, in 1986, that 'every American is now considered a potential ethnic' (p. 33).

Several indicators initially supported the legend that ethnicity was fading or eroding away. First there was the declining importance of the 'Little Italys' and so forth as the children of immigrants moved from the city centres and tenements into the suburbs (Barton 1975: 20, Nelli 1970: 209). The Near West Side district of Chicago, for example, had an Italian population of 1,860 in 1970, compared with over 13,000 in 1920 (Nelli 1983: 175). This movement reflected a second factor, the upward mobility into skilled and white-collar occupations of what had been a largely unskilled immigrant labour force. Barton's data from Cleveland show that such mobility did not occur uniformly, but in due course the second generation 'broke decisively from the entrance status' (1975: 5). Thirdly, there was decline of the formerly thriving immigrant associational life: the clubs and societies, the foreign language press, and the ethnically specific theatre and vaudeville. Fourthly, the parochial school system, which had *inter alia* offered support for mother-tongue teaching, never really captured the loyalty of groups such as the Italians, most of whom preferred to place their children in the public schools. Fifthly, there was the apparent general absorption of 'American' culture, and sixthly there was intermarriage.

Studies in the 1920s had continued to report a very high degree of inmarriage for groups such as Italians, Poles, and Jews (Taylor 1971: 269–70). Barton, however, argues that the introduction of the Quota Acts, which led to a reduction of new entrants, meant that immigrants had increasingly to seek partners outside traditional sources (1975: 3). Research in the 1940s, however, suggested that while marriage outside the ethnic group was increasing, the choice of spouse was still limited by religious affiliation (Kennedy 1944; see also Gordon 1964: 123, Taylor 1971: 276 ff.). This so-called 'triple melting pot thesis' indicated that there were three pools within which marriage occurred: Catholic, Jewish, and Protestant. 'Marital relationships', says Barton, 'were selective, and these choices represented the remorseless decline in the second generation's participation in the ethnic community but also allowed a continuing pattern of association within a larger religious community' (1975: 167).

This thesis offered an early modification of the standard view of assimilation, but not until the 1960s was there a serious questioning of the whole argument. An important clarifying contribution came from Gordon (1964), who suggested that although acculturation had occurred, structural assimilation had not. By this he meant that although the cultural practices of second and later generation immigrants embraced values similar to those of their compatriots at large, their effective and affective social relationships continued to be with others of the same or similar ethnic background. Gordon further proposed that such relationships were contained within class-based sectors of each ethnic group, portraying American society as composed of what he called, somewhat infelicitously, 'ethclasses'. Thus, studies such as Gans's account (1962) of second-generation working-class Italian-Americans in Boston in the 1950s showed that such groups were 'ethnically (and class) enclosed, structurally, but overwhelmingly acculturated to an American working-class way of life' (Gordon 1964: 205). Gans himself previously suggested a similar process among second-generation Jewish immigrants (1956a, 1956b), but added that although moving away from traditional forms of the religion, they continued to express their identity through what he called 'symbolic Judaism': the elaboration of a Jewish 'objects culture', a Jewish popular culture, a Jewish cuisine, and a preoccupation with 'the problems of being Jewish in America' (1956a: 427–8). He later developed and generalized this theme in an account of what he called (1979) 'symbolic ethnicity', an idea taken up inter alia by Alba (1990) and Waters (1992).

Beyond the Melting Pot was very much about politics, and it is perhaps in politics that ethnic identity most obviously continued to be salient. To date, John F. Kennedy is the only non-Protestant ever to be elected President of the USA, and Kennedy's election, right at the beginning of the 'ethnic revival', as it is often called, may have had some part in generating it. It was in local politics, however, that ethnicity was most conspicuous. If one wonders what happened to ethnicity between, say, 1924 and 1960, Bayor's account of New York politics in the inter-war years provides some of the answers: it was, in a sense, never absent. Consider the following extract from a speech by a New York City Italian political leader in 1968:

Staten Island, where I grew up, was dominated by the Irish. The Congressman, the Senator and one or two Assemblymen were Irish. The other Assemblyman and the City Councilman were of German extraction. All the judges were Irish. No judge was of Italian descent. No Italian-American was considered for public office, although the Italian-Americans constituted about 25 per cent of the Staten Island population (in Bayor 1978: 32).

The language of politics was soaked in ethnicity, and Bayor's material (p. 42 ff.) reveals how political actors were invariably assumed to be ethnic collectivities ('the Jews say this', 'the Italians want that', 'the Irish feel thus'), and the actions of political leaders largely ethnically motivated (see Woods (ed.) 1902, *passim*, for a description of ethnic politics in Boston at the end of the nineteenth century). Political leaders were primarily interested in the advancement of their own ethnic group, and used ethnicity to secure their power bases. Bayor's account of the politics of New York's long-serving mayor, Fiorello La Guardia, shows that while other factors, such as a commitment to welfare programmes, may well have been important, in city politics in the USA, ethnicity was, generally, 'more than an influence on events; it is commonly the source of events. Social and political institutions do not merely respond to ethnic interests; a great number of institutions exist for the purpose of serving ethnic interests' (Glazer and Moynihan 1970: 310).

Politics in the cities, which traditionally hinged on ward organization and patronage, stimulated and reinforced this tendency (see Nelli's description of Chicago's 19th Ward in the early years of this century, 1970: 95 ff., and Jane Addams's struggles with the prevailing system, Davis 1967: 151 ff.). Ethnic groups in America were, moreover, part of global diasporas, and never fully insulated from the politics of their 'old countries'. The events in Europe in the 1930s, for example, had profound effects on Italian and Jewish communities, and the ongoing significance of the Irish question needs no underlining (see Bayor 1978: 119 ff. for the Italians). In the post-war period, the establishment of the state of Israel and its fluctuating fortunes, was a constant element in the politics of the Jewish community, especially in New York (Glazer and Moynihan 1970: 292).

Another factor commonly held to have sustained ethnic politics (or perhaps influenced the recrudescence of ethnicity) in the 1960s was the influx into Northern cities after World War II of a large Black population, migrating from the South, and of 'Hispanic' immigrants of Puerto Rican and Central and South American origin. In the politics of the period claims to resources were made, and to an extent met, on the basis of ethnic, or more accurately racial, identity, and, as Handlin observed, an 'ethnic' identity, one which was non-WASP became an 'asset' (1973: 276). 'WASP' means 'White Anglo-Saxon Protestant', a term which Higham believes first appeared in print in 1964 (1984: 13; it is not in Glazer and Moynihan). To second and third generation descendants of the new immigration (the 'white' ethnics) it appeared that advantage was to be gained by stressing their own particularity. (By the 1970s 'ethnic' meant those of non-WASP, non-Black, non-Hispanic, non-Asian origin, Novak 1971: 46–7, and note how they had now become 'white'.) Thus, as Nelli says, 'the ethnic consciousness that formed in the black ghettos of American cities during the 1950s and 1960s played a central role in the development of the ethnic awareness that emerged among Italians, Poles, and other white groups in the late sixties and seventies' (1983: 174). The changing role of the state as the provider of welfare meant that ethnic identity became a vehicle through which resource demands were made on the system (Glazer and Moynihan 1975: 8–9). It became a ' "strategic site", chosen by disadvantaged persons as a new mode of seeking political redress in the society' (Bell 1975: 169, Glazer and Moynihan 1975: 10). Greer has also suggested that analysis of the public school system revealed a 'terribly underestimated social and economic immobility' among the children and grandchildren of the new immigration, and that this was 'a serious factor encouraging the current rediscovery of ethnicity by white working-class groups, particularly by the Italians and Slavs in Boston, New York, Baltimore, Cleveland, Pittsburgh and Detroit' (1972: 86). A sense of relative deprivation prevailed. It seemed to the white ethnics that 'doors were opened to blacks everywhere in this city [New York], which would never have been opened to a Pole or a Slovak with similar credentials' (Glazer and Moynihan 1970: lxxv). Their response came close to open racism.

If the new ethnicity had its roots in the political process, and in part was a product of government action to rectify ancient inequities (Loveland 1990: vii), it invaded other areas too. Writers, such as Nelli, Novak, and Rolle sought to define or redefine the 'ethnic' heritage. Sometimes this meant little more than locating individual success stories: celebrating Italians, Poles, Ukrainians, etc. who had become famous business leaders, politicians, film stars, lawyers, professors, and baseball players. Sometimes it entailed a revaluation of the past. Whereas the previous generation had despised and rejected its ancestry, their children, the third generation of immigrant origin sought it out: 'in search of their self-identity [they] have re-examined the experiences of the immigrant generation and take pride in what their parents abhorred: the peasant origins of their grandparents and the miserable living and working conditions they encountered and endured in core-area tenement neighbourhoods' (Nelli 1983: 175).

To an outside observer this was noticeable in the films of the period. Hollywood had in the past neglected ethnicity almost entirely. There was a New-York based Yiddish language cinema which flourished in the 1930s (see D. S. Cohen (ed.) 1990), and there were aberrations such as the 'Cohens and Kellys' comedies of the 1920s. But few if any films prior to 1960 dealt seriously with the experience of immigration into the USA or even so much as mentioned the ethnic dimension of American society. The 'gangster' pictures of the 1930s ('Mother of Mercy, is this the end of Rico?') may have been about criminals of Italian origin, but they were not about ethnicity. In the 1970s, however, a kind of ethnic cinema became the rage. From *Pay or Die!* (1960), through *The God-father* (1972), *Mean Streets* (1973), and *Goodfellas* (1990), the cinema consciously portrayed Italian communities of the first, second, and third generations in a quite different way. Rolle refers to Martin Scorsese, who was responsible for several such films, and for promoting 'Italian' actors like Robert De Niro, as an 'ethnic director' (1980: 116). He is that, but of course not that alone (see Thompson and Christie (eds.) 1989). It would be equally misleading to portray George V. Higgins, whose writing documents, *inter alia*, the Irish political culture of Massachusetts, as in any simple sense an 'ethnic novelist'. Television, too, presented an image of greater ethnic diversity. The main characters in the police series *Hill Street Blues*, for example, included an Italian, an Hispanic, a Central European, two kinds of Jews, and two different sorts of Blacks. Such films and programmes reflected an underlying reality in which in the 1970s 'men and women were more likely to choose ethnicity as an anchor for life styles, values and tastes' (Handlin 1973: 276).

What was going on? The ethnicity of the period was not a 'revival', but signified the appearance, in a new form, in the public arena, of a type of relationship that had flourished in an earlier epoch. The politics of the 1960s, and the changing composition of urban populations, partly explain this up-surge, as does the arrival from the late 1960s onwards of new waves of immi-grants (Jones 1992). It may also have reflected deeper changes. As so often, Higham points us in a fruitful direction. He deeply regretted what had come to pass, though felt that by the mid-1980s the 'passion of hyperethnicity' that characterized the previous twenty years had begun to cool. Reflecting on the reasons for what many describe as the 'persistence' of urban ethnicity, he argued that there were long-term social and economic shifts in American soci-ety in which 'the trend toward a rigid, absolutistic definition of roles and identities, which arose in the eighteenth century, is now being reversed' (1984: 245). Referring to 'the weakening of social boundaries', and the resultant 'mul-tiplication of small audiences, specialized media, local attachments, and partial identities which play into one another in ways we cannot yet understand' (p. 248), he thus begins to outline a possible framework for the discussion of ethnic and cultural pluralism in post-industrial, postmodern societies which later chapters explore.

8

A 'magpie society'? From 'Assimilation' to 'Integration' in Britain and France

The West Indian or Asian does not, by being born in England become an Englishman. In law he becomes a United Kingdom citizen by birth; in fact he is a West Indian or an Asian still. Unless he be one of a small minority— for number, I repeat again and again, is of the essence—he will by the very nature of things have lost one country without gaining another, lost one nationality without acquiring a new one.

(Enoch Powell, in Smithies and Fiddick 1969: 77.)

A young North African born in France and having, in theory, lived here continuously between the ages of thirteen and eighteen, automatically acquires French nationality at the age of eighteen, but does not feel any more French, and is not thought of as any more French by his community.

(Jean-Yves le Gallou, in Silverman 1992: 135.)

1. Britain and the construction of Britishness

These two quotations, one by a well-known Conservative British parliamentarian, and former minister, the other by the French Secretary-General of the new right Club de l'Horloge, illustrate a common concern with the *assimilability* of peoples of immigrant origin who in the late twentieth century formed substantial minorities within the two countries. It would, however, be a mistake, to imagine that the supposed problem of assimilating such peoples was one wholly constructed by right-wing politicians such as Enoch Powell or Yves le Gallou. The debate cuts across the political spectrum, throwing together unexpected allies (Lapeyronnie 1992: 13). It is also an international debate. Germany, Switzerland, Scandinavia, Belgium, Holland, Canada, Australia, as well as Britain, France, and as we saw in the previous chapter, the USA, have all questioned whether, and if so on what terms, they should accommodate peoples of other cultural and ethnic backgrounds. This chapter examines the British response in the period 1960 to the present, with supplementary material on France. The experience of these two countries and that of the USA is in many ways comparable. Although there are important differences between them, all three have abandoned the policies of out-and-out assimilation which characterized earlier periods and now espouse more pluralistic solutions described variously as 'integration', 'insertion', or 'multiculturalism'. What these mean in practice is the subject of this chapter and the next.

In the late 1980s and early 1990s numerous socio-historical studies appeared in Britain concerned with the distinct but related phenomena of nationalism and patriotism. This interest in matters which in Britain, compared with France, had mostly been passed over in silence, was stimulated by the emergence during the 1980s of what seemed to many historians to be an unwonted, and unwanted, nationalism in political discourse. For Samuel and the contributors to the three volumes on *Patriotism* which he edited in 1989, the defining moment was the Falklands War of 1982 (Samuel 1989a: x). For others, the entire decade was one in which 'the past seem[ed] to be up for grabs, a chest of props and togs ready-to-wear in almost any costume drama, available to fulfil all manner of fantasies' (Porter 1992: 1). It was as if politicians had read and absorbed a seminal work of the period, and were busily engaged in inventing or reinventing traditions in an anachronistic nationalist vein (Hobsbawm and Ranger (eds.) 1983).

There were, of course, genuine, and long-standing, anxieties about the implications for a British economy, polity, and culture of a Europe that was moving steadily from a 'Community' to a 'Union'. Hugh Gaitskell, then leader of the Labour Party, had opposed entry to the European Economic Community in 1962, declaring it would mean the end of 'a thousand years of [British] history'. The process of unification, which culminated in the early 1990s in the Maastricht Treaty, generated misgivings in other countries, too: did we really want that kind of Europe? There was, however, a darker side. From the popular press with its jokes about 'Frogs' and 'Krauts', to the constant background of racism and racist violence at street level, Britain seemed an increasingly ugly, nationalistically minded society. The lager-swilling young men rampaging through the cities of Europe dressed in Union Jack shorts and T-shirts may have been untypical, but they offered a compelling, and repellent, vision of the new Britain.

This is the wider context of change within which the present chapter explores the development of British ethnic relations during the years 1960–90, concentrating on the impact on British society of the immigration of what came to be called 'New Commonwealth' citizens. In examining that impact, and the responses to it, six themes emerge:

The politicization of immigration and the enacting of legislation which controlled and restricted entry to Britain, and redefined British nationality;
The development by the central state of policies and legislation governing 'race relations', as they were called;

The development by the local state of 'anti-racist' and 'multicultural' policies and practices, especially in education, designed to combat what were seen to be outstanding problems of day-to-day living in contemporary Britain;
The reaction by some communities to these same problems which began to take them in a 'separatist' direction;
The constant interplay between several models of British society which might be variously described as 'rejectionist', 'assimilationist', 'integrationist', or 'multiculturalist';
Overall an unsteady lurch towards a form of pluralism ('integration') which events such as the so-called Rushdie affair tested to its limits.

Crucial in these developments were debates about British (or English) identity: the ambiguity is important but difficult to resolve. In Britain, to an even greater extent than in the USA or France, there has always been vagueness about national identity (Robin Cohen 1994). It has tended to be formulated implicitly rather than explicitly, represented through clichés about the past which supposedly conjure up a 'spirit', rather than offer any precise definition. The important questions (Who is 'in'? Who is 'out'? Who can join? Who cannot?) are rarely addressed directly. Serious academic study of the representation of British identity, both in the present and in other periods, is relatively recent, and much of this recent work has concerned the eighteenth and early nineteenth centuries: there is much less on the crucial years 1880–1920, though Noel Annan's account of British preparatory and public schools during and after World War I contains a great deal of relevant information (Annan 1990: 37–51). One excellent example is Linda Colley's *Britons: Forging the Nation 1707–1837* (1992).

Colley is partly concerned with what the French call *nationalisation*, the way in which peoples such as the French or British were brought within a framework of common economic, political, and social institutions. That this was a long-drawn-out process was demonstrated for France by Eugen Weber (1976), who showed that it is very difficult to speak of a French 'nation' much before 1914, if then. As well as the development of a national economic infrastructure, and the evolution of a political elite which incorporated representatives from all British regions, Colley is also concerned with 'Britishness', and with loyalty to the emergent entity (patriotism). Her principal theme, therefore, is forging (a nice, ambiguous word) an identity. In the early eighteenth century Britain was 'less a trinity of three self-contained and self-conscious nations than a patchwork in which uncertain areas of Welshness, Scottishness and Englishness were cut across by strong regional attachments, and scored over again by loyalties to village, town, family and landscape' (1992: 17). Britishness, the common national identity, was thus 'superimposed over an array of internal differences'. This happened 'in response to contact with the Other, and above all in response to conflict with the Other' (p. 6), crucially with France, the image of alterity par excellence in this period (see also Cottrell 1989: 261, 269). British identity was construed as an essentially *Protestant* one, and the principal contrast was with France as a *Catholic* country whose population was seen stereotypically as poor, oppressed, 'ignorant and credulous' (Colley 1992: 36).

Surel (1989: 23) has suggested that a 'national' image is one 'projected by a social category within [a] nation'. Whether always true or not, in the British case, as Colley shows, the projection of Britishness by the ruling elite was an important element in the development of the identity. Indeed, much of Colley's account is do with the making of 'a new unitary ruling class' (p. 163), a *British* ruling class, which through its education was inducted into a form of 'patrician patriotism' (p. 168). This enabled them to act as representatives of an identity, and leaders of a cause, in support of which, they mobilized thousands of ordinary men, women, and children, literally in the Napoleonic Wars. The theme of Protestant Britain versus Catholic France was expressed and reinforced in new royal ritual and local ceremonial, and in the images of patriotic figures such as Mr and Mrs 'John Bull', and Britannia (Dresser 1989, Surel 1989). Upper-class patriotism elaborated this concept of Britishness by establishing connections with such things as 'public schools, fox-hunting, a cult of military heroism and of a particular brand of "manliness", the belief that stately homes are part of the nation's heritage, a love of uniform' (Colley 1992: 193).

These ideas did not penetrate society uniformly or evenly. Colley's analysis of recruitment through the defence of the realm returns of 1803 shows that there were differences between regions, and between town and country: the former were more readily co-opted into the national endeavour (p. 300). Moreover, 'patrician' patriotism was contested by another which drew on a tradition of the English as 'uniquely free and distinctive people who could keep alien and arbitrary rule at bay' (p. 112; see also Colley 1989). There was in eighteenth-century Britain, as in America in the same period, a radical and progressive sense of 'patriot', as someone opposed to corrupt government (Cunningham 1989: 57–8 ff., Newman 1987: 35). Associated with this was the belief that Britain had a special, providential status: favoured by God, it was obliged to undertake a mission which would spread its blessings throughout the world (Cunningham 1989: 75, Wolfe 1989: 197 ff.) The radical view succumbed to the patrician during the Napoleonic Wars but resurfaced in mid-century Chartism (Cunningham 1989, Finn 1993). By the end of the nineteenth century, however, the patrician view was thoroughly in the ascendancy, and patriotism, along with the providential mission, had been definitively co-opted as 'a key component of the ideological apparatus of the imperialist state' (Cunningham 1989: 77).

The detailed work undertaken by Colley (and Newman) has yet to be done for a later period (though see Robbins 1988). None the less, Colley's view that Britishness was constructed negatively by contrast with an 'Other', and positively by reference to certain beliefs, values, and institutions located in an historical tradition, has important implications for the understanding of nationalism in late twentieth-century Britain. Samuel carried us forward into more recent times in a brilliant survey of what it meant to be 'British' (or perhaps

'English') in the inter-war period and later (1989*a*: xxii–xxviii). The dominant conception of Britishness, which he believes did not finally dissolve until the mid-1970s (p. xxvii), was constituted, above all, through a way of life, with lots of little symbols as well as some big ones: democracy, Empire, public service, but also gardening, Big Ben, and cricket. Interestingly, while Mrs Thatcher struck the big symbols (though not, as it happens, that of public service) very effectively, her successor, John Major, played the little ones: not so much 'Vitai lampada' as 'Miss Joan Hunter Dunne'.

These ways of defining Britishness are not inherently racial. They could, however, easily be reworked in racial terms by designating those who shared these traditions as stemming from some natural 'stock', and were in late nineteenth-century conceptions of an 'Anglo-Saxon heritage' (see Chapter 7). Lugard and others of his generation were quite explicit about this. Although from the mid-twentieth century onwards a racial perspective has rarely been on view in public discourse, it has never been far beneath the surface, and in the 1980s it seemed to many that race re-emerged 'as a primary metaphor of nationality' (Samuel 1989*a*: xxxiii).

2. Britain and Commonwealth immigration

All the 'core' countries of Western Europe attracted large numbers of immigrants after 1945, not least to fill the gaps in manpower that the war had created. Although Britain drew in workers from Southern Europe (notably Italians), as well as retaining the services of exile groups such a Poles or Ukrainians, the bulk of those entering came from its colonial (increasingly ex-colonial) territories, initially the West Indies, thereafter South Asia. By the 1980s these immigrants and their descendants born and brought up in this country formed a substantial minority, or set of minorities, in British society. The 1991 census (Table 3) recorded 5.5 per cent of the population, some three million people, describing themselves as 'non-white', about half, including the majority of the one million or more Muslims, born in the UK (Layton-Henry 1992: 16, Modood 1992*a*: 260).

Three points about post-war immigration need underlining. First, it was required by the British economy, especially for those sectors which the indigenous population began to desert through upward mobility. Secondly, colonial and Commonwealth immigrants had a special legal and civil status with right of entry into the UK, and the same rights as other citizens including the vote. Their situation was thus very different from that of citizens from other countries, and from that of immigrants in, for example, France and Germany. Thirdly, whether from the Caribbean or South Asia, they were perceived to be 'different' from the native population: people of different racial, cultural, and linguistic stock who had moreover in the recent past been British 'subjects', that is subjected to British colonial rule.

Whether Britain is or is not fundamentally (and irredeemably) a racist country, its 'New Commonwealth' immigrants were undeniably perceived (and

Table 3. *Ethnic Composition, British Population, 1991*

Place of birth	Males UK	Males Outside UK	Females UK	Females Outside UK	Total UK	Total Outside UK	Total All
Total	24,776,117	1,798,837	26,366,605	1,947,285	51,142,722	3,746,122	54,888,844
White	24,073,295	993,084	25,658,866	1,148,549	49,732,161	2,141,633	51,873,794
non-White	702,822	805,753	707,739	798,736	1,410,561	1,604,489	3,015,050
% non-White	2.84	44.79	2.68	41.02	2.76	42.83	5.49
Black Caribbean	128,378	111,106	139,959	120,521	268,337	231,627	499,964
Black African	38,339	68,461	38,994	66,568	77,333	135,029	212,362
Black Other	73,618	13,895	77,044	13,844	150,662	27,739	178,401
Indian	178,871	244,020	173,602	243,762	352,473	487,782	840,255
Pakistani	122,808	122,764	117,750	113,233	240,558	235,997	476,555
Bangladeshi	30,131	54,813	29,548	48,343	59,679	103,156	162,835
Chinese	22,876	54,793	21,800	57,469	44,676	112,262	156,938
Other Asian	21,547	72,058	21,722	82,207	43,269	154,265	197,534
Other	86,254	63,843	87,320	52,789	173,574	116,632	290,206
'Black'	240,335	193,462	255,997	200,933	496,332	394,395	890,727
'Asian'	376,233	548,448	364,422	545,014	740,655	1,093,462	1,834,117

Source: 1991 Census.

received) through a framework of racial categories and stereotypes which, as Rex (1970, Rex and Tomlinson 1979) argued, derived from the experience of empire. As Holmes points out:

Sophisticated, historically-based theories of British superiority over Europeans and an historically derived, scientific-based racism which postulated a belief in inherent White supremacy, were thin on the ground after 1945. However, less precise antipathies were in constant circulation in Britain and at times combined with perceptions of immediate threats from immigrants or refugees to generate public opposition towards such groups which could be exploited for political advantage (1988: 271–2).

During the 1950s the Conservative government became increasingly concerned at the seemingly rapid increase in immigration, especially from the Caribbean. The then Prime Minister, Winston Churchill, of whom Roberts (1994: 211) has said 'he spoke of certain races with a virulent Anglo-Saxon triumphalism', worried that the result would be a 'magpie society', which 'would never do' (Roberts 1994: 225, Layton-Henry 1992: 31). The terms on which this 'non-white' minority, concentrated in certain jobs and areas of residence, coexisted with the majority population, came forcibly to public attention through the race riots which broke out in London (Notting Hill) and Nottingham in 1958. The riots were, however, the tip of an iceberg of racism which extended across many sectors of economic and social life (jobs, housing, education, the health services, sport), and which manifested itself in discriminatory practices, hostility, abuse, and direct violence. The existence of this racism was used by some as an excuse to question the desirability of admitting non-Whites into Britain, and bring racial thinking out into the open. Thus, in 1958 one MP stated in Parliament: 'the core of the problem is coloured migration. We must ask ourselves to what extent we want Great Britain to become a multi-racial community . . . a question which affects the future of our race and breed is not one we should merely leave to chance' (in Layton-Henry 1992: 73).

Against this background the Conservative government passed the Commonwealth Immigrants Act of 1962, a major step controlling admission to the UK (Holmes 1988: 260 ff.) By restricting the right of entry previously available to colonial and ex-colonial subjects, the Act represented a break with the imperial tradition, 'our great metropolitan tradition of free entry from every part of Empire' as one Conservative cabinet minister called it (in Foot 1969: 18). This legislation did little to appease racist sentiment of the kind which feared Britain becoming 'a coffee-coloured nation' (in Foot 1969: 108), and which demanded much tougher measures. In the general election of 1964 racism surfaced strongly in certain Midlands constituencies where one Conservative, on an openly racist platform, won the Smethwick seat against the national trend to Labour. Holmes cites an extract from the candid diary of the Labour cabinet minister Richard Crossman, who reflected that:

Ever since the Smethwick election it has been quite clear that immigration can be the greatest political vote loser for the Labour Party if one seems to be permitting a flood of immigrants to come in and blight the central area of our cities (vol. i, pp. 149–50, in Holmes 1988: 266).

A Labour government legislated further restrictions in the Commonwealth Immigration Act of 1968 described by Layton-Henry as a 'major erosion of the grand expansive ideal of British imperial citizenship' (1992: 53).

This was not the end of it. At this juncture came the intervention from Enoch Powell, who articulated as clearly as anyone the anti-immigrant viewpoint, and placed it in a theoretical and ideological framework of longer-term significance. Speaking at Birmingham in 1968 (in Smithies and Fiddick 1969: 35–43) Powell referred to a 'national danger':

We must be mad, literally mad, as a nation to be permitting the annual inflow of some 50,000 dependants, who are for the most part the material of the future growth of the immigrant-descended population. It is like watching a nation busily engaged in heaping up its own funeral pyre (p. 37) . . . To be integrated into a population means to become for all practical purposes indistinguishable from its other members. Now, at all times, where there are marked physical differences, especially of colour, integration is difficult enough though, over a period, not impossible . . . to imagine that such a thing [to integrate in this sense] enters the heads of a great and growing majority of immigrants and their descendants is a ludicrous misconception, and a dangerous one to boot (p. 42) . . . Now we are seeing the growth of positive forces acting against integration, of vested interests in the preservation and sharpening of racial and religious differences, with a view to the exercise of actual domination, first over fellow-immigrants, and then over the rest of the population . . . As I look ahead, I am filled with foreboding. Like the Roman, I seem to see 'the River Tiber foaming with much blood.' That tragic and intractable phenomenon which we watch on the other side of the Atlantic . . . is coming upon us by our own volition and own neglect (p. 43).

He returned to these themes at Eastbourne in November (in Smithies and Fiddick 1969: 63–77). It was 'a grotesque supposition', he argued, 'to suppose that the habits of the great mass of immigrants, living in their own communities, speaking their own languages and maintaining their native customs, will change appreciably in the next two or three decades' (p. 71). There were 'detachments . . . encamped in certain areas of England . . . still to a large extent a part, economically and socially, of the communities from which they have been detached and to which they regard themselves as belonging' (p. 75). At Wolverhampton during the 1970 General Election, he declared: 'There are at the moment parts of this town which have ceased to be part of England, except in the sense that they are situated within it geographically' (in Wood (ed.) 1970: 101). Yet, 'we are told in terms of arrogant superiority that we have got a "multi-racial society" and had better like it' (in Smithies and Fiddick 1969: 69). And, more stridently,

Newspapers like the Sunday Times denounce it as 'spouting the fantasies of racial purity' to say that a child born of English parents in Peking is not Chinese but English, or that a child born of Indian parents in Birmingham is not English but Indian. It is even heresy to assert the plain fact that the English are a white nation (in Wood (ed.) 1970: 109–10).

Much has been written about Powell's intervention in the debate, and of the response it generated in many quarters, not least among the skilled working class (Barker 1981, Cohen 1994, Foot 1969, Gilroy 1987). It was in the course of the Eastbourne speech that Powell made the famous remark cited at the beginning of this chapter. Hearing it at the time, I had to wonder whether he referred to someone like myself, descended from Italian immigrants. A moment's reflection made it obvious that these were not included among those whom Powell abjured, and wished to send home. For although he always made much of quantity ('numbers are of the essence' was constantly on his lips), it was clear that it was people of Asian and West Indian *stock* (racial and cultural) who could never hope to aspire to being British, who could not be, and in his view did not wish to be, absorbed in British society.

This was not the first time that such arguments had been advanced, as the debate about the 'New Immigrants' in the USA makes clear. In Britain, too, at the beginning of the twentieth century the same point had been made about Jewish immigrants from Eastern Europe (Cesarani 1996: 62, Cohen 1994: 43 ff.). Holmes (1988: 68) cites the *East London Advertiser* of 1899: 'People of any other nation, after being in England for only a short time, assimilate themselves with the native race and by and by lose nearly all their foreign trace. But the Jews never do. A Jew is always a Jew.' The 1901 census recorded 290,000 aliens in the UK, out of a population of forty-two million. Over half were based in London, with about 35,000 in the East End borough of Stepney (Royal Commission on Alien Immigration 1903: 14). Many were Jews, of whom 120,000 entered Britain between 1875 and 1914 (Layton-Henry 1992: 6). Concentrated in the East End, they were said to form 'a compact non-assimilating community', which did not intermarry, but remained 'a solid and distinct colony' (Royal Commission on Alien Immigration, p. 6). In this they were compared unfavourably with the Huguenots, who 'frankly accepted the nationality of the country of their adoption and mixed their blood with ours by intermarriage, retaining neither their racial pride nor exclusiveness' (evidence to Royal Commission on Immigration, p. 23). This is not the place to consider what actually happened to the Jewish population in Great Britain (see *inter alia* Feldman 1989), but it is significant that the Aliens Act of 1905, the first major legislation controlling immigration into this country, was seen by Powell as restricting the entry of Jews to numbers which enabled 'us' 'to learn to live together' (in Smithies and Fiddick 1969: 125; for the background to the Royal Commission and the 1905 Aliens Act see Holmes 1988: 70, 72–3, Layton-Henry 1992: 7, Sponza 1988: 187).

Immigration continued to be a potent factor in British politics throughout the 1970s: it is said that Mrs Thatcher's remarks about Britain being 'swamped by people with a different culture' (in Layton-Henry 1992: 94, and elsewhere), and her promise to be very strict in controlling immigration, helped her win the 1979 election. Further legislation in 1971 and 1982 built on that of 1962 and 1968 to redefine British nationality in terms of *jus sanguinis* (Layton-Henry 1992: 191 ff., Cesarani 1996: 62, Cohen 1994): the nation was reconstituted as a *Volk*, rather than an association: 'Whereas it was enough for a person to have been born on British soil or in British territorial waters, to be regarded as British, this is no longer sufficient. The person must also have been born to parents of whom one is a British citizen' (Goulbourne 1991: 119). Although non-whites were never *formally and specifically* excluded from citizenship of the United Kingdom, immigration restriction, the practices of immigration officers at ports of entry, and the redefinition of British nationality were taken to signal that *informally* they were in effect denied membership of the British nation, just as the literacy clauses of the US Immigration Act of 1917 in practice bore most heavily on immigrants from South, East, and Central Europe. 'Blackness and Englishness' were, as Gilroy phrased it, 'constructed as incompatible, mutually exclusive identities' (1993*a*: 27), or more succinctly, as in the title of his 1987 book: *There ain't no Black in the Union Jack*.

3. Assimilation to integration

Serious urban disorder in the 1980s pointed up the tensions. Even if the riots were caused by economic and social problems (unemployment, poor housing and schooling, police harassment), they were also quite centrally to do with the failure of ethnic minorities to be accorded a legitimate place in *British* society (Layton-Henry 1992: 137). This is a bleak picture, but it is only one side of the story. First, alongside measures to restrict immigration and redefine nationality, there was legislation which attacked racism. In the same year as the 1968 Commonwealth Immigration Act, the Labour government also passed a Race Relations Act, the first in a series of measures tackling racial and other kinds of discrimination. These included the establishment of institutions such as the Race Relations Board, the Community Relations Commission, and the Commission for Racial Equality, and the 1976 law which attacked both direct and indirect forms of racial discrimination (Layton-Henry 1992: 53 ff., 60). Secondly, at the level of the local state, there was in the 1970s and 1980s a commitment to combat racism through policies of 'anti-racism' and 'multiculturalism', especially in education.

These measures generated a great deal of debate (there is an enormous literature about multicultural education from the 1970s and early 1980s), with supporters and opponents from across the political spectrum. Through much of the argument run terms such as 'assimilation', 'integration', 'multiculturalism', 'pluralism', and 'separatism'. All are ambiguous, and sometimes used interchangeably: 'integration' for 'assimilation', 'multiculturalism' or 'pluralism' for 'integration', 'separatism' for 'pluralism': the discourse is not noted for its precision. None the less, it is possible to identify three main positions informing political and other attitudes (others will be discussed in later chapters). One says, quite simply, that there is a British (or English) tradition and a British stock, defined by a mixture of racial identity and cultural practice, into which those of Afro-Caribbean or Asian origin do not and cannot fit, except perhaps as temporary helots. This 'rejectionist' standpoint was broadly the view of Enoch Powell. Another, the classic 'assimilationist' perspective, argues that there should be no deviation from British cultural tradition, but accepts that others may be accommodated within it: they are welcome to stay if they wish, but must become like 'us'. The third may be called 'integration'.

'Integration' covers a wide area. One sense is well expressed by Smithies and Fiddick in an attempt to sort out the vocabulary of Enoch Powell, who clearly used 'integration' as a synonym for 'assimilation' in his Birmingham speech of 1968 (see Smithies and Fiddick 1969: 37):

Implicit in integration is that the minorities may retain whatever religious and cultural characteristics they choose—provided these characteristics are not incompatible with the harmony of the whole society. Some of the minority culture will remain within the minority, as has, for instance, Jewish worship in synagogues, and some of it will spread through the community, particularly in universal areas such as food, language and clothing (Smithies and Fiddick 1969: 61).

They clearly follow the then Labour Home Secretary, Roy Jenkins, in a much-quoted remark in 1966:

Integration is perhaps a rather loose word. I do not regard it as meaning the loss, by immigrants, of their own national characteristics and culture. I do not think we need in this country a 'melting pot', which will turn everybody out in a common mould, as one of a series of carbon copies of someone's misplaced vision of the stereotyped English-man . . . I define integration, therefore, not as a flattening process of assimilation but as equal opportunity, coupled with cultural diversity, in an atmosphere of mutual toler-ance (Jenkins 1967: 267).

This 'Jenkins formula' (Rex 1995: 80–1) is very close to the viewpoint adopted in the Canadian Royal Commission on Bilingualism and Biculturalism of 1969: 'Integration . . . does not imply the loss of an individual's identity and original characteristics or of his original language and culture', cited by Bissoondath, 1994: 209. No assimilation in the traditional sense, but equal opportunity, cultural diversity, and tolerance.

In Britain, then, 'integration' came to mean a stand against racial and ethnic discrimination while allowing some room for ethnic difference. Bullivant, adopting the term from Higham (Bullivant 1983: 243 citing Higham *Send these to me*, 1975 edition: 242–3), calls this 'pluralistic integration', and signals ap-proval of a system in which there is participation on the basis of equality, within a framework of common legal and political institutions, but with some degree of recognition for diversity and specificity. Rex (1996: 2) calls this 'egalitarian multiculturalism', though simply to equate it with the widely used (and abused) term 'multiculturalism' would be misleading (see Chapter 9). It was this kind of pluralism which pervaded public policy in a remarkably consistent way from the mid-1960s at least until the late 1980s. Compare, for example, 'the Jenkins formula' with that expounded in the following extract from a letter from the then Conservative Minister of State at the Home Office (John Patten) to a group of Asian community leaders in July 1989:

Modern Britain has plenty of room for diversity and variety . . . Putting down new roots in a new community does not mean severing the old. No one would expect or indeed want British Muslims, or any other group, to lay aside their faith, traditions or heritage. But the new roots must be put down, and go deep, too . . . I would emphasise that greater integration in the sense of a fuller participation in British life does not mean forfeiting your faith or forgetting your roots. Muslims cannot and should not be expected to do this, nor Hindus or Sikhs, or Catholics or Jews. But between all these groups there should be a shared link—the link of being settled in Britain with all that involves . . . At the heart of our thinking is a Britain where Christians, Muslims, Jews, Hindus, Sikhs and others can all work and live together, each retaining proudly their own faith, but each sharing in common the bond of being by birth or choice, British (included as an appendix in Commission for Racial Equality 1990b: 84–7).

Poulter, who also cites the Jenkins speech, refers to a letter from Mr Patten's superior, then Douglas Hurd, who in the same period told an audience at the opening of a mosque in Birmingham: 'No-one is asking you to abandon either your faith or your traditions' (in Poulter 1990: 5). Clearly Patten and Hurd shared the same discourse, and perhaps the same speech-writer. Not that the position taken by a Labour Home Secretary in 1966 and a Conservative Minister of State in 1989 was exactly the same. The latter was fuller and reflected developments of the intervening twenty-five years (for example, in the emphasis on 'British'). None the less, the common concerns with equal opportunity and tolerance of cultural diversity (Poulter 1990: 5) indicate considerable continuity in British state policy throughout the period. That policy has been by no means without its critics, many of them very severe, as we shall see in Chapter 9.

4. Multiculturalism and anti-racism

'Integration' connoted vague and overlapping social possibilities rather than a clear-cut project. Policies within the local state in Britain, in their own vague way, were located within this discourse, addressing the same underlying, badly articulated, questions. Often enough, they were no more than *practical* responses to the problems faced by teachers in large, ethnically mixed comprehensive schools in the 1970s and 1980s. Confronted by increasing intakes of 'immigrant' children, and dealing daily with multi-ethnic and multicultural classes in schools in which there was often considerable ethnic tension, teachers looked for solutions to their difficulties, and often had to think in new ways (Foster 1990: 34–6). The so-called multicultural curriculum seemed to offer a way forward. What teachers of the time were seeking is well illustrated in the remarks recorded by Foster in his survey of one such school: 'respect', 'toleration', 'sensitivity towards others', 'understanding' of different cultures and ethnic groups; fostering a positive ethnic 'identity', 'self-image', 'pride in blackness' (1990: 39).

Such teachers were trying to address two problems. One, conceived as specific to ethnic minorities (a term which gradually replaced 'immigrants' in British discourse), and possibly specific to certain groups among them, was educational underachievement. The Rampton Report (1981) had concluded that fundamental to the widely reported educational failure (relative to other children) of young Black West Indians was low self-esteem, and this derived from the racist nature of the British education system, and of British society as a whole. On these grounds, if on no other, teachers in many schools sought to redress matters by adopting pedagogic materials and methods which would help promote a 'positive' identity. The second problem was of equal concern to ethnic minority and ethnic majority children. In the hope that this would enable ethnic minorities to feel that their traditions were valued, not despised, and help majority children place their own practices in a broader, more relativistic perspective, teachers sought to make a place in the curriculum for non-British literature, culture, and history. Provided this type of teaching was 'across the curriculum' (in maths, history, the performing arts, political education, and in language), and not simply a token gesture towards Islam, Buddhism, or Hinduism in religious studies, it was strongly supported by a second inquiry, the Swann Report (1985), which argued that a multicultural perspective in education was desirable for all pupils (and teachers). It was not intended to benefit only blacks or other ethnic minorities, but to offer, as the Report's title put it, an *Education for All*.

Halstead's account (1988) of anti-racist and multicultural education in Bradford in the 1980s shows how these issues were presented by the then Conservative-controlled local education authority's policy:

within the framework of a common school curriculum . . . to seek ways of preparing all children and young people for life in a multicultural society; to counter racism and racist attitudes, and the inequalities and discrimination which result from them; to build on and develop the strengths of cultural and linguistic diversity; to respond sensitively to the special needs of minority groups (in Halstead 1988: 23).

From this approach stemmed two sorts of practice. With regard to religion, for example, there was an emphasis on 'equal respect', and 'positive image', coupled with a policy of granting 'multi-cultural concessions' to ethnic minority groups. The latter policy aimed at ensuring that schools were 'never in a position to require pupils to act in a way that is contrary to their . . . religious and cultural beliefs' (p. 36). This meant allowing children to adopt certain kinds of dress, for classes or for sporting activities, providing *halal* meat for school meals, and so on (Halstead 1988: 45–6). The policy of emphasizing a positive image meant the incorporation of appropriate materials in the curriculum. Foster, for example, describes the use of novels by Trinidadian authors in English classes (1990: 79), and in one science course called 'Seeds of History' the use of materials which the teacher described as 'non-elitist, multicultural, anti-racist, anti-sexist, and environmentally conscious', emphasizing scientific discoveries which could be attributed to 'Third World' peoples (p. 69).

These modest reforms were not as radical as those which the Swann Report envisaged, and a long way from proposals for 'multi-ethnic' education in the USA (see the discussion on multiculturalism in Chapter 9). They did not, and at the level of the school, could not, tackle wider issues of equality of opportunity, the importance of which were stressed in John Rex's review of the Swann Report (Rex 1989). Rex's title ('Equality of Opportunity, Multiculturalism, Anti-Racism, and "Education for All"') points to three elements each of which, he argued, were of great importance in addressing issues of pluralism in British society. He was, however, sceptical of anti-racist teaching which sometimes degenerated into treating teachers and pupils 'as delinquents . . . in some sense being punished for their racist crimes' (Rex 1989: 20). The 'moralistic excesses' (Gilroy 1992: 49) of such an approach have posed many difficulties for its radical critics (P. Cohen 1992), who feel they must oppose a discourse in which blacks are always and only constituted as helpless victims (Gilroy 1993*a*: 3, 5), but who must also distance themselves from anti-racism's opponents on the new right (for example in Palmer (ed.) 1987; see also Back 1996: 2–3, Bonnet 1997, Modood 1997, Wieviorka 1997, for British experience, and Bernstein 1995 for an account of what is called 'diversity training' in the USA).

Referring to the two kinds of multicultural practices outlined above, Halstead points out that 'equal respect' ('education for all', as it were) stemmed as much as anything from what educationists saw as the needs of white pupils. The policy of 'multi-cultural concessions', however, was often a response to pressures from outside the school, from the parents of ethnic minority children and their religious and political leaders. In Bradford there was a political imperative, which influenced all political parties, to meet demands from a substantial, and growing, ethnic minority population which formed an influential sector of the city's voters (Halstead 1988: 24). One focus for pressure, especially from Muslim families, was single-sex education, and ethnic minorities in Bradford lobbied successfully for the retention of single-sex schools within the authority. Another was the 'mother-tongue' issue, which emerged against a background of increasing linguistic diversity in British cities.

Studies by the Linguistic Minorities Project (1985), revealed that in the early 1980s in Bradford some 18 per cent of all schoolchildren were bilingual, half of them speakers of Punjabi, while in the London Borough of Haringey bilinguals made up 31 per cent of all children enrolled in the authority's schools (see also

Halstead 1988: 14–15). This raised the question whether or not the 'home language' language of immigrants should be promoted in the educational system, and if so how. In many countries there is an informal and unofficial 'ethnic school' sector, concerned principally with the 'mother tongue' of immigrants and their children, offering an education external and supplementary to the official (state or private) school system (Grillo 1989: 110–16). From the mid-1970s there was increasing pressure to include ethnically specific language teaching of this kind within the mainstream education system. One reason was the development of European Community policy for the children of migrant workers which proposed that their education should seek to maintain their linguistic and cultural ties with their countries of origin. Parents, too, especially those of Asian origin, already making extensive private provision for mother-tongue teaching within the ethnic school sector, began to demand that the burden be taken on by the state system. Although seeing linguistic diversity as a positive resource, and in general declaring itself 'for' the mother tongues, the Swann Report believed mother-tongue maintenance should be left to the ethnic school sector. Bilingual education or support for mother- tongues posed problems of organization and resources (not least the adequate supply of trained teachers and appropriate teaching materials), and raised concerns about separatism (Swann Report: 406–7). Thus, for a mixture of pedagogic, practical, and political reasons, the British education system placed the burden of providing mother-tongue teaching on the communities themselves.

This discussion of multiculturalism, inside and outside the battleground of education, is continued in the next chapter, but first, a comparison with French experience will be found instructive.

5. France: between assimilation and difference

Max Silverman begins his *Deconstructing the Nation: Immigration, Racism and Citizenship in Modern France* with a reference to the so-called 'headscarf' episode of 1989. This episode, 'the French Rushdie affair' (Modood 1992*a*: 261), revolved around an incident at a school near Paris in which three young Muslim female pupils were suspended because they insisted on attending wearing the head covering which they claimed their religion required. In a detailed discussion entitled 'Headscarves and the Enlightenment' (pp. 111–18), Silverman shows that it brought to the forefront of French politics the tension between two competing ideologies, one stressing assimilation, or at any rate limited integration, of immigrants and ethnic minorities, and one involving greater recognition of the right to be different. Responses to the incident cut across the traditional political spectrum of left and right, creating strange alliances.

The politics of the case (see also Hargreaves 1995) were complex and multi-layered. They turned on a ruling by the then Minister of Education, Lionel Jospin, who on appeal permitted the youngsters to return to school wearing their headscarves. The reaction to this decision, says Silverman, revealed that the case was interpreted in a discourse which saw it in terms of a 'binary opposition between secularism and difference' (1992: 112). Thus, many on the left, or rather many of those who stressed the secular nature of the republican tradition in general, and the secular (non- or even anti-religious) nature of the republican school in particular, supported the original suspension. Headscarves signalled religion, in this instance a religion seen as a particularly oppressive and obscurantist one (Islam), which had to be kept out of the schools at all costs. Others, while adhering to the principal of secularism, felt that to support the rejection of the children was to play into the hands of the Front National, which had based its anti-immigrant campaigns on the defence of French culture. There was also, they believed, a danger that it would create martyrs for those elements in the Muslim communities in France who would prefer separate institutions. This idea that support for difference was reactionary, and would ultimately lead to separate development, was forcibly expressed by the historian Michael Winock in an article in *L'Événement du Jeudi* (9–15 Novembre 1989):

Two scenarios can be imagined. Either we are disposed to allow the formation—contrary to our tradition—of religious communities living according to their own rules . . . ghettos in society, a state within a state, with its own specific laws, customs, tribunals; and then we enter into the logic of segregation in the name of 'difference.' Or, faithful to our history, we believe that Muslims can, if they want, become French citizens, in which case their religion—a minority religion in a pluralist society—will accept the concessions which Catholicism was obliged to make in the past (cited in Silverman 1992: 113).

It is interesting that the seemingly innocuous matter of headscarves should excite such passion in France in the late 1980s and early 1990s (the reverberations of the affair continued for several years, Hargreaves 1995) when similar matters had been debated and resolved with much less rancour in Britain a decade earlier. The comparison was not lost on the French, and running through the debate about the affair was an explicit contrast between French, British, and American policies and experience in this area. Britain and America were seen as subscribing to what the French termed an 'Anglo-Saxon' conception of ethnic relations, much more pluralistic than their own. The President of the Council for Integration, set up in 1990 partly in response to the headscarf affair (Silverman 1992: 66), drew attention to these two contrasting conceptions as follows:

One is based on the right of ethnic minorities, of communities; this is the concept which has been adopted in the Anglo-Saxon countries but it is also prevalent in Europe, notably Eastern Europe. The other concept is ours, French but also continental, based on individual adhesion . . . (Those who talk of communities) are wrong. It's another way of imprisoning people within ghettos rather than affirming their right to opinions as individuals (cited in Silverman 1992: 4).

Similarly, Harlem Désir, head of the radical organization 'SOS-Racisme', commented in 1989 that

a model which has come from elsewhere is establishing itself little by little in our towns: that of the Anglo-Saxon world. It is a most serious challenge to the French melting-pot. How many ghettos do we have to have to introduce a specific policy? (Cited in Silverman 1992: 116).

The self-styled French concept reflects the long-standing French republican tradition discussed in previous chapters. As Hargreaves argues,

the republican-inspired idiom of nationhood . . . is strong not only among French elites but also among the public at large. There is a wide consensus in favour of the view that citizenship is to be reserved for members of the nation, and that the nation should be open to people of foreign origin who have internalised its norms . . . While open at the level of political incorporation, the assimilationist aspect of this idiom is closed to cultural difference (1995: 176).

The concern with ghettos, closed off from French society, in Winock's phrase 'a state within a state', brings to mind Clermont-Tonnerre's fear that the Jews might constitute a 'nation within a nation'. The French model gives primacy to the individual, and emphasizes individual assimilation (see also Silverman 1992: 4). The 'Anglo-Saxon' model, on the other hand, as the French see it, is based on the 'recognition of differences and special provision for minorities' (Silverman 1992: 4). This view of British and American practice represents a somewhat simplistic French reading of the situation in those countries, and as Silverman also says, French practice often 'belies the universalist ideology' (p. 4). Certainly in Britain neither ideology nor practice can in any simple way be described as according recognition to difference. In both France and Britain there is a complex interplay, ideologically and practically, between assimilation, integration, pluralism, and separatism.

France always had a much more substantial immigrant population than Britain before c.1960, and immigration was always a much more salient factor in French politics. Wihtol de Wenden's account (1988) of the debates surrounding immigration from the 1850s to the 1930s shows that although the assimilationist view (that immigrants could and should be absorbed in French society by becoming French citizens) generally prevailed, there were periods when public opinion also revealed a tendency to regard immigrants as a threat to national and ethnic unity. Thus in the late nineteenth century and again in the 1930s there was a marked rise in xenophobia, which in the 1930s certainly occurred at a time of high unemployment and international tension (Wihtol de Wenden 1988: 53–9; see also Chapter 6).

The immigrants of earlier periods were mostly of European origin: Belgians, Italians, and in the inter-war years, Poles. Immediately after World War II, immigration remained predominantly European, mainly from Southern Europe, including Italy, Spain, and later Portugal, but from the 1950s onwards migrants from the colonies and former colonies of North Africa, principally Algeria, but also Tunisia and Morocco, arrived in large numbers. At first most were single men who lived and worked in France often for very long periods while maintaining homes and families in their countries of origin where they eventually expected to return. In the 1960s and 1970s, however, increasing numbers stayed, and brought their families across. This *immigration sédantarisée*, as the French came to call it, was heavily concentrated in the suburbs of the major industrial cities, usually in the high-rise apartment blocks of what were termed *Zones à Urbaniser en Priorité*, or 'ZUPs'. There was in these areas a growing population of young people of North African origin, but born and brought up in France, who in the 1970s and early 1980s began to appear in great numbers in the school system.

After 1973, says Wihtol de Wenden, immigration became an increasingly important political issue in France, especially in the difficult economic climate following the oil price increases of 1970s. As in Britain, politicians responded with measures which progressively tightened controls over entry. Unlike Britain, however, where proposals for 'repatriation' were for the most part associated only with the extreme right, French governments of the orthodox right and left both offered financial incentives to encourage migrants to return to their countries of origin, a policy which was supported by the Algerian government anxious about the security of its citizens in what was seen to be an increasingly hostile, racist climate (Wihtol de Wenden 1988: 248). These two lines of attack on what were seen as the 'problems' of immigration and immigrants (see Grillo 1985) characterized governments of both right and left from the mid-1970s onwards, albeit with different emphases in different periods. The mainstream political parties, across the spectrum, were thus in accord in their response to the increasingly strident opposition to immigration and immigrants voiced by the extreme right represented by Le Pen's *Front National* (Frybès 1992: 91), a much more powerful and enduring force in French politics than its equivalents, the National Front or the British National Party, ever were in Britain.

Policies addressing the social and cultural needs of immigrants also evolved. These had two aims: to facilitate the retention of language and culture of those who would eventually return to their countries of origin, and to ease the integration, or what was called *insertion* into French society, of those legitimately in France and who wished to stay (Hargreaves 1995: 195). Mother-tongue teaching was thought to have a part to play in the former policy, and the French government was quite receptive to European Community initiatives in this area. By the late 1970s, following bilateral agreements with various sending countries, language courses were made available in French primary schools for children from Portugal, Italy, Tunisia, Spain, Morocco, Turkey, Yugoslavia, and eventually Algeria (Grillo 1989: 120). Supplementary schooling, including language tuition, has in France tended to be provided by organizations sponsored by the consulates of countries such as Italy and Algeria (in the latter case through the Amicale des Algériens en Europe), and is similarly concerned with providing for children who will eventually return 'home'.

Cultural policies concerned with 'insertion' faced a number of obstacles, not least residential concentration, and the educational disadvantages experienced by schoolchildren which blocked their entry into more qualified occupations (Wihtol de Wenden 1988: 203). In general, however, they emphasized the importance of those immigrants who remained in France becoming an integral part of *French* society. None the less, in the early 1980s the Mitterand government enacted a number of measures which moved in a more pluralistic direction. Foremost among these was a relaxation of the Law of 1901 governing foreign clubs and societies, one consequence of which was the emergence of large number of ethnically specific associations (Frybès 1992: 103): Wihtol de Wenden estimates that by 1984 there were 4,200 (1988: 364). *Inter alia*, many mosques were founded, over 1,000 by the mid-1980s (Hargreaves 1995: 122). The relaxation of the law did not, of course, create these associations. Their emergence was a response in various ways (and ways which varied from one ethnic group to another, Wihtol de Wenden 1988: 366 ff.) to a reality in which ethnic minorities (that term is not used in France) felt it important to organize themselves to express their own specific needs.

For North Africans, in particular, says Wihtol de Wenden, associational activities around religion and language provided a basis for a 'community existence' (1988: 363). This led to some associations placing such emphasis on the culture of origin that they became wrapped up in themselves and thus, in the view of Frybès, 'an obstacle to integration' (1992: 104). These associations must be seen as grappling with the issue of 'difference', on one level as a matter of personal, individual identity, on another as a matter of the rights of collectivities to be different, to maintain a distinctive way of life. Through the 1970s and 1980s the rhetoric through which this issue was addressed switched frequently, as immigrants and their children, especially those of North African origin, and their French supporters cast around for a language with which to express their sense of the problem, and its solution. Thus the slogans which have at various times signalled the perspective of the moment have called for the 'right to difference', the 'right to be different', the 'right of indifference', 'equal rights', 'civil rights', and a 'new citizenship' (Wihtol de Wenden 1988: 363).

Summarizing the experience of the 1980s and 1990s, Hargreaves (1995: 203) suggests that France was faced by a choice between three policies: pluralism, exclusion, or what he calls 'co-option'. The latter, which was the predominant policy from the mid-1980s, and exemplified the approach of the mainstream parties of both right and left, 'tolerates differences but seeks to ensure that minorities limit their distinctive patterns of behaviour in ways that are compatible with the dominant cultural norms' (p. 203). This makes it seem very close to what was called 'integration' in Britain, and the underlying issue has been much the same in both countries: what kind of room should there be for those whose origin is not French (or British), socially, culturally, or racially?

By comparison with Britain, there has been very little in the way of multicultural education (Grillo 1989: 127), and Lapeyronnie indicates the sort of dilemma in which French educationists find themselves:

Le choix d'une politique d'éducation privilégiant le multiculturel n'est pas toujours exempt d'un racisme avoué ou non: à chacun sa culture. A l'inverse, le choix d'une politique d'intégration scolaire totale n'est pas plus exempt d'une xénophobie avouée ou non qui se traduit par le mépris des cultures d'origine et le refus de les prendre en considération (1992: 12–13; compare Frybès 1992: 109).

Running through the debate has been the fear of those on the left that to stress difference carries with it the danger of racism. Silverman alludes to this difficulty when he refers to the 'ambiguities of the discourse of cultural differences . . . which traverse[d] the Right and the Left' (1992: 94). This is an old issue: see, for example, the position taken by Gobineau on nineteenth-century colonialism (in Chapter 5). Silverman, good republican that he seems to aspire to be, at times places far greater stress on the dangers of emphasizing difference than he does on its potential as a resource. The response is understandable in a context where Le Pen opposed the education minister's action in reinstating the Muslim children after the headscarf incident, seeing it his duty to protect French culture menaced by Islam (Wihtol de Wenden 1988: 332), while other elements of the extreme right supported the children. In a curious way, and for reasons of its own, discussed in the next chapter, 'the language of cultural difference [was] appropriated by the New Right' (Silverman 1992: 117). In consequence, the left was bereft of grounds on which to discuss difference. Silverman traces this development to Giscard d'Estaing's Minister for Immigration, Paul Dijoud, who in the 1970s tried to introduce policies which would foster a modicum of respect for the culture of immigrants (1992: 115). Silverman argues that Dijoud 'racialized' the issue of difference. By this he means that the Minister placed cultural differences in a discourse within which they could only be treated as racial: the policy of fostering difference was bound to be received within a framework of racist perceptions. 'Anti-racism', says Silverman (1992: 122) was thus 'caught between assimilation and difference', or rather, 'perpetually locked into the classic topography of assimilation *or* difference' (p. 123). The question posed, in 1990, by SOS-Racisme illustrated this dilemma: 'How to be anti-racist, therefore "differentialist", without effacing the aspiration to the universal present in all people?' (in Silverman 1992: 123).

This question could be put another way: what kind of ethnic and cultural pluralism is possible (or desirable) in societies committed to universalistic, democratic ideals? How far can or should one 'be French differently' (Silverman 1992: 146)? Can there be 'a new way of being British after all this time' (Kureishi 1989: 286, see also Modood 1992*b*)? This is the dilemma of nation-states which had previously espoused ideals of assimilation, and in the case of Britain and France of post-imperialist polities coming to terms with the internal and the international consequences of the end of empire. But the question which is posed, although taking a particular form in Britain, and another in France, is of much wider significance. Although we live in recognizably multiracial, multicultural, and multilingual societies, only a narrow range of cultural values is still considered legitimate and we are far from seeing multiculturalism as 'benefit and resource for the whole society' (Saifullah Khan 1980: 76). Ernest Gellner (1983: 55), who has questioned the viability of cultural pluralism in modern industrial nation-states, would view this as a sad, though inevitable, outcome of the structural conditions which gave rise to that type of political formation. Yet the claims of pluralism, or at any rate the particularistic claims of cultural minorities have become increasingly loud and widespread in the last decades of the twentieth century. They will not go away. Policies of assimilation reflected what Gellner has called an 'objective need' for homogeneity in the emergent nation-states of the nineteenth century. The demands for pluralism may well reflect, if not an 'objective need' for heterogeneity or pluralism, then at the very least the presence of conditions under which it has become a serious social possibility.

9

Multiculturalism and Beyond

Are we to remain prisoners of the past, insisting on a unitary image of a
Briton as a person who is white, Christian, clean-shaven, wearing a suit or
skirt? Or should we start conceiving a pluralistic image of being a Briton,
possibly black or brown, Hindu or Muslim, wearing a turban or kanga or
sari?

(Hiro 1991: 313.)

On the one side . . . is the vision of an increasingly unified society . . . the
symbol of the melting pot. On the other . . . a vision of persistent
separateness . . . of a society that is in some basic sense pluralistic or
irreconcilably divided.

(Higham 1984: xi.)

1. Modes of pluralism in contemporary societies

In Britain and other countries with similar patterns of ethnic and cultural
diversity, policy in the 1980s and 1990s stood within the messy middle of the
spectrum from assimilation to separatism (Modood *et al*. 1994: 4). As we saw in
Chapter 8, this is often signalled by the vague words and phrases used to
describe this condition. Whatever the terminology, crucial questions remain:
how much diversity, of what kind, and on what basis? What kind of pluralism
is possible or desirable in countries like Britain, France, and the USA, where
there is commitment to universalistic, democratic ideals? What room can or
should such societies allow for being French or British or American 'differently'? During the 1990s a number of important contributions were made to
such debates, mainly by political philosophers in North America (including
Kymlicka 1995a, 1995b, Taylor 1994). I will address some of the normative
issues in this chapter and the next, but for the moment I wish to look more
closely at what is happening in certain societies in the late twentieth century
from within a social scientific perspective.

There are many forms of ethnic and cultural pluralism, and they must not be
confused. Confining attention to countries such as Britain, France, the USA, and

Canada and specifically excluding consideration of other types of contemporary social and political formation, I argue that in these 'post-industrial' societies three emergent modes of pluralism, three pluralistic projects, may be identified: 'multicultural pluralism' (or more simply 'multiculturalism'); 'institutional pluralism' (or more simply 'separatism'), and what has come to be called 'hybridity'. The first two are examined in this chapter, the third in Chapter 10. But it is not enough to identify and describe these three projects, and distinguish them from other social and political agendas. We must ask why the late twentieth century has seen this push towards pluralism. Chapter 10 seeks to locate this impulse in the type of society and economy, 'post-industrial' and 'postmodern', widely believed characteristic of the world of the 'North' as we approach the millennium.

2. Cultural pluralism: the history of an idea

Assimilation, whether into 'Anglo-Conformity' or the melting pot, was not the only model for the development of American society. From time to time a different way was proposed, though generally rejected, one which came to be known as 'cultural pluralism'. In the early twentieth century a mild form of 'celebrating' immigrant cultures was not uncommon. For Jane Addams 'diversity of creed was part of the situation in American Settlements, as it was our task to live in a neighborhood of many nationalities and faiths' (1960 (1910): 308). The celebration of difference was in her case conjoined with a liberal outlook that led her to take up the cause of minorities generally: she was a strong supporter of black rights (A. F. Davis 1967: 102), and invited Du Bois to lecture at Hull-House (Addams 1960 (1910): 183). Going beyond this, Claghorn's review of immigrants and the law in the 1920s came close to arguing, in a way which moved in a direction opposite to Americanization, that judges needed to know the language of the immigrants who came before them (1923: 186). She also cited with approval a Boston Italian newspaper (the *Italian Voice*) which, noting the existence of judges with Irish, French, and Jewish names, called for similar representation for the 'Italian race' (in Claghorn 1923: 197–8). Claghorn also approved of the Jewish Court of Arbitration established in 1920 in New York City. Similar to the consistory courts in France, this comprised a rabbi, a justice, and a businessman or lawyer who dealt with civil cases involving disputes between members of Jewish congregations, and domestic problems (Claghorn 1923: 217–18). This court, said Claghorn, 'works rapidly, cheaply, and understandingly, for one group of foreign-born clients . . . [and] might well serve as a model for other communities' (p. 219).

Towards the end of their study, in a section entitled 'Perpetuation of groups impossible', Park and Miller, who also approved of the experiment with the New York Kehillah (see also Wirth 1928: 270), raised the question of 'the ideal character of our national life—whether we shall strive for a uniform or diversified type of culture and whether the perpetuation of immigrant traits and organizations will accomplish this diversity' (1921: 296). They argued, however, that if an immigrant group were separated from American society 'it will be pauperized in even the culture which it brings . . . No existing state or nation, and certainly no nation within a nation can create alone the values necessary to a high degree of efficiency' (p. 306). Their language brings to mind Clermont-Tonnerre on French Jews, though Paul Gilroy has pointed out that Martin Delany, an early black nationalist, and the first black officer in the United States Army, used the term 'nation within a nation' in 1852 to refer, *inter alia*, to the 'coloured people of the United States' (Gilroy 1993*b*: 22). For Park and Miller, ethnically specific institutions were valuable if, and only if, they assisted the movement towards assimilation, which they believed they did. They were important as transitional arrangements, a view supported by Covello (1967: 412; compare Nelli 1970: 200).

One theorist of the earlier period, still widely cited (Glazer 1997: 85–7), argued for something much more substantial. This was Horace Kallen, who if he did not invent the term cultural pluralism (Sollors, 1986: 181, and others attribute it to him; Bullivant 1983: 112, to John Dewey), was its key exponent. Higham has referred to the 'chronic indistinctness of the pluralist idea in ethnic relations' (1984: 198). Kallen's meandering writing is indeed difficult to follow or criticize! His later work especially (1956) is so abstract that it is almost impossible to divine what he actually means, or rather what his beliefs might mean, in practice, on the ground (as Walzer, 1995: 145, puts it Kallen 'rarely advanced much beyond glowing description and polemical assertion'). His ideas, although vague and unspecific, perhaps because vague and unspecific, were none the less influential: Covello, for example, certainly drew inspiration from him, as did the workers associated with the New Jersey Ethnic Survey. This Survey, details of which were rescued from the obscurity of the archives by David Cohen in the 1980s, was undertaken in the late 1930s as part of a programme funded by the Federal Writers Project (an offshoot of the New Deal) to send amateur reporters into working-class areas to locate and record the experiences of immigrants in their own words (D. S. Cohen (ed.) 1990: 10 ff.). It belonged, says Cohen, to a wider movement which sought to sustain cultural diversity and looked to Kallen as its spokesman.

Kallen came to prominence through a series of articles during World War I which criticized the then prevailing mood of Americanism, and attacked the Americanization campaign, which he believed, like other kinds of assimilation theory and practice, expressed an 'authoritarian monism of culture' (1956: 99). He proposed instead a wide-ranging form of cultural pluralism which he believed inherent in and justified by the 'American Idea' (Gordon 1964: 141–53, Higham 1984: 206 ff.). In his 1916 article on the 'Meaning of Americanism' (republished in 1924), he argued strenuously that compared to Europe, where 'nationality is a thing spontaneous and natural rather than voluntary, rooted in hereditary groupings far more than in reason' (1924: 51), the USA ('a union of states, not a consanguineous nationality') was a 'mosaic of peoples, of different bloods and of different origins' (p. 58), where citizenship was based on 'free assent' (p. 60). The Americanization programme, he believed, reflected the demand for standardization and uniformity emanating from the industrial mode of production and consumption. This industrial imperative also required mobility, which 'reinforces the need of the immigrant to learn English—for a lingua franca intelligible everywhere becomes indispensable' (p. 85). Pursuit of the goal of 'unison' would, however, involve the 'complete nationalization of education, the abolition of every form of parochial and private school, the abolition of instruction in other tongues than English, and the concentration of the teaching of history and literature upon the English tradition' (p. 119).

On the other hand, 'Men . . . cannot change their grandfathers' (p. 122), and there must be an alternative to Americanization. This Kallen sought in 'harmony' which, starting from existing ethnic and cultural diversity, 'would seek to provide conditions under which each might attain the cultural perfection that is proper to its kind'. He rejected the examples of the Ottoman and Austro-Hungarian Empires where the 'union of nationalities is . . . based more on inadequate force than on consent'. (They were 'plural societies' in Furnivall's sense, a notion which Kallen anticipates up to a point.) Instead he found appropriate models in Britain and Switzerland, especially the latter (p. 122). The ideal was a federal, multilingual, republic, 'a democracy of nationalities, co-operating voluntarily and autonomously through common institutions in the enterprise of self-realization through the perfection of men according to their kind' (p. 124). Drawing on Sir Henry Maine's distinction between 'status' and 'contract', Kallen envisaged a society consisting of congeries of status groups entered by birth ('a diversity of natural, organic groups', p. 200), conjoined into a federated state by contractual union. English would provide a common language, but 'each nationality would have for its emotional and involuntary life its own peculiar dialect or speech, its own individual and inevitable aesthetic and intellectual forms' (p. 124). Finding in the Jewish quarter of New York a community 'autonomous in spirit and self-conscious in culture', he located in the Kehillah something close to what he appeared to mean by cultural pluralism (see especially Kallen 1924: 113–14).

Kallen's vision for America represented a 'strong' version of cultural pluralism, one which in terms of the institutions its members inhabited was not far short of separatism, or at any rate involved a high degree of institutional pluralism, that is a configuration in which across a wide range of institutions, or possibly across some of them, there is provision for ethnically specific and separate arrangements (below). It is not clear what he really had in mind, however. Although he rejected the Habsburg and Ottoman Empires as models, something close to what he may have envisaged was perhaps revealed in Solomon Bloom's idyllicized and romanticized portrayal (in the magazine *Commentary* in 1947) of his childhood in the town of Harlau, Romania, before World War I, cited by Moynihan (1993: 132–5) in a chapter entitled 'Before the fall'.

According to Bloom, before 'nationalism crushed Rumania's design for living', Harlau was 'a living organism functioning through ethnic divisions of labour' (in Moynihan, p. 139), in which the various ethnic groups 'lived together in relative harmony, indeed synergy', as Moynihan puts it (p. 135). Kallen's America was never really thought through as a practical project. His vision was an innocent, naive one, with little sense of the politics or economics, or of any specific social context: he believed, for example, that hostility to outsiders was 'universal and endemic' (1956: 33). Moreover, as Higham points out (1984: 210), he had almost nothing to say about the situation of America's blacks (see also Glazer 1997: 111). Although cognizant of the position of the Negro in the South (1924: 237), he never considered how cultural pluralism might address existing inequalities.

Running through his work, that of the Federal Writers (Cohen (ed.) 1990), and of others such as Louis Adamic (1940), who took up Kallen's cultural pluralism using Walt Whitman's phrase 'a nation of nations' (Gordon 1964: 156, Sollors 1986: 239–40), was a strong sense of German romanticism. Higham finds this romanticism underlying all kinds of cultural pluralist thinking (1984: 210), with its emphasis on 'folk' culture and language, and on the idea of a national community. Compared with the proponents of assimilation, for whom the individual freedom it entailed was fundamental, cultural pluralists stressed that 'the persistence and vitality of the group comes first' (Higham 1984: 235). The contrast between group and individual, expressed by Clermont-Tonnerre, is an important one, and raises major questions to which we will return.

Although Kallen was influential, it was not his 'strong' version of cultural pluralism which commanded attention but rather his more general call for the recognition of cultural diversity (for example, in the 1920s movement for what was called 'intercultural education', Gollnick and Chinn 1986: 24). This tended to mean respect for cultural specificity within an overarching Americanism, and in practice came to little more than the 'celebration' of cultural difference of the kind which characterized the activities of the settlement workers in the early years of the twentieth century. Not until the 1960s, with the emergence of the black civil rights movement on the one hand, and the 'new ethnicity' on the other, did demands for a more substantial form of cultural pluralism begin to be voiced, principally in the field of education.

A landmark of that era was the formation of the 'National Coalition for Cultural Pluralism' which in elaborating its vision defined cultural pluralism as:

a state of equal co-existence in a mutually supportive relationship within the boundaries or framework of one nation of people of diverse cultures with significantly different patterns of belief, behavior, color, and in many cases with different languages. To achieve cultural pluralism, there must be unity with diversity. Each person must be aware of and secure in his own identity, and be willing to extend to others the same respect and rights that he expects to enjoy himself (Stent *et al.* 1973: 14, cited in Bullivant 1983: 114).

Bullivant (1983: 113) points out that 'unity with diversity' is a typical formulation of Kallen's. Like Kallen, the Coalition also proposed that cultural pluralism should be seen as an alternative to assimilation, indeed 'a negation' of it, which as well as requiring 'the same fair share' for all ethnic and cultural groups also demanded 'the right not to assimilate' (Stent *et al.* 1973: 16–17, cited in Bullivant 1983: 115). Bullivant links the work of the Coalition with the Ethnic Heritage Studies Program Act of 1972 ('Title IX'), which *inter alia* called for 'recognition of the heterogeneous composition of the Nation and of the fact that in a multiethnic society a greater understanding of the contribution of one's own heritage and those of one's fellow citizens can contribute to a more harmonious, patriotic, and committed populace' (in Bullivant 1983: 121).

The Act was, says Bullivant, decidedly anti-assimilationist, and thus in tune with a great deal of thinking in educational circles. One important influence was the 1972 report of a Commission on Multicultural Education established by the American Association of Colleges of Teacher Education entitled *No One Model American* from which Bullivant cites the following extracts:

Multicultural education is education which values cultural pluralism [and] rejects the view that schools should seek to melt away cultural differences or . . . merely tolerate cultural pluralism . . . [It] recognizes cultural diversity as a fact of life in American society, and it affirms that this cultural diversity is a valuable resource that should be preserved and extended . . . To endorse cultural pluralism is to endorse the principle that there is no one model American . . . Cultural pluralism is more than a temporary accommodation to placate racial and ethnic minorities. It is a concept that aims toward a heightened sense of being and wholeness of the entire society based on the unique strengths of each of its parts (cited in Bullivant 1983: 124–5).

The contemporaneous development of thinking about multicultural education in Britain towards the end of the 1970s, which entered its period of florescence in the 1980s and was endorsed by the Swann Report (Verma 1990: 52–3), was discussed in the previous chapter.

The cultural pluralism characterizing thinking in Britain and the USA, the vague, ill-defined, ambiguous set of ideas which commanded general support both inside and outside the world of education, corresponded roughly to what Gordon (1975: 105) has called 'liberal pluralism'. The keynote was participation plus diversity, and it is around questions concerning these (how much and what kind?) that the debate has revolved in Britain and other countries which to a greater or lesser extent espouse pluralistic principles. What pluralism means in practice, of course, varies hugely. It is not a fully worked out theory or programme nor a readily identifiable social state. It is an emergent phenomenon, the outcome of a multiplicity of international, national, and perhaps above all local and specific accommodations on a range of issues which Waardenburg (1988) calls 'test cases'. Some of these, headscarves in France, the Rushdie affair in Britain, question the 'terms of engagement' (Parekh 1995: 310) whereby immigrants enter the society, and probe definitions of acceptable pluralism to their very limits.

3. Against multiculturalism

This brief history shows that multicultural pluralism (let us go with the current jargon and say multiculturalism for short) is not as recent a phenomenon as is sometimes supposed. None the less it has not been constantly on the social agenda, and certainly in Britain in the late 1980s and early 1990s it moved out of the political limelight, though still much discussed in academic and educational circles. In North America, on the other hand, during the same period it became the focus for a virulent debate, especially in the USA, where it was caught up in the controversy over 'political correctness'. The academic and polemical literature grew exponentially: figures from the Nexis database cited by Glazer (1997: 7) reveal no references to multiculturalism in 1988, thirty-three in 1989, 1,500 in 1994.

Both Glazer and Goldberg (1994), from different perspectives, agree that multiculturalism, like the earlier cultural pluralism of Horace Kallen, was a response to the monoculturalism (Goldberg 1994: 3–4) which characterized earlier policies of Americanization and assimilation Thus, for Glazer, multiculturalism is:

a position-taking stance on the racial and ethnic diversity of the United States. It is a position that rejects assimilation and the 'melting pot' image as an imposition of the dominant culture, and instead prefers such metaphors as the 'salad bowl' or the 'glorious mosaic' in which each ethnic and racial element in the population maintained its distinctiveness (1997: 10).

More specifically, both see multiculturalism (like the 'ethnic revival') stemming from the Civil Rights movement of the 1960s, and the failure of policies of integration. For Glazer, it is 'the price America is paying for its inability or unwillingness to incorporate into its society African Americans, in the same way and to the same degree it has incorporated so many groups' (1997: 147). In Canada, on the other hand, according to Bissoondath (1994), multiculturalism followed a different trajectory and stemmed from the need to formulate a political response to the separatist demands of French-speaking Quebec. In both the USA and Canada (and Britain and France) the focal point of debate about multiculturalism has been education. Goldberg begins and ends his discussion (1994) with the university, and Glazer (1997: chapter 2) provides a riveting if scarifying account of the proceedings of commissions of inquiry concerned with redefining the curriculum to take into account multicultural principles in California and New York (the outcome of the latter, in which Glazer himself participated, provoked Schlesinger's ferocious attack, 1992).

Many observers have proposed that multiculturalism takes 'strong' and 'weak' forms (see my own suggestion, outlined earlier, that forms of pluralism fall along a spectrum). Glazer, for instance, writes of a 'militant multiculturalism' (1997: 11). This, presumably, is the opposite of what Goldberg calls 'weak' multiculturalism:

a strong set of common, universally endorsed, centrist values to which everyone— every reasonable person irrespective of the divisions of race, class, and gender—can agree. These universal principles are combined with a pluralism of ethnic insight and self-determination provided no particularistically promoted claim is inconsistent with the core values (1994: 16).

This milk-and-water version he condemns as 'implicit monculturalism dressed up as weak pluralistic multiculturalism' (ibid.). Perhaps he would so describe Rex's 'egalitarian multiculturalism' (Rex 1996: 2). Eriksen, too, writing from the perspective of the ethnography of Mauritius, identifies as a strong form of multiculturalism that which rejects ideologies of human rights and individual liberty (1997: 66). Eriksen's strong version, which he contrasts unfavourably with the multiculturalism actually found in Mauritius, is comparable to the 'communal option' discussed below, in which pluralism is formally recognized across a range of public institutions and practices.

Multiculturalism, both strong and weak, has its critics, often in unexpected alliances: 'strange bedfellows', as Schmuhl (1995: 145) describes them. There are six principal areas of controversy, problems with multiculturalist theory and practice: (1) multiculturalism's implicit essentialism; (2) the system of categorization which underpins it; (3) the form that multicultural politics takes; (4) the ritualization of ethnicity often associated with it; (5) the elision of race (and class) that it appears to entail; and (6) the attack on the 'common core' which it represents. (See also Eriksen, 1997: 66, and Glazer, 1997: 34.) Many of these criticisms stem from a focus on 'culture'. During the 1970s, as British educationists worked their way through the minefield of competing terms ('multiracial', 'multi-ethnic', 'multicultural', etc.) in an effort to identify the nature of the project in which they were engaged, there emerged a consensus around 'culture' as 'the central all-embracing concept' (Bullivant 1983: 41). This happened, suggests Bullivant, in part because it was a term which would (so it was believed) be readily understood outside the ranks of the professional educational experts. And it was, of course, not only in education that a discourse of multicultural pluralism predominated. Along with other observers Bullivant sees this as a dubious emphasis: 'a seductive trap' (1983: 133). By defining the key features of social relations and the groups which compose society as 'cultural', other interpretative frameworks are precluded, notably those which would emphasize race and racism (Bullivant 1983: 229, 232), or class. Rattansi (1992) calls this 'cultural essentialism', or more fully 'cultural and ethnic essentialism': multiculturalism conceives of society as a population of 'ethnic groups' defined by their presumed (or claimed) cultural specificity and distinctiveness (Sahgal and Yuval-Davis 1992: 15, Anthias and Yuval-Davis 1993: 158).

The charge of essentialism is frequently made, but rarely argued persuasively. 'In the present deconstructive moment', says Werbner, 'any unitary conception of a "bounded" culture is pejoratively labelled naturalistic and essentialist' (1997*a*: 3–4). She is one of the few to try to tease out an operational meaning for the term:

To essentialise is to impute a fundamental, basic, absolutely necessary constitutive quality to a person, social category, ethnic group, religious community or nation. It is to posit falsely a timeless continuity, a discreteness or boundedness in space, and an organic unity. It is to imply an internal sameness and an external difference or otherness (1997*b*: 228).

Essentializing involves categorizing (below) and stereotyping, and is a way of thinking and acting which treats individuals as if they were 'essentially' defined, that is their subjectivity is determined, by membership of a particular category, in this case their cultural/ethnic group. In multiculturalism, therefore, culture plays the part of race and sex in other discourses (feminist thinking about sex and gender has been highly influential in the anti-essentialist critique of multiculturalism). Ethnic groups are seen as 'self-evident, quasi-biological collectives of a reified "culture"' (Baumann 1997: 222) and there is a refusal to accept that that culture is constructed within those 'communities' themselves. Appiah, too, argues that multiculturalism is based on 'conceptions of collective identity that are remarkably unsubtle in their understandings of the process by which identities, both individual and collective, develop' (1994: 156).

Essentialism is not only found in Western societies, in Western 'Orientalism', for example, or in the way that countries such as Britain or Sweden deal with their ethnic minorities. Werbner's excellent account (1979*b*: 231 ff.) of the origins and development of the Rushdie affair shows how much essentializing there was on all sides, including that of Iranian Islamic 'fundamentalists'. Essentialism has also characterized debates about 'blackness' from early discussions of *négritude* to the present day, and some argue that such essentialism may well have strategic value in political struggles: that there is a necessary and acceptable form of 'strategic essentialism' (Spivak 1987; see also Werbner 1997*b*: 240, Bonnet 1997: 187; see also Bissoondath 1994: 163, for an account of the way in which the word 'racialized' is used in a non-pejorative sense by certain black Canadians).

Secondly, categorization. Earlier, I drew attention to Richard Jenkins's argument about the importance of categorization in the social and political processes concerned with the construction of identity (1994: 197), and numerous examples have been cited in previous chapters. Multiculturalism, it is argued, creates and/or works with existing ethnic and cultural categories and essentializes them. Cohen (1997: 136) cites the argument that in Britain, '"South Asian" is made an inclusive [category], almost inadvertently, through the power of Western liberal-democratic discourses, which require a single fabricated "culture" for their multicultural ideologies and policies'. This can happen for the best of reasons. Thus following anti-discrimination and monitoring legislation, US agencies adopted a limited number of categories for reporting purposes: 'blacks', 'Hispanics', 'Asian', and 'other' (Glazer 1995: 128). It is all too easy to stereotype. Les Back (1996: 153) quotes one young black South Londoner saying he would much rather be reading Shakespeare, but all he can find in his youth centre's library are books about Rastafarianism. These 'unitary definition[s] of "blackness"' do not go unopposed (Back 1996: 152), none the less, the 'ethnic dialectic' would suggest that such categories are not simply invented but emerge in complex interaction of the kind which in Southall (London) leads to the emergence of an 'Asian' culture constructed by young people whose families are of diverse South Asian origin (Baumann 1997: 217–18).

In multiculturalism 'all families are extended, children respect their elders, religious faith is total and unquestioning, and women are veiled creatures living in the shadows' (Ali 1992: 109). The process of defining, or, more strongly, constituting social (and political actors) through a stereotypical and essentialized 'culture' (rather than, say, their relationship to the means of production), and thus by their ethnic identity, appears in many different guises, in both British and American society. Consider, for example, the school system portrayed in Gollnick and Chinn's textbook on *Multicultural Education in a Pluralistic Society* (1986) intended for trainee teachers and social workers. Schools should, they argue, have a multicultural curriculum pervading the classroom and the school environment at all times. Ethnicity permeates the life of all children outside school, and the school must reflect this reality, albeit in a positive way:

Bulletin boards, resource books, and films that show ethnic diversity should constantly reinforce these realities . . . Too often minorities are not seen on bulletin boards or included in the reading lists when students study biographies, the basic food groups, labor unions, or the environment . . . It is the educator's responsibility to ensure that ethnic groups become an integral part of the total curriculum (Gollnick and Chin 1986: 93).

'Start "where people are"', they enjoin (p. 269), with what children bring to the school and the classroom, and that means with their ethnic identity. By stressing ethnicity within the total school environment, down to the minutiae of verbal interactions within the learning process, they seem to be saying to teachers: Whether you know it or not, whether *they* know it or not, your students bring their ethnicity with them. There is an *assumption* that students will be defined by their ethnically distinct cultures, and this assumption seems almost designed to elicit an appropriately ethnic response. As Waters comments, 'The expectation in American society that everyone has an ethnic identity in addition to being American is often institutionalized in elementary school projects where children are given the assignment of researching their roots' (1990: 59). Waters also discovered that while interviewing her American informants 'individuals remembered an ancestry that was not even consciously a part of what they believed their ethnic origins to be' (1990: 23). That such a response can be elicited was found in surveys by the Linguistic Minorities Project (1985): asking pupils in British schools to reflect on their home language or dialect made them conscious of a sociolinguistic identity in a way they had not been before the study.

In discussing the rights and wrongs of British social work practice which insists on 'same race' adoption and fostering, Paul Gilroy argues that 'emphasizing ethnic particularity has become an important means to rationalize the practices of [social service] departments. It organizes their clients into discrete groups with separate needs and problems which have been identified as expressive of the various cultures they inhabit' (1987: 66). Encouragement of ethnic diversity may mean that people are 'positively forced to adorn themselves with an ethnic label, whether they want to or not' (Eriksen 1993: 143, 1997: 62). One should not, however, overemphasize the ability of institutions such as schools and social services to 'generate' ethnicity and cultural diversity. It is important not to deny the existence of distinct cultural practices and collectivities: multiculturalism does not conjure ethnic and cultural groups from nothing. If categorized as ethnic, people are almost obliged to respond as ethnic, though it is never as simple a one-way affair as that suggests. As with the 'invented' tribes of colonial Africa, or the categories of the Ottoman millet system, multiculturalism sometimes reflects an underlying reality, sometimes creates it, sometimes shapes it in a particular way.

Thirdly, as these examples suggest, categorization and stereotyping have an important political aspect, indeed several. First there is what Goldberg (1994: 26) calls 'managed or corporate multiculturalism'. These are 'tools for . . . maintaining a constriction of diversity that otherwise might be unmanageable and overwhelming from the standpoint of bureaucratic and administrative technologies' (ibid.: 29). This is a point that is frequently made in Europe, including Britain (Rex 1996: 2). For example, Rex points out that several 'Councils of Mosques' which exist in Britain in fact originated with municipal councils (1996: 230). Multiculturalism is thus seen as a way of controlling minorities, 'as a manipulative policy through which the state seeks to control minorities through selected elders, reifying and rendering static the notion of minority cultures' (Rex 1996: 58; see also Rex and Drury (eds.) 1994, and Hannerz 1996: 158 on Sweden). In the British context, such a conception fits well with the traditions of a polity which once ruled a multicultural empire through a system of indirect rule (Ali 1992: 104, Goulbourne 1991: 104, Sahgal 1992: 167–8). That a similar process has characterized American cultural pluralism shows, however, that it is not confined to post-imperial societies, and cannot be explained solely as the residue of a colonial heritage. This is not to say that the management of multiculturalism takes the same form. Evidence from Britain (and other European countries, see Grillo 1985), as well as from the USA and Canada, suggests that essentialism is politicized in different ways. The manner in which cultural blocks are given political and social space is often very different and in all likelihood heavily influenced by prevailing patterns of political culture. If British (or French) colonial experience offers one model through which notions of ethic essentialism are articulated politically, an American tradition of interest-group pluralism offers another. And there may be other, simpler, ways in which multiculturalism gets caught up in politics. Thus in Canada, where according to a Canadian source cited by Bissoondath (1994: 40), it became a 'slush fund to buy ethnic votes', multiculturalism was a device used by national politicians in the struggle over independence for French-speaking Quebec. French particularism was submerged by multiculturalism: it became only one among many (Bissoondath 1994: 62).

A frequent charge made against managed multiculturalism, especially where it operates through systems equivalent to some form of 'indirect rule', is that it supports the most conservative elements in ethnic minority communities: old against young, men against women (Rex 1996: 58–9, Rex and Drury (eds.) 1994, Waldron 1995: 109; see also below). Thus Kymlicka argues that demands for the outlawing of 'group libel' made in Britain during the Rushdie affair stemmed from Muslim leaders who wished to 'control apostasy within the Muslim community, rather than to control the expression of non-Muslims' (1995a: 43). On the other hand, he also believes that there was 'little support for the imposition of internal restrictions amongst the members of minority groups themselves' (ibid.: 41). 'Internal restrictions' involve the application of (generally illiberal) principles which are specific to particular minority cultures.

The institutional fostering of ethnic and cultural diversity may select which diversity to permit, and which groups are to be recognized as culturally significant. Gollnick and Chinn, for example, by defining ethnicity as something based on 'national origin' discover that, for their purposes, Jews are not an ethnic, but a religious group (1986: 71). They are therefore represented in the multicultural curriculum and the multicultural school in a different way from, say, Italians. The institutional promotion of certain ideas and procedures through which the management of multiculturalism is articulated sometimes forces groups to represent themselves in a certain way (see Radtke 1994: 36, for a German example). In Britain, this was illustrated in the courts in the case of *Mandla* v. *Lee* (in Poulter 1986: 185 ff.). This involved a Sikh boy who was refused entry to a private school because he and his family said he must wear the customary Sikh turban. The case, brought by the family under the 1976 Race Relations Act, eventually went on appeal to the House of Lords, who had to determine whether Sikhs as a group were covered by the Act. Although the lower courts had decided that on biological grounds Sikhs were not an ethnic group, their Lordships, reflecting on the meaning of ethnicity in the 1976 Act, concluded that it involved more than biology. They therefore proposed that an ethnic group was one which had seven 'essential' (*sic*) characteristics: a shared history and consciousness; a distinct cultural tradition; 'common geographical origin or descent from a small number of common ancestors'; a common language and literature; and 'being a minority or being an oppressed or a dominant group within a larger community' (Poulter 1986: 186). By these criteria it was accepted that Sikhs were an ethnic group and the 1976 Act applied in their case. Likewise, a 1994 court ruling determined that the harassment of an Irishman through the repetition of mindless jokes constituted an infringement of this law, and thus brought the Irish within the terms of the Act.

It is these kind of considerations which in fact lead Werbner to defend multicultural politics and, in an attempt to find what she calls a non-essentialist mode of representation (1997b: 229), to distinguish between 'modes of objectification' and 'modes of reification', the latter 'essentialist in the pernicious sense'. Multiculturalism, she argues, 'empowers morally and aesthetically imagined communities', (1997b: 247). Bureaucracy essentializes, but its 'fictions of unity' (p. 241) are different from the essentialist constructs of racism. The objectification is situational and pragmatic and intended to serve principles of equity and 'redistributive justice' (p. 248).

Fourthly, the ritualization of ethnicity. Institutionally engendered or legitimated multiculturalism, managed multiculturalism, takes strong or weak forms. Sometimes it is mere tokenism of the sort that in Britain is referred to, contemptuously, as 'saris, samosas, and steel bands' (Joly 1992: 134; Kanneh's phrase is 'calcified autonomies', 1995: 70). This tokenism highlights a simple range of what are believed to be appropriate visual cues of typical (and generally harmless) diversity, as frequently happens in those carnivals which represent the ethnic as 'folk', and which 'turn ethnic groups into the museums of exoticism' (Bissoondath 1994: 111). A good example was the opening ceremony for the 1994 World Cup on Soldier Field, Chicago, in which each competing nation was represented by members of an appropriate ethnic association from the city (thus making the performance as much about the USA as it was about world soccer) in an endless parade of castanets, clogs, and coloured robes. Cultural diversity thus becomes a stereotyped symbolic dance for a ceremonial occasion: ritual ethnicity in every sense. (See M. Davis 1992: 80–1 for an account of a similar process in Los Angeles.)

Fifthly, the elision of race and class. A major difficulty with the cultural emphasis is that although multiculturalism generally espouses some form of relativism, in societies such as Britain and France cultures are routinely compared and evaluated against each other. This has posed particular problems for the left in the face of what has been termed the 'racialization of culture' in the theorizing of the so-called 'new right'. Barker has described *The New Racism* as an ideology in which theories of race are 'concealed inside apparently innocent language' about culture (Barker 1981: 3). The argument is that in the 1970s and 1980s, the new right reworked the historic themes of racial difference and hierarchy through a discourse of culture. 'Race' was redefined as cultural difference: Mrs Thatcher's reference to 'swamping' is frequently cited as an instance of this (Goldberg 1993: 73). Gilroy, and others, also point to the way in which through a discourse of 'mugging', gangs, and drugs, criminality 'was gradually identified as an expression of black culture' (Gilroy 1987: 109). Apparently, though only apparently, eschewing biology, the new racism had at its centre a theory of human nature, the idea that it was 'natural to form a bounded community, a nation, aware of its differences from other nations. They are not better or worse. But feelings of antagonism will be aroused if outsiders are admitted. And there grows up a special form of connection between a nation and the place it lives' (Barker 1981: 21). Seidel, who develops Barker's argument through a study of articles in the *Salisbury Review* and similar writing in France by the Groupement de Recherche et d'Études pour la Civilisation Européenne (GRECE), concludes that the new right emphasis on cultural difference meant that a slogan such as 'le droit à la différence' was therefore 'very ambiguous' in its implications (Seidel 1986*a*: 129).

Was there anything really new about the new racism? Racial and cultural themes have always been intertwined in xenophobic discourse in Europe and the USA, not least in the late nineteenth century. The link between criminality and culture made in the case of the black population of London in the 1980s is not very different from that made in 1911 by the United States Commission on Immigration with reference to the Italian population of New York. Gilroy sees the 'novelty' of the new racism in its linking of 'discourses of patriotism, nationalism, xenophobia, Englishness, Britishness, militarism and gender difference into a complex system which gives "race" its contemporary meaning' (1987: 43). Yet, as Colley has shown, that linkage had already been made in the eighteenth century. Moreover, it is not at all clear that the theorists of the *Salisbury Review* or GRECE have much influence or significance outside the intellectual milieus they inhabit; that, for example, the 'new racism' legitimizes the 'old racism' at street level in London or Paris. There was nothing new, for instance, in the scurrilous poem about the black British Member of Parliament, Bernie Grant, which Gilroy found in a pamphlet distributed on the streets of London (1992: 54), and its perpetrators were unlikely to have sought justification in the pages of sophisticated journals (Anthias and Yuval-Davis 1993: 57, Lutz, Phoenix, and Yuval-Davis 1995: 7). On the other hand, as in France, sensitivity to the way in which race/culture was reworked in the discourse of the new right, made many on the left deeply suspicious of any statement about cultural difference. It was readily assumed that remarks about 'culture' were in fact coded ways of speaking about 'race' (Goldberg 1993: 73), and hence the 'real' issue was racism, *tout court*.

If the elision of race is paramount for some, for others it is the diversion from economic problems (Eriksen 1997: 66), or the glossing over of questions of class (Glazer 1997: 16), though Modood (1997: 157) applauds the way in which multiculturalism rectifies the denial of difference between Afro-Caribbeans and Asians found in previous race-class models. For others the key issue is the extent and type of diversity it promotes: will multiculturalism go too far, and destroy the common ground of British or French or US society?

Although anti-racist, multicultural, and multilingual education made only modest headway in Britain during the 1980s, in many schools the ethos was quite different from that which prevailed in the monocultural educational system of the 1960s. Latterly, however, such advances as had been achieved were attacked from the right. The case of Ray Honeyford, the Bradford head teacher who was removed from his post after parents had protested at what they alleged were racist elements in his criticism of multiculturalism, was taken up by the new right in a renewed defence of the traditional, assimilationist, school (Halstead 1988). Historically, British schools, explicitly or implicitly, have always been concerned with maintaining a language (English) and mainstream British culture. Doyle's account of the development of the teaching of English in the early part of this century shows how that culture was seen as a 'transcendental essence inhering within an "organic" national language and a humanistic literary tradition' (Doyle 1989: 59). That this was and remains the dominant view was confirmed by a statement by Sir Keith Joseph, Secretary of State for Education, shortly before he left the office: 'Our schools should transmit British culture, enriched as it has been by so many traditions . . . It would be unnecessary . . . and I believe wrong, to turn our education system upside down to accommodate ethnic variety or to jettison those many features and practices which reflect what is best in our society and its institutions' (*Guardian*, 22 May 1986). This affirmation of the 'British' tradition in education was confirmed by later legislation, principally the Education Reform Act of 1988, and the 'National Curriculum', which placed 'a standard language, a definitive canon of English literature and a single, shared narrative of the nation's history' (Donald and Rattansi 1992: 5) once again at the core of the school's endeavour (see also Foster 1990, Goulbourne 1991, Hiro 1991, Verma (ed.) 1989). This perspective was reinforced in 1996 by the government's chief adviser on the curriculum who called for the 'development of a British cultural identity in all schoolchildren, regardless of their ethnic background' (*Guardian*, 19 July 1995).

In more general terms, Bissoondath (1994: 71) believes that Canadian multiculturalism has 'eradicated the centre'. What he means is that 'the historical centre and the sense of national self it offered are, for all intents and purposes, no more. A void remains, a lack of a new and definable centre' (ibid.: 77). Similarly, Bernstein (1995: 357) cites approvingly the view expressed in the USA that multiculturalism is an 'assault on the nation . . . on the idea that we are a nation', and worries that it will all end in ethnic conflict as in Bosnia. Kymlicka dismisses such concerns. Fears of separatism are unfounded: 'Even the most politicized ethnic groups are not interested in reconstituting themselves as distinct societies or self-governing nations alongside the mainstream society' (Kymlicka 1995a: 67). Not only that, but demands for cultural rights on the part of immigrant groups are in fact intended to *aid* their integration (ibid.:

176), just as the 'ethnic revival' in the USA expressed a wish for recognition within the 'mainstream society' (ibid.: 98).

Kymlicka's critique of Glazer (1995) and of Walzer (1995) perhaps misses the point: their concerns are those of Enlightenment liberals and represent a French-style 'republican' rejection of particularism rather than a right-wing defence of the status quo. In fact, both Kymlicka and Glazer agree that excessive demands for diversity on the part of immigrant minorities are unwarranted (see Glazer 1995: 135). In their case, 'The expectation of integration is not unjust' (Kymlicka 1995*a*: 96). They themselves decided to move to the receiving societies and in doing so 'voluntarily relinquish some of the rights that go along with their original national membership' (compare Bernstein 1995: 162). 'It is absurd,' says Rex, 'for some Muslims to suggest that they can turn established Western societies into Islamic states':

immigrant communities should, as many do, accept that living in a society with its own language, religion, economic system, law, folk customs and school system, means that they must pay a price for their chosen situation. What they have to do is to learn to be culturally bilingual, to be able to operate within the institutions of their society of settlement as well as maintaining their own solidary culture (1996: 162).

But if for some multiculturalism conceded too much, for others it conceded too little.

4. Public and private domains

In a review of the Swann Report, Rex distinguished public and private domains and insisted on the need for equality of opportunity (not special provision) within the public arena. However, he goes on:

If there is only one culture in the public domain and that culture is the culture of equal opportunity, there is no reason at all why any society should insist that the norms which govern familial and community life, including such matters as marriage arrangements and religious practices, should be the same for all (1989: 14).

This he describes as 'multiculturalism in a situation of equality of opportunity' (p. 19). Verma, on the other hand, while accepting that under conditions of cultural pluralism, 'the vast majority' of those matters which distinguish one group from another 'belong in the domain of private life' (1990: 49), elsewhere appears to envisage a stronger version, with pluralism in the public domain. This 'implies that certain ethnic groups (defined by combination of religion, ethnicity or cultural values) are both relatively endogamous, and strive to retain their distinctive cultural identity through some degree of institutional separation' (1989: 238). This comes close to what Gordon (1975: 106) has called 'corporate pluralism' in which 'racial and ethnic groups are formally recognized as legally constituted entities with official standing in the society'.

Rex later conceded that the public/private distinction is difficult to operationalize in areas such as education or social work and religion (1995: 83 ff.), and poses a special problem for Islam because of the ways in which ideals and practice address and invade the public sphere (ibid.: 91); the term 'civil society' might be more helpful, but not decisively so. None the less, if 'public domain' refers to law, politics, and the economy, as Rex himself proposes (1996: 18), it points to an important area of contemporary society from which Rex believes ethnicity should be banished. To do otherwise raises the danger of replacing the ideals of egalitarian multiculturalism with pluralism of a Furnivall–Smith kind (ibid.: 20). The idea that cultural diversity is for the domestic sphere, for the private world of the family etc., not for the public world of political relations, is something which Parekh believes to have been fundamental to the 'liberal integrationism' characteristic of British policy since the 1960s (1990: 64). It certainly represents the view of someone like Glazer: 'To me . . . the overall direction of American society has been towards a society with a common identity, based on common ideals, one in which group identities are respected as private and individual choices but in which these identities are strictly excluded from a formal, legal, constitutional role in the polity' (1995: 137–8). Ethnicity is 'symbolic' in Gans's sense (1979), and should remain so.

Although Parekh is opposed to minority cultures being thus confined to the 'private realm' (1990: 67), what he advocates is no more (but no less) than a widening and deepening of liberal integrationism to offer more room for diversity in the public arena than exists at present, for example through the provision of mother-tongue teaching and bilingual education in schools. At the same time minorities 'must accept the full obligations of British citizenship', and acquire mastery of the English language and British history (p. 70). Similarly, he rejects any form of legal pluralism: 'Britain cannot allow separate legal systems for different communities without violating the fundamental principles of common citizenship and equality before the law' (p. 72). None the less, he is convinced that 'the distinct character of ethnic communities needs to be recognised by our legal system', and the law 'can and should accommodate acceptable cultural differences without violating these principles' (p. 72).

Legal pluralism, the coexistence of two or more distinct legal systems, characterized British and French colonial systems under policies of 'association' and indirect rule, as it did the Ottoman Empire. In British India, for example, Hindus and Muslims were governed, so far as family law was concerned, by separate codes, such as the Muslim Personal Law (Hooker 1975: 95 ff., Brass 1991: 80–2), and Muslims in French North Africa had their own *statut personnel*. Indeed, Hooker (in 1975) appeared to suggest that Muslims resident or domiciled in France '*continue* to be governed by Islamic law unless they renounce their personal statute in accordance with the law of 10 September 1946' (pp. 212–13, my emphasis). In support of this he cites the judgement in the case of *Fatma Kali* v. *Hamache* of 1957 which confirmed that 'Whereas the Moslem rules were legally adopted by the French Parliament for French Moslems in Algeria, so the French courts must apply, purely and simply, to their class of citizens, the statute which is specific to it and has been legally recognized for it' (in Hooker 1975: 213). 'Continue' gives the misleading impression that a practice that in the colonial period was an extension of a right available to French Muslim citizens when resident in their home department was maintained after Algerian independence. It is none the less interesting that a form of legal pluralism existed for Muslim residents in *metropolitan France* during the earlier period.

Poulter, whose *English Law and Ethnic Minority Customs* provides an excellent textbook style guide to the important legal decisions in this field to 1986, argues elsewhere that the English legal system has in fact 'accommodated divergent ethnic and religious practices and beliefs in a constructive manner' (1990: 16; see also Parekh 1995: 314), and favours maintaining the current 'legal monism' coupled with 'flexibility to accommodate the cultural needs of the ethnic minority communities' (p. 22). The scope for traditional customary practice to be supported by English courts appears to be enormous (see Norgren and Nanda 1988 for an account of American experience). Take, for example, the case of *Alhaji Mohammed* v. *Knott* (1969). This involved a Nigerian who had married under Islamic law, and brought to England, a 13-year-old girl. When he took her for medical treatment, the doctor informed the police, and in due course the court committed her into care under the Children and Young Persons Act of 1963, as being in moral danger. This was overturned on appeal, with the Lord Chief Justice stating that the case could not be judged by reference to local, British standards: 'it could only be said that she was in moral danger if one was considering someone brought up and living in our way of life'. To do otherwise would be to ignore 'the way of life in which she was brought up, and her husband was brought up' (in Poulter 1986: 20). (Sexual intercourse in this instance would not be unlawful as the two partners were 'validly married'.)

In *Mohammed* v. *Knott* the law is a long way from 'the man on the Clapham omnibus' as the arbitrator of reasonableness. Similarly, and perhaps equally problematically given current British practice, courts have supported arranged marriages. In *Hirani* v. *Hirani* (1983), the court ruled that opponents of an arranged marriage had to demonstrate that the threats or pressure to undertake the marriage were such as to destroy the validity of any assent. Poulter calls this the 'overborne will' theory, and adds: 'The dilemma posed by arranged marriages is to distinguish between proper and improper pressures imposed not by the other party to the marriage but by the petitioner's own family and the wider ethnic community' (p. 31). Thus the existing law gives a great deal of room for ethnically specific practices, and Poulter looks at a number of areas where it might be further amended or changed, to widen the scope or simply to clear up uncertainties. These range from the recognition of polygamous marriages (p. 58); 'defining who are members of a family in the eyes of the law' (p. 96); *talaq* divorces (under Islamic rules), and 'extrajudicial consensual divorces' in general (p. 125); rules governing the fostering of children, and their discipline (pp. 145–

70); scarification and tattooing (pp. 148 ff.); and the alignment of Muslim graves in cemeteries (p. 241).

None the less, the scope for expanding the recognition of other cultural practices if considerable, is not limitless. The possible extension of the law of blasphemy, perhaps via a new concept of 'group libel', to cover religions other than Christianity was widely debated in the wake of the Rushdie affair, and rejected as a possible option by the government among others (Commission for Racial Equality 1990*b*). Poulter (1986: 156 ff.) provides an account of the discussion surrounding the Prohibition of Female Circumcision Act of 1985 which illustrates one way limits are imposed. The Bill, while outlawing most types of female circumcision, wished to exclude from the prohibition certain kinds of operations in the genital region which were necessary on medical grounds. These included the recognized medical practice of 'trimming' carried out in a very small number of cases each year on women who believe that their genitalia are in some way abnormal. In a first attempt to exclude this practice from prohibition, the Government included a clause which would have stated that when such an operation was proposed on the grounds of the mental health of the patient 'no account shall be taken of the effect on that person of any belief on the part of this or any other person that the operation is required as a matter of custom or ritual' (p. 157). The Commission for Racial Equality, however, argued that such a clause would 'suggest that some reasons for [the] state of mind [of the patient] may be acceptable and others, broadly confined to those which might affect persons of African origin or descent are not', and this, in the Commission for Racial Equality's view, would be discriminatory. In response, the Government minister concerned stated that 'the essential purpose of the whole Bill . . . is to prevent acts of cruelty or harm from being performed under the cloak of custom or ritual . . . *these particular customary practices are not compatible with the culture of this country*' (in Poulter 1986: 158, my emphasis). In the event, after considerable discussion in the House of Lords, agreement was reached on a clause which simply stated that among operations excluded from the prohibition were those which were 'necessary for the physical or mental health of the person on whom [they are] performed'.

Although both Poulter and Parekh argue that the range of customary cultural practices recognized as valid by the courts might be increased, they are adamant in their opposition to any form of institutionalized legal pluralism, as advocated by some Muslim groups (Parekh 1990: 72, Poulter 1990: 21, Goulbourne 1991: 237). Hiro, on the other hand, has called precisely for legal pluralism of this kind, advocating the introduction of a distinct code of Muslim personal law similar to that in operation in British India, and still available to Muslims in that country (Hiro 1991: 312). Modood, making a similar comparison with colonial India, and referring to a delegation which put the case for such a law to the Home Office in 1989, also notes that some Muslims have begun calling for the implementation in Britain of a 'variation of the *millat* system' (1992*a*: 273). In the area of education (separate schools), law (specifically family law), and to a degree political representation (the Muslim Parliament, which Samad also likens to the millet system, 1992: 517, or in another context debates about black sections in the British Labour Party, Layton-Henry 1992: 163 ff.), there was during the 1980s pressure for some form of institutionalized, publicly recognized, separatism, especially on the part of British Muslims. These pressures are seen as a severe test of any policy of pluralistic integration. As the Home Minister, John Patten, put it in 1989: If there is in Britain 'plenty of room for diversity and variety', there is none for 'separatism or segregation' (in appendix in Commission for Racial Equality 1990*b*: 84), a sentiment echoed by Frybès (1992), Lapeyronnie (1992), Yuval-Davis (1992), Parekh, Poulter, and many others across the political and ethnic spectrum in both Britain and France (see Rex 1996 and contributors to Rex and Drury 1994).

5. Institutional pluralism

Despite the state's attempt to restore an assimilationist perspective in British education, many people remained committed to a multicultural outlook: Hiro notes in the third edition of his book *Black British, White British* that since it first appeared in the early 1970s, 'my idea of social pluralism has become accepted wisdom' (1991: vii). The pluralism that was accepted, however, was always one confined within certain limits. Thus Jeffcoate (1984: 118), who described himself as a 'modified' pluralist, spoke for many when he declared that he did not believe British society could or should tolerate every instance of cultural diversity: for example, and they are all Islamic, female circumcision, the subordination of women, and *halal* meat. He likewise opposed mother-tongue maintenance within the school system, and any religious provision, particularly of Islamic doctrine, but supported the right of children to wear ethnically specific school dress (1984: 125). Whether or not Jeffcoate was correct in labelling his views 'modified pluralism', he was undoubtedly typical of many teachers of the period who were concerned to maintain an *integrated* education system, education for all, perhaps in another sense. Certainly, throughout the 1980s the views of central and local government, as well as those of educationists (as represented by the Swann Report's majority conclusions in this area, pp. 501 ff.) opposed any form of *separate* or special education for the children of ethnic minorities. Some kind of separatism has, however, long been permitted within the private and voluntary-aided school sector in Britain.

The desirability of a different, in a sense ethnically specific, kind of schooling for some pupils was recognized by the Education Acts of 1902, 1906, and 1944 which designated a 'voluntary-aided' sector of schools run by the Church of England, Catholics, Jews, and Methodists, overseen by the state. In 1988 there were some 5,000 such schools, most of them Christian. Twenty-one were Jewish, but none represented faiths such as Islam or Hinduism (Commission for Racial Equality 1990*c*: 4). There were, on the other hand, a number of *private*

Muslim schools offering full-time education. (These are quite different from the supplementary classes found in the informal ethnic schools sector.) One prominent private Muslim school in the 1980s was the Islamia Primary School which opened in *c.*1983 with the backing of Yusuf Islam, the former pop singer and convert to Islam Cat Stevens. In 1993, when visited by a reporter from the *Independent* newspaper, the school which had over 100 pupils was housed in the former Kilburn Grammar School buildings, which the Islamia Schools Trust had bought for £2.5m. (The buildings also contained the Private Secondary Islamia Girls School.) The primary school's syllabus was devoted to an Islamic education for between 15 per cent and 20 per cent of the time, including study of the Arabic language, the Islamic religion, and 'how to live as a Muslim'. The rest of the syllabus was more orthodox, covering English, mathematics, and science. (The school was particularly proud of its science facilities.) The reporter commented: 'In many respects its classrooms resemble those of any primary school . . . But there are differences. Some of the writing is in Arabic—all children learn Arabic as a second language—and the paintings and drawings are almost exclusively abstract and geometric, with not a human figure or animal in sight.' This was explained to the reporter as ensuring that the followers of Islam are 'not tempted to worship idols' (*Independent*, 4 April 1993). There were some 20 such private schools at this time, with a total enrolment of over 2,000 (*Independent*, 7 February 1991; five years later there were about 40, Runnymede Trust 1997: 18). They were fee-paying (the Islamia primary school charged parents £1,100 per annum, *Independent*, 20 August 1993), and clearly offered only limited opportunities for the great majority of parents. Yet there was a substantial demand for them: Islamia claimed a waiting list of over 1,000. (Khanum 1992 describes a Muslim girls school in Bradford.)

The Swann Committee had considered the extension of the voluntary-aided sector to include Muslim schools. The majority report had opposed this, though a minority entered a dissenting note (p. 515). From the early 1980s onwards, there were numerous attempts to take over local authority schools as Muslim educational establishments with voluntary-aided status. In 1983, for example, the Muslim Parents Association in Bradford, arguing that Muslims should have the same rights as other faiths, had sought to acquire and reorganize several schools (primary, middle, and secondary) in the city. Not all Muslims were in support of this proposal which was opposed by the city's Council of Mosques, the Asian Youth Movement, and the Community Relations Council, and eventually rejected by the local authority (Halstead 1988: 44–5). Halstead comments: 'For many people, it appears that the call for the establishment of Muslim voluntary-aided schools marks the limit of what can be tolerated in a multi-cultural society, and it is the only serious request from a minority group in Bradford so far to meet with an outright refusal' (1988: 45).

In the late 1980s and early 1990s several similar proposals were made in West Yorkshire, the London area, and in Glasgow, relying on the older legislation concerning voluntary-aided status or the new so-called 'opting out' provisions of the 1988 Education Reform Act. None has been successful to date. In the early 1990s the Islamia School tried twice to gain funded status, but permission was refused by the Secretary of State. The benefits for the school would have been huge: it would have received reimbursement for all of its recurrent expenditure, including salaries, and for 85 per cent of its capital costs (*Independent*, 4 April 1993). By the summer of 1994 the latest of these proposals had reached an advanced stage of local agreement (*Guardian*, 31 May 1994), a bid by a private Muslim girls high school to become 'Britain's first state-funded Muslim school' receiving the support of community leaders and the local council. It only remained for the Education Secretary (then Gillian Shephard) to give approval, but this she refused (*Guardian*, 17 February 1995).

Such proposals had the backing, on equity grounds, of the Commission for Racial Equality. In a pamphlet which reviewed arguments for and against such developments, the Commission concluded that desire for separate, voluntary-aided schools was not necessarily a sign that groups wish to segregate themselves. They also reflected a wish to 'opt in':

The spokespeople of the Islamia Schools Trust, the Seventh day Adventists and the Orthodox Jewish community in Hackney, for example, all of whom are actively seeking voluntary status for existing schools, share an impressive degree of unity in declaring their desire to be part of the state system, not only to benefit from it but to be integrated into it and to contribute to it. They do not want to be trapped in the private sector (Commission for Racial Equality 1990c: 16).

In any event, the education system must not discriminate against a particular religion, such as Islam. As an editorial in the *Independent* argued, there was an equity argument for allowing Muslims to have their own schools (20 August 1993). The issue was raised again in 1997 by the Runnymede Trust in its consultation paper on 'Islamophobia', and in January 1998 the new Labour Government finally conceded the point. (According to Roosens 1989: 143, Islamic schools have the right under Belgian law to state subsidies, but by the early 1990s no such schools had been created (Nielsen 1995: 74–5). Islamic religious instruction is, however, widely available in state schools.)

It is not clear that 'opting in' reflects all opinion within the Muslim community. Foremost among supporters of the separate school idea was the so-called 'Muslim Parliament'. In October 1990 Dr Kalim Saddiqi (who had Iranian backing) announced the intention of establishing such a body, with some 150 'MMPs' who would promote the interests of Muslims up and down the country (*Independent*, 29 October 1990; see also Rex 1995: 91, 1996: 233). In January 1991 a letter from Musadiq Dhalla of the *Muslim News*, referring to a comparison which had been made with the Jewish Board of Deputies and the Synod of the Church of England, pointed out that: 'The Board of Deputies aspires to the successful integration of the Jewish community into British society, while the Muslim parliament is based on a strategy of creating separate institutions.' So far as his own publication was concerned, it was believed that 'The Muslim community has to organise itself . . . politically and economically, to fully participate in British society without losing its Islamic identity' (*Independent*, 8 January 1990). When the parliament eventually met for the first time in early 1992, high on its agenda was education, with calls for the immediate establishment of Muslim voluntary-aided schools, and, eventually, an Islamic university (*Independent*, 5, 7 January, 19 March 1992). The parliament, whose members one influential Muslim has described as 'hand-picked and [without] very high standing in the Muslim community' (Ahsan 1994: 352), also attacked the Commission for Racial Equality, and called for its abolition, for 'rejecting the centrality of religion and trying to assimilate Muslims into accepting "false national, racial or linguistic identities" '. The Commission, it said, was trying to 'ensure that Muslims and their religion would be reduced to a series of rituals so that gradually Muslims would become like British Christians' (*Independent*, 24 August 1992). As earlier in Bradford, many Muslims themselves (including, for example, parents in cities such as Glasgow, *Independent*, 28 August 1991) continued to oppose proposals for separate schools (Modood *et al.* 1994: 53 ff.), and were hostile to the idea of a Muslim parliament. A correspondent in the *Independent* (25 June 1991), warning against the setting up of Muslim schools, reminded readers that 'the hardliners are far from representative of the majority' of Muslims, and the academic, Akbar Ahmed advised that 'the further you pull away from the mainstream, the more isolated the community becomes' (*Independent*, 19 June 1991).

Two events influenced the development of the debate about separatism within the Muslim community in the early 1990s: the Gulf War, and the Rushdie affair (see Werbner 1994 for an account of the former). Dr Saddiqi, who reportedly said on television that Salman Rushdie 'should be taken to Iran to face trial' (*Independent*, 30 December 1990) admitted that the Muslim parliament 'would not have come into being without the momentum of the Rushdie affair'. The significance of that episode as a test case of pluralism in Britain needs little underlining. For many Muslims, as Hiro suggests, it became a focus for the many difficulties which they felt they and their families encountered in living according to the tenets of Islam in a society which was Christian on the one hand and secular on the other (Hiro 1991: 182 ff.; see further Samad 1992, and Ahsan 1994: 352–4, who also mentions the significance for the emergent solidarity of British Muslims of Muslim–Hindu conflict in India). It also brought out a strong, at times racist, strain of anti-Islamic feeling (as did the Gulf War), which was as apparent among liberal intellectuals as in the popular press (Hiro 1991: 312). As Gilroy remarked, many on the left 'found their common-sense commitment to a principled form of cultural relativism tested to the limit by the sight of book burnings' (1993*a*: 57). Like separate schools, these things were beyond the pale of what could be tolerated by British society.

Samuel has suggested that recent immigrants seem less interested in integration than previous generations, and that 'British society seems to have lost its assimilative power' (1989*b*: xxxiv; see also Ballard 1994: 28, and Calleo 1995: 17, and Schmuhl 1995: 143, for the USA). Moves towards separatism, on the part of Muslims and other ethnic minorities, partly reflect a desire to create institutions in which life can be led in accordance with ethnically or religiously specific beliefs and values which emanate from elsewhere. They also respond to a felt need to erect barriers of protection against rejection by the dominant society. In an obituary of Kalim Saddiqi (*Guardian*, 20 April 1996), Tariq Ali commented that '[Saddiqi] found support among many of the young Muslims in Britain. During the 1960s and 1970s, Asian youths had been attracted to secular projects . . . but during the 1980s a new generation, alienated from mainstream politics of any kind, began to find a new identity in religion.' Samad's careful account (1992) of the progress of the Rushdie affair in the city of Bradford (see also Rex 1996: 234 ff.) shows how the response, especially among young Muslims, must be understood against a longer term background of economic recession and local events such as Honeyford's intervention in the schools' debate. Rejected on racist or quasi-racist grounds, many in the ethnic minorities concluded that 'their humanity must be found in communities external to the mainstream of society into which they were and are being born' (Goulbourne 1991: 122).

6. Against the communal option

Kymlicka believes there is little support for separatism on the part of ethnic minorities: Muslim educational demands he dismisses as 'atypical' (1995*a*: 177). Certainly, on practical grounds alone, it is very difficult to envisage a 'federal' solution for ethnic minorities in Europe which lack a territory (Habermas 1994: 128). None the less that there is some support for some form of separatism is abundantly clear.

Goulbourne is extremely hostile to this 'communal option', which he describes as 'highly dangerous' (1991: 14): 'the increasing desire of many individuals to be part of an identifiable group, and for each group not only to exist almost entirely within its own confines but also to ensure that individuals conform to the supposed norms of the group' (ibid.: 13). He sees support coming partly from ethnic minorities themselves, for whom separatism appears the only way in which they can preserve a distinct cultural identity in a hostile social environment (p. 73), and partly from the British preference for a mode of social organization derived from a colonial tradition of the Dual Mandate (p. 50). 'In post-imperial Britain', he argues, 'the overwhelming impact of much state action . . . has been to create a new Britain in which discrete communities, defined in terms of colour/race/culture, have little in common with each other' (p. 25). Encouragement of the communal option, he adds, represents a 'commitment to a future in which the non-white minorities have no place, or if they are to have a place this must be outside of the mainstream of social and political life enjoyed by the majority of the population' (p. 231). The emergent model would replicate the colonial-type plural society in Furnivall's sense in which

each so-called racial group should live apart, attend separate schools, belong to separate social and sporting clubs, participate in different areas of the economy . . . In short, that the different groups of people in Britain enjoy only a *market relationship*; people of African, Asian and European backgrounds increasingly meet only where they buy and sell commodities (ibid.; compare Furnivall 1948: 304).

Goulbourne overemphasizes the extent to which this type of model is the product of *conscious* state policy, which in Britain (and France) has consistently *opposed* any formal separatism (for example in education), though a belated move towards the acceptance of separate private (voluntary-aided) Muslim schools might prove him right. None the less, he is correct to suggest that the encouragement of multiculturalism engenders conditions under which the communal option becomes a serious social possibility. Although seeking to 'legitimize heterogeneity in British national culture' (Yuval-Davis 1992: 283), multicultural policies have paradoxically 'created a space for separatist and fundamentalist movements which seek to impose uniformity and homogeneity on all their adherents' (ibid.). By creating opportunities for the formation of cultural blocks, multiculturalism has enabled interest groups (or fractions claiming to represent the interests of particular groups) to emerge through a dialectical process (Anthias and Yuval-Davis 1993: 38, Sahgal and Yuval-Davis 1992: 14).

The idea of a positive, identity-affirming separatism is, of course, advocated by others besides ethnic minorities. For example, Peter Tatchell, a well-known, and controversial, gay rights activist in Britain in the 1980s and 1990s, although acknowledging the progress made in the status of gay people in the twenty-five years following the Stonewall riots, has argued that much of this progress stemmed from the actions of gays themselves. This led him to the conclusion that the way forward for gays was 'self-help and community empowerment'. With an emphasis on self-reliance, he believes,

we can create our own homo-affirming community and safe queer space where we do not have to justify ourselves or plead with heterosexuals for acceptance. We can give each other the support that straight society denies us. Developing the lesbian and gay community as a focus of counter-culture and counter-power helps undermine the grip that homophobia has on our lives. A well organised, powerful queer community is more difficult for straights to ignore. From a position of strength, we can better challenge hetero-supremacism (*Observer*, 19 June 1994).

Substituting 'black' or 'Muslim' for 'queer', 'gay', etc., 'white' for 'heterosexual' or 'straight', 'racism' for 'homophobia' in that extract reveals a high degree of similarity between arguments proposed on the part of what are otherwise very different minorities, and perhaps displays the extent that the discourse of one draws on the rhetoric of the other.

Separatism of this kind may well take the form, not of the social pluralism of colonial societies, which Goulbourne fears, but of American-style political pluralism, with which he is also uncomfortable (1991: 232). In this, socially, culturally, economically, and *politically* distinct minorities are regarded as legitimate interest groups who compete to advance their cause (Hobsbawm 1992: 155). This is the style of politics advocated in the USA by Iris Marion Young, who believes disadvantaged minorities should be 'provided with public funding to enable them to formulate their own policy initiatives [with] policy-makers . . . obliged to take these views into account' (Phillips 1993: 116). Young also envisages what is sometimes called a 'rainbow' coalition linking minorities of all kinds including blacks, Native Americans, Hispanics, gay men, lesbians, the working class, the elderly, the poor, the mentally and physically disabled, and women (Phillips 1993: 93, citing Young 1989: 261; see also Kymlicka 1995*a*: 145). This is an unlikely alliance in the British context, where feminists and Muslim separatists have been at odds over education and the Rushdie affair.

The debate about whether and on what terms societies such as France and Britain should accommodate Islam has provided a major test for ideas of pluralism of both an integrationist and separatist kind. In numerous ways, the Islamic presence now makes itself felt in the daily life of many of the countries of Western Europe. The Rushdie affair or the 'Headscarves' may catch the headlines, but for some two decades now it has been in myriad events of a less dramatic though no less complex kind that the social and cultural issues raised by that presence have emerged. What does a substantial, growing immigrant Islamic population mean for European countries? What does living in Europe mean for Muslims or those of Muslim origin? The contributors to Gerholm and Lithman's collection (1988) provided a timely opportunity for a comparative assessment of these questions, offering material from a wide range of countries which, *inter alia*, showed the diversity of the Islamic population of Europe. A wide range of national and regional groupings of migrants, and hence of varieties of Islam, have come to the receiving countries, and emerge, in the migrant situation. This ethnic diversity, reflected in organizational diversity, has meant that nowhere does a single group emerge as representative of 'the' Muslim community. In fact, the latter does not exist and this frequently poses problems for the institutions of the receiving society. The activities of sending society governments, who attempt in various degrees to form their Muslims into a community and represent it, add a further complication.

Though there is, therefore, a great diversity of environments within which possible expressions of Islam, collective and individual, can occur, common to many groups and individuals is the desire to 'make a place' for the religion (Joly 1988). Compared with France, where the matter of headscarves proved a major stumbling block, Britain has generally made much greater room for Islam than have many other countries. None the less, the Rushdie affair revealed major tensions and differences, on all sides, as well as major misunderstandings as to the nature of other parties' concerns (compare, for example, Modood 1992*a* and

Yuval-Davis 1992 for various shades of Muslim and non-Muslim opinion). There is moreover widespread throughout Europe what amounts to a 'great fear' of Islam, or rather of an imagined Islam of a fundamentalist kind (a 'misrecognized' Islam, it might be called, see Gilsenan 1982). This has been accompanied by what has been described as a 'racialization' of Islam which is represented not as a body of religious doctrine, open to all who aspire to membership of the world community of the religion (Mashuq Ibn Ally 1990: 22), but as the property of non-Western groups (specifically of Asian origin in Britain), and thus an ethnic, or rather racial, trait (Sahgal and Yuval-Davis 1992: 15, Anthias and Yuval-Davis 1993: 53, and Kushner 1996: 135 for an interesting example). 'Muslim' has thus become a demonized ethnic category.

The Rushdie affair illustrated this, bringing out a strain of anti-Asian, even racist, sentiment even among liberal intellectuals (Gilroy 1993a, Hiro 1991, Weldon 1989). This meant that many Asian and black intellectuals had to walk a fine line: supporting Rushdie's right to publish but condemning the 'anti-Muslim and anti-third world sentiments' (Bhabha 1989: 35) to which the affair gave expression. In their 'nervous shuffle' (Kanneh 1995: 71) they also felt obliged to distance themselves from what was conventionally described as Muslim 'fundamentalism' (Yuval-Davis 1992). Thus Bhabha (1989: 35): 'Those of us who have experienced the authoritarian and patriarchal conditions of orthodox communities, of any colour or creed, and have witnessed their attempts to stifle dissent and discussion, can never endorse demands for censorship and unquestioned conformity.' The point recalls debates among French Jews for whom the privilege of belonging to a self-governing community was double-edged, entailing subjection to the rabbinate and a particular form of conservative Judaism.

Modood has denied that in the British context fundamentalism in the strict sense had much to do with the response of the Asian community to the Rushdie affair (see also Parekh 1995: 307–8, for a summary of Muslim complaints against Rushdie, and Schnapper 1994, who rightly emphasizes the diversity of Islam in Europe). For British Muslims, many of whom criticized the stand taken by London-based intellectuals, 'the reduction of their religion to a selfish sexual appetite [in the *Satanic Verses*] was no more a contribution to literary discourse than pissing upon the Bible is a theological argument' (Modood 1992a: 269). None the less, fear of an imagined fundamentalism has been an important influence on thinking about Islam and about Asian minorities in Britain, for example in debates over separate schools (Commission for Racial Equality 1990c: 16 ff.) Halstead (1988), locating his discussion of multicultural education in wider debates about pluralism, concluded that for there to be any society at all there has to be common ground in 'a basic social morality', 'commitment to the pluralist ideal', and 'the acceptance of a common system of law and government' (p. 217). This common ground, these shared values, are threatened by 'groups whose fundamental commitments include the acceptance of a divine order of authority that affects every area of their lives and prevents them from *celebrating* a diversity which includes groups totally antipathetic to their own beliefs and values' (p. 219). He suggests that although Muslims share certain values of British society, they are none the less representative of groups which are 'reluctant to accept a liberal framework of values as a basis for educational decision-making' (pp. 227–8).

Thus, in the 1980s and 1990s local and global forces conspired to construct 'Muslim' as an ethnicized and racialized social category in Britain and other countries of Europe, and Muslims themselves increasingly made common cause across divisions of origin, language, and sect (P. Lewis 1994, Samad 1992, A. Shaw 1994). And 'however much [young British Bengalis] may seek to identify themselves as British', say Gardner and Shukur, '[they] regularly find that others assume them to be first and foremost Muslim' (1994: 162).

10

Pluralism and the Postmodern Condition

> Yannick Noah, the flamboyant French former tennis star, is causing uproar
> on the airwaves with a rap version of the Marseillaise . . . The song . . .
> ends with a plea for 'liberté, fraternité et diversité'.
>
> (*Guardian*, 17 September 1997.)

1. From the patrimonial to the post-industrial

Let me recall the argument of this book. I have been concerned with plural
societies, and began by asking how the political process, working through the
authoritative institutions of society (the state), shapes and reproduces difference. The state has in turn been seen as embedded in a wider system of
economy, culture, and technology, and so the emphasis has been on exploring
the politicization of difference in the context of particular configurations of
state and society. Two such configurations have received special attention: the
patrimonial state and the modern, industrial, nation-state. In these two, the
terms which best describe the place accorded to difference of the kind which
is generally called 'ethnic' are, respectively, incorporation and assimilation. In
the patrimonial state, ethnic and cultural difference did not, normally, pose any
great difficulty so long as the groups which constituted the polity (and early
states were often highly mixed linguistically and culturally) paid their dues,
literally and metaphorically. The Ottomans are particularly instructive in this
regard. They 'cared less about how their empire was run so long as each of their
dominions provided them with a steady supply of revenue' (Ingrao 1996: section 3). As Mansell says: 'The Ottoman government was more interested in
raising revenue than saving souls' (1995: 48).

Patrimonial rulers rarely attempted to spread uniformity of culture unless,
like some, but by no means all, Islamic (and Christian) polities, they were
committed (as the Ottomans were not) to proselytizing on behalf of their
religion. Modern nation-states, on the other hand, have been grounded in the
fostering of common identities and homogeneous cultures. Whether their
nation-building ideologies were of *Gemeinschaft* or *Gesellschaft* type, their rulers
eschewed difference, and promoted the homogenization which the economic,
social, and political configuration demanded. And in pursuing such goals they

invaded and captured the institutions of civil society. Colonialism was in this respect ambivalent: 'patrimonial' in so far as it emphasized the extraction of resources, 'modern' in so far as the colonial powers believed they had a mission to uplift and transform their colonial subjects.

Nation-building in Europe and elsewhere often incorporated linguistically, culturally, and economically disparate regions within a single polity. Many were 'mosaic' states (Strayer 1963), consisting of diverse localities pulled together, often unwillingly, under the hegemony of some powerful 'centre'. Elsewhere (Grillo 1980) I have called them 'disjunctive' societies because the incorporative process sustained, but also created, various kinds of differentiation and difference between and within the constituent elements, and therefore they contain the seeds of their own dissolution. Much has been written about the integration or rather disintegration (actual or potential) of such societies: for many, 'the crisis of the nation-state' refers precisely to this. As I pointed out in Chapter 1, however, there are many crises, and this study has not really been concerned with that of the incomplete incorporation of regional, ethnic, or linguistic 'minorities'. The focus, especially in the latter half of the book, has been rather on integration of another kind.

Various nation-states apparently committed to a *Gesellschaft*, or associational, ideology of the nation-state, and to assimilative goals, have at times entered periods of social and cultural crisis around those objectives: 'crises of assimilation'. Chapters 6 to 9 explored these as they affected Britain, France, and the USA in the last decades of the nineteenth and twentieth centuries. In that last period there has been a new emphasis on difference, in terms of the demands made on society by many of its members, and what has been described as an upsurge in ethnic and cultural pluralism. That pluralism, however, takes different forms, and manifests itself in somewhat different strategic demands: multiculturalism and institutional pluralism, discussed in Chapter 9, and hybridity, examined below. I noted in Chapter 7 that in contemplating the 'revival' of ethnicity in the late twentieth-century USA, the historian John Higham made a valuable proposal in attempting to relate that phenomenon to long-term social and economic change. The present chapter develops that suggestion by seeking to locate the demand for pluralism, and the 'upsurge' or 'persistence' of ethnicity, in contemporary forms of postmodern, post-industrial state, economy, and society. It then discusses the much debated notion of 'hybridity' before returning to consider whether, despite all that has been said, despite all the criticisms, there is realistically any alternative to multiculturalism as a means of dealing with difference.

2. Pluralism and postmodernity

'Why? Why pluralism now?' Hassan's question (1987: 167), posed from within postmodern literary theory, referred not to pluralism of a social, political, or cultural kind but to an intellectual, critical, and 'methodological' pluralism, found in postmodern writing, film, architecture, and so on, where 'all styles are dialectically available in an interplay between the Now and the Not-Now' (ibid.: 171). None the less, that same question is appropriate for a different context, that of the cultural and ethnic pluralism of contemporary Britain, France, and the USA. Why *these sorts of pluralism now*? Specifically, what connection might be made between pluralism and the condition referred to as 'postmodernity'? Gilroy's sense that the syncretism or hybridity which he explores in relation to black identity must be understood with reference to the contemporary economic and political (as well as intellectual) contexts in which they occur is a strong indication that there are issues to be addressed. But what constitutes the 'postmodern' and (closely related term) the 'post-industrial' condition?

A distinction should be drawn between *postmodernity* as a descriptive and analytical category and *postmodernism* as an intellectual enterprise or philosophical project. One may be highly sceptical about the latter while accepting that 'post-industrial', and more recently 'postmodern', are concepts of considerable value in assisting us to grasp and explain significant features of the contemporary condition, at least in the 'West', or the 'North'. 'North', of course, does not refer to a location on the globe. It is not a geographical expression so much as a social, economic, and political one, referring to the rich and powerful 'advanced' industrial countries found mostly (but by no means exclusively) in the north-western 'quadrisphere' of the planet.

My own scepticism about the intellectual enterprise derives from the damage that postmodernism as philosophical project has done to my own discipline. There have been several controversies of a deep and at times bitter kind in social anthropology, for example over structuralism and interactionism in the 1960s, Marxism and feminism in the 1970s, and semantic and applied anthropology in the 1980s. Though no holds were barred, these controversies did not affect the core of the subject: anthropology is a broad church able to accommodate a wide variety of adherents. But disputes associated with the self-styled 'postmodernist' intervention have posed a real danger of a sort of China Syndrome, a meltdown of the core.

Postmodernism in anthropology has strong affinities with postmodernism at large and in other disciplines: irony and self-reference, an emphasis on meta-narratives, a stress on language games, a shared sense of what some call 'a crisis of representation in the human sciences' (Marcus and Fischer 1986: 8). Postmodernist anthropology has taken seriously the notion that anthropologists 'construct' their data, and therefore what is central is the process of construction. This has led to an emphasis on the 'how' of gathering what become 'data' (that is fieldwork), and the way that 'data' are placed in the public domain (that is through ethnography). This in turn has led to a stress on the anthropologist as 'author', on his or her 'authority', and on the relationship between anthropologist and 'subject'. The flavour of this intervention is aptly summarized in the following:

A post-modern ethnography is a co-operatively evolved text consisting of fragments of discourse intended to invoke in the minds of both reader and writer an emergent fantasy of a possible world of commonsense reality, and thus to provoke an aesthetic integration that will have a therapeutic effect (Tyler 1986: 125).

Geertz, in many respects a prominent fellow-traveller of postmodernism, none the less recognizes the difficulties with this approach:

If anthropologists were to stop reporting how things are done in Africa and Polynesia, if they were instead to spend their time trying to find double plots in Alfred Kroeber or unreliable narrators in Max Gluckman, and if they were seriously to argue that Edward Westermarck's stories about Morocco and those of Paul Bowles relate to their subject matter in the same way, and with the same means and the same purposes, matters would indeed be in a parlous state (1988: 1–3).

Unfortunately, what Geertz suggested as unthinkable has happened, and parts of anthropology are in consequence indeed in a parlous state. The ethnographer has become more important than the 'ethnographed', indeed postmodernists would argue that it is impossible to write about them, and thus everything is reduced to reflexivity. On the whole, I agree with Firth, who has described himself as a 'a modified empiricist': 'The world may be an illusion— I know of no means of proving it is not. But it is expedient to behave *as if* there be a substantial reality that can be encountered, with chartable effect and some possibility of prediction' (1989: 50).

There is, however, a side to this which is potentially more important and interesting. There is an ambiguity in postmodernist writing in the social sciences: are we dealing with an intellectual stance (on language and so forth) or type of culture and society whose features are captured by the phrase 'postmodern'? Or both? When Tyler says 'A post-modern ethnography is fragmentary because it cannot be otherwise' (1986: 131), does he speak philosophically, or is he referring to that 'thing of shreds and patches' (Hannerz 1992: 34), the postmodern culture which ethnography attempts to capture? 'The breaking up of the grand narratives', says Lyotard, referring to what in his view is one of the principal features of the postmodern condition, 'leads to what some authors analyze in terms of the dissolution of the social bond and the disintegration of social aggregates into a mass of individual atoms thrown into the absurdity of Brownian motion' (Lyotard 1986: 15). This much cited passage represents what might be called a 'Heraclitan' view of society ('Everything is in a state of flux and nothing remains the same'). How far can such views of the contemporary social condition be justified, and in what way can they be related to discussions of difference?

3. The postmodern and the post-industrial

Concepts of the postmodern and post-industrial intersect each other in numerous ways. As Rose (1991: 21) points out, definitions of the two have been elaborated alongside and in relation to each other. Best known, and most persuasive, of the attempts to connect the two has been that of Lyotard, who, citing Bell and Touraine, identified the postmodern as the cultural aspect of the post-industrial. Elaborating this, Jameson has glossed postmodernity as involving

the production of postmodern people capable of functioning in a very peculiar socio-economic world indeed, one whose structure and objective features and requirements—if we had a proper account of them—would constitute the situation to which 'postmodernism' is a response (1991: xv).

So what, then, are the features of the 'very peculiar world' to which postmodernism is a response and for which it is a preparation?

The term post-industrial has been in circulation for most of this century. Rose (1991: xi) dates it to *c*.1914, though at that time it was used by American syndicalist critics of the 'modern' industrial system to refer to certain social, economic, and political alternatives to it. The ideas behind this original usage were in essence anti- rather than post-Fordist, and it might be said that Kallen's proposals on cultural pluralism in the 1920s fell within this camp. In the 1960s and 1970s, however, the term reappeared in a different guise, used as a convenient way of summarizing the apparent changes (mainly of a socio-economic kind) in the 'advanced' industrial economies of North America and Western Europe in the affluent years which followed World War II. It was this notion of 'post' or 'advanced' industrial society which informed, *inter alia*, my own account of immigration in Lyon, France, in the 1970s (Grillo 1985). 'Industrial', 'post-industrial', 'modern', 'postmodern' (and 'early' or 'patrimonial') are ideal-type constructs through which social scientists carve up semantically what is in reality a continuum. Contrasts between modern and postmodern, or industrial and post-industrial inevitably hide continuities and emphasize discontinuities between one era or form of polity and another, as Gilroy, for example, is well aware (1993*b*: 2, 42). None the less, it is important to try to grasp some sense of the difference between 'then' and 'now', and of the significance of changes that have occurred in the course of the twentieth century.

By the late 1970s writers such as Dahrendorf (1959), Bell (1973), and Touraine (1974), had appeared to define a post-industrial form of society of which the following were the principal features. There was, first and foremost, the central and growing importance of scientific knowledge in the organization of both production and consumption. This involved the ever wider application of 'advanced' technologies based on electronics, nuclear physics, chemistry, micro-biology, and latterly genetics. Linked to that was the demand for highly skilled manpower, at many different levels of skill, with a consequent growth of a white-collar, white-coated labour force (and an education system to match). Industrial production was becoming more and more specialized by unit (within the production process), and by region. This created greater geographical interdependence, and interdependence between industries, but also led to greater inter-regional and inter-industrial disparities. Specialization and concentration meant that the economic and occupational profiles of different regions diverged. At the extreme, some flourished, others became wastelands. The organization of production and consumption was continually increasing in scale, with a corresponding centralization of key decisions at higher and higher levels, including, supranational levels. Organizationally, 'rational', bureaucratic modes of operation prevailed. The 'managerial revolution', however, meant that the simple idea of the ownership of the means of production became a problematic, and increasingly irrelevant means of differentiating between those who had power and privilege and those who did not.

In the 1960s and 1970s there was, generally speaking, a high wage economy, at least in the North/West, though there were great disparities, some of which represented an overturning of traditional differentials: nineteenth-century labour aristocracies found themselves displaced from their once pre-eminent position. At the same time, and despite the growth of the white-collared, white-coated labour force, the work of the clerk and the secretary (what the French call *employés*) became increasingly similar to that of the factory worker in a Fordist-style production system. The 'deskilling' of many tasks due to technological change often meant that the gap between traditionally skilled and unskilled occupations declined. The lowest paid jobs in the older, declining industries, or the deskilled sectors of the industries, were given over to the least-favoured elements of the population, immigrants and women. These changes were accompanied by a high degree of *physical*, and a significant degree of *social*, mobility with the break-up (and breakdown) of traditional industrial and urban communities (old industries, inner cities), and what was seen as increasing individuation and isolation.

In all the economies of the 'quadrisphere', the tertiary (service) sector became increasingly important. This was related to the growing significance of *consumption*. But production and consumption were in turn closely linked, with the latter controlled, tailored, and consciously oriented through advertising. There was homogenization, but also, in different ways and at different levels, heterogenization of patterns of consumption. Products became standardized, but a much wider range of goods became more readily available, and there was greater variety in patterns of consumption by individual consumers. At the same time, the language of 'consumerism' spread to services which had previously been thought of in non-commercial terms, and there was a shift in the focuses of conflict both within the production system and outside of it. Summarizing some of these changes, the French sociologist Alain Touraine called the emerging formation a 'programmed society':

A new society is now being formed. These new societies can be labelled post-industrial to stress how different they are from the industrial societies which preceded them, although—in both capitalist and socialist nations—they retain some characteristics of these earlier societies. They may also be called technocratic because of the power that dominates them. Or one can call them programmed societies to define them according to the nature of their production methods and economic organisation (Touraine 1974: 3).

An important feature of the post-industrial society in this sense, which demonstrated a significant continuity with its predecessor albeit in an accentuated form, was, or appeared to be, the power of the state to define and regulate the economic and social order. Young, writing in 1976, characterized the immediately preceding decade as one in which there was a 'centrality of the state system as authoritative arena' (1976: 73). There had been 'progressive expansion in generalized expectations as the role of the state; continuing accretion of the power capabilities of the state . . . and the force of the international system in enforcing the maintenance of the existing state system'. The state was the prime mover in moulding and developing the economy, and in mobilizing resources, human and physical, and in creating the framework of boundaries and infrastructure (the bounded infrastructure) within which economy and society operated. There was a 'growing capacity of the state', and

The state system, in roughly its present form, is hardening into an iron grid fixing the most basic parameters of politics. The yearly increments of power of their coercive instruments, improving communications networks, ever more numerous public bureaucracies, new technologies of control—all these strongly flowing currents merge into a powerful tide of central power (Young 1976: 518).

At the risk of allowing a proliferation of terminology to add further confusion (and *pace* Giddens 1991: 27 ff., 243), it seems in retrospect preferable to use the term 'high' modernity for the social, political, and economic formations which emerged in the transatlantic democracies after World War II (Wagener 1992: 475). This was modernity at its apogee. The society described by Young, Touraine, and others, which Bell called post-industrial, was, suggests Wagener, the product of a particular configuration of state and politics: a 'Keynsian', interventionist, welfare-oriented state, and 'competitive party democracy' (ibid.). Wagener is, in this regard, in broad agreement with Rosanvallon, who characterized the post-war world as one in which

democratic industrial societies . . . developed either implicitly or explicitly, within the framework of the Keynsian compromise which regulated relations between the economic and social spheres in the manner of a positive sum-game. The foundations of this model were the growth of the welfare state and collective bargaining. The welfare state governed relations between the state and the working class and reflected the latter's economic and political power (1988: 213).

This, of course, was within the 'quadrisphere'.

In the period from the 1970s to the 1990s, however, in what Rosanvallon calls (p. 213) the 'post-social-democratic' era, further changes undermined this kind of formation, involving *inter alia* a shift from a 'Keynsian' to a neo-liberal, 'Washington', consensus. Keane pulls some of the threads together by drawing attention to the way in which, after the 1970s, the Western economies (and one might add, after the 1980s, those of the East) were forced into major restructuring in response to the apparent failure of previously successful social and economic strategies, which now seemed unable to cope with 'deindustrialization' and widespread unemployment. There was also a major shift in the organization of production: 'Fordism' gave way to 'Post-Fordism' (Murray 1990). In sum,

disintegration of the old technological paradigm based upon continuous-flow industries and the assembly-line system and the introduction of a great number and variety of process innovations . . . based on new microelectronics technologies . . . [has] forced trade unions into defensive (and often self-regarding) strategies . . . thrown into question the official post-war commitment to greater equality of opportunity . . . and severely undermined the capacity of the Keynsian welfare state to fulfil effectively its commitment to high levels of employment (Keane 1988a: 8).

The cause, says Keane, was to be found in changes in the international monetary system, and in the emergence of a 'new international division of labour', all with important implications for the nation-state as a form of social and political organization. It was the sense of rapid and dramatic change which informed the political manifesto aptly entitled 'New Times':

The 'New Times' argument is that the world has changed, not just incrementally but qualitatively, that Britain and other advanced capitalist societies are increasingly characterised by diversity, differentiation and fragmentation, rather than homogeneity, standardization and the economies and organizations of scale which characterised modern mass society (Hall and Jacques 1990: 11).

Crawford Young, a perceptive and prescient writer (see, for instance, his remarks about ethnicity and nationalism in the Soviet Union and Yugoslavia, and about South Africa, 1976: 10–11, 105), failed to foresee two ways in which the social, economic, political, and cultural systems of 'high' modernity would be transformed. Although recognizing the growing importance of multinational corporations, he believed that economic organization and decision-making would continue to be bounded by the nation-state: 'No doubt such transnational bodies as multinational corporations are of significant scale and import—but the fundamental cellular composition of the international system remains tied to the nation-state' (Young 1976: 81). Yet many observers point to the 1980s and 1990s as decades in which there was a vast increase in the *globalization* of economic (as well as social and cultural) relations. For Jameson, it is this *transnational* character of business which is the predominant feature of what he calls 'late capitalism' (1991: xx). The globalization or transnationalization of production, distribution, and exchange (banking, stock markets, debt, the 'new international division of labour', the relocation of production to Third World countries, mass international transportation systems, new communication technologies, the media, etc)., accompanied by new forms of international organization, had important implications for the nation-state as site of social, economic, and political relations.

Melucci argues that the state has been 'replaced from above by a tightly interdependent system of transnational relationships and subdivided from below into a multiplicity of partial governments' (1988: 257). For these and other reasons it no longer seems to be the 'iron grid' which Young envisaged. Rather than an inexorable increase in strength, what seems to be widespread is the *weakness* of the state, its incapacity to resolve the problems it is obliged to address. This view is not universally shared. Hobsbawm, for one, has continued to believe that despite international migration, industrial zones, offshore financial centres, etc., the powers of the state remain undiminished:

Quite apart from the continued importance of state direction, planning and management even in countries dedicated in theory to neo-liberalism, the sheer weight of what public revenue and expenditure represent in the economies of states, but above all their growing role as agents of substantial redistributions of the social income by means of fiscal and welfare mechanisms, have probably made the national state a more central factor in the lives of the world's inhabitants than before (1992: 182).

Robin Cohen also points out that although withdrawing from the economy, the state retains a strong political presence, controlling migration and 'galvaniz[ing], although with diminishing capacity, a single identity around a national leadership, common citizenship and social exclusion of outsiders' (1997: 156). Hannerz (1996) entitles one chapter: 'The withering away of the nation?', with a question mark, and argues that it is not so much withering away as changing with the growth of 'transnational imagined communities' (1996: 90). None the less, the evidence for what Waters (1995: 98–100) has called 'disétatization' is widespread. It is readily apparent in much of Africa, for example, or Latin America, and across great swathes of South and Central Asia and Eastern Europe (Ronald Cohen 1993: 232, 248–51), but it is also in the 'advanced' industrial countries, where sometimes for ideological reasons there was, through the 1980s, a 'selective withdrawal of state power from civil society' (Keane 1988a: 9). Global economic neo-liberalism in particular represented a 'central challenge' to the Keynesian 'promise . . . to take full responsibility for the economic welfare of a given population through the deft exercise of the power of its state' (Dunn 1995: 12).

There were, of course, important tendencies of long duration, which run through both the era of 'high' modernity, and that which followed. One of these concerns changes in the form of the occupational base, and relates to what many observers have seen as a progressive disintegration of the classic forms of social and political organization associated with modernity. In many respects it is the displacement of 'class' from centre stage which has appeared to be the most important shift in the transition from modern to post-industrial and perhaps postmodern society (see *inter alia* Samuel 1989*b*: xxxiii). Touraine and his colleagues link this displacement of class with the emergence of 'new' social movements based on gender or sexuality, on regional or ethnic identity, or on some special interest or a non-class-based ideology such as environmentalism. Jameson, though sceptical of the view that these new movements come out of the 'void left by the disappearance of social classes', none the less understands why this should appear to be so in an era of 'global reconstruction of production and . . . radically new technologies' (1991: 319).

4. Postmodern sociality and the politics of difference

Maffesoli, in a paper which investigates, somewhat misleadingly, 'neo-tribalism', contrasts 'modern' and 'postmodern times'. In the former there were 'individuals' whose place in the social and economic order was defined by their 'function' within it. In the contemporary world there has occurred a 'process of deindividuation'. Individuals are replaced by 'persons' ('polysemantic, poly-phonic', Maffesoli 1988: 141), and collective solidarities based on function have given way to 'emotional communities' (p. 146). This 'neo-tribalism', says Maffesoli, 'refuses to be identified with specific political endeavours, does not conform to any single definite structure, and has as its sole raison d'être the preoccupation with the collectively lived present' (p. 146). He has in mind the 'spectacle [of] contemporary megalopolises' where there is a multiplicity of eclectic lifestyles and representations of self (for example, punks), which change from year to year, and which generate mutual sympathies of an extremely fluid and fluctuating character. Adherents are continually 'zipping from one group to another' (p. 147), and, echoing Lyotard, it is this which creates the 'impression of an atomization' (p. 148).

There is a similarity between the thinking of Maffesoli and that of the French sociologist Baudrillard, whom Lyotard himself cites in this connection. Maffesoli's and Baudrillard's vision of a multiplicity of transient collectivities, of a polyphony of voices in cities transformed by post-industrialism, is widely echoed elsewhere. Samuel, for example, refers to 'the building of a whole way of life out of alternative lifestyles or even popular music', and notes the way in which 'style aristocracies hold the passes between capitalism and consumer; segmentation of the market encourages the growth of minority tastes' (Samuel 1989*b*: xxxiii). How useful is such a vision in helping identify a relationship between ethnic and cultural pluralism and the current condition? It would certainly be misleading to suppose that ethnic and cultural difference involves simply a pluralism of *style*, that it is a matter of the 'media and the market'

(Jameson 1991: 220). Some forms of ethnicity do undoubtedly become entangled with what Jameson calls the 'obscene consumerist pluralism of late capitalism' (1991: 323), but most do not. Nor is it simply a matter of choice: as Sollors notes, 'if voluntary or multiple-choice ethnicity is possible, then what is the *substance* of ethnicity in America?' (1986: 33). It is equally unhelpful to reduce ethnicity to the individual search for place within a complex society. Fischer, writing of the tentative nature of ethnic identity in the contemporary USA, as that emerges in some autobiographies, uses the phrase 'finding a voice' (Fischer 1986: 196), a notion which also appears in work on literature produced by *les beurs* (Hargreaves 1991, 1995), second-generation North African immigrants in France. 'Being Chinese-American', says Fischer, 'exists only as an exploratory project' (1986: 210).

This approach, redolent of 'the disintegration of social aggregates into a mass of individual atoms' has its limits. Following Gans (1956a, 1956b, 1979) there has been considerable discussion in American sociology of the notion of 'symbolic ethnicity'. The suggestion is that many Americans have a 'taste . . . for ethnicity in a mild form, without strong commitments to ethnicity as a social bond' (Alba 1990: 251). There is adherence to cultural markers of identification (cuisine, saints' days, life cycle rituals) which are 'somewhat intermittently and consciously maintained' (Waters 1990: 116). The result is a 'fragile and thin layer' (Alba 1990: 121) of ethnically specific cultural expressions of identity 'alloyed to a larger body of common American culture'. Although it is not just a matter of talk, certainly in the USA there is a great deal of talk (at the very least talk) about ethnic and cultural pluralism. In Alba's survey (1990: 79) 'Discussing your ethnic background with someone else' was the second most frequently cited 'ethnic experience', after eating ethnic cuisine. Nevertheless symbolic ethnicity has very little practical impact in the everyday world of the middle-class white American suburbanites who espouse it. For such Americans 'ethnic' identity is highly flexible, and largely a matter of choice: evidence reported by Waters (1990: 40) shows the extent to which informants changed their ethnic identification between interviews a year apart. Within certain limits, says Alba, 'whites are largely free to identify themselves as they will and to make these identities as important as they like' (1990: 295). This is manifestly not true of other Americans: 'the ways in which ethnicity is flexible and symbolic and voluntary for white middle-class Americans are the very ways in which it is not so for non-white and Hispanic Americans' (Waters 1990: 156). Consider, for example, the 'exploratory project' of a Korean-American in Los Angeles in the early 1990s: find a corner grocery shop, stay open all hours, and get a .38 Police Special for protection.

There are other ways of understanding ethnic and cultural pluralism under conditions of post-high-modernity (see further below), but one question should not be evaded: *why* ethnicity? As Breines suggests, it is necessary to ask 'why our age finds it so intensely important to *have* any sort of ethnic identity in the first place' (Breines 1992: 539). Compared with the past, when similarity formed their basis, political demands and identities are now more often couched in language of 'difference' (Goulbourne 1991: 12, Samuel 1989a: xx). How should we understand what has been variously described as this 'new politics of difference' (Phillips 1993: 144, Hall 1992a: 257), this 'new "identity" politics' (Silverman 1992: 124, Brunt 1990: 152), and the 'politics of recognition' (Taylor 1994).

A useful starting point is Wagener's discussion of the sociology of postmodernity (1992) where he adapts Giddens's term 'disembedding' (Giddens 1991). Though not concerned with ethnic and cultural pluralism, Wagener's account of the 'disembedding' which has accompanied the social and economic change associated with post-industrialism provides a context in which a discussion of contemporary pluralism may be located. Wagener argues that postmodernism as philosophy, rather than being a *product* of post-industrial society, is a *response* to it. Postmodern theorists in the late twentieth century are, he suggests, reacting to contemporary economic, social, and political change, and their reaction resembles that of the 'crisis-of-modernity' theorists at the end of the nineteenth century. There was, then too, a widespread sense of social and political crisis which accompanied the transition to 'modern' society. This in turn 'followed on, or went along with, a disembedding process of grand scale' (p. 482). Major changes in the order of society, major social disruptions stemming from rapid industrialization and urbanization, ripped people from long-established ways of living in an era when, in Europe and the USA, there was also an upsurge in xenophobia. The disruption was, however, eventually resolved through a 'reembedding' of the population of modern societies along lines of class and nation (compare Glazer and Moynihan 1975: 18), and the first half of the twentieth century may be characterized as a period in which the 'organization of society's individuals as members of a class or nation was more or less successfully or disastrously tried' (Wagener 1992: 482). In the late twentieth century there have once again been major changes in the order of society which have resulted once again in widespread social 'disembedding', not least from class and nation. In postmodern and post-industrial societies there has been a crisis of the nation-state accompanied by a crisis of class as a mode of organization and identification. Thus far, however, 'nothing comparable to the organization of the society's individuals during the first period [has] happened' (Wagener 1992: 483). There has, as yet, been no comparable 'reembedding'.

Wagener's comparison of two periods of 'disembedding' brings to mind the suggestion sometimes made that postmodernity is a condition of displacement that could occur at any time in history. To use 'postmodern' in this way is not especially helpful as it destroys its historic specificity. (It would not be useful to write about 'postmodernity' in the context of, say, late fifth-century Athens or *fin de siècle* Paris). None the less, the suggestion that the symptoms of what is currently called 'postmodernity' have occurred in other periods deserves attention. This brings to mind Durkheim's concept of 'anomie', the structural condition of 'deregulation' which Durkheim observed in certain periods in nineteenth-century France. These periods of deregulation and disembedding may in turn be correlated, at least in the 'quadrisphere', though, increasingly during the late twentieth century, across the globe as a whole, with periods of severe economic depression, themselves perhaps identifiable as low points in a long-term Kondratieff cycle. (Interestingly, Stuart Hall notes one criticism of the 'New Times' argument: that what was portrayed were the conditions on the upward slope of a 'Kondratiev' curve, 1990: 122.)

This wider context inevitably takes us some way beyond our immediate concerns, and we must return to the principal theme, and consider how ethnic and cultural pluralism might appear in this scenario. Are 'ethnics' to be seen, perhaps like coal miners, as left behind, relics of modernity, or is ethnicity, if not a product of postmodernity, a response to it?

5. Why pluralism? Why now?

In the nineteenth and early twentieth centuries the solution to the problems of an industrializing, urbanizing society involved a consolidation of the assimilative state. In France, for example, *nationalisation* pressed ahead from the time of the Third Republic, drawing citizens ever more closely into state structures, guaranteeing the advantages of citizenship, extending means of communication, and so on, reaching its apogee in the years after World War II (Noiriel 1992: 179). Kallen's cultural pluralism was a response precisely to that kind of solution (1924: 9 ff., 84). It represented a Romantic reaction to the fulfilment of the Enlightenment dream, comparable to the poet Mistral's seeking in Provençal regionalism a bulwark against late nineteenth-century industrialization (Grillo 1989). In what ways is pluralism now a product of, or a reaction to, the international development of capitalism, easy and rapid means of international transport and communication, the emergence of supranational institutions, and other social and economic changes characterisic of the contemporary condition? That there is such an effect is widely accepted. Hall, for example, writes of globalization 'powerfully dislocating national cultural identities' (1992b: 299), generating a 'fragmentation of cultural codes . . . multiplicity of styles, emphasis on the ephemeral, the fleeting, the impermanent, and on difference and cultural pluralism' (ibid.: 302). Moreover, through flexible specialization and niche marketing globalization, 'actually exploits local differentiation' (p. 304). Thus:

As a tentative conclusion it would appear that globalization *does* have the effect of contesting and dislocating the centred and 'closed' identities of a national culture. It does have a pluralizing impact on identities, producing a variety of possibilities and new positions of identification, and making identities more positional, more political, more plural and diverse (Hall 1992b: 309).

Thus, one way of approaching the question is a macroscopic one, stressing the decline of the nation-state as the principle focus of economic, political, and social activity. The nation-state, squeezed from above and from outside no longer shapes things as it once did and is in retreat.

At the same time, as Bell suggested long ago, the new forces and institutions operating at a multinational, supranational, global level have as yet 'no real "civil theology" to bind them' (1975: 144). They do not, and cannot, provide a moral force, organize a community, command personal loyalty, provide a basis for identification. The relevance of this to ethnic and cultural pluralism lies in Bell's view that where this civil theology is absent, then 'one finds the centrifugal forces of separatism gaining strength'. The link between the breakdown of the nation-state and enhanced space for ethnic and cultural pluralism is also made explicit by Ronald Cohen: 'increased localism and the active dismantling of centralized governmental control along with a worldwide movement for increased democratization, means that pluralism is on the rise' (1993: 251). Mass communications, the mobility of capital, international migration, adds Goulbourne, have 'helped to undermine the continuing relevance of the nations-state duo' (1991: 219). Ironically, mass communications and mobility of labour were often the very things which the nation-state made possible, and vice versa.

Hannerz, seeking a way of signalling the interdependence of social, cultural, economic, and political relations which characterize contemporary experience, has promoted the phrase 'global ecumene' (1992, 1996), meaning roughly the totality of the known world, which nowadays is coterminous with the planet. A consequence of existing in such a world is that essentialist visions of culture and society become 'unviable' (Werbner 1997a: 6). There is, however, what seems to be a paradox here: 'It is a feature of the contemporary world that groups and individuals apparently become more similar and more different at the same time . . . although people in a certain sense become more similar because of modernization, they simultaneously become more distinctive' (Eriksen 1993: 147). Globalization brings with it 'powerful centripetal waves of cultural homogenisation' (Eriksen 1993: 149; compare Hall 1992b: 313, Waters 1995: 136), yet globalization has also been accompanied by massive movement of population, voluntary and involuntary, in what Castles and Miller (1993) have called *The Age of Migration*. 'All societies', says Taylor, 'are becoming increasingly multicultural, while at the same time becoming more porous . . . more open to international migration; more of their members live the life of diaspora, whose center is elsewhere' (1994: 63). New migrations, new diasporas, new 'localisms' are constantly emerging (Eriksen 1993: 150), and new choices have to be made: to be Asian or West Indian or English or British or Asian *and* West Indian *and* English *and* British, and perhaps 'European' as well (Goulbourne 1991: 5). At the same time, 'unable to control the social relations in which they find themselves, people have shrunk the world to the size of their communities and begun to act politically on that basis' (Gilroy 1987: 245). So the nation-state retreats, ethnic and cultural pluralism advance; and the more they advance, the less the nation-state becomes capable of acting.

6. Cosmopolitans, transnationals, and hybrids

To say 'pluralism advances' of course begs the question: pluralism of what kind? As Hall comments: 'The trend towards "global homogenization" . . . is matched by a powerful revival of "ethnicity", sometimes of the more hybrid or symbolic varieties, but also frequently of the exclusive or "essentialist" varieties' (1992*b*: 313). There are manifestly different ways of living 'pluralistically', and some of these become apparent if, in keeping with the notion of globalization and all it entails, we focus on the migrant. Migration and diaspora are key terms in current debates in social and cultural studies with migrants celebrated as archetypal hero(ines)/victims. Obliged to live within and between cultures, they must, metaphorically and usually practically, be multilingual and mul-ticultural. Yet their multiculturalism (polyphonic, syncretic, hybrid) is very different from that described in previous chapters.

In Bhabha's view, the most productive contribution to the Rushdie debate came from feminists,

concerned less with the politics of textuality and international terrorism, and more with demonstrating that the secular, global issue lies uncannily at home, in Britain—in the policies of local government and the race relations industry; in the 'racialization of religion' in multicultural Britain; in the imposition of homogeneity on 'minority' populations in the name of cultural diversity or pluralism (Bhabha 1994: 229).

The position he takes on the affair thus broadens the issues to encompass the wider debate about pluralism in Britain. This is of a piece with his general position on culture and society in a post-colonial world which he signals through the word 'hybridity' (or 'hybridization'). Writers such as Bhabha and Gilroy reject both separatism and, as Bhabha's remark cited above indicates, much of what passes for multiculturalism in British policy. His starting point is an '*inter*national culture, based not on the exoticism of multiculturalism or the diversity of cultures, but on the inscription and articulation of culture's hybridity' (1994: 38). Culture is seen as a dynamic force, 'an enactive, enunciatory site' (p. 178), and to that extent all cultures are 'hybrid', though Bhabha is particularly concerned with the hybridity which occurred in the colonial period (in India, for example), and currently in a post-colonial world. I return to hybridity in a moment; but it is useful first to look at two other ways in which plurality is experienced.

The old term 'cosmopolitans' has recently been resurrected to refer to com-munities which transcend national boundaries: scholars, scientists, artists, femi-nists, advocates of human rights, socialists (Waldron 1995: 102). In another category would be the officials of international organizations such as the UN or the European Union in Brussels, dreaming of 'European citizenship' (Shore and Black 1994). These are carriers of a 'transnational culture' (Hannerz 1992: 249), not confined to a single nation or state. Hannerz rightly points to an earlier discussion of the cosmopolitan intellectual by Karl Mannheim (1936), though Mannheim himself wanted to distinguish between the conservative 'cosmopolitic' intellectual and the progressive internationalist (1952: 168), and it would be interesting to consider the differences between the cosmopolitans of Mannheim's generation and those of Hannerz's (the Saids, for example, the Spivaks, and the Gilroys). Manifestly the global ecumene of the year 2000 is different from that of 1900 or 1930 or even 1960. The same applies to another category for whom the term 'transnational' might be the most appropriate (following Hannerz 1996, Kearney 1995, Rex 1996, and Werbner 1997a).

Transnationals are migrants who differ from cosmopolitans in that 'their loyalties are anchored in translocal social networks . . . rather than the global ecumene' (Werbner 1997a: 12). Their situation is typical of many international labour migrants and so-called diasporic communities. (The term 'diaspora' has expanded far beyond its original sense and now refers to a wide range of migrant and exile groups to the point where virtually everyone now has a diaspora. Cohen, 1997, attempts to institute some rigour into the discussion.) Pakistani migrants (extensively studied by Werbner), Sikhs, a favourite example of Rex's, and Senegalese street traders in France, Italy, and other countries are excellent illustrations of the phenomenon of transnationalism. The Senegalese may be based in a city or region, but are mobile within their country of (temporary) residence, between that and other countries in which their trading networks are established, and between them and their home regions in Senegal (Bruno Riccio, personal communication). Latino migrants in Sacramento whom M. P. Smith (1992) describes through an adaptation of Rosaldo's metaphor of 'border crossings', provide another example. Transnational migration of this kind is, of course, far from a recent phenomenon, and the differences between the form it takes now and what happened in the past deserve much fuller consideration than can be accorded here.

Transnationals, like cosmopolitans, are likely to be multilingual and multicultural, but their situation, their multiculturalism, must be distinguished from that of a third category: hybrids. 'Hybridity' is an awkward word. It appears to have entered postmodern and post-colonial critical theory via architecture: Rose draws attention to the way in which Jencks (1978) used it 'to describe the complexity of codes in postmodern architecture' (1991: 105). For the literary critic Hassan, 'hybridization' (the 'mutant replication of genres', 1987: 170) is one of eleven 'definiens' of postmodernism along with indeterminacy, fragmentation, decanonization, and so on (1987: 168–72). It is somewhat puzzling, however, that this word, which is of course a biological metaphor, should appear innocently in post-colonial theoretical writing, unless of course intended as a deliberate, ironic gesture of defiance against the 'degeneracy' (cultural and physical) of 'miscegenation' or 'mongrelization' presumed by racist thought (Young 1995: 10). Papastergiadis (1997: 258) in fact suggests this may be the case with Rushdie: Cohen (1997: 130) and Waldron (1995: 93) both cite Rushdie's own assessment (1991) that the *Satanic Verses* 'celebrates hybridity, purity, intermingling . . . It rejoices in mongrelization'.

In earlier anthropological literature on the Caribbean, 'hybrid' was certainly used biologically, to refer to people of mixed racial origin (Smith 1965: 6), though it was also used metaphorically as in 'cultural hybridism' (ibid.: 172, Wolf 1962: 254). None the less, it is not pedantry to insist that whether or not the intent is ironic, biological metaphors need to be used with great care when referring to culture and identity, not least when, as a good dictionary would remind us, hybrids are sterile (Cohen 1997: 131, Young 1995: 8). The same applies to another metaphor widely used in this context: schizophrenia. Gilroy, who employs 'hybridity' in *The Black Atlantic*, signals as possible alternatives 'creolisation', 'métissage', 'mestizaje' (1993*b*: 2). 'Hybridity' does not appear in earlier work (1987), where he uses 'syncretism' instead, and this may be preferable.

Hybridity signals a range of themes, and perhaps now carries too much baggage. For Bhabha it refers to what happens culturally in the 'third space', the 'interstitial passage between fixed identifications' (1994: 4): this is where multilingualism and multiculturalism is made possible and their creative potential exploited. The concept also draws on the Bakhtinian concept of 'heteroglossia', the juxtaposition of voices within texts (Papastergiadis 1997: 267–8, Werbner 1997*a*: 4–5, Young 1995: 20), and perhaps on a Lévi-Straussian notion of *bricolage* (Back 1996: 5). Thus, as Gilroy implies, it has to do with linguistic and cultural syncretism and with creolization (Hannerz 1992, 1996). Hybridity therefore celebrates polyphony and creativity. As Rushdie says, it also 'rejoices in mongrelization', perhaps in a biological rather than cultural sense, appealing simultaneously to a social, cultural, and physical 'Brazilianization', as it were, or at any rate imagined Brazilianization, from which would emerge new social and cultural forms, and new persons. Thus Back: 'Young people . . . are creating cultures that are neither simply black nor simply white. These syncretic cultures produce inter-racial harmony while celebrating diversity . . . and result in volatile cultural forms that can be simultaneously black and white' (1996: 159). And consider Bissoondath's 'new vision of Canadianness . . . a Canada where inherent differences and inherent similarities meld easily and where no one is alienated with hyphenation. A nation of cultural hybrids, where every individual is unique, every individual distinct . . . a cohesive, effective society enlivened by cultural variety: reasonable diversity within vigorous unity' (1994: 224). In a curious way does not this echo nineteenth-century visions of the 'melting pot'?

What emerges from Gilroy and Bhabha is that multiculturalism, and still more separatism, are underpinned by a static view of culture and cultural production and by cultural essentialism. There is an underlying sense of cultural difference as 'fixed, solid almost biological properties of human relations' (Gilroy 1987: 39). The result has been to promote a 'pseudo-pluralism' in which 'a culturally defined ethnic particularity has become the basis of political association' (ibid.). This reification and freezing of culture is something that Gilroy finds in 'Afro-centricity', a form of separatism which operates with an 'essentialist' view of black culture and identity (1993a: 122, 197, 1993b: 31). This 'desire to anchor themselves in racial particularity' (1993b: 86) runs counter to the historic hybrid or syncretic character of black (and other) cultures which have always been in a constant state of renewal. Ethnicity, says Gilroy, is an 'infinite process of identity construction' (1993b: 223; compare Hall 1992a), and the reification of culture through both multiculturalism and separatism seeks to impose an unacceptable block on that process. As Sollors remarks, 'Perhaps ethnic scholars ought to develop as much joy in syncretism as they have found in purity and authenticity in the past' (1986: 246).

For Gilroy, what is paramount has been the development of black culture and identity in a dynamic way within the context of what he calls a *Black Atlantic*: 'A new structure of cultural exchange has been built up across the imperial networks which once played host to the triangular trade', that is slavery (1987: 157). These networks have four nodes: the Caribbean, USA, Europe, and Africa, the limits, in broad terms, of the black diaspora, with London, in the 1980s and 1990s, 'an important junction point' in this 'web' of black political culture and identity (1993a: 141). In his view, therefore, the process of cultural production transcends the traditional boundaries of nation-states, and must be seen in relation to the 'transnational character of modes of production, social movements and informational exchanges' (1993a: 71). In similar fashion, new information and communication technologies 'have taken all nationalisms away from their historic association with the technology of print cultures' (1993a: 192).

This intersection of the local and the global in the production of culture and identity may at first sight be thought of as a problem of interest only to cosmopolitan intellectuals. Comments by Bhabha might seem to confirm this. Referring to 'the people of the pagus—colonials, postcolonials, migrants, minorities—wandering peoples who will not be contained within the Heim of the national culture and its unisonant discourse' (1990: 315), he gives the appearance, at times, of locating them in some universal Paris: 'Gatherings of exiles and émigrés and refugees, gathering on the edge of "foreign" cultures; gathering at the frontiers; gatherings in the ghettos or cafés of city centres; gathering in the half-life, half-light of foreign tongues' (p. 291). Here 'hybrid' appears to mean marginal, and the marginality, the cultural doubleness of the migrant or exile, is an old theme (Sollors 1986: 243, 252). Another, perhaps better sense of what hybridity means at the street level emerges from Gilroy. He remarks of one record, the 1990 hit by the 'Impressions' entitled 'Proud of Mandela', that it

brings Africa, America, Europe, and the Caribbean seamlessly together. It was produced in Britain by the children of Caribbean and African settlers from raw materials
supplied by black Chicago but filtered through Kingstonian sensibilities in order to pay
tribute to a black hero whose global significance lies beyond the limits of his partial
South African citizenship and the impossible national identity which goes with it (1993b:
95).

The 'fusion and intermixture' he commends is revealed in the work of another
group, 'Fun-Da-Mental', whose leader is Haq Qureishi, Pakistani-born but who
grew up in Bradford. Known at school as 'Pete', but calling himself 'Propa-
Gandhi', he sees their songs and lyrics opposing the idea of Asians as passive
recipients of racial abuse. 'Seize the time', for example, contains the lines:
'We're ready for a collision with the opposition | It won't be a suicide mission
| And one thing about me, I'm not afraid to die'. The rap style enables the
writer of an article (Caroline Sullivan) to describe the group as 'half-West
Indian/half-Pakistani', a music for which, 'ironically', as she says, 'most of their
audience is white' (*Guardian*, 17 June 1994; see also Gardner and Shukur 1994,
and Hutnyk 1997).

Some of the most interesting writing on hybridity has come from cultural
studies concerned with popular music. This may lead to the reproach that it is
'far too *textual*', as Wolff (1992: 557) says of Smith's account of Latino creative
endeavours to 'make a space' for identity at the intersection of the global and
local ethnic identity. Certainly Smith's study is partly textually based, in a
manner reminiscent of Gilroy (see, for example, the description of Latino
identity in song, 1992: 516–23), but he goes far beyond the text to provide an
institutionally rooted, though not institutionally confined, rendering of how
ethnicity operates in a postmodern, post-industrial, transnational environment.
There is also what Back (1996: 11) calls a 'small but significant literature' dealing
with multiracial areas of Britain which describes how new, syncretic cultures
are emerging among gangs of young people. Back himself and in an earlier
study, Roger Hewitt (1986), both describe how young people from racially
mixed South London housing estates have begun to develop a common culture. Hewitt shows how black (British, Jamaican) language and music has
'hegemonic authority' (p. 81) in the clubs and on the streets, and this leads to
some white youths adopting black speech and lifestyle. Both Hewitt and Back
stress that in the clubs and on the playgrounds a novel culture was being
negotiated. 'Young white and black people', says Back, 'construct an alternative
public sphere in which truly mixed ethnicities develop' (Back 1996: 158), and
this to an extent transcends the barriers of race.

Those who write about hybridity are in the main optimists, seeing in it a way
forward out of the quagmire of essentialism and multiculturalism. Others are
not so sanguine, and Back himself stresses the need for caution in 'projecting
romantic and utopian desires on to the accounts and interpretations of the
culture of young people' (1996: 1). In Hewitt's study, relationships did not

survive much beyond the mid-teens and leaving school, and Back found that young Vietnamese were excluded by both blacks and whites. Friedman and Hutnyk both criticize hybridity on political grounds. For Friedman it is elite, cosmopolitan idealism, and far removed from the 'Balkanisation and tribalisation experienced at the bottom of the system' (1997: 85). Hutnyk describes it as 'a rhetorical cul-de-sac which trivialises Black political activity' (1997: 128). 'This view of the world seems very happy to identify differences and celebrate multiplicities', he says, and continuing in Dave Spart vein, 'but does little in the way of organizing political alliances across these differences. It is all well and good to theorise the diaspora, the post-colony and the hybrid; but where this is never interrupted by the necessity of political work, it remains a vote for the status quo' (Hutnyk 1997: 134). He is right, of course, to point to the need to address 'the contextualising conditions in which these [cultural] phenomena exist' (ibid.), but his own agenda seems as devoid of substance as those he criticizes.

7. Coda

What now, then? What will eventually happen in postmodern and post-industrial societies is unclear because not yet determined. It is not obvious what kind of pluralism will prevail: institutional pluralism (what the French would call *ghettoisation*), the messiness of multiculturalism, or that hybridity which, argues Gilroy (1987: 219), comes from 'stepp[ing] outside the confines of modernity's most impressive achievement—the nation-state'. (None would have pleased Gellner, for whom 'in a mobile world of overlapping communities, the diversity of communal visions is a problem, not a solution', 1987: 168.) Ironically, the globalization which encourages hybridity also fosters conditions where separatism and other forms of particularism might flourish. In the deregulated political and moral economies of the late twentieth century, where there has been 'a disintegration of social aggregates', where there are only 'individuals', and 'no such thing as society', institutional pluralism and hybridity are both understandable responses to the multiply riven, media-driven, anarchic, postmodern, post-industrial wastelands inhabited by many ethnic minorities in Britain, France, and the USA, a landscape vividly portrayed in the mid-1990s in the French film *La Haine*.

For most of us, I suspect, the problem remains one of navigating between the 'Scylla of universalism and the Charybdis of differentialism' (Wieviorka 1997: 149). Much has been written in the 1990s about the rights of cultural and ethnic minorities, and it is clear from the work of Kymlicka that liberals can justify a wide range of group-specific rights of the kind which go with a relatively strong form of multiculturalism. Although much less familiar with the position of minorities such as Muslims in Europe than he is with racial and ethnic minorities in North America, Kymlicka provides a convincing *philosophical* basis for a politics of difference from a liberal perspective. On the other hand, like Taylor (1994), he has a less sure grasp of questions of power, and as his comments on numerous issues suggest, of the day-to-day practicalities of living in a multicultural society: his suggestion that 'shared identity' will provide the basis for unity in multinational states (1995*a*: 187 ff.) seems to beg all the questions of what and how.

My own feeling is that matters are determined less by philosophy than by *rapports de force*, and I make no claim to have any answers. None the less, like Rex, Werbner, and others, I believe that so far as migrants are concerned a non-essentializing version of 'egalitarian' multiculturalism, if that is possible, one which provides for a genuine integration, is probably the least-worst solution. Perhaps Noah Yannick is right: *liberté, fraternité,* AND *diversité.* A 'politically re-configured' multiculturalism (the phrase is Back's, 1996: 251), however, re-quires a strong national and local state prepared to intervene directly in society's affairs, for and on behalf of egalitarian multiculturalism's ideals, and willing to tolerate a vibrant, ethnically and culturally diverse, civil society. Under modernity, the state acknowledged it had such an interventionist role, though usually it intervened to suppress rather than promote difference. Goulbourne has called for it to 'resume its historical responsibilities' (1991: 238), though not necessarily its traditional stance. Whether there is the will or the ability or the resources remains to be seen, but it would be safest to assume that we will have to learn to do without it.

LIST OF REFERENCES

ABBOTT, E. (ed.) (1924). *Immigration: Select Documents and Caserecords* (Chicago: University of Chicago Press).

——(ed.) (1926). *Historical Aspects of the Immigration Problem* (Chicago: University of Chicago Press).

ABRAHAMS, I. (1932 (1896)). *Jewish Life in the Middle Ages* (London: Edward Goldston).

ADAMIC, L. (1940). *From Many Lands* (New York: Harper & Row).

ADDAMS, J. (1960 (1910)). *Twenty Years at Hull-House* (New York: Macmillan).

AFIGBO, A. E. (1972). *The Warrant Chiefs: Indirect Rule in Southeastern Nigeria, 1891–1929* (London: Longman).

AHSAN, M. M. (1994). 'Islam and Muslims in Britain', in H. Mutalib and T. ul-U. Hashmi (eds.), *Islam, Muslims and the Modern State* (London: Macmillan), 339–61.

ALBA, R. D. (1990). *Ethnic Identity: The Transformation of White America* (New Haven: Yale University Press).

ALBERT, P. C. (1992). 'Israelite and Jew: How did Nineteenth-Century French Jews Understand Assimilation?', in J. Fraenkel and S. Zipperstein (eds.), *Assimilation and Community: The Jews in Nineteenth-Century Europe* (Cambridge: Cambridge University Press), 88–109.

ALI, Y. (1992). 'Muslim Women and the Politics of Ethnicity and Culture in Northern England', in G. Sahgal and N. Yuval-Davis (eds.), *Refusing Holy Orders* (London: Virago Press), 101–23.

ALLEN, W. E. D. (1963). *The Problems of Turkish Power in the Sixteenth Century* (London: Central Asian Research Centre).

ANDERSON, B. (1983). *Imagined Communities* (London: Verso).

ANDERSON, P. (1974). *Lineages of the Absolutist State* (London: New Left Books).

ANDRIC, I. (1994 (1945)). *The Bridge over the Drina* (London: Harvill).

ANNAN, N. (1990). *Our Age: Portrait of a Generation* (London: Weidenfeld & Nicolson).

ANTHIAS, F., and YUVAL-DAVIS, N. (1993). *Race, Nation, Gender, Colour and Class and the Anti-Racist Struggle* (London: Routledge).

APPIAH, A. (1994). 'Identity, Authenticity, Survival: Multicultural Societies and Social Reproduction', in A. Gutmann (ed.), *Multiculturalism: Examining the Politics of Recognition* (Princeton: Princeton University Press), 149–64.

APTHORPE, R. (1968). 'Does Tribalism really Matter?', *Transition*, 37: 18–22.

Archives Parlementaires (1995). *Archives Parlementaires de 1787 à 1860*, Série 1: *1787–1799* (Paris: CNRS).

ARNAKIS, G. C. (1969). *The Near East in Modern Times*, v/1: *The Ottoman and the Balkan States to 1900* (Austin and New York: Pemberton Press).

ARTINIAN, V. (1988). *The Armenian Constitutional System in the Ottoman Empire, 1839–63* (Istanbul: Privately published).

AZARYA, V. (1988). 'Jihads and Dyula States in West Africa', in S. N. Eisenstadt, M. Abitbol, and N. Chazan (eds.), *The Early State in African Perspective* (Leiden: E. J. Brill), 109–33.

BACK, L. (1996). *New Ethnicities and Urban Culture: Racisms and Multiculture in Young Lives* (London: UCL Press).

BALLARD, R. (1994). 'The Emergence of Desh Pardesh', in R. Ballard (ed.), *Desh Pardesh: The South Asian Presence in Britain* (London: Hurst), 1–36

BANKS, M. (1996). *Ethnicity: Anthropological Constructions* (London: Routledge).

BARDAKJIAN, K. B. (1982). 'The Rise of the Armenian Patriarchate of Constantinople', in B. Braude and B. Lewis (eds.), *Christians and Jews in the Ottoman Empire* (New York: Holmes & Meier), 89–100.

BARKER, M. (1981). *The New Racism* (London: Junction Books).

BARRÈS, M. (1925 (1902)). *Scènes et doctrines de nationalisme* (Paris: Plon).

BARTH, F. (1959). *Political Leadership Among the Swat Pathan* (London: Athlone Press).

——(1969). 'Introduction', in F. Barth (ed.), *Ethnic Groups and Boundaries* (London: Allen & Unwin), 18–22.

——(ed.) (1969). *Ethnic Groups and Boundaries* (London: Allen & Unwin).

BARTON, J. (1975). *Peasants and Strangers: Italians, Rumanians and Slovaks in an American City, 1890–1950* (Cambridge, Mass.: Harvard University Press).

BAUMANN, G. (1997). 'Dominant and Demotic Discourses of Culture: Their Relevance to Multi-Ethnic Alliances', in P. Werbner and T. Modood (eds.), *Debating Cultural Hybridity: Multi-Cultural Identities and the Politics of Anti-Racism* (London: Zed Books), 209–25.

BAYOR, R. H. (1978). *Neighbours in Conflict: The Irish, Germans, Jews and Italians of New York City, 1919–1941* (Baltimore: John Hopkins University Press).

BEATTIE, J. (1971). *The Nyoro State* (Oxford: Clarendon Press).

BELL, D. (1973). *The Coming of Post-Industrial Society* (London: Penguin Books).

——(1975). 'Ethnicity and Social Change', in N. Glazer and D. P. Moynihan (eds.), *Ethnicity: Theory and Experience* (Cambridge, Mass.: Harvard University Press), 141–74.

BERNSTEIN, R. (1995). *Dictatorship of Virtue* (New York: Vintage Books).

BETTS, R. F. (1961). *Assimilation and Association in French Colonial Theory, 1890–1914* (New York: Columbia University Press).

——(1976). *The False Dawn: European Imperialism in the 19th Century* (Oxford: Oxford University Press).

——(1985). *Uncertain Dimensions: Western Overseas Empires in the Twentieth Century* (Oxford: Oxford University Press).

BHABHA, H. K. (1989). 'Beyond Fundamentalism and Liberalism', *New Statesman*, 39/2: 34–5.

——(1990). 'Dissemination', in H. K. Bhabha (ed.), *Nation and Narration* (London: Routledge), 291–322.

——(1994). *The Location of Culture* (London: Routledge).

BIRNBAUM, P. (1989). 'Les Juifs entre l'appartenance identitaire et l'entrée dans l'espace public: La Révolution française et le choix des acteurs', *Revue Française de Sociologie*, 30/3–4: 497–510.

——(1992). 'Accepter la pluralité: Haines et préjugés', in J.-F. Sirinelli (ed.), *Histoire des Droites en France*, iii: *Sensibilités* (Paris: Gallimard), 424–72.

BISSOONDATH, N. (1994). *Selling Illusions: The Cult of Multiculturalism in Canada* (London: Penguin).

BONNET, A. (1997). 'Constructions of Whiteness in European and American Anti-Racism', in P. Werbner and T. Modood (eds.), *Debating Cultural Hybridity: Multi-Cultural Identities and the Politics of Anti-Racism* (London: Zed Books), 173–92.

BORAH, W. (1982). 'The Spanish and Indian Law: New Spain', in G. A. Collier, R. I. Rosaldo, and J. D. Wirth (eds.), *The Inca and Aztec States 1400–1800: Anthropology and History* (New York: Academic Press), 265–88.

BRASS, P. R. (1991). *Ethnicity and Nationalism: Theory and Comparison* (New Delhi: Sage).

BRAUDE, B. (1982). 'Foundation Myths of the Millet System', in B. Braude and B. Lewis (eds.), *Christians and Jews in the Ottoman Empire* (New York: Holmes & Meier), 69–88.

——and LEWIS, B. (1982). 'Introduction', in B. Braude and B. Lewis (eds.), *Christians and Jews in the Ottoman Empire* (New York: Holmes & Meier), 1–36.

BREINES, P. (1992). 'Comments on Smith and Wagener', *Theory and Society*, 21/4: 533–41.

BROWN, L. C. (1996). 'The Setting: An Introduction', in L. C. Brown (ed.), *Imperial Legacy: The Ottoman Imprint on the Balkans and Middle East* (New York: Columbia University Press), 1–12.

BRUNT, R. (1990). 'The Politics of Identity', in S. Hall and M. Jacques (eds.), *New Times* (London: Lawrence & Wishart), 150–9.

BUCI-GLUCKSMANN, C. (1980). *Gramsci and the State* (London: Lawrence & Wishart).

BULLIVANT, B. (1983). *The Pluralist Dilemma in Education: Six Case Studies* (Sydney: Allen & Unwin).

BYRNES, R. F. (1950). *Antisemitism in Modern France*, i: *The Prologue to the Dreyfus Affair* (New Brunswick, NJ: Rutgers University Press).

CALLEO, D. P. (1995). 'America's Federal Nation State: A Crisis of Post-Imperial Viability?', in J. Dunn (ed.), *Contemporary Crisis of the Nation State?* (Oxford: Blackwell), 16–33.

CALNEK, E. E. (1976). 'The Internal Structure of Tenochtitlan', in E. J. Wolf (ed.), *The Valley of Mexico* (Albuquerque: University of New Mexico Press), 287–302.

——(1982). 'Patterns of Empire Formation in the Valley of Mexico, Late Postclassical Period, 1200–1521', in G. A. Collier, R. I. Rosaldo, and J. D. Wirth (eds.), *The Inca and Aztec States 1400–1800: Anthropology and History* (New York: Academic Press), 43–62.

CARLSON, R. (1975). *The Quest for Conformity: Americanization Through Education* (New York: Wiley).

CASTLES, S., and MILLER, M. J. (1993). *The Age of Migration: International Populations Movements in the Modern World* (London: Macmillan).

CESARANI, D. (1996). 'The Changing Character of Citizenship and Nationality in Britain', in D. Cesarani and M. Fulbrook (eds.), *Citizenship, Nationality and Migration in Europe* (London: Routledge), 57–73.

——and FULBROOK, M. (1996). 'Introduction', in D. Cesarani and M. Fulbrook (eds.), *Citizenship, Nationality and Migration in Europe* (London: Routledge), 1–14.

CHAPMAN, M. (1978). *The Gaelic Vision in Scottish Culture* (London: Croom Helm and Montreal: McGill-Queen's University Press).

——McDONALD, M., and TONKIN, E. (1989). 'Introduction—History and Social Anthropology', in E. Tonkin, M. McDonald, and C. Chapman (eds.), *History and Ethnicity* (ASA Monographs, 27; London: Routledge), 1–21.

CHARBONNIER, G. (1969). *Conversations with Claude Lévi-Strauss* (London: Cape).

CLAESSEN, H. J. M. (1978a). 'Early State in Tahiti', in H. J. M. Claessen and P. Skalnik (eds.), *The Early State* (The Hague: Mouton), 441–67.

——(1978b). 'The Early State: A Structural Approach', in H. J. M. Claessen and P. Skalnik (eds.), *The Early State* (The Hague: Mouton), 533–96.

——and SKALNIK, P. (1978a). 'The Early State: Theories and Hypotheses', in H. J. M. Claessen and P. Skalnik (eds.), *The Early State* (The Hague: Mouton), 3–29.

————(1978b). 'The Early State: Models and Reality', in H. J. M. Claessen and P. Skalnik (eds.), *The Early State* (The Hague: Mouton), 637–50.

————(eds.) (1978). *The Early State* (The Hague: Mouton).

——and VAN DE VELDE, P. (1987). 'Introduction', in H. L. M. Claessen and P. Van de Velde (eds.), *Early State Dynamics* (Leiden: E. J. Brill), 1–23.

CLAGHORN, K. H. (1923). *The Immigrant's Day in Court* (New York: Harper).

CLENDINNEN, I. (1991). *Aztecs: An Interpretation* (Cambridge: Cambridge University Press).

COHEN, A. (1969). *Custom and Politics in Urban Africa* (London: Routledge & Kegan Paul).

——(1974). *Two-Dimensional Man* (London: Routledge & Kegan Paul).

——(ed.) (1974). *Urban Ethnicity* (ASA Monographs, 12; London: Tavistock Publications).

COHEN, D. S. (ed.) (1990). *America: The Dream of my Life* (New Brunswick, NJ: Rutgers University Press).

COHEN, P. (1992). ' "It's Racism what Dunnit": Hidden Narratives in Theories of Racism', in J. Donald and A. Rattansi (eds.), *'Race', Culture and Difference* (London: Sage Publications), 62–103.

COHEN, ROBIN (1994). *Frontiers of Identity: The British and the Others* (London: Longman).

——(1997). *Global Diasporas: An Introduction* (London: UCL Press).

COHEN, RONALD (1967). *The Kanuri of Bornu* (New York: Holt, Rinehart & Winston).

——(1970). 'Incorporation in Bornu', in R. Cohen and J. Middleton (eds.), *From Tribe to Nation in Africa: Studies in Incorporation Process* (Scranton, Pa.: Chandler), 150–74.

——(1978a). 'State Origins: A Reappraisal', in H. J. M. Claessen and P. Skalnik (eds.), *The Early State* (The Hague: Mouton), 31–75.

——(1978b). 'Ethnicity: Problem and Focus in Anthropology', *Annual Review of Anthropology*, 7: 379–403.

——(1978c). 'Introduction', in R. Cohen and E. Service (eds.), *Origins of the State* (Philadelphia: ISHI), 1–20.

——(1993). 'Conclusion: Ethnicity, the State and Moral Order', in J. Toland (ed.), *Ethnicity and the State* (New Brunswick, NJ: Transaction Publishers), 231–58.

——and MIDDLETON, J. (1970). 'Introduction', in R. Cohen and J. Middleton (eds.), *From Tribe to Nation in Africa: Studies in Incorporation Process* (Scranton, Pa.: Chandler), 1–34.

COHEN, W. B. (1971). *Rulers of Empire: The French Colonial Service in Africa* (Stanford, Calif.: Hoover Institution Press).

——(1980). *The French Encounter with Africans: White Response to Blacks, 1530–1880* (Bloomington: Indiana University Press).

COLE, J. (1977). "Anthropology Comes part-way Home: Community Studies in Europe', *Rev. Anthropol.* 6: 349–78.

COLLEY, L. (1989). 'Radical Patriotism in Eighteenth-Century England', in R. Samuel (ed.), *Patriotism: The Making and Unmaking of British National Identity*, i: *History and Politics* (London: Routledge), 169–87.

——(1992). *Britons: Forging the Nation 1707–1837* (London: Pimlico).

COMMISSION FOR RACIAL EQUALITY (1990a). *Britain: A Plural Society; Report of a Seminar* (Discussion Paper No. 3; London: Commission for Racial Equality).

——(1990b). *Law, Blasphemy and the Multi-Faith Society; Report of a Seminar* (Discussion Paper No. 1; London: Commission for Racial Equality).

——(1990c). *Schools of Faith: Religious Schools in a Multicultural Society* (London: Commission for Racial Equality).

CONRAD, G. W., and DEMAREST, A. A. (1984). *Religion and Empire: The Dynamics of Aztec and Inca Expansion* (Cambridge: Cambridge University Press).

CONTAMINE, P. (1992). 'Jeanne d'Arc dans la mémoire des droites', in J.-F. Sirinelli (ed.), *Histoire des Droites en France*, ii: *Cultures* (Paris: Gallimard), 399–435.

COOK, M. A. (1976). 'Introduction', in M. A. Cook (ed.), *A History of the Ottoman Empire to 1730: Chapters from the Cambridge History of Islam and the New Cambridge Modern History* (Cambridge: Cambridge University Press), 1–9.

COTTRELL, S. (1989). 'The Devil on Two Sticks: Franco-Phobia in 1803', in R. Samuel (ed.), *Patriotism: The Making and Unmaking of British National Identity*, i: *History and Politics* (London: Routledge), 259–74.

COVELLO, L. (1967). *The Social Background of the Italo-American School Child* (Leiden: E. J. Brill).

CROWDER, M. (1967). *Senegal: A Study of French Assimilation Policy* (London: Methuen & Co.).

CUNNINGHAM, H. (1989). 'The Language of Patriotism', in R. Samuel (ed.), *Patriotism: The Making and Unmaking of British National Identity*, i: *History and Politics* (London: Routledge), 57–89.

DAHRENDORF, R. (1959). *Class and Class Conflict in Industrial Society* (London: Routledge & Kegan Paul).

DAVIES, N. (1973). *The Aztecs: A History* (London: Macmillan).

DAVIES, N. (1980). *The Toltec Heritage from the Fall of Tula to the Rise of Tenochtitlan* (Norman: University of Oklahoma Press).

——(1987*a*). *The Aztec Empire: The Toltec Resurgence* (Norman: University of Oklahoma Press).

——(1987*b*). *The Toltecs: Until the Fall of Tula* (Norman: University of Oklahoma Press).

DAVIS, A. F. (1967). *Spearheads for Reform* (New York: Oxford University Press).

DAVIS, J. (1977). *People of the Mediterranean* (London: Routledge & Kegan Paul).

DAVIS, M. (1992). *City of Quartz: Excavating the Future in Los Angeles* (London: Vintage).

DAVIS, P. (ed.) (1977 (1920)). *Immigration and Americanization: Selected Readings* (Folcroft, Pa.: Folcroft Library Editions).

DELPECH, F. (1976). 'L'Histoire des Juifs en France de 1780 à 1840', in B. Blumenkranz and A. Soboul (eds.), *Les Juifs et la Révolution Française* (Paris: Privat), 3–46.

D'INNOCENZO, M., and SIREFMAN, J. P. (eds.) (1992). *Immigration and Ethnicity: American Society—'melting pot' or 'salad bowl'?* (Westport, Conn.: Greenwood Press).

DONALD, J., and RATTANSI, A. (1992). 'Introduction', in J. Donald and A. Rattansi (eds.), *'Race', Culture and Difference* (London: Sage Publications), 1–8.

DOYLE, B. (1989). *English and Englishness* (London: Routledge).

DRESSER, M. (1989). 'Britannia', in R. Samuel (ed.), *Patriotism: The Making and Unmaking of British National Identity*, iii: *National Fictions* (London: Routledge), 26–49.

DRUMONT, E. (1886). *La France juive* (Paris: Marpon & Flammarion).

DUNN, J. (1995). 'Introduction: Crisis of the Nation State?', in J. Dunn (ed.), *Contemporary Crisis of the Nation State?* (Oxford: Blackwell), 3–15.

——(ed.) (1995). *Contemporary Crisis of the Nation State?* (Oxford: Blackwell).

DURAN, F. D. (1964). *The Aztecs: The History of the Indies of New Spain*, trans. with notes by D. Heyden and F. Horcasitas (New York: Orion Press).

DURKHEIM, E. (1964). *The Division of Labour in Society* (New York: Free Press of Glencoe).

EISENSTADT, S. N., ABITBOL, M., and CHAZAN, N. (1988). 'The Origins of the State Reconsidered', in S. N. Eisenstadt, M. Abitbol, and N. Chazan (eds.), *The Early State in African Perspective* (Leiden: E. J. Brill), 1–27.

EKEH, P. P. (1990). 'Social Anthropology and Two Contrasting Uses of Tribalism in Africa', *Comparative Studies in Society and History*, 32/4: 660–700.

ELIAS, N. (1978). *The Civilizing Process*, i: *The History of Manners* (Oxford: Blackwell).

——(1982). *The Civilizing Process*, ii: *State Formation and Civilization* (Oxford: Blackwell).

EPSTEIN, A. L. (1978). *Ethos and Identity* (London: Tavistock Publications).

EPSTEIN, M. (1982). 'The Leadership of the Ottoman Jews in the Fifteenth and Sixteenth Centuries', in B. Braude and B. Lewis (eds.), *Christians and Jews in the Ottoman Empire* (New York: Holmes & Meier), 101–15.

ERIKSEN, T. H. (1993). *Ethnicity and Nationalism: Anthropological Perspectives* (London: Pluto Press).

——(1997). 'Multiculturalism, Individualism and Human Rights: Romanticism, the Enlightenment and Lessons from Mauritius', in R. Wilson (ed.), *Human Rights, Culture and Context: Anthropological Perspectives* (London: Pluto Press), 49–69.

EVANS-PRITCHARD, E. E. (1937). *Witchcraft, Oracles and Magic among the Azande* (Oxford: Oxford University Press).

——(1971). *The Azande: History and Political Institutions* (Oxford: Clarendon Press).

FARDON, R. (1987). '"African Ethnogenesis": Limits to the Comparability of Ethnic Phenomena', in L. Holy (ed.), *Comparative Anthropology* (Oxford: Blackwell), 168–88.

FAROQHI, S. (1984). *Towns and Townsmen of Ottoman Anatolia: Trade, Crafts and Food Production in an Urban Setting, 1520–1650* (Cambridge: Cambridge University Press).

——(1994). 'Part II. Crisis and Change, 1590–1699', in H. Inalcik and D. Quataert (eds.), *An Economic and Social History of the Ottoman Empire, 1300–1914* (Cambridge: Cambridge University Press), 411–636.

FELDMAN, D. (1989). 'Jews in London, 1880–1914', in R. Samuel (ed.), *Patriotism: The Making and Unmaking of British National Identity*, ii: *Minorities and Outsiders* (London: Routledge), 207–29.

FEUERWERKER, D. (1976). *L'Émancipation des Juifs: De l'Ancien Régime à la fin du Second Empire* (Paris: Albin Michel).

FINDLEY, C. V. (1980). *Bureaucratic Reform in the Ottoman Empire: The Sublime Porte, 1789–1922* (Princeton: Princeton University Press).

FINN, M. C. (1993). *After Chartism: Class and Nation in English Radical Politics, 1848–1874* (Cambridge: Cambridge University Press).

FIRTH, R. (1989). 'Fact and Fiction in Ethnography', in E. Tonkin, M. McDonald, and C. Chapman (eds.), *History and Ethnicity* (ASA Monographs, 27; London: Routledge), 48–52.

FISCHER, M. (1986). 'Ethnicity and the Post-Modern Arts of Memory', in J. Clifford and G. Marcus (eds.), *Writing Culture* (Berkeley: University of California Press), 194–233.

FOOT, P. (1969). *The Rise of Enoch Powell* (London: Cornmarket Press).

FORTES, M. (1975). 'Isaac Schapera: An Appreciation', in M. Fortes and S. Patterson (eds.), *Studies in African Social Anthropology: Essays Presented to I. Schapera* (London: Academic Press), 1–6.

——and EVANS-PRITCHARD, E. E. (1940). 'Introduction', in M. Fortes and E. E. Evans-Pritchard (eds.), *African Political Systems* (London: Oxford University Press), 1–23.

————(eds.) (1940). *African Political Systems* (London: Oxford University Press).

FOSTER, P. (1990). *Policy and Practice in Multicultural and Anti-Racist Education: A Case Study of a Multi-Ethnic Comprehensive School* (London: Routledge).

FRAENKEL, J. (1992). 'Assimilation and the Jews in Nineteenth-Century Europe: Towards a New Historiography?', in J. Fraenkel and S. Zipperstein (eds.), *Assimilation and Community: The Jews in Nineteenth-Century Europe* (Cambridge: Cambridge University Press), 1–37.

FRAZEE, C. A. (1983). *Catholics and Sultans: The Church and the Ottoman Empire, 1453–1923* (Cambridge: Cambridge University Press).

FRIEDMAN, J. (1997). 'Global Crises, the Struggle for Cultural Identity and Intellectual Porkbarrelling', in P. Werbner and T. Modood (eds.), *Debating Cultural Hybridity: Multi-Cultural Identities and the Politics of Anti-Racism* (London: Zed Books), 70–89.

FRYBÈS, M. (1992). 'France: Un équilibre pragmatique fragile', in D. Lapeyronnie (ed.), *Immigrés en Europe: Politiques locales d'intégration* (Paris: La Documentation française), 83–110.

FURNIVALL, J. S. (1948). *Colonial Policy and Practice* (Cambridge: Cambridge University Press).

GANS, H. (1956a). 'American Jewry: Present and Future', *Commentary* 21/5: 422–30.

——(1956b). 'The Future of American Jewry', *Commentary*, 21/6: 555–63.

——(1962). *The Urban Villagers* (New York: Free Press of Glencoe).

——(1979). 'Symbolic Ethnicity: The Future of Ethnic Groups and Cultures in America', *Ethnic and Racial Studies*, 2/1: 1–20.

GARDNER, K., and SHUKUR, A. (1994). ' "I'm Bengali, I'm Asian, and I'm living here": The Changing Identity of British Bengalis', in R. Ballard (ed.), *Desh Pardesh: The South Asian Presence in Britain* (London: Hurst), 142–63.

GEERTZ, C. (1963). 'The Integrative Revolution: Primordial Sentiments and Civil Politics in the New States', in C. Geertz (ed.), *Old Societies and New States* (Chicago: Chicago University Press), 105–57.

——(1988). *Works and Lives: The Anthropologist as Author* (Oxford: Polity Press).

GELLNER, E. (1983). *Nations and Nationalism* (Oxford: Basil Blackwell).

——(1987). *Culture, Identity and Politics* (Cambridge: Cambridge University Press).

GERHOLM, T., and LITHMAN, G. Y. (eds.) (1988). *The New Islamic Presence in Western Europe* (London: Mansell Publishing Ltd.).

GERTH, H. H., and MILLS, C. W. (eds.) (1961). *From Max Weber: Essays in Sociology* (London: Routledge & Kegan Paul).

GIBB, H. A. R., and BOWEN, H. (1957). *Islamic Society and the West*, i: *Islamic Society in the Eighteenth Century*, part II. (Oxford: Oxford University Press).

————(1963). *Islamic Society and the West*, ii (Oxford: Oxford University Press).

GIBSON, C. (1964). *Aztecs under Spanish Rule* (Stanford, Calif.: Stanford University Press).

——(1967). *Tlaxcala in the Sixteenth Century* (Stanford, Calif.: Stanford University Press).

GIDDENS, A. (ed.) (1986). *Durkheim on Politics and the State* (Cambridge: Polity Press).

——(1991). *Modernity and Self-Identity: Self and Society in the Late Modern Age* (Cambridge: Polity Press).

GILROY, P. (1987). *There ain't no Black in the Union Jack: The Cultural Politics of Race and Nation* (London: Hutchinson).

——(1992). 'The End of Antiracism', in J. Donald and A. Rattansi (eds.), *'Race', Culture and Difference* (London: Sage Publications), 49–61. Orig. pub. in W. Ball and J. Solomos (eds.), *Race and Local Politics* (London: Macmillan, 1990).

——(1993a). *The Black Atlantic: Modernity and Double Consciousness* (London: Verso).

——(1993b). *Small Acts: Thoughts on the Politics of Black Culture* (London: Serpent's Tail).

GILSENAN, M. (1982). *Recognizing Islam* (London: Croom Helm).

GIRARD, P. (1976). *Les Juifs de France de 1789 à 1860* (Paris: Calmann–Levy).

GIRARDET, R. (1966). *Le Nationalisme français, 1871–1914* (Paris: Armand Colin).

GLAZER, N. (1995 (1983)). 'Individual Rights against Group Rights', in W. Kymlicka (ed.), *The Rights of Minority Cultures* (Oxford: Oxford University Press), 123–38.

——(1997). *We are all Multiculturalists now* (Cambridge, Mass.: Harvard University Press).

——and MOYNIHAN, D. (1970). *Beyond the Melting Pot*, 2nd edn. (Cambridge: MIT Press).

—————(1975). 'Introduction', in N. Glazer and D. Moynihan (eds.), *Ethnicity: Theory and Experience* (Cambridge, Mass.: Harvard University Press), 1–26.

GLUCKMAN, M. (1963). *Order and Rebellion in Tribal Africa* (London: Cohen).

—————(1965). *Politics, Law and Ritual in Tribal Society* (Oxford: Blackwell).

GODECHOT, J. (1976). 'La Révolution Française et les Juifs (1789–1799)', in B. Blumenkranz and A. Soboul (eds.), *Les Juifs et la Révolution Française* (Paris: Privat), 47–70.

GOLDBERG, D. T. (1993). *Racist Culture, Philosophy and the Politics of Meaning* (Oxford: Blackwell).

—————(1994). 'Introduction: Multicultural Conditions', in D. T. Goldberg (ed.), *Multiculturalism: A Critical Reader* (Oxford: Blackwell), 1–41.

GOLLNICK, D. M. and CHINN, P. C. (1986). *Multicultural Education in a Pluralistic Society* (Columbus, Oh.: Charles Merrill).

GOODY, J. (1962). *Death, Property and the Ancestors* (London: Tavistock).

GORDON, M. (1964). *Assimilation in American Life* (New York: Oxford University Press).

—————(1975). 'Towards a Theory of Ethnic Group Relations', in N. Glazer and D. Moynihan (eds.), *Ethnicity: Theory and Experience* (Cambridge, Mass.: Harvard University Press), 84–110.

GOULBOURNE, H. (1991). *Ethnicity and Nationalism in Post-Imperial Britain* (Cambridge: Cambridge University Press).

GRAMSCI, A. (1978). *Selections from the Prison Notebooks of Antonio Gramsci*, ed. and trans. Quentin Hoare and Geoffrey Nowell-Smith (London: Lawrence & Wishart).

GRANT, M. (1916). *The Passing of the Great Race* (New York: Charles Scribner's Sons).

GREER, C. (1972). *The Great School Legend: A Revisionist Interpretation of American Public Education* (New York: Viking Press).

GRILLO, R. D. (1974). 'Ethnic Identity and Social Stratification on a Kampala Housing Estate', in A. Cohen (ed.), *Urban Ethnicity* (ASA Monographs, 12; London: Tavistock), 159–85.

—————(1980). 'Introduction', in R. D. Grillo (ed.), *'Nation' and 'State' in Europe: Anthropological Perspectives* (London: Academic Press), 1–30.

—————(1985). *Ideologies and Institutions in Urban France: The Representation of Immigrants* (Cambridge: Cambridge University Press).

—————(1989). *Dominant Languages* (Cambridge: Cambridge University Press).

GUTMANN, A. (1994). 'Introduction', in A. Gutmann (ed.), *Multiculturalism: Examining the Politics of Recognition* (Princeton: Princeton University Press), 3–24.

HABERMAS, J. (1994). 'Struggles for Recognition in the Democratic Constitutional State', A. Gutmann (ed.), *Multiculturalism: Examining the Politics of Recognition* (Princeton: Princeton University Press), 107–48.

HACKER, J. R. (1982). 'Ottoman Policy towards the Jews and Jewish Attitudes toward the Ottomans During the Fifteenth Century', in B. Braude and B. Lewis (eds.), *Christians and Jews in the Ottoman Empire* (New York: Holmes & Meier), 117–26.

HALL, S. (1990). 'The Meaning of New Times', in S. Hall and M. Jacques (eds.), *New Times* (London: Lawrence & Wishart), 116–33.

HALL, S. (1992a). 'New Ethnicities', in J. Donald and A. Rattansi (eds.), *'Race', Culture and Difference* (London: Sage Publications), 252–9.

—— (1992b). 'The Question of Cultural Identity', in S. Hall, D. Held, and T. McGrew (eds.), *Modernity and its Future* (Cambridge: Polity Press), 274–316.

—— and JACQUES, M. (1990). 'Introduction', in S. Hall and M. Jacques (eds.), *New Times: The Changing Face of Politics in the 1990s* (London: Lawrence & Wishart), 11–22.

HALSTEAD, M. (1988). *Education, Justice and Cultural Diversity: An Examination of the Honeyford Affair, 1984–85* (London: Falmer Press).

HANDLIN, O. (1973). *The Uprooted*, 2nd edn. (Boston: Little, Brown & Co.).

HANNERZ, U. (1992). *Cultural Complexity: Studies in the Organization of Meaning* (New York: Columbia University Press).

—— (1996). *Transnational Connections: Culture, People, Places* (London: Routledge).

HARGREAVES, A. (1991). *Voices from the North African Immigrant Community in France* (New York and Oxford: Berg).

—— (1995). *Immigration, 'race' and ethnicity in Contemporary France* (London: Routledge).

HARTMANN, E. G. (1948). *The Movement to Americanize the Immigrant* (New York: Columbia University Press).

HASSAN, I. (1987). *The Postmodern Turn* (Columbus, Oh.: Ohio University Press).

HEWITT, R. (1986). *White Talk, Black Talk: Interracial Friendship and Communication amongst Adolescents* (Cambridge: Cambridge University Press).

HICKS, F. (1987). 'First Steps towards a Market-Integrated Economy in Aztec Mexico', in H. J. M. Claessen and P. Van de Velde (eds.), *Early State Dynamics* (Leiden: E. J. Brill), 91–107.

HIGHAM, J. (1984). *Send these to me: Immigrants in American Society*, 2nd edn. (Baltimore: Johns Hopkins University Press).

—— (1988). *Strangers in the Land: Patterns of American Nativism, 1860–1925* (New Brunswick, NJ: Rutgers University Press).

HIRO, D. (1991). *Black British, White British*, 3rd edn. (London: Grafton Books).

HOBSBAWM, E. (1992). *Nations and Nationalism since 1780*, 2nd edn. (Cambridge: Cambridge University Press).

—— and RANGER, T. (eds.) (1983). *The Invention of Tradition* (Cambridge: Cambridge University Press).

HOLMES, C. (1988). *John Bull's Island: Immigration and British Society, 1871–1971* (London: Macmillan).

HONT, I. (1995). 'The Permanent Crisis of a Divided Mankind: "Contemporary Crisis of the Nation State" in Historical Perspective', in J. Dunn (ed.), *Contemporary Crisis of the Nation State?* (Oxford: Blackwell), 166–231.

HOOKER, M. B. (1975). *Legal Pluralism: An Introduction to Colonial and Neo-Colonial Laws* (Oxford: Clarendon Press).

HUTNYK, J. (1997). 'Adorno at Womad', in P. Werbner and T. Modood (eds.), *Debating Cultural Hybridity: Multi-Cultural Identities and the Politics of Anti-Racism* (London: Zed Books), 106–36.

HYMAN, P. A. (1992). 'The Social Contexts of Assimilation: Village Jews and City Jews in Alsace', in J. Fraenkel and S. Zipperstein (eds.), *Assimilation and Community: The Jews in Nineteenth-Century Europe* (Cambridge: Cambridge University Press), 110–29.

INALCIK, H. (1973). *The Ottoman Empire: The Classical Age, 1300–1600* (London: Weidenfeld & Nicolson).

——(1976). 'The Rise of the Ottoman Empire', in M. A. Cook (ed.), *A History of the Ottoman Empire to 1730* (Cambridge: Cambridge University Press), 10–53.

——(1994). 'Part I. The Ottoman State: Economy and Society, 1300–1600', in H. Inalcik and D. Quataert (eds.), *An Economic and Social History of the Ottoman Empire, 1300–1914* (Cambridge: Cambridge University Press), 9–409.

INGRAO, C. (1996). *Ten Untaught Lessons about Central Europe: An Historical Perspective* (full text available at: gopher://gopher.ttu.edu:70/00/Pubs/lijpn/HABS/Papers/lessons).

ITZKOWITZ, N. (1996). 'The Problem of Perceptions', L. C. Brown (ed.), *Imperial Legacy: The Ottoman Imprint on the Balkans and Middle East* (New York: Columbia University Press), 30–8.

JAMESON, F. (1991). *Postmodernism or, the Cultural Logic of Late Capitalism* (Cambridge, Mass.: Harvard University Press).

JEFFCOATE, R. (1984). *Ethnic Minorities and Education* (London: Harper & Row).

JENCKS, C. (1978). 'Why Post-Modernism?', *Architectural Design*, 48/1: 11–26; 43–58.

JENKINS, R. (1967). *Essays and Speeches* (London: Collins).

JENKINS, RICHARD (1994). 'Rethinking Ethnicity: Identity, Categorization and Power', *Ethnic and Racial Studies*, 17/2: 197–223.

JENNINGS, R. (1976). 'Urban Population in Anatolia in the Sixteenth Century: A Study of Kayseri', *International Journal of Middle East Studies*, 7/1: 21–57.

——(1978). 'Zimmis (non-Muslims) in early 17th Century Ottoman Judicial Records', *Journal of the Economic and Social History of the Orient*, 21/3: 225–93.

JEWSIEWICKI, B. (1989). 'The Formation of the Political Culture of Ethnicity in the Belgian Congo, 1920–1959', in L. Vail (ed.), *The Creation of Tribalism in Southern Africa* (Berkeley: University of California Press), 324–49.

JOLY, D. (1988). 'Making a Place for Islam in British Society', in T. Gerholm and Y. V. Lithman (eds.), *The New Islamic Presence in Western Europe* (London: Mansell Publishing Ltd.), 32–52.

——(1992). 'Grande-Bretagne: Minorités ethniques et risques de ségrégation', in D. Lapeyronnie (ed.), *Immigrés en Europe: Politiques locales d'intégration* (Paris: La Documentation française), 111–43.

JONES, M. A. (1960). *American Immigration* (Chicago: University of Chicago Press).

——(1992). *American Immigration*, 2nd edn. (Chicago: University of Chicago Press).

JUST, R. (1989). 'Triumph of the Ethnos', in E. Tonkin, M. McDonald, and M. Chapman (eds.), *History and Ethnicity* (ASA Monographs, 27; London: Routledge).

KALLEN, H. M. (1916). 'The Meaning of Americanism', *Immigrants in America Review*, 1: 12–19.

——(1924). *Culture and Democracy in the United States* (New York: Boni & Liveright).

KALLEN, H. M. (1956). *Cultural Pluralism and the American Idea* (Philadelphia: University of Pennsylvania Press).

KANNEH, K. (1995). 'When Culture becomes Race', in M. Dunne and T. Bonazzi (eds.), *Citizenship and Rights in Multicultural Societies* (Keele: Keele University Press), 69–78.

KARPAT, K. (1985). 'The Ethnicity Problem in a Multi-Ethnic Anational Islamic State', in P. Brass (ed.), *Ethnic Groups and the State* (London: Croom Helm), 94–114.

KARTTUNEN, F. (1982). 'Nahuatl Literacy', in G. A. Collier, R. I. Rosaldo, and J. D. Wirth (eds.), *The Inca and Aztec States 1400–1800: Anthropology and History* (New York: Academic Press), 395–417.

KAVIRAJ, S. (1995). 'Crisis of the Nation-State in India', in J. Dunn (ed.), *Contemporary Crisis of the Nation State?* (Oxford: Blackwell), 115–29.

KEANE, J. (1988a). 'Introduction', in J. Keane (ed.), *Civil Society and the State: New European Perspectives* (London: Verso), 1–31.

——(1988b). 'Despotism and Democracy', in J. Keane (ed.), *Civil Society and the State: New European Perspectives* (London: Verso), 35–71.

KEARNEY, M. (1995). 'The Local and the Global: The Anthropology of Globalization and Transnationalism', *Annual Review of Anthropology*, 24: 547–65.

KEDWARD, H. R. (1965). *The Dreyfus Affair* (London: Longman).

KENNEDY, R. J. R. (1944). 'Single or Triple Melting Pot? Intermarriage Trends in New Haven, 1870–1940', *American Journal of Sociology*, 49/4: 331–9.

KHANUM, S. (1992). 'Education and the Muslim Girl', in G. Sahgal and N. Yuval-Davis (eds.), *Refusing Holy Orders* (London: Virago Press), 124–40.

KORMAN, G. (1967). *Industrialization, Immigrants, and Americanizers: Two Views from Milwaukee, 1866–1921* (Madison: State Historical Society of Wisconsin).

KRAUT, A. M. (1982). *The Huddled Masses: The Immigrant in American Society, 1820–1921* (Arlington Heights Ill.: Harlan Davidson).

KUNT, I. M. (1974). 'Ethnic-Regional (Cins) Solidarity in the Seventeenth Century Ottoman Establishment'. *International Journal of Middle East Studies*, 5: 233–9.

——(1982). 'The Transformation of Zimmi into Askeri', in B. Braude and B. Lewis (eds.), *Christians and Jews in the Ottoman Empire* (New York: Holmes & Meier), 55–68.

——(1983). *The Sultan's Servants: The Transformation of Ottoman Provincial Government, 1550–1650* (New York: Cambridge University Press).

KUREISHI, H. (1989). 'London and Karachi', in R. Samuel (ed.), *Patriotism: The Making and Unmaking of British National Identity*, ii: *Minorities and Outsiders* (London: Routledge), 270–87.

KURTZ, D. V. (1978). 'The Legitimation of the Aztec State', in H. J. M. Claessen and P. Skalnik (eds.), *The Early State* (The Hague: Mouton), 169–89.

KUSHNER, T. (1996). 'The Spice of Life? Ethnic Difference, Politics and Culture in Modern Britain,' in D. Cesarani and M. Fulbrook (eds.), *Citizenship, Nationality and Migration in Europe* (London: Routledge), 125–45.

KYMLICKA, W. (1995a). *Multicultural Citizenship: A Theory of Liberal Rights* (Oxford: Clarendon Press).

——(1995b). 'Introduction', in W. Kymlicka (ed.), *The Rights of Minority Cultures* (Oxford: Oxford University Press), 1–27.

LAFAYE, J. (1976). *Quetzalcoatl and Guadalupe: The Formation of Mexican National Consciousness, 1531–1813* (Chicago: University of Chicago Press).

LAPEYRONNIE, D. (1992). 'Les Politiques locales d'intégration des immigrés en Europe', in D. Lapeyronnie (ed.), *Immigrés en Europe: Politiques locales d'intégration* (Paris: La Documentation française), 5–17.

LAYTON-HENRY, Z. (1992). *The Politics of Immigration: Immigration, 'Race' and 'Race relations' in Post-war Britain* (Oxford: Blackwell).

LEACH, E. R. (1954). *Political Systems of Highland Burma* (London: Bell).

——(1961). *Rethinking Anthropology* (London: Athlone Press).

LEON-PORTILLA, M. (1963). *Aztec Thought and Culture* (Norman: University of Oklahoma Press).

LEVTZION, N. (1988). 'Islam and State Formation in West Africa', in S. N. Eisenstadt, M. Abitbol, and N. Chazan (eds.), *The Early State in African Perspective* (Leiden: E. J. Brill), 98–108.

LEWIS, B. (1963). *Istanbul and the Civilization of the Ottoman Empire* (Norman: University of Oklahoma Press).

LEWIS, M. D. (1962). 'One Hundred Million Frenchmen: The "Assimilation" Theory in French Colonial Policy', *Comparative Studies in Society and History*, 4/2: 127–53.

LEWIS, P. (1994). 'Being Muslim and being British: The Dynamics of Islamic Reconstruction in Oxford', in R. Ballard (ed.), *Desh Pardesh: The South Asian Presence in Britain* (London: Hurst), 58–88.

LINGUISTIC MINORITIES PROJECT (1985). *The Other Languages of England* (London: Routledge & Kegan Paul).

LOCKHART, J. (1982). 'Views of Corporate Self and History in some Valley of Mexico Towns: Late Seventeenth and Eighteenth Centuries', in G. A. Collier, R. I. Rosaldo, and J. D. Wirth (eds.), *The Inca and Aztec States 1400–1800: Anthropology and History* (New York: Academic Press), 367–94.

——(1992). *The Nahuas after the Conquest* (Stanford, Calif.: Stanford University Press).

LOIZOS, P. (1975). *The Greek Gift* (Oxford: Basil Blackwell).

LOVELAND, C. (1990). 'Introduction—Cultural Pluralism'. *Proteus*, 7/1: vi–viii.

LUGARD, F. E. (1922). *The Dual Mandate in British Tropical Africa* (Edinburgh: Blackwood).

LUTZ, H., PHOENIX, A., and YUVAL-DAVIS, N. (1995). 'Introduction: Nationalism, Racism and Gender—European Crossfires', in H. Lutz, A. Phoenix, and N. Yuval-Davis (eds.), *Crossfires: Nationalism, Racism and Gender in Europe* (London: Pluto Press), 1–25.

LYBYER, A. H. (1966 (1913)). *The Government of the Ottoman Empire in the Time of Suleiman the Magnificent* (New York: Russell & Russell).

LYNCH, J. (1958). *Spanish Colonial Administration, 1782–1810* (London: Athlone Press).

LYOTARD, J.-F. (1986). *The Postmodern Condition: A Report on Knowledge* (Manchester: Manchester University Press).

McALLISTER, L. N. (1984). *Spain and Portugal in the New World, 1492–1700* (Oxford: Oxford University Press).

MCDONALD, M. (1986). 'Celtic Ethnic Kinship and the Problem of being English', *Current Anthropology*, 27/4: 333–41, 344–7.

MCGOWAN, B. (1981). *Economic Life in Ottoman Europe: Taxation, Trade and the Struggle for Land, 1600–1800* (Cambridge: Cambridge University Press).

MAFEJE, A. (1971). 'The Ideology of "Tribalism"', *Journal of Modern African Studies*, 9/2: 253–61.

MAFFESOLI, M. (1988). 'Jeux de masques: Postmodern tribalism', *Design Issues*, 4/1–2: 141–51.

MAIR, L. (1928). *The Protection of Minorities* (London: Christophers).

——(1963). *New Nations* (London: Weidenfeld & Nicolson).

MALGLAIVE, G. (1942). *Juif ou Français?* (Vichy: Éditions CPRN).

MALINOWSKI, B. (1941). 'An Anthropological Analysis of War', *American Journal of Sociology*, 46: 521–50.

——(1947). *Freedom and Civilisation* (London: Allen & Unwin).

MANNHEIM, K. (1936). *Ideology and Utopia* (London: Routledge & Kegan Paul).

——(1952). *Essays on the Sociology of Knowledge* (London: Routledge & Kegan Paul).

MANNING, P. (1988). *Francophone Sub-Saharan Africa, 1880–1985* (Cambridge: Cambridge University Press).

MANSEL, P. (1995). *Constantinople: City of the World's Desire, 1453–1924* (London: John Murray).

MARCUS, G. (1986). 'Contemporary Problems of Ethnography in the Modern World System', in J. Clifford and G. Marcus (eds.), *Writing Culture* (Berkeley: University of California Press), 165–93.

——and FISCHER, M. (1986). *Anthropology as Cultural Critique* (Chicago: University of Chicago Press).

MARX, R. (1976). 'La Régéneration économique de Juifs d'Alsace à l'époque révolutionnaire et napoléonienne', in B. Blumenkranz and A. Soboul (eds.), *Les Juifs et la Révolution Française* (Paris: Privat), 105–20.

MASHUQ IBN ALLY (1990). 'Second Introductory Paper', in Commission for Racial Equality (ed.), *Law, Blasphemy and the Multi-Faith Society* (Discussion Papers, 1; London: Commission for Racial Equality), 21–31.

MAUROIS, A. (1934). *Lyautey* (Paris: Plon).

MAURRAS, C. (1954). *Œuvres capitales*, ii: *Essais politiques* (Paris: Flammarion).

——(1972). *De la politique naturelle au nationalisme intégral: Textes choisies*, F. Natter, C. Rousseau, and C. Polin, (Paris: Vrin).

MAURRUS, M. R. (1971). *The Politics of Assimilation: A Study of the Jewish Community at the Time of the Dreyfus Affair* (Oxford: Clarendon Press).

MELUCCI, A. (1988). 'Social Movements and the Democratisation of Everyday Life', in J. Keane (ed.), *Civil Society and the State: New European Perspectives* (London: Verso), 245–60.

MEMMI, A. (1973). *Portrait du Colonisé, Précédé du Portrait du Colonisateur* (Paris: Payot).

MICHELET, J. (1973 (1846)). *The People* (Urbana: University of Illinois Press).

MIDDLETON, J. (1960). *Lugbara Religion* (Oxford: Oxford University Press).

MODOOD, T. (1992a). 'British Asian Muslims and the Rushdie Affair', in J. Donald and A. Rattansi (eds.), *'Race', Culture and Difference* (London: Sage Publications), 260–77. Orig. pub. in *Political Quarterly*, 61/2 (1990), 143–60.

——(1992b). *Not easy being British: Colour, Culture and Citizenship* (London: Runnymede Trust & Trentham Books).

——(1997). '"Difference", Cultural Racism and Anti-Racism', in P. Werbner and T. Modood (eds.), *Debating Cultural Hybridity: Multi-Cultural Identities and the Politics of Anti-Racism* (London: Zed Books), 154–72.

——BEISHON, S., and VIRDEE, S. (1994). *Changing Ethnic Identities* (London: Policy Studies Institute).

MOULINAS, R. (1976). 'Les Juifs d'Avignon et du Comtat et la Révolution Française', in B. Blumenkranz and A. Soboul (eds.), *Les Juifs et la Révolution Française* (Paris: Privat), 143–82.

MOYNIHAN, D. P. (1993). *Pandaemonium: Ethnicity in International Politics* (Oxford: Oxford University Press).

MURRA, J. V. (1982). 'The Mit'a Obligations of Ethnic Groups to the Inka State', in G. A. Collier, R. I. Rosaldo, and J. D. Wirth (eds.), *The Inca and Aztec States 1400–1800: Anthropology and History* (New York: Academic Press), 237–62.

MURRAY, R. (1990). 'Fordism and Post-Fordism', in S. Hall and M. Jacques (eds.), *New Times: The Changing Face of Politics in the 1990s* (London: Lawrence & Wishart), 38–53.

NADEL, S. F. (1940). 'The Kede: A Riverain State in Northern Nigeria', in M. Fortes and E. E. Evans-Pritchard (eds.), *African Political Systems* (Oxford: Oxford University Press), 165–95.

——(1942). *A Black Byzantium* (London: Oxford University Press).

——(1954). *Nupe Religion* (London: Routledge & Kegan Paul).

NAIRN, T. (1977). *The Break-up of Britain: Crisis and Neo-Nationalism* (London: New Left Books).

NECHELES, R. (1971). *The Abbé Grégoire, 1787–1831: The Odyssey of an Egalitarian* (Westport, Conn.: Greenwood Publishing Co).

——(1976). 'L'Émancipation des Juifs, 1787–1795', in B. Blumenkranz and A. Soboul (eds.), *Les Juifs et la Révolution Française* (Paris: Privat), 71–86.

NELLI, H. (1970). *Italians in Chicago, 1880–1930: A Study of Ethnic Mobility* (New York: Oxford University Press).

——(1976). *The Business of Crime: Italians and Syndicated Crime in the United States* (New York: Oxford University Press).

——(1983). *From Immigrants to Ethnics: the Italian Americans* (Oxford: Oxford University Press).

NEWMAN, G. (1987). *The Rise of English Nationalism: A Cultural History, 1740–1830* (London: Weidenfeld & Nicolson).

NICHOLLS, D. (1974). *Three Varieties of Pluralism* (London: Macmillan).

NIELSEN, J. (1995). *Muslims in Western Europe*, 2nd edn. (Edinburgh: Edinburgh University Press).

NOIRIEL, G. (1992). *Population, Immigration et identité nationale en France, IX–XX siècle* (Paris: Hachette).

NORGREN, J., and NANDA, S. (1988). *American Cultural Pluralism and the Law* (New York: Praeger).

NOVAK, M. (1971). *The Rise of the Unmeltable Ethnics* (New York: Macmillan).

OFFNER, J. (1984). *Law and Politics in Aztec Texcoco* (Cambridge: Cambridge University Press).

PALMER, F. (ed.) (1987). *Anti-Racism: An Assault on Education and Value* (London: Sherwood).

PAPASTERGIADIS, N. (1997). 'Tracing Hybridity in Theory', in P. Werbner and T. Modood (eds.), *Debating Cultural Hybridity: Multi-Cultural Identities and the Politics of Anti-Racism* (London: Zed Books), 257–81.

PAREKH, B. (1990). 'Britain and the Social Logic of Pluralism', in Commission for Racial Equality (ed.), *Britain: A Plural Society* (Discussion Papers, 3; London: Commission for Racial Equality), 58–76.

——(1995 (1990)). 'The Rushdie Affair: Research Agenda for Political Philosophy', in W. Kymlicka (ed.), *The Rights of Minority Cultures* (Oxford: Oxford University Press), 303–20.

PARK, T., and MILLER, H. A. (1921). *Old World Traits Transplanted* (New York: Harper).

PATTERSON, T. C. (1991). *The Inca Empire: the Formation and Disintegration of a Pre-Capitalist State* (New York and Oxford: Berg).

PEEL, J. D. Y. (1983). *Ijeshas and Nigerians: The Incorporation of a Yoruba Kingdom 1890s–1970s* (Cambridge: Cambridge University Press).

——(1989). 'The Cultural Work of Yoruba Ethnogenesis', in E. Tonkin, M. McDonald, and C. Chapman (eds.), *History and Ethnicity* (ASA Monographs, 27; London: Routledge), 198–215.

PHILLIPS, A. (1993). *Democracy and Difference* (Oxford: Polity Press).

PITT-RIVERS, J. (1954). *The People of the Sierra* (London: Weidenfeld).

PORTER, R. (1992). 'Introduction', in R. Porter (ed.), *Myths of the English* (Cambridge: Polity Press), 1–11.

POULTER, S. M. (1986). *English Law and Ethnic Minority Customs* (London: Butterworth).

——(1990). 'Cultural Pluralism and its Limits: A Legal Perspective', in Commission for Racial Equality (ed.), *Britain: A Plural Society* (Discussion Papers, 3; London: Commission for Racial Equality), 3–28.

POUSSOU, J.-P., and MALINO, F. (1992). 'Le Peuple sans droits', in Y. Lequin (ed.), *Histoire des étrangers et de l'immigration en France* (Paris: Larousse), 251–69.

PRATT, J. (1980). 'A Sense of Place', in R. D. Grillo (ed.), *'Nation' and 'State' in Europe: Anthropological Perspectives* (London: Academic Press), 31–43.

RADTKHE, FRANK-OLAF (1994). 'The Formation of Ethnic Minorities and the Transformation of Social into Ethnic Conflicts in a So-Called Multi-Cultural Society—the Case of Germany', in J. Rex and B. Drury (eds.), *Ethnic Mobilisation in a Multi-Cultural Europe* (Aldershot: Avebury), 30–7.

RAMPTON REPORT (1981). *West Indian Children in our Schools*, A. Rampton, Chairman (Cmnd. 8273; London: HMSO).

RANGER, T. (1983). 'The Invention of Tradition in Colonial Africa', in E. Hobsbawm and T. Ranger (eds.), *The Invention of Tradition* (Cambridge: Cambridge University Press), 211–62.

——(1989). 'Missionaries, Migrants and the Manyika: The Invention of Ethnicity in Zimbabwe', in L. Vail (ed.), *The Creation of Tribalism in Southern Africa* (Berkeley: University of California Press), 118–50.

RAPHAEL, F. (1976). 'Les Juifs d'Alasace et la conscription au dix-neuvième siècle', in B. Blumenkranz and B. Soboul (eds.), *Les Juifs et la Révolution Française* (Paris: Privat), 121–42.

RÄTHZEL, N. (1995). 'Nationalism and Gender in West Europe: The German Case', in H. Lutz, A. Phoenix, and N. Yuval-Davis (eds.), *Crossfires: Nationalism, Racism and Gender in Europe* (London: Pluto Press), 161–89.

RATTANSI, A. (1992). 'Changing the Subject? Racism, Culture and Education', in J. Donald and A. Rattansi (eds.), *'Race', Culture and Difference* (London: Sage Publications), 11–48.

REBÉRIOUX, M. (1975). *La République radicale? 1898–1914* (Paris: Éditions du Seuil).

RENAN, E. (1869). 'La Part de la famille et de l'état dans l'éducation', in *Œuvres complètes (1947–1961)*, i (Paris: Calman-Levy), 523–42.

——(1871). 'Nouvelle lettre à M. Strauss', in *Œuvres complètes (1947–1961)*, i (Paris: Calman-Levy), 449–62.

——(1873). 'La Société berbère', in *Œuvres complètes (1947–1961)*, ii (Paris: Calman-Levy), 550–75.

——(1882*a*). 'Qu'est-ce qu'une nation', in *Œuvres complètes (1947–1961)*, i (Paris: Calman-Levy), 887–906.

——(1882*b*). 'Réponse au discours de reception de M. Cherbuliez', in *Œuvres complètes (1947–1961)*, i (Paris: Calman-Levy), 779–98.

REX, J. (1970). *Race Relations in Sociological Theory* (London: Weidenfeld & Nicolson).

——(1989). 'Equality of Opportunity, Multiculturalism, Anti-Racism, and "Education for All"', in G. K. Verma (ed.), *Education for All: A Landmark in Pluralism* (London: Falmer Press), 11–25.

——(1995). 'The Political Sociology of a Multicultural Society', in M. Dunne and T. Bonazzi (eds.), *Citizenship and Rights in Multicultural Societies* (Keele: Keele University Press), 79–94.

——(1996). *Ethnic Minorities in the Modern Nation State* (London: Macmillan).

——and DRURY, B. (eds.) (1994). *Ethnic Mobilisation in a Multi-Cultural Europe* (Aldershot: Avebury).

——and TOMLINSON, S. (1979). *Colonial Immigrants in a British City* (London: Routledge & Kegan Paul).

RICARD, R. (1966 (1933)). *The Spiritual Conquest of Mexico* (Berkeley: University of California Press).

RIPLEY, W. Z. (1899). *Races of Europe* (London: Kegan Paul).

ROBBINS, K. (1988). *Nineteenth Century Britain: Integration and Diversity* (Oxford: Oxford University Press).

ROBERTS, A. (1994). 'Churchill, Race and the "Magpie Society" ', in *Eminent Churchillians* (London: Weidenfeld & Nicolson), 211–41.

ROBERTS, P. (1912). *The New Immigrants: A Study of the Industrial and Social Life of Southeastern Europeans in America* (New York: Macmillan).

ROBERTS, S. H. (1963 (1926)). *The History of French Colonial Policy, 1870–1925* (London: Frank Cass).

ROLLE, A. (1980). *The Italian Americans: Troubled Roots* (New York: Free Press).

ROOSENS, E. E. (1989). *Creating Ethnicity: The Process of Ethnogenesis* (London: Sage).

ROSANVALLON, P. (1988). 'The Decline of Social Visibility', in J. Keane (ed.), *Civil Society and the State: New European Perspectives* (London: Verso), 199–220.

ROSE, M. (1991). *The Post-Modern and the Post-Industrial* (Cambridge: Cambridge University Press).

ROUNDS, J. (1982). 'Dynastic Succession and the Centralization of Power in Tenochtitlan', in G. A. Collier, R. I. Rosaldo, and J. D. Wirth (eds.), *The Inca and Aztec States 1400–1800: Anthropology and History* (New York: Academic Press), 63–89.

ROUSSEAU, J.-J. (1964). 'Considérations sur le gouvernement de Pologne', in B. Gagnebin and M. Raymond (eds.), *Œuvres complètes*, iii (Paris: Gallimard), 951–1041.

ROWE, J. H. (1982). 'Inca Policies and Institutions relating to the Cultural Unification of the Empire', in G. A. Collier, R. I. Rosaldo, and J. D. Wirth (eds.), *The Inca and Aztec States 1400–1800: Anthropology and History* (New York: Academic Press), 93–118.

ROYAL COMMISSION ON ALIEN IMMIGRATION (1903). *Report of the Royal Commission on Alien Immigration* (British Parliamentary Papers, ix; London: HMSO).

RUNCIMAN, W. G. (ed.) (1978). *Max Weber: Selections in Translation* (Cambridge: Cambridge University Press).

RUNNYMEDE TRUST (1997). *Islamophobia: its Features and Dangers* (London: Runnymede Trust).

RUSHDIE, S. (1991). *Imaginary Homelands* (New York: Vikas).

RUSINOW, D. (1996). 'Yugoslavia's Disintegration and the Ottoman Past', in L. C. Brown (ed.), *Imperial Legacy: The Ottoman Imprint on the Balkans and Middle East* (New York: Columbia University Press), 78–99.

RUSTOW, D. (1996). 'The Military Legacy', in L. C. Brown (ed.), *Imperial Legacy: The Ottoman Imprint on the Balkans and the Middle East* (New York: Columbia University Press), 246–60.

SAHGAL, G. (1992). 'Secular Spaces: The Experience of Asian Women Organizing', in G. Sahgal and N. Yuval-Davis (eds.), *Refusing Holy Orders* (London: Virago Press), 163–95.

—— and YUVAL-DAVIS, N. (1992). 'Introduction: Fundamentalism, Multiculturalism and Women in Britain', in G. Sahgal and N. Yuval-Davis (eds.), *Refusing Holy Orders* (London: Virago Press), 1–27.

SAIFULLAH KHAN, V. (1980). 'The "Mother Tongue" of Linguistic Minorities in Multicultural England', *Journal of Multilingual and Multicultural Development*, 11: 71–88.

SAMAD, Y. (1992). 'Book Burning and Race Relations: Political Mobilisation of Bradford Muslims', *New Community*, 18/4: 507–19.

SAMUEL, R. (1989a). 'Preface' and 'Introduction', in R. Samuel (ed.), *Patriotism: The Making and Unmaking of British National Identity*, i: *History and Politics* (London: Routledge), pp. x–lxvii.

——(1989b). 'Introduction', in R. Samuel (ed.), *Patriotism: The Making and Unmaking of British National Identity*, ii: *Minorities and Outsiders* (London: Routledge), pp. ix–xxxiv.

SCHAM, A. (1970). *Lyautey in Morocco: Protectorate Administration, 1912–1925* (Berkeley: University of California Press).

SCHLESINGER, A. M. J. (1992). *The Disuniting of America: Reflections on a Multicultural Society* (New York: W. W. Norton).

SCHMUHL, R. (1995). 'America and Multiculturalism', in M. Dunne and T. Bonazzi (eds.), *Citizenship and Rights in Multicultural Societies* (Keele: Keele University Press), 141–52.

SCHNAPPER, D. (1994). 'Conclusion: Muslim Communities, Ethnic Minorities and Citizens', in B. Lewis and D. Schnapper (eds.), *Muslims in Europe* (London: Pinter), 148–60.

SEIDEL, G. (1986a). 'Culture, Nation and "Race" in the British and French New Right', in R. Levitas (ed.), *The Ideology of the New Right* (Cambridge: Polity Press), 107–35.

——(1986b). *The Holocaust Denial: Antisemitism, Racism and the New Right* (Leeds: Beyond the Pale Collective).

SHAW, A. (1994). 'The Pakistani Community in Oxford', in R. Ballard (ed.), *Desh Pardesh: The South Asian Presence in Britain* (London: Hurst), 35–57.

SHAW, S. J. (1976). *History of the Ottoman Empire and Modern Turkey*, i: *The Empire of the Gazis: The Rise and Decline of the Ottoman Empire, 1280–1808* (Cambridge: Cambridge University Press).

SHIFFERD, P. A. (1987). 'Aztecs and Africans: Political Process in Twenty-Two Early States', in H. J. M. Claessen and P. Van de Velde (eds.), *Early State Dynamics* (Leiden: E. J. Brill), 39–53.

SHORE, C., and BLACK, A. (1994). 'Citizens' Europe and the Construction of European Identity', in V. A. Goddard, J. R. Llobera, and C. Shore (eds.), *The Anthropology of Europe: Identities and Boundaries in Conflict* (Oxford: Berg), 275–98.

SILVERMAN, M. (1992). *Deconstructing the Nation: Immigration, Racism and Citizenship in Modern France* (London: Routledge).

——(1996). 'The Revenge of Civil Society: State, Nation and Society in France', in D. Cesarani and M. Fulbrook (eds.), *Citizenship, Nationality and Migration in Europe* (London: Routledge), 146–58.

SIMON, R. (1982). *Gramsci's Political Thought* (London: Lawrence & Wishart).

SKALNIK, P. (1978). 'The Early State as Process', in H. J. M. Claessen and P. Skalnik (eds.), *The Early State* (The Hague: Mouton), 597–618.

SMITH, A. D. (1995). *Nation and Nationalism in a Global Era* (Cambridge: Cambridge University Press).

SMITH, M. G. (1960a). *Government in Zazzau, 1800–1950* (London: Oxford University Press).

——(1960b). 'Social and Cultural Pluralism in the Caribbean', *Annals of the New York Academy of Science*, 83/5: 76.

SMITH, M. G. (1965). *The Plural Society in the British West Indies* (Los Angeles: University of California Press).

SMITH, M. P. (1992). 'Postmodernism, Urban Ethnography, and the New Social Space of Ethnic Identity', *Theory and Society*, 21/4: 493–531.

SMITHIES, B., and FIDDICK, P. (1969). *Enoch Powell on Immigration* (London: Sphere Books).

SOLLORS, W. (1986). *Beyond Ethnicity: Consent and Descent in American Culture* (Oxford: Oxford University Press).

SOUTHALL, A. (1956). *Alur Society* (Cambridge: Heffer).

——(1965). 'Typology of States and Political Systems', in F. Eggan and M. Gluckman (eds.), *Political Systems and the Distribution of Power* (London: Tavistock), 113–40.

——(1970a). 'Incorporation among the Alur', in R. Cohen and J. Middleton (eds.), *From Tribe to Nation in Africa: Studies in Incorporation Process* (Scranton, Pa.: Chandler), 71–92.

——(1970b). 'The Illusion of Tribe', *Journal of Asian and African Studies*, 5/1–2: 28–50.

——(1976). 'Nuer and Dinka are People: Ecology, Ethnicity and Logical Possibility', *Man*, NS 11/4: 463–91.

——(1988). 'The Segmentary State in Africa and Asia', *Comparative Studies in Society and History*, 30/1: 52–82.

SPENCER, J. (1989). 'Anthropology as a Kind of Writing', *Man*, 24/1: 145–64.

SPIVAK, G. (1987). *In Other Worlds: Essays in Cultural Politics* (London: Methuen).

SPONZA, L. (1988). *Italian Immigrants in Nineteenth-Century Britain: Realities and Images* (Leicester: Leicester University Press).

STEIN, B. (1980). *Peasant State and Society in Medieval South India* (Delhi: Oxford University Press).

STEINBERG, J. (1987). 'The Historian and the Questione della Lingua', in P. Burke and R. Porter (eds.), *The Social History of Language* (Cambridge: Cambridge University Press), 198–209.

STENT, M. D., HAZARD, W. R., and RIVLIN, N. H. (eds.) (1973). *Cultural Pluralism in Education: A Mandate for Change* (New York: Appleton-Century-Crofts).

STRAYER, J. R. (1963). 'The Historical Experience of Nation-Building in Europe', in K. W. Deutsch and W. J. Foltz (eds.), *Nation Building* (New York: Atherton Press), 17–26

SUGAR, P. F. (1977). *Southeastern Europe under Ottoman Rule, 1354–1804* (Seattle: University of Washington Press).

SUREL, J. (1989). 'John Bull', in R. Samuel (ed.), *Patriotism: The Making and Unmaking of British National Identity*, iii: *National Fictions* (London: Routledge), 3–25.

SWANN REPORT (1985). *Education for All: Report of the Committee of Inquiry into the Education of Children from Ethnic Minority Groups*, Chairman Lord M. Swann (Cmnd. 9453; London: HMSO).

SZÜCS, J. (1988). 'Three Historical Regions of Europe: An Outline', in J. Keane (ed.), *Civil Society and the State: New European Perspectives* (London: Verso), 291–332.

TAYLOR, C. (1994). 'The Politics of Recognition', in A. Gutmann (ed.), *Multiculturalism: Examining the Politics of Recognition* (Princeton: Princeton University Press), 25–74.

TAYLOR, P. (1971). *The Distant Magnet* (London: Eyre & Spottiswood).

TESTER, K. (1992). *Civil Society* (London: Routledge).

THOM, T. (1990). 'Tribes within Nations: The Ancient Germans and the History of Modern France', in H. K. Bhabha (ed.), *Nation and Narration* (London: Routledge), 44–70.

THOMAS, H. (1993). *The Conquest of Mexico* (London: Hutchinson).

THOMPSON, D., and CHRISTIE, I. (eds.) (1989). *Scorsese on Scorsese* (London: Faber & Faber).

TODOROV, T. (1993). *On Human Diversity: Nationalism, Racism and Exoticism in French Thought* (Cambridge, Mass.: Harvard University Press).

TODOROVA, M. (1996). 'The Ottoman Legacy in the Balkans', in L. C. Brown (ed.), *Imperial Legacy: The Ottoman Imprint on the Balkans and Middle East* (New York: Columbia University Press), 45–77.

TOLAND, J. D. (1987). 'Discrepancies and Dissolution: Breakdown of the Early Inca State', in H. J. M. Claessen and P. Van de Velde (eds.), *Early State Dynamics* (Leiden: E. J. Brill), 138–53.

——(1988). 'Inca Legitimation as a Communication Process', in R. Cohen and J. Toland (eds.), *State Formation and Political Legitimation* (New Brunswick, NJ: Transaction Publishers).

TOSH, J. (1973). 'Colonial Chiefs in a Stateless Society: A Case-Study from Northern Uganda', *Journal of African History*, 14: 473–90.

TOURAINE, A, (1974), *The Post-Industrial Society* (London: Wildwood House).

TULLY, J. (1995). 'The Crisis of Identification: The Case of Canada', in J. Dunn (ed.), *Contemporary Crisis of the Nation State?* (Oxford: Blackwell), 77–96.

TURNER, F. J. (1920). *The Frontier in American History* (New York: Henry Holt).

TYLER, S. (1986). 'Post-Modern Ethnography', in J. Clifford and G. Marcus (eds.), *Writing Culture* (Berkeley: University of California Press), 122–40.

URSINUS, M. O. H. (1993). 'Millet', in C. E. Bosworth, E. Van Donzel, W. P. Heinrichs, *et al.* (eds.), *The Encyclopedia of Islam,* new edn. (Leiden: Brill), 61–4.

VAIL, L. (1989). 'Introduction: Ethnicity in Southern African History', in L. Vail (ed.), *The Creation of Tribalism in Southern Africa* (Berkeley: University of California Press), 1–19.

——and WHITE, L. (1989). 'Tribalism in the Political History of Malawi', in L. Vail (ed.), *The Creation of Tribalism in Southern Africa* (Berkeley: University of California Press), 151–92.

VANSINA, J. (1978). 'The Kuba State', in H. J. M. Claessen and P. Skalnik (eds.), *The Early State* (The Hague: Mouton), 359–80.

VERMA, G. K. (ed.) (1989). *Education for All: A Landmark in Pluralism* (London: Falmer Press).

——(1990). 'Pluralism: Some Theoretical and Practical Considerations', in Commission for Racial Equality (ed.), *Britain: A Plural Society* (Discussion Papers, 3; London: Commission for Racial Equality), 44–57.

VINCENT, J. (1993). 'Ethnicity and the State in Northern Ireland', in J. Toland (ed.), *Ethnicity and the State* (New Brunswick, NJ: Transaction Publishers), 123–46.

WAARDENBURG, J. (1988). 'The Institutionalization of Islam in the Netherlands, 1961–86', in T. Gerholm and Y. V. Lithman (eds.), *The New Islamic Presence in Western Europe* (London: Mansell Publishing Ltd), 8–31.

WAGENER, P. (1992). 'Liberty and Discipline: Making Sense of Postmodernity, or, once again, toward a Sociohistorical Understanding of Modernity', *Theory and Society*, 21/4: 467–92.

WALDRON, J. (1995 (1992)). 'Minority Cultures and the Cosmopolitan Alternative', in W. Kymlicka (ed.), *The Rights of Minority Cultures* (Oxford: Oxford University Press), 93–119.

WALZER, M. (1995 (1980)). 'Pluralism: A Political Perspective', in W. Kymlicka (ed.), *The Rights of Minority Cultures* (Oxford: Oxford University Press), 139–54.

WARNER, M. (1991). *Joan of Arc* (London: Vintage).

WATERS, M. (1995). *Globalization* (London: Routledge).

WATERS, M. C. (1990). *Ethnic Options: Choosing Identities in America* (Berkeley: University of California Press).

——(1992). 'The Construction of a Symbolic Ethnicity: Suburban White Ethnics in the 1980s', in M. D'Innocenzo and J. P. Sirefman (eds.), *Immigration and Ethnicity: American Society—'Melting pot' or 'salad bowl'?* (Westport, Conn.: Greenwood Press), 75–90.

WEBER, E. (1976). *Peasants into Frenchmen: The Modernization of Rural France 1870–1914* (London: Chatto & Windus).

WEBER, M. (1947). *The Theory of Social and Economic Organisation* (New York: Free Press).

——(1978). *Economy and Society: An Outline of Interpretative Sociology*, ii, ed. G. Roth and C. Wittich (Berkeley: University of California Press).

WEIL, P. (1996). 'Nationalities and Citizenships: The Lessons of the French Experience for Germany and Europe', in D. Cesarani and M. Fulbrook (eds.), *Citizenship, Nationality and Migration in Europe* (London: Routledge), 74–87.

WEISSLEDER, W. (1978). 'Aristotle's Concept of Political Structure and the State', in R. Cohen and E. Service (eds.), *Origins of the State* (Philadelphia: ISHI), 187–204.

WEISSMANN, N. (1964 (1938)). *Les Janissaires: Étude de l'organisation militaire des ottomans* (Paris: Librairie Orient).

WELDON, F. (1989). *Sacred Cows* (London: Chatto).

WERBNER, P. (1994). 'Islamic Radicalism and the Gulf War: Lay Preachers and Political Dissent among British Pakistanis', in B. Lewis and D. Schnapper (eds.), *Muslims in Europe* (London: Pinter), 98–115.

——(1997a). 'Introduction: The Dialectics of Cultural Hybridity', in P. Werbner and T. Modood (eds.), *Debating Cultural Hybridity: Multi-Cultural Identities and the Politics of Anti-Racism* (London: Zed Books), 1–26.

——(1997b). 'Essentialising Essentialism, Essentialising Silence', in P. Werbner and T. Modood (eds.), *Debating Cultural Hybridity: Multi-Cultural Identities and the Politics of Anti-Racism* (London: Zed Books), 226–56.

WHITMAN, W. (1926). *Leaves of Grass* (New York: Doubleday).

WHYTE, W. F. (1955). *Street Corner Society* (Chicago: Chicago University Press).

WIEVIORKA, M. (1997). 'Is it so difficult to be an anti-racist', in P. Werbner and T. Modood (eds.), *Debating Cultural Hybridity: Multi-Cultural Identities and the Politics of Anti-Racism* (London: Zed Books), 139–54.

WIHTOL DE WENDEN, C. (1988). *Les Immigrés et la politique* (Paris: Presses de la Fondation Nationale des Sciences Politiques).

WINOCK, M. (ed.) (1993). *Histoire de l'extrême droite en France* (Paris: Éditions de Seuil).

WIRTH, L. (1928). *The Ghetto* (Chicago: University of Chicago Press).

WITTEK, P. (1938). *The Rise of the Ottoman Empire* (London: Royal Asiatic Society of Great Britain and Ireland).

WOLF, E. (1962). *Sons of the Shaking Earth* (Chicago: Chicago University Press).

WOLFE, J. (1989). 'Evangelicalism in Eighteenth-Century England', in R. Samuel (ed.), *Patriotism: The Making and Unmaking of British National Identity*, i: *History and Politics* (London: Routledge), 188–200.

WOLFF, J. (1992). 'The Real City, the Discursive City, the Disappearing City: Postmodernism and Urban Sociology', *Theory and Society*, 21/4: 553–60.

WOOD, J. (ed.) (1970). *Powell and the 1970 Election* (Kingswood, Surrey: Elliott Right Way Books).

WOODS, R. (ed.) (1898). *The City Wilderness* (Boston: Houghton, Mifflin).

——(ed.) (1902). *Americans in Process: A Settlement Study* (Boston: Houghton, Mifflin).

WORSLEY, P. (1957). *The Trumpet shall Sound* (London: MacGibbon and Kee).

YOUNG, C. (1976). *The Politics of Cultural Pluralism* (Madison: University of Wisconsin Press).

——(1985). 'Ethnicity and the Colonial and Postcolonial State in Africa', in P. Brass (ed.), *Ethnic Groups and the State* (London: Croom Helm), 57–93.

YOUNG, I. M. (1989). 'Polity and Group Difference: A Critique of the Ideal of Universal Citizenship', *Ethics*, 99: 250–74.

YOUNG, R. (1995). *Colonial Desire: Hybridity, Theory, Culture and Race* (London: Routledge).

YUVAL-DAVIS, N. (1992). 'Fundamentalism, Multiculturalism and Women in Britain', in J. Donald and A. Rattansi (eds.), *'Race', culture and difference* (London: Sage Publications), 278–91.

ZANGWILL, I. (1909). *The Melting Pot* (New York: Macmillan).

INDEX